Latin American
Unification

Latin American Unification

A History of Political and Economic Integration Efforts

Salvador Rivera

McFarland & Company, Inc., Publishers

Jefferson, North Carolina

LIBRARY OF CONGRESS CATALOGUING-IN-PUBLICATION DATA

Rivera, Salvador, 1957–
    Latin American unification : a history of political and
economic integration efforts / Salvador Rivera.
        p.   cm.
    Includes bibliographical references and index.

    ISBN 978-0-7864-7625-1
    (softcover : alkaline paper) ∞

    1. Latin America—Politics and government.
    2. Confederation of states—Latin America—History.
    3. Latin America—Economic integration.   4. Latin
    America—Economic conditions.   I. Title.
    F 1410.R495 2014
    980—dc23   2013044339

BRITISH LIBRARY CATALOGUING DATA ARE AVAILABLE

On the cover: Ibero-American Summit, November 2007, Santiago,
Chile (courtesy Presidency of the Nation of Argentina)

Manufactured in the United States of America

McFarland & Company, Inc., Publishers
    Box 611, Jefferson, North Carolina 28640
        www.mcfarlandpub.com

In loving memory
of my father Salvador Rivera who
would have been pleased to see this book,
and
for my lovely and caring wife, Rosina

ACKNOWLEDGMENTS

This historical study is the result of many years of research. With time, the author's indebtedness rises. The following individuals merit recognition for their assistance. Librarians and archivists were critical to the completion of this study. Both Nancy Niles and Francine Apollo, inter-loan librarians of the State University of New York, enthusiastically secured much of the material used. Ms. Kristen Nyitray, of the Special Collections Section of the State University of New York at Stony Brook, meticulously provided me with all requested documentation. Kathryn I. Dyer provided documents from the Central Intelligence Agency. I wish to applaud Dick Averson for his ceaseless advice and consultation.

Michelle McKowen from the Council on Foreign Relations assisted me with sources from that organization. The staff at the ALADI Library in Montevideo, Uruguay, was always welcoming and enthusiastic in assisting and providing me with new sources. Mario Farachio of the Uruguayan Senate gave generously of his time in identifying sources. Carla Macario, formerly with the United Nations Economic Commission for Latin America, provided valuable insight into available Latin America historical sources. Interviews with Gustavo Magariños, Hector Carlevaro, Alberto Methol Ferré, Marcos Methol Ferré, Guzmán Carriquiry, Elbio C. Pezzati, Daniel Szabo, Víctor Urquidi, Tomás A. Musich, Hector N. di Biase and Mrs. Eliana Díaz de Prebisch added insight into the complex integration problems of the 1960s. Professor Dick Averson was always on hand to review the manuscript as proofreader and as a friend. Last, but not least, I thank my wife Rosina for her enthusiastic moral support that helped make this work possible.

TABLE OF CONTENTS

PREFACE

This historical study is about attempts to promote the political and economic union of Latin America over the last two centuries. It is both an intellectual and political history. The movement is important because every generation of Latin Americans has known some effort to create a unified Latin America. Latin Americans were the first Third World people to recognize the need for a development program that would ameliorate political, economic and social problems. The policy they suggested was regional integration, referred to as unionism. A review of the literature showed that no comprehensive historical analysis of the Latin American integration effort exists; hence, this study seeks to remedy the situation. The focus herein is on the unionists and their rationale for restructuring the Latin American political system. These unionists campaigned for an integrated Latin America because they were dissatisfied with the political and economic fragmentation that had emerged. For these unionists the inadequacies of the state system were considered an impediment to furthering modernity.

This is the first comprehensive historical study of Latin American unionism in the English language. Extensive research in Spanish language sources did not yield anything sufficiently thorough. The few books I found in Spanish often ignored certain time periods or did not investigate them sufficiently. Those that examined the modern period failed to consider past efforts, while those that studied earlier attempts were outdated.

The few English language monographs on integration that do exist primarily examine the Latin America Free Trade Association (LAFTA) or the Central American Common Market (CACM). Though they served as useful guides they did not provide an overall or satisfying examination of the Latin American experience. Most of these monographs were produced by economists or political scientists whose disciplinary concerns did not fulfill the need for an all-encompassing historical study; thus, I initiated the research and writing of this work.

In the last 190 years various approaches have been utilized by Latin Americans in pursuit of regional integration. The integration effort has undergone four stages of evolution. The first phase began in the 1820s with political leaders such as Simón Bolívar initiating the Panama Congress and was then superseded in the second period by the intellectuals of the 1860s. The third stage began in the 1950s when technocrats working through the United Nations Economic Commission for Latin America and the Caribbean (ECLAC) suggested the economic unification of the region. The fourth stage began in the late 1980s to 1990s with the return of democracy to the region, when political leaders resumed a proactive approach to the integration movement by launching the Common Market of the South (Mercado Común del Sur, or MERCOSUR). Since that time presidents and their assigned technocrats and diplomats have been given the task of consolidating that organization, as evinced by the dramatic political effort to incorporate the left-wing Venezuelan government of Hugo Chávez.

Although unionists continue to articulate the older political and cultural rationales for the unionist cause, these arguments do not carry the same weight as they did in the past. Indeed, the impetus for the fourth stage has been not only the re-institutionalization of democracy, but the ever-increasing economic competition between states. By the late 1980s the Latin American states faced the combined economic weight of the European Union and the emergent North American Free Trade Agreement (NAFTA), alongside the traditional competition from the United States, Japan and emerging Asian economies.

Though this study deals with trade policy and the evolution of the contemporary Latin American trade blocs in the latter chapters, it is not about commercial policies or trade blocs per se. The concern of the narrative is the drive to the ultimate goal of political union between Latin Americans. Consequently, the work will not discuss NAFTA or the new emerging Trans Pacific Partnership (TPP), since their objective is not an all–Latin American state. Likewise, the book will not examine the Central American Integration System or the Bolivarian Alliance because the former has little economic or political potential to promote further integration, unless it joins MERCOSUR, and the latter organization exists only on paper as an ideological bloc. The objective of contemporary unionists is increasing the economic coadunation of Latin America. They reason that since economic decisions made by a supranational body are ultimately political in nature, the integration movement will eventually transition to a higher level.

The principal method of research was to examine the unionists' own words, which have been gleaned from a large collection of primary and secondary materials. The primary sources are mainly from documentary collections;

others are memoirs. Interviews with participants also proved particularly helpful regarding the complex issues surrounding the integration movement. The narrative format was influenced by Mark Van Aken's work on Pan-Hispanism and the writings of Pascaline Winand and Carl H. Pegg, who examined the origins of European integration.

A quick note on the usage of diacriticals: Certain commonly used terms in English, such as the names of countries, have been utilized without diacritical marks as that is the common practice in the United States. However, for Spanish language sources, accents were employed. For example, in English language sources Mexico is spelled without the accent over the letter e. In Spanish language quotations, titles from articles/books or citations the county will appear as México. There is an exception to this rule. For Spanish/Portuguese language footnotes and bibliography the place of publication is cited using English usage (i.e. Mexico), with the publisher's name in Spanish.

Many Spanish and Portuguese names, terms and countries have accents in their native language. The reader should be aware that some foreign place-names that do not contain foreign accents may carry diacritical marks in other languages. For example, Brasilia does not carry the accent in Spanish, but in Portuguese it does: Brasília. In Spanish language sources I kept words as they appeared in that language even if they were of Portuguese origin. When these terms were utilized in Portuguese literature the appropriate diacriticals were employed.

It is imperative that the work of the unionists not be forgotten. Their struggles reverberate throughout the entire Latin American experience. The individuals who promoted political and economic unification were firm believers in enlightenment theory, with its emphasis on the ability of humankind to effect progress and change. The unionists have consistently argued that a change in the political structure of Latin America would create a more just society. It is significant that not once did the unionists ever call for the use of war as a means of reaching their goal, as is the case with the unification movements of other countries. Latin American unionism has always proffered a peaceful transition from fragmentation to federal, confederal or common-market type organizations as mechanisms that could replace the dominant state system. With the dawn of MERCOSUR they are on the verge of slowly reaching that objective. The past and present endeavors of unionists serve to link an entire community though time and space.

INTRODUCTION

This book is a study of an intellectual and political movement that has sought to promote the political and economic unification of Latin America. The effort has been known by different terms: unionism, the integration movement, continentalism, continental nationalism, Pan-Hispanism, and Pan-Latin-Americanism. It is in fact a nationalist campaign that views the region as one nation fragmented into many states. In this study the terms unionism, unionist and integration will be employed to refer to this struggle and its advocates. Every generation of Latin Americans has witnessed some effort to promote the political and/or economic unification of the region. Until recently these efforts have been stymied. In recent times (since the 1950s), Latin American trade blocs have been formed in order to facilitate regional integration. The supporters of these organizations have had different motives. Most proponents have shied away from openly supporting eventual political coadunation, claiming that the purpose of the blocs is strictly to expand trade. Nonetheless, unionists have supported these trade blocs as the most likely mechanism for eventually creating a politically unified state. The development of the Common Market of the South (MERCOSUR) trade bloc suggests it is becoming a reality.

The movement's advocates have scarcely envisioned Latin American unification without Brazil; consequently the term Hispanic will also be used to include Brazil, which is a correct use of the term as the Iberian Peninsula was originally named "Hispania" by the ancient Roman Empire. The term Pan-American(ism) has been used erroneously by some writers to refer to efforts promoting an all–Latin-American state. The concept is a term coined by the United States Secretary of State, James Blaine, in the 1880s to promote binding Inter-American free trade agreements between the U.S. and Latin America; hence the term is inappropriate for usage when discussing the political unification efforts of the region, since unionist plans have always excluded Washington.

This study accomplishes its goal by examining the writings of the numerous unionists who have advanced the integration movement. This study does not posit any theories or models; I leave this to political scientists. The narration and documentation will provide more than sufficient information to support whatever theory they choose to elaborate or criticize. The work does argue that the movement has been thwarted by the state system and the political class, which defended the state system until the 1990s when a number of countries became more amenable to some level of economic integration, however limited. It is the political class that has been the sword and shield of the state system in Latin America. This stratum has always held the power to initiate or thwart political and economic integration. The narrative conclusively shows that this group has frustrated the movement via overt hostility or inertia. The political class has controlled foreign policy in Latin America, whether it is in the form of a dictatorship or of representative government. It is a tenet of political science that foreign relations are the prerogative of the executive branch of government, but legislatures also play a crucial role in determining the course of any such policy. Ultimately, it is legislatures that accept or reject a foreign policy such as political or economic integration. It must be borne in mind that both executive and legislative branches can effectively deal with foreign policy issues without formally confronting such matters, which also constitute a political position. As an example, some of the mechanisms utilized by political figures in the past for dealing with unionism have been to simply ignore the movement, to claim that political or economic unification is impossible, to belittle the movement, to claim that geography impedes unification, or to subvert from within. For instance, in 1960 one Brazilian businessman told U.S. foreign policy experts that his country would kill integration with kindness. A particularly deadly approach for dealing with unionists came in the 1960s with implementation of the Latin American Free Trade Association (LAFTA). Political figures decided to wash their hands of the project by delegating the organization to technocrats situated within sectoral commissions that represented various industries. The task of the individuals who sat on these committees was to determine what tariff reductions would be made for their industry. The members of these commissions were not elected to these positions and had almost carte blanche to protect the interests of the groups they represented. This meant that behind the scenes, special interests could operate without public scrutiny, thus protecting political forces from the grasp of public opinion. Eventually, tariffs concessions ceased and LAFTA became moribund by 1967, officially disbanding in 1980. Recently, some countries have undermined the unionist movement by forming bilateral free trade agreements with Washington.

The failure of LAFTA could not, however, quench the idea of unification for unionists, and by 1990 the idea resurfaced with the appearance of the Treaty of Asunción (1991), which created the Common Market of the South (MERCOSUR). For all its problems, which are publicly highlighted in the press by its enemies, the organization stands firm more than 20 years later and continues to grow. The recent incorporation of Venezuela and a formal request by the Ecuadorian and Bolivian governments (summer 2012) for full accession to MERCOSUR highlight the continued potency of the unionist movement and its logical benefits.

The movement for political unification is the result of independence from Spain. With the rupture of the old political bonds came recognition soon after independence that the old empire had provided the Latin Americans with many benefits and a gemeinschaft. With independence a new nationalism known as unionism was born that condemned the multiplicity of new states. It soon became obvious to unionists that the affairs of the region required a new state system capable of dealing with a multitude of new problems, such as military coups, political chaos, wars, border disputes and internal revolts, that could not be adequately dealt with by the new political units. Ironically, unionism arose at a time when local political leaders sought unbridled political control over their territories and began to exacerbate the fragmentation of the region in order to consolidate their power, which led to numerous power struggles. These conflicts led to dictatorship and stifled any viable efforts at promoting social equality. Unionism gave hope that it could strengthen democracy and enhance equality amid the obvious fact that the new states could not reach that objective.

With separation from Spain and Portugal, the problem of promoting economic growth quickly became apparent as the economies of Europe and the United States grew at dramatic rates. The people of Latin America were now forced to ponder proposals for the economic progress of their lands. The first viable proposal for such progress was unionism. The Ibero-Americans became the first Third World people to posit a program for economic development that would use the mechanism of political integration. It was argued that political union would also create more favorable conditions for the advancement of viable representative government and lead to greater social equality. Despite many failures to implement this objective, the allure of unionism's potential is so potent that its promotion continues unabated to this day in the form of economic integration, with the hope by many that it will lead to a political union. Although the unionist movement is usually identified as a Pan-Hispanic or Latin-American movement, it is not solely for those of Hispanic background. It has always been recognized that people of other racial, ethnic, and religious backgrounds, with their own identities, exist in the region. This condition has increased with immigration. Unionism is a flexible movement that has made it expressly clear that the movement is to promote the interests of the people of Latin America, rather than any one group. The concept of Latin America embraces the uniqueness and importance of the commonality of culture over bloodline. Even before the term was coined by the French, the people of the region accepted the intellectual premise that culture was what formed nationality, as proposed by José María Samper in the 1800s. This premise was absolutely essential if the idea of a common Latin American nationality was to exist.

The most salient feature of Latin American culture has been its ability to absorb people of different races, ethnicities and languages into its fold. This is clearly seen in Latin America with both the Spanish and Portuguese colonial traditions. The flexibility of this universalism hails back to the Roman absorption of various ethnic-linguistic groups in the Italic peninsula and Western Europe. Some groups continue with their own racial, ethnic, and religious identities, but this does not detract from the utility or desirability of the term, as these groups depend on Latin institutions, such as courts, science, and alphabet. It denotes a culture rather than a bloodline. It is a malleable term that does not focus on a specific gene pool, recognizing that the region consists of many different racial backgrounds. This universalism found recognition with the term La Raza Cósmica, adopted by José Vasconcelos, originally utilized for describing Mexico's racial and cultural assimilation process, but now commonly used throughout Latin America. Vasconcelos subtitled his work the "Misión de la Raza Iberoamericana," clearly indicating a uniquely American view of the American.[1] Vasconcelos argued that those who denied the Latin heritage of the Indian and black were the dupes of British and American imperialism.[2] His assertion made it clear that it was the people of the region and not an extraterritorial political or cultural force that would define who was a Latin American and who was not. He reminded his readers that the Hispanic political and cultural legacy served the interests of all people of the region regardless of their racial background.[3]

A note on some terms: Political integration shall refer to the status of a number of states who concede some level of their political sovereignty to a centralized, state-run organization or government. A body such as MERCO-SUR is an organization controlled by formal states, but it cannot be considered a government. The ultimate objective of unionists is to create and secure state power, as that is the agglutination that will achieve their objectives. The term elites will refer to political figures, businessmen (foreign and domestic), technocrats, bureaucrats and intellectuals who have a major ability to influence political events beyond their own personal vote in elections. Some of these individuals and groups are visible. Most are unknown to the public. Some may reside in Latin America; others may live outside the region. An example would be the media, a large percentage of which is controlled by U.S. corporations and their executives.

This book focuses on the most important and most promising of unionist activities. Not every Latin American trade bloc is examined. The Central American Integration System (Spanish acronym SICA) and the Andean Community will not be discussed, because these organizations do not have the potential for an all–Latin-American organization. The SICA is an organization with limited objectives, and its member states have engaged in bilateral trade agreements with the United States, hence limiting its utility to unionists. Inquiries have been sent by MERCOSUR to Nicaragua and El Salvador so as to encourage their entry into the South American organization without affirmative results at this time. The Andean community is only mentioned with respect to the negative role it played with respect to LAFTA. It has also heavily engaged in bilateral free-trade agreements with countries outside the region, thereby defeating the purpose of a customs union or common-market organization. Only MERCOSUR has this potential, as it is geographically the largest, has a larger population (internal market), has the most resources, and continues to add viable new member states; consequently it has the most flexibility to deal with a number of issues.

The study examines the movement as it has evolved through its four phases. The following chapters examine these stages. Chapter I argues that the many explanations alleging impediments to Latin American political and economic integration are erroneous. An examination of the region within the context of the independence movement and the first plans for political coordination is made in the second chapter. The first phase of the unionist movement in which political unification was undertaken by official state representatives is explored in Chapters III–V. Chapter VI reviews the second phase of the unionist movement ushered in by intellectuals disillusioned by political efforts. It was the hope of these activists in the nineteenth century that they could convince massive numbers of people of the logic of their cause and hence initiate a movement that political figures would have to respond to. This did not materialize in the nineteenth century. However, as Chapter VII notes, the intellectuals of the twentieth century fared somewhat better as the result of appealing to a more educated and politically proactive population. It was their objective to instill in Latin Americans a "continental consciousness." While they failed to make political inroads prior to the 1950s, they did succeed in promoting a broader awareness of Latin America and its common problems to the people of the region, hence laying the intellectual groundwork for future unionist activity. Their work helped to create a respectable environment for postwar efforts initiated by technocrats to promote economic integration. The work of the twentieth century intellectuals was so prominent that they even managed to excite university students into pro-unionist activism.

The third phase of the unionist movement, which was initiated by technocrats in the postwar era, is examined in Chapters VIII–IX. These chapters discuss the evolution of LAFTA as the product of the work of Raúl Prebisch and his team at the United Nations Economic Commission for Latin America (UNECLA, or simply ECLA) and the political class within each state. It also covers LAFTA's demise at the hands of the member states, via the sectoral commissions that refused to make any further concessions. Chapter X covers the impact of the United States on the Latin American integration movement during the 1950s and '60s. Readers will observe that presidents Eisenhower, Kennedy and Johnson, foreign policy experts at the State Department, and the Council on Foreign Relations did not ignore the movement, as the chapter provides a detailed scrutiny of the concerns of the United States, demonstrating that serious and positive consideration was given to the movement.

Chapter XI introduces the reader to the fourth stage, which was again dominated by Latin American political forces in a renewed and committed effort to develop a viable economic integration with MERCOSUR. The origins of the bloc stem from the re-democratization of the southern zone and the ever-increasing global economic competitiveness. It covers the origin of the organization and its early years. The chapter utilizes a thematic approach rather than a strictly chronological one, which should make it easier for the reader to follow many of the complicated political maneuvers followed by both the pro-MERCOSUR faction and its enemies. A special investigation studies the herculean effort of Venezuela to enter the MERCOSUR bloc as a plenary member. It examines the struggle between pro–Venezuelan forces within Venezuela and the bloc's members, as well as the efforts of anti–Chávez factions to thwart the entry of Caracas into MERCOSUR. The chapter also surveys Washington's shift away from a pro–Latin-American economic integration policy to one of hostility via its own free-trade organizations and treaties (killing with kindness). Resistance to these Washington-inspired initiatives by states and popular groups within the MERCOSUR countries is analyzed. A discussion of the Union of South American Nations (UNASUR) is conducted, but as that organization is still congealing only time will be able to reveal its ultimate course. The final chapter concludes with a brief review of the major issues discussed and an analysis of the integration movement's future prospects.

A word on sources: this study initiated a massive and exhaustive search for research materials. The reader will find a rich depository of primary and secondary sources in both English and Spanish. Materials were utilized from international organizations, foreign diplomatic archives, the Central Intelligence Agency, unionist writers as well as from non-governmental organizations in Latin America and the United States. A review of the literature indicates that this work has utilized the most exhaustive and useful bibliography of unionism. Additional material was gathered from numerous interviews and correspondence with contributors to the Latin American integration movement. Some participants are well known and others will be introduced to the public for the first time via this publication. All of them have been as significant as they have been perspicacious. It is my hope that this work will satisfy the reader's historical curiosity on the topic and stimulate further research on unionism.

I

IMPEDIMENTS TO POLITICAL UNION IN LATIN AMERICA

As long as we are not able to correct our concepts, it will not be possible to influence the physical environment to make it serve our purposes.—José Vasconcelos, *La Raza Cósmica*, 1925

The beginning of the independence movement in Latin America induced a number of political and intellectual figures to question the political wisdom of the emerging nation-state system in the region. Serious concerns were raised after the new state system was created, and efforts were immediately undertaken to reverse the trend of political fragmentation towards the reconstruction of a politically unified Latin America. These efforts persisted for two centuries and encountered numerous obstacles.

Several problems can be identified as impediments to the political and economic unification of Latin America since these states gained independence. These matters have been addressed from the beginning of the independence movements to the present time. The most serious of them have been

- political fragmentation;
- nationalism, claims of impossibility and the state;
- race, nationality and civilization;
- separation: imperial administration and geography; and
- political and socio-economic differences in Latin America.

Political Fragmentation

The most serious dilemma for unionists occurred at the moment the Latin Americans began their revolutions, when they immediately began to

11

fragment into various political units that eventually frustrated future efforts to promote political unification.[1] The inability of the Spanish-Americans to preserve the political union provided by the Spanish monarchy stemmed from their failure to create an organization similar to the Continental Congress, created by the United States in 1775. Such an organization might have allowed them to coordinate more effectively their political and military policies during the wars for independence. In spite of the fact that the Spanish-Americans assisted one another in various military campaigns, these activities were conducted without the benefit of a centralized political organ. Their reluctance to create a unified political system, however weak, laid the foundation for the later political fragmentation that beset the region.

The various administrative units that proclaimed their independence under Spanish rule in the early 1800s usually operated their military autonomously and self-sufficiently, although there were a few noteworthy occasions when Spanish-American military commanders came to the assistance of other countries and armies, as did José de San Martín. The Spanish-Americans refused to consider the slightest possibility for a formal alliance of states solely for the duration and conduct of military operations against Spain, which undoubtedly prolonged the conflict. This policy was fueled by the desire of each administrative political unit, which was under the leadership of the pre-eminent city in its region, to become politically independent. The new political entities that were formed, as well as the groups that governed them, made firm commitments to maintain their power and were unwilling to allow political control to slip away from them. It is a maxim of political science and historical experience that political power gained is not readily relinquished. The history of the region demonstrates the poignancy of that observation.

Nationalism, Claims of Impossibility and the State

The degree to which nationalism has been an impediment to political integration is subject to debate. Nationalism has certainly been a problem for unionists in the twentieth century, when governments chose to exploit it, but in the nineteenth century nationalism was a doctrine of elites that was not always shared or understood by the broad mass of people, who had to be inculcated with new notions regarding their relationship to the new states.

It is generally recognized that the region was afflicted by a provincialism that arose from geography, but it is difficult to determine to what degree nationalism was a nineteenth century problem in Latin America, since both sentiments can be confused and often coexist. Nationalism is a belief that is created over many years, or even decades. In Latin America this nationalism germinated in the nineteenth century and came to fruition in the twentieth century. Contrary to what might be believed, overt and hostile nationalism has not been the primary obstacle to closer political and economic union among the Latin American states.

A close study of the historical literature from the nineteenth and twentieth centuries reveals that very few, if any, individuals openly condemned any form of integration based on the premise of uniqueness of nationality, or that the population of one country was incompatible with that of another. If writers secretly harbored such views, few were bold enough, or sufficiently honest, to commit them to writing or public discourse. It is rare to find any writer propagating such views. Likewise, it does not appear that loyalty to the nation-state or reconciling one's place of birth (nationality) with being a member of a larger Latin American civilization has posed a problem for most Latin American writers and political figures who dealt with the issue of integration. Historically, the overwhelming majority of writers and political figures have extolled the fraternity of the Latin American states and the virtues of alleged brotherhood. These intellectuals defined Latin America as possessing an Iberian heritage. As a result of this perception, these individuals applauded what they viewed as the likeness of language, customs, religion, law and history.

The argument that Latin American political or economic union is impossible due to size has proven to be a much more devastating argument than nationalism against the formation of an effective integration program. This view has historically asserted that it is not possible to integrate the diverse interests of so many states because they cover such a large land mass on which population centers are separated by great distances. Nevertheless, integration as a concept has proven to be an intellectually acceptable doctrine for many people; hence its permanent popularity. Only the crudest and most insensitive individuals have come forth to openly oppose or belittle integration efforts.

Opposition to political and/or economic integration presented a major problem for its opponents because the burden of explaining their prejudice against brotherhood and cooperation has fallen on them.[2] Nevertheless, the assertion of impossibility has provided an intellectually acceptable screen for those seeking to disguise their true animosity towards the concept. Elbio C. Pezzati, a former member of the Uruguayan Senate associated with the political center and a supporter of his country's integration efforts, explains the dilemma facing opponents and obstructionists of political union and economic integration: "It is impossible to reject integration publicly. To openly proclaim an opposition to integration invites condemnation as a voice against progress and reason. Integration has been perceived and continues to be seen as the vanguard of progress. It represents fraternity and cooperation. How can anyone publicly condemn the concept without appearing to be an enemy of progress and humanity before the eyes of the entire world?"[3]

The claim of impossibility has traditionally allowed opponents of integration the benefit of utilizing "plausible deniability," thus allaying any suspicious motives concerning their position on the matter, while maintaining their credibility before the public and history. It has also provided a historical explanation for several generations of Latin Americans seeking to understand why efforts to promote integration have proven futile. The strength and power of the impossibility theory cannot be underestimated. This historical interpretation has served to sow apprehension among many supporters of integration who would publicly forego espousing their beliefs for fear of being ridiculed. It should not be surprising that the assertion of impossibility has become a self-fulfilling prophecy.

The history of the integration movement clearly demonstrates that the existence of numerous governments in Latin America has posed a greater problem for integrationists than nationalist sentiment. The nationalism and patriotism of the region gradually evolved from the new political units and were encouraged as the essential prerequisites required for maintaining loyalty from their citizens. The complexity of the situation can best be understood by recognizing that most serious proposals for political or economic integration have required initiatives to come from ruling political circles. Nevertheless, the goal of creating a unified Latin American state has persistently eluded them.

In the many conferences held to discuss potential political or economic integration, the Ibero-American governments continuously and militantly refused to agree to what extent, if any, their states would surrender legal or political sovereignty. Thus, one of the major impediments that integrationists faced was not nationalism or questions of nationality but rather an ideological bulwark supporting the total sanctity of the state as the ultimate raison d'être. This situation was considered so deplorable by some that Manuel Matta, a Chilean writer of the 1860s, lamented that Latin American leadership had become the victim of a sorcerer's "evil spell" conjured up in order to beguile their unification efforts.[4]

Thus, the appearance of the new political structures created a much more complex and insuperable obstacle to political or economic union among the Latin American states than anyone could have foreseen during the wars for independence. In spite of the many conferences held in the nineteenth and twentieth centuries to promote the integration of the region, disagreements and problems have always arisen among political elites for a number of reasons.

The bases of these polemics have included border disputes, economic considerations, puerile political egotism, concerns about inheriting problems from neighboring countries, and the sentiment that integration is unnecessary or impossible.

Race, Nationality and Civilization

In the first half of the nineteenth century, a few Pan-Hispanic writers who subscribed to racial ideology spoke about the need for unification for the "Spanish race." These essayists depicted those born in Spain, or Americans (Creoles) sired by Spanish parents, as the group to be unified. These ideologues adamantly rejected any political or cultural bond that would include both the African and Indian. This definition of the "Spanish race" would have excluded the majority of people living in Ibero-America, who were of African or American Indian ancestry, from participating in any political activity within their society. Yet, Spaniards writing in 1836 referred to the inhabitants of Latin America as the "Hispano-Indian race," a clear indication that they understood this mixture formed the largest single racial component in that region.[5] The Spanish Chargé for Nicaragua and Costa Rica, Facundo Goñi, observed that "what is called the Hispanic American race has only a small portion of Spanish blood."[6]

The narrow view of the "Spanish race" of uniquely European origin did not find a receptive audience with enlightened Latin Americans, who for the most part rejected the narrow and pedantic perspective of a racial standard, at least since the middle of the nineteenth century. Such a dogmatic perspective would have placed serious limits on any society seeking to build a viable state, if it indeed sought effective loyalty from its people. Despite the fact that the racialist perspective had only minimal success in Latin America, its supporters proved boisterous, with serious and negative implications for unionists. Their ideology maintained that political unification in the region was impossible due to the multiplicity and incompatibility of the various races in Latin America. Likewise, their perspective included no place for other races in the political culture of such a state.

One of the most prominent proponents of the "Spanish race" ideology was Francisco Muñoz del Monte, whose influence was prominent in the 1850s. He was born in Santo Domingo, Dominican Republic, of Spanish origin. He believed that the Latin American states would eventually undergo a thorough political "reorganization" which would involve some type of unification.[7] Nonetheless, he maintained that the wide variety of races in Latin America made it difficult, if not impossible, for Latin Americans to effect a genuine political union.[8] In his writings, he argued that the Indian and the African could play no significant role in a reorganized Latin America due to their alleged "physical and intellectual inferiority."[9]

Muñoz asserted that Latin America was in reality "Europe transported to the New World.... The Indian does not figure as a part of the population; he has no role in political and civil society, he is the pariah of American civilization. As for the Negro, or African race..., it is a foreign, accidental, and anomalous importation that has no civil status in the few countries where it unfortunately exists. Its probable destiny is to disappear from America."[10] A large percentage of the population of Ibero-America was in fact Native American or black, which ultimately meant that the views of Muñoz would eventually have to be rejected if any serious plan for political integration was to be contemplated.

The first unionist intellectual to openly challenge Muñoz del Monte was his contemporary, the prominent writer José María Samper from Colombia. Samper, like Muñoz del Monte, was a supporter of political unification but differed radically in his views of race and nationality. He argued that the two elements, however diverse, were not inimical to the development of a politically integrated state and completely rejected the viewpoint of Muñoz del Monte. Samper boldly and proudly asserted, "Our race is one." His writing reflected a genuine appreciation for the propagation of enlightenment theory that began in the seventeenth and eighteenth centuries and stated that all societies had the ability to create a better life for their people, regardless of bloodline, through the restructuring of their political units. These advanced ideas were aggressively challenged by the nineteenth century social theories of Scientific Racism and Social Darwinism, which threatened liberal political, economic and social reforms in many societies.

Samper made it explicitly clear he was not referring to a single bloodline but to a culture and a civilization. He wrote:

> What constitutes the unity of a human family, of a complete race, is the grouping of language, religion, climate, traditions, genuine character, tendencies, basic institutions and common interests. Race is not a physical form so much as it is a moral form. It is in the intimate analogies, that effect the nations in their moral and intellectual life, in their literature, their history and their legislation.... It is here that the physical traits should be sought that make the various countries a great community.[11]

Samper acknowledged that the population of Spain was not a truly Latin population in the biological sense but rather an amalgamation of various bloodlines that had filtered into that land over thousands of years as the result of Spain's geographical position at the Mediterranean crossroads of both European and Asiatic civilizations. Upon the discovery and settlement of the Western Hemisphere, Spanish society had produced new racial types via miscegenation.[12] Samper ridiculed the idea of a purely Spanish or Latin race as a "fascinating sophism" and recognized the importance of the various racial strains in Latin America and their socio-economic historical impact on the development of Latin American society. He also called for the elimination of the term *race* from the dictionary, an enlightened idea for the world of 1858, which had been heavily influenced by the Social Darwinism and Scientific Racism of Herbert Spencer, and suggested replacing it with the concept of "civilization."[13]

Samper ridiculed the popular "struggle of the races" theory, which had become prominent in the 1850s and 1860s, as "chimerical." Ever cognizant of the antagonisms among different nationalities, he suggested that the so-called struggle between the races was not a conflict between races per se, so much as conflicts between "ideas and interests" that became unique to various nationalities, such as the religious-ideological struggles that pitted Roman Catholic Spain against anti–Catholic England. He maintained that these antagonisms had been exacerbated by the rivalry between the Anglo-Saxon and Latin civilizations that had been transplanted to the Western Hemisphere.[14]

Samper's perspicacious distinctions allowed unionists to speak of a civilization revolving around culture rather than bloodline, thus providing integration supporters with an opportunity to escape the burdensome and erroneous implications of the new racist theories that had evolved. His successful intellectual retorts placed the racists on the defensive, which allowed integrationists the opportunity to promote the utilization of all the human resources available to their respective states and the entire region. Like many unionists, Samper understood that a viable unification program could never take place if it propagated the inherent biological inferiority of any particular group. He understood that a project for Latin American union could not be built solely on the alleged superiority or claims to uniqueness of a single bloodline. All serious integration proposals have recognized this reality.

Separation: Imperial Administration and Geography

One of the alleged hindrances to political or economic unity in Latin America has been the political and geographical separation of the Ibero-American colonies. These divisions have been a problem for integrationists.

It is not clear that these forms of separation made political fragmentation inevitable, but they certainly did complicate the integration process. Both Spain and Portugal ruled their colonies with similar administrative structures, although the policies they followed varied. Spain ruled her colonies in Latin America by tying them to a highly centralized policy in which the political, administrative and economic bonds between the Latin American territories were linked exclusively to the imperial bureaucracies. This meant that political and commercial groups focused exclusively on satisfying their own unique interests and the interests of the metropolis. In the later colonial period, various regions of Spanish America were given additional administrative responsibilities and discretion, but continued to be subordinate to the viceroyalty, which was the highest administrative body whose director, the viceroy, was directly responsible to the monarch.

Portuguese-speaking Brazil was ruled similarly to Spanish-America, with a viceroy and political subdivisions. Brazil, however, was spared the ordeal of the fragmentation because it maintained a monarchy after independence, which limited the effectiveness of secessionist movements that appeared after independence. The Spanish and Portuguese administrative systems both produced a myopic political-administrative-geopolitical perspective in which elites focused upon their unique regional problems and on relations with the metropolis, instead of the other regions in Latin America. In the early colonial period, rivalries between Spain and Portugal helped to heighten this myopia between the Latin Americans. This was ameliorated between 1580 and 1640, when Spain and Portugal were united under the Spanish crown; but after 1640 relations between the Spanish Empire and Portuguese-speaking Brazil returned to an atmosphere of suspicion and constant border clashes, usually centered in what is now Uruguay.

Geography was a determining factor in shaping the Spanish and Portuguese administrative organizations. The Spanish monarchy created the various administrative units of its empire based on the natural geographical divisions that existed. When the independence movement arose, these various administrative units proclaimed themselves to be sovereign independent states. Even the countries created to serve as buffer states, such as Bolivia and Uruguay, had previously served as administrative units whose borders were based solely on the geography of their territory. The natural barriers between the various administrative units of the Iberian American colonies limited commercial, political and social intercourse among them and continued to do so after the dawn of independence, leading in turn to a provincialism that has always attended the region, creating to a sense of self-sufficiency and introversion as in Brazil.

The problem of fragmentation is not unique to Latin Americans. This geopolitical dilemma occurred in other civilizations at different times, most notably that of the ancient Greeks. The development of the Greek polis (irrespective of political structure), which arose from its physical environment, not only created totally autonomous and inward-looking societies that promoted *esprit de corps* and the ability to maintain self-sufficiency, but also served to cause the Hellenes a number of inextinguishable and agonizing problems. When the Ibero-Americans became independent of Spain and Portugal, they had to confront the same negative and insuperable dilemmas that the political culture of the ancient Greeks was unable to resolve.

Many Latin American writers have blamed the harsh topography of the region as the principal reason for its political fragmentation. No other cultural-linguistic region of the world possesses such a large, rugged and diverse geography as Latin America. The area spans two continents. It is divided by massive mountain ranges where in some cases there are no viable passes for hundreds of miles except at very high altitudes. It is separated by vast plains, deadly deserts, monstrous jungles, and even the ocean. In this era of modern and comfortable air transportation, it is difficult to comprehend the vast dangers and physical hardships posed by travel prior to the late twentieth century. Until that era, this rugged geography was largely inaccessible due to the region's lack of infrastructure, which did not facilitate trade. Roads were nonexistent over vast portions of Latin America. There was also a lack of bridges and canals. Only the most desperate, enterprising, or adventurous individual would dare to brave the passage of any of the mountain chains, deserts, or jungles that claim huge portions of Latin American territory. Railroads did not appear until about the 1870s and only in the few countries that satisfied the commercial demands of the industrial and imperial powers.

Until the dawn of modern technology, transportation was by foot or horse. In many cases it was quicker to travel by sea, which meant that the economic and social intercourse of the Latin Americans was stronger with Europe, and in some cases with the United States, than with the rest of Ibero-America. Communications were also poor. For example, until about the 1940s, telephone calls had to be channeled through New York City. It was more likely for Latin American diplomats to meet each other in Paris or Washington, D.C., than in Bogotá or Rio de Janeiro.[15]

The opponents of integration have traditionally claimed that both the harsh geography and the provincialism that it sired made the political union of Latin America impossible. Both factors are related to each other and contributed to the difficulties unionists would encounter, but these problems have not demonstrated the alleged historical inevitability of the failure of unionist efforts. The harsh geography did not necessarily constitute a problem for the creation of an integrated state, although it did complicate the process. A close examination of the region's political evolution shows that the intimidating topography of the two continents did not impede centralized political control by the Spanish and Portuguese thrones, which allowed considerable discretion to their viceroys and sub-regional administrators in governing these huge territories. Likewise, the governance of the independent Latin American states was not impeded solely by the harsh terrain that most of the countries possess. Consequently, a viable and convincing explanation that the creation of a unified Ibero-America failed, or is impossible to construct, due exclusively to possession of a peculiar geography, is untenable.

Political and Socio-Economic Differences in Latin America

Difficulties in cementing an integrated Latin America have also arisen from the region's distinct political systems and relationships among various socio-economic groups. These myriad differences have existed in practically every Latin American state. By 1830, the majority of the Latin American states had gained their independence and had established republican governments. Brazil was the only independent Latin American state to establish and maintain a monarchy, which lasted until 1889. The presence of the Brazilian throne made it difficult for republican adherents to incorporate it into any integration plans, although Brazil was occasionally invited to attend integration conferences because it was felt by the Spanish-Americans to be an integral member of the Latin American family. Brazil was also the last South American state to abolish slavery; abolition occurred in 1888, long after most of the other Latin American states had eliminated that institution. It was also the earliest Latin American state to espouse the idea that it might become a superpower, a concept conspicuously absent from the other Latin American states except Argentina.

Cuba and Puerto Rico were left out of most integration proposals because they remained colonies of the Spanish Crown until 1898, when they were taken over by the United States. Puerto Rico formally became a possession of the United States, achieving commonwealth status in 1952, which it currently maintains. Cuba was given a provisional government, subject to North American control of its foreign policy as a result of the Platt Amendment of 1901. Panama was also left out of many of the early proposals because it would not become an independent country until 1903, when a U.S.–sponsored revolution succeeded in separating it from Colombia for "international use" in the building of the Panama Canal, a remarkable engineering feat made possible by modern technology and financing from the United States government.

At the beginning of the independence period, Latin Americans also possessed different stages of socio-economic development within their borders, as they did at the dawn of the twentieth and twenty-first centuries. All of them had large cities, coexisting with agricultural systems. In most of Latin America, agriculture was controlled by the gentry and the church. These two groups controlled the most productive and modern agricultural establishments, which effectively denied the rest of the population the possibility of competing with the larger landlords. In some regions, agriculture was heavily dependent on the use of common lands. In other areas agriculture was attended by small yeoman farmers. In countries such as Argentina and Uruguay, which had vast tracts of land, there existed an acute labor shortage in agriculture during various time periods due to the small population in those countries. This demographic problem resulted in massive European immigration, leading to major changes in the racial and ethnic composition of the two states.

In addition to all the elements of civilized society, there existed in Latin America large numbers of people who lived in distinctly socio-economic groups. There were many people who continued to live in communal agricultural settlements. These individuals were usually of Indian descent and tilled the land much as their ancestors had. In some cases, they produced only for themselves, although many supplied the market. Likewise, at the dawn of the twentieth century nomadic Native American tribes maintained their centuries-old existence in northern Mexico and Chile. In the Amazon basin of Brazil large numbers of Native Americans still continue their isolation from the modern-day industrialized giant which that society has become.

The various levels of development made integration a difficult enough task within individual Ibero-American states, especially because political figures chose to unnecessarily accentuate the differences among the numerous states. With all these many problems, it is not surprising that political and economic integration has not proceeded along a smooth path. In spite of the aforementioned obstacles, the various governments of the region that came into existence did succeed in consolidating political control over their countries. However, from a political and economic perspective the new independent states faltered. They had difficulties implementing effective representative government. Broad sectors of the population remained outside the political process. In the economic realm the new states faced serious problems financing their governments and even more difficulty repaying obligations. This failure eventually led to problems with foreign governments seeking to collect debts.

A united Latin America might have been able to reach these goals sooner by providing easier access to resources, irrespective of the structure that might have been erected.

Nevertheless, jungles, mountains, diverse bloodlines, the doctrine of impossibility and socio-economic differences could not stem the enthusiasm and hope that come from ideas. Ideas have a power of their own that transcend both distance and time. The concepts of brotherhood, cooperation and the possibilities of systematizing and rationalizing the political and economic systems of Latin America were too powerful and intoxicating to be cast aside. The rich lode of feasibilities that could grow from a political union was too powerful and lucrative to be ignored. Someone, or some group, would have to be bold enough to seize the initiative and promote the germination of a unified political system. Thus, Latin Americans eagerly began discussing the possibilities of creating a politically unified state.

Many of these unionists would be denounced as dreamers, but without a dream to hold onto, humans and societies stagnate and fail to reach their full potential. The eventual descent into political chaos and cynicism meant many people in Latin America would face a spate of intractable problems.

II

Revolution, Independence and Early Initiatives for Political Union

Boastful patriotism is not satisfied with presenting its heroes as unities of a continental movement, but as autonomous, not realizing that in acting this way, it belittles rather than exalts them.
—José Vasconcelos, *La Raza Cósmica*, 1925

The Revolutionary Period

The first recommendations for political integration in Latin America arose as quickly as the wars for independence began. The call for political unification came not from the general population, but from a small portion of elite society that recognized the perils that would result from a multiplicity of governments. These suggestions came primarily from political and military leaders who hoped to see a viable re-unified state come to fruition. Ironically, these first supporters of political integration continue to be portrayed as dreamers. A closer analysis will reveal that they were in fact hard-nosed statesmen and military leaders who grappled successfully with difficult political and military issues and the problems these entailed. They were individuals who grasped a keenly pragmatic view of political reality, and also possessed the confidence that came from public support, from their responsibilities, and from groups that had placed them in positions of power.

The call for political integration revolved mainly around four important concerns: (1) the military defense of the newly established states and the maintenance of their territorial integrity, (2) the establishment and consolidation of friendly relations among them, (3) the pursuit of an active foreign policy

23

abroad that could make a significant contribution to their interests and prestige, and (4) the desired ability to create and implement policies for alleviating
social and economic problems common to all of them. The latter objective
was also the first plan in Latin America intended to promote economic development.

Despite many calls for closer political integration during the early revolutionary period, these proposals were generally ignored by most ruling circles,
who sought to maintain political control over the regions they inhabited. With
the dawn of the independence movement in Latin America there appeared an
ardent, almost unquenchable desire by local groups to control the various
administrative regions of the all–Hispanic state (Spanish empire) that they
had inherited. These local political figures had long been denied the great
esteem that political service and policy-making provide to their practitioners.
With revolutionary ferment spreading to all parts of Hispanic America, ruling
groups that had been starved of this much-desired recognition were anxious
to wrest control from the Spanish oligarchy that operated the imperial bureaucracy.

In the ensuing discussion about the reorganization of Latin America,
some elites proffered the possibility of close military political alliances; others
sought closer political coordination among some regions of Latin America
rather than the political integration of all of Latin America. These new political
forces were not interested in sharing their political power with any other
groups in Latin America. This strong desire for maintaining political control
of the newly established states could not be stemmed by the proponents of
political integration. Nevertheless, a few individuals continued to express their
desire for maintaining a politically unified Latin America, beginning a long
and dynamic tradition of promoting its political unification. The first group
was a small number of politicians and military leaders seeking some level of
integration during this period of the wars for independence. After independence, these politicians would work with their diplomats in order to reach this
objective.

The separatist-independence movement in Latin America formally began
with the establishment of the first revolutionary council (junta) in Venezuela.
Almost immediately the junta expressed a perspicacious concern over the
future political organization of Latin America. On April 27, 1810, the council
issued a statement in which it asked the other Hispanic-American regions to
"contribute to the great work of creating a Spanish American confederation."[1]
A diplomatic mission was sent to Britain led by Simón Bolívar, who was to
negotiate with Richard Wellesley as his counterpart.[2] The Venezuelan delegation was given instructions to persuade the British king, George III, "to

complete the grand work of confederating the scattered sections of America."
The British government expected the political outcome of the Latin American
upheavals to conclude with the eventual independence of the Spanish colonies,
but it was also assumed that they would form a federal union.[3]

In spite of the enthusiasm of pro-integration supporters, the new governments of Latin America were slow to respond to the Venezuelan junta's call
for unity. On September 18, 1810, the governing junta of Buenos Aires sent a
representative to the *cabildo* (city council) of Santiago de Chile. The Argentine
envoy, Antonio Álvarez Jonte, carried a note stating, "The general interests of
America require that all the countries be reunited fraternally and that we
should concentrate in sustaining this aspect of the monarchy, free of the risks
bringing us close to the ruin of Spain by accelerating closer union and relations
conducive to our countries."[4]

Álvarez Jonte's mission was doomed to failure because of competing ideas
about integration within the Buenos Aires junta. The radical Jacobin secretary
of that junta was Mariano Moreno, who led the campaign against the idea of
creating a general congress that would seek a measure of political union. In
the official 1810 journal of the junta, Moreno vociferously and successfully
laid the foundation for the political and legal arguments against the continuing
political union of Latin America. He argued that once the Spanish crown had
relinquished power, or been denied political control over a region, sovereignty
automatically passed to each administrative unit. Moreno emphatically lobbied
against the argument that the political unity provided by the Spanish monarchy could be utilized to establish political integration, arguing that the unity
provided by the crown did not necessarily ensure the continuation of political
links once it had been displaced. Such a union could only be created by a joint
agreement among the various political units. He claimed that the massive size
of Latin America made any move towards political integration unfeasible, and
that the immense distances between Latin America's urban centers made "communication impossible" even with Mexico, more so than with "with Russia or
Tartary." He asked rhetorically, "Who could harmonize the wills of men who
inhabit a continent, where distances are counted by thousands of leagues?
Where would be fixed the great congress and how would it provide for the
urgent necessities of people of whom it could have no news except after three
months? It is a chimera to pretend that all of Spanish America should form a
single state." Instead of promoting a single state, the Latin Americans, Moreno
wrote, should settle for a close political and military alliance, and a federal
form of government should be contemplated only for future consideration.[5]
Moreno neglected to publicly acknowledge that none of the city councils
(*cabildos*) were democratically elected. Nor were the people of any of these

regions consulted. In order to deal with these fundamental issues, some form of representative congress needed to be created in order to legitimize Moreno's pompous presumptions. Hence, the *cabildos* had no legitimate legal right to dismantle the unified Latin American entity because the people could not give their consent to continue unification, or to part ways as city-states with large hinterlands. Moreno also ignored the fact that the territorial-administrative units whose sovereignty he defended were not created by democratic means, nor had there been any efforts considered that would have allowed the populace to decide if they wished to maintain unity.[6]

In 1812 the Chilean Camilo Henríquez reiterated Moreno's concerns about the impediment to political integration posed by Latin America's great distances. He claimed, "America is so vast and our geniuses are too diverse for all to receive laws from a single legislative body. At best, there could be formed an assembly of plenipotentiaries to agree on certain indispensable points, thus, such an assembly does not appear necessary." Henríquez caustically demonstrated his true views on unification efforts when he belittled and ridiculed the integration idea: "It truly presents itself to the fancy with a very august aspect, but it will not advance beyond the fancy." He added sarcastically that an American congress might be a possibility in the year 2440.[7]

Egaña, O'Higgins, San Martín and Artigas

Another call for political unification came in 1810, when Juan R. Egaña, who has been described as both a Chilean and a Peruvian, called for a confederation rather than a federal state. This prominent republican, essayist and intellectual served as a member of the first Chilean Congress, and eventually was exiled by Royalist forces between 1814 and 1817. He elaborated on his plan for unification in a declaration entitled "Proyecto de una Declaración de los derechos del pueblo de Chile," in which he posited the following observations and objectives: (1) "The countries of America require ... that they reunite for their external security against the projects of Europe, and to eliminate wars between them," (2) "It is very difficult that every country sustain itself even by force from dangers as an isolated sovereignty," and (3) "The day that America reunites in a Congress, it will be as a nation, of both continents.... Her voice will speak to the rest of the globe, her voice will be respectable and her resolutions difficult to contradict."[8]

Egaña argued that although many people considered the political union of Latin America difficult and unlikely, there was in fact no logical reason or impediment to its implementation. Consequently, he wrote, "Why should it be difficult? Since its justice and necessity are well known." He claimed that the idea had political and moral support from all of Latin America, although he did not specify from which sectors this enthusiasm sprang. Taking note of arguments that foreign governments would be opposed to unification, he argued that its implementation could not and should not be "contradicted" by foreign governments if it was the will of Latin Americans. Egaña's perception that political integration could be readily facilitated by Latin American society was influenced by his recognition that Ibero-Americans were related by blood, language, political and economic relations, laws, customs, religion and above all else an "urgent necessity to implement" such a union. He thought that a sincere attempt by state leaders to call on their people for supporting such a proposal was all that was needed to achieve the goal.[9] Egaña's statements contained the same concerns and proposals that would be echoed by proponents of political unification in Latin America during the next two centuries. His successors would face the same dilemmas that he faced: the old Spanish-Portuguese administrative borders, geographical barriers and narrow self-interest. They would also display the same intensity and enthusiasm for the cause.

A few years later, Bernardo O'Higgins, the liberator of Chile, also issued a statement calling for political unification. This declaration, made on May 6, 1818, called for a "great confederation of all the American continent capable of sustaining its political and civil liberty." In spite of the prestige O'Higgins enjoyed, it does not appear that he or his immediate political circle pursued this goal with any significant zeal.[10]

Another important partisan of political integration was José de San Martín, the liberator of Argentina and an influential figure in the liberation of Chile and Peru. He, like others, was frustrated by the long years of war against Spain, and recognized that the source of this long, drawn-out conflict was the lack of political and military coordination that had resulted in six years of war and military stalemates. He complained that this condition arose from "the lack of military leaders and disunion that are the causes of our problems," although, he added, both situations "could be remedied." The general emphasized that the "Americans of the United Provinces had no other objective in the revolution, other than the emancipation from Spanish iron, and belonging to one union." San Martín referred to both objectives as "the cause of the American continent," which, he argued, would ultimately bring order and progress to the region.[11]

San Martín claimed to have no personal political ambitions or ideologies. He prided himself on his all–American, apolitical, pro-integration stance, claiming on December 5, 1820, in Supe, Peru: "My ambition is limited to securing the independence of America ... and to look at all the American states whose forces are under my command as brother states all of which are interested in a wonderful and similar end." The liberator of South America would hold these sentiments to his last days. In a letter to General Guido, dated October 20, 1845, he expressed his concerns about Latin American political factionalism and European political interference in the region, which served to reinforce his pro-unionist stance: "I do not belong to a single party, I reiterate, I belong to the American party, and as such, cannot look without great emotion at the insults that are made towards America."[12]

San Martín was unquestionably one of the most apolitical of all generals that Latin America has produced. However, as time went on he became increasingly alienated from his people. This coincided with the growth of established Latin American governments that descended into civil war and political chaos. The growing anarchy later led San Martín to claim that monarchy in South America would have facilitated its political reunification and order. Any proposal, however, for the re-establishment of a monarch always brought swift and severe reaction from republicans, who always outnumbered royalists in the post-independence era. Whether he actually might have considered accepting the throne himself, as was claimed, is unclear. How serious or politically active San Martín was in supporting these schemes is also unknown.

If San Martín did indeed support royalist policies, it was only because his country and most of the other states in the region had slipped into anarchy, and he could see no other alternative. Ironically, this man, who had served the people of Latin America with such devotion, lacked the influence to overcome the unyielding behavior of the new regional political class, whom he despised and blamed for the problems of the area. San Martín was later forced into political exile and died in France in 1850, forgotten by Latin Americans of his day. His body was later sent to the National Cathedral of Argentina in Buenos Aires, where he is now hailed as a great hero for his military acumen and nonpartisan leadership. For the integrationists, the use of his name did not help their cause; indeed, the inability of unionists to exploit his prestige serves to highlight the obstreperous difficulties they would face.

At the same time that Egaña, O'Higgins, San Martín and Bolívar were promoting the ideal of political integration, José Gervasio Artigas, the colorful liberator of the Banda Oriental, known today as Uruguay, was also supporting political integration. Artigas, who was born in 1764 and died in exile in Paraguay in 1850 (the same year San Martín passed away), spent his life fighting the Spanish, the Argentines, the Portuguese and later the Brazilians, who at various times ruled or controlled his country. Over a lengthy period of time coinciding with the revolutionary struggles, he reiterated the need for closer political ties between the Spanish-American states. In a letter dated December 7, 1811, addressed to the junta of Paraguay, Artigas lamented that Latin America had broken into various states, creating a "deformed body" incapable of meeting the dynamic needs of modern nationhood.[13] In a note sent to the government at Buenos Aires on June 29, 1813, he preached the utility of political integration, declaring that "only union can place the seal on our work, thus securing the guarantee of such a union."[14] While in the midst of fighting his guerrilla war against the Spaniards, he stressed the military necessity for a more coordinated political and military policy that could only come from some modicum of political integration. "We should not have in sight only what we can do respectively, but what all the reunited countries could do," he wrote to the city council of Montevideo on May 9, 1815, "because wherever the peninsulares [Spaniards] present themselves, they would have to confront all Americans."[15] A few years later, in a letter to Simón Bolívar of July 29, 1819, Artigas again emphasized the benefits of political union. Latin America, he wrote, urgently required integration, and it could be readily achieved because the region was "intimately united by natural bonds and reciprocal interests.... I cannot be more expressive in my desires when I offer your excellency the most cordiality for greater harmony and the closest union."[16] Artigas died disappointed that his efforts for a dynamic, prosperous and respected Latin America that was to have come from unification had eluded him, and so many other men who were as pragmatic as they were idealistic.

Proposal of Bernardo Monteagudo

A strong supporter of political integration in Latin America during the 1820s was the political figure Bernardo Monteagudo, who had directed vehement political attacks against the Argentine federalists. He was born in Tucumán, in the Viceroyalty of La Plata (the future Argentina), in 1785, of humble origin and out of wedlock. His mother was of Creole peasant stock and his father, Miguel Monteagudo, born in Cuenca, Spain, served as a cavalryman in the regular Spanish army in the Buenos Aires intendancy. His father later served as mayor of Jujui, also part of the future Argentina. The political activities of the elder Monteagudo served to heighten young Bernardo's interests in the politics of his time.[17]

Bernardo Monteagudo eventually earned a name for himself as a journalist in Buenos Aires, until he was exiled due to the many enemies he made. He called for a strong central government in Argentina to deal with its myriad problems and viewed Latin America's chaos as the logical product of its political factionalization. In 1820, he articulated the view that these conditions made Latin America unsuitable for the adoption of political institutions similar to those of Great Britain or the United States. Shortly after patriot forces liberated Peru, Monteagudo was named foreign minister of that country, but his unpopularity with conservatives led to his dismissal from that post. Eventually he left that country, where he is still viewed as a tyrant. Monteagudo was a hard-core Jacobin who constantly sought to recruit men for his causes. His biographer, C.L. Fregeire, described him as a passionate man of "fiery mentality," who could not under any circumstances be considered a statesman.[18]

Monteagudo's contribution to the cause of Latin American unification took the form of a short essay in favor of political integration, published posthumously in 1825 after his assassination in Lima, Peru. The purpose of the work was to garner support for the Panama Congress, which had been called and organized by Simón Bolívar. The essay called for the creation of a confederation of the Spanish-speaking countries of the region. It did not discuss political structure, preferring instead to comment on those problems of Latin America that could be impacted by political integration. As early as 1813, Monteagudo wrote, "Our force will be born of such a union.... The enemies of the American cause would tremble before such a formidable body. Why can't New Granada and Venezuela make a solid union? And why can't all of southern America reunite under a centralized government?"[19]

In his essay, Monteagudo stressed the need for domestic tranquility throughout Latin America. His own country, Argentina, was the scene of internal chaos and a vicious civil war between nationalists (centrists) and federalists. The chaos caused by this struggle left Monteagudo bitterly opposed to the federalists, whom he blamed for Argentina's troubles. His desire to see internal order restored prompted him to write his treatise. He wrote that political integration would provide the "respect, credit and power due an assembly of our plenipotentiaries that will eventually form a solemn guarantee of our territorial independence and internal peace." The convinced unionist emphasized that "the internal peace of the confederation would be equally guaranteed with the existence of such an assembly, because the interests of each confederate would be examined with the same jealousy and impartiality" that each of the individual states possessed.[20]

His observation echoes statements made in the *Federalist Papers*, written by Alexander Hamilton, John Jay and James Madison, in which they claimed that the diversity of interests throughout the new country would prevent any one interest or region from predominating over any other. There is no evidence, however, that Monteagudo was influenced by the *Federalist Papers*, or that he had even read them. It is possible that he reached this conclusion independently, in the same manner that scientists working separately often reach identical solutions.

Like Bolívar and others, Monteagudo was concerned about a possible attempt by Spain and the Holy Alliance (an alliance composed of Austria, Prussia and Russia designed to crush democratic political movements) to reinstall a monarchical form of government in Spanish America in the name of legitimacy. He applauded the efforts undertaken at the Panama Congress, claiming, "We hope that in the year twenty-five [1825] the Hispanic-American federation will be realized, under the auspices of an assembly whose political foundation should be to consolidate the rights of the countries, and not that of some families."[21] Monteagudo recognized the political realities of Latin America and expressed apprehension about the entry of Brazil into a political union. He opposed it not for cultural reasons, but because the monarchy of Pedro I was incompatible with republican government. Furthermore, the Brazilian crown was closely associated with the Holy Alliance and had intimate family ties to European royalty. As an ardent liberal and republican, Monteagudo argued that the Brazilian throne could not be included in a political union because the regime of Pedro I was not a truly liberal state, or even a constitutional monarchy. He complained that "that sovereign does not demonstrate the respect that he owes to liberal institutions whose spirit placed the scepter in his hands."[22]

The opposition of Monteagudo and other republicans to Brazilian membership in the proposed union arose from the unique historical circumstances surrounding the establishment of the Brazilian monarchy. During the Napoleonic invasion of Portugal, the prince regent, João VI, fled to Brazil, where he became king in 1816. He returned to Portugal in 1821 amidst rumblings of disaffection that clamored for independence. Anticipating a republican initiative to politically separate Portugal and Brazil, the monarch advised his son (who resided in Brazil) to take control of the independence movement if possible. When the political separation between the two realms became inevitable, Pedro I, the son of the Portuguese monarch, declared independence from his father's kingdom. This peculiar political development gave rise to Monteagudo's conviction that Brazil would decide to serve as a "barracks" for the Holy Alliance "as it surely is for the secret agents of the Holy Alliance."[23]

A major problem facing Monteagudo was his association with Jacobinism. His ideological affinity with this radical and popular ideology concerned many people. The harsh and disorderly regime of the Jacobins in France, with its legacy of state-sponsored intimidation and terrorism, had frightened many people. The experience served as a warning to other societies that rapid political and social change could always go awry. Monteagudo's close association with Simón Bolívar raised questions regarding the motives of Bolívar, as well as the desirability of creating a politically unified Latin American state that might result in a continental Jacobin government.

Monteagudo's work concerning political unification reveals a major conceptual flaw. In his proposal he continually wrote of the need for federation and confederation, using these two terms synonymously without contrasting their variances. Why this discrepancy occurred remains unclear. If Monteagudo did discern the differences, he did not discuss them for the benefit of his readers, although Latin American political figures would carefully scrutinize both forms of government in later integration conferences. The two systems are not identical, but refer to distinct forms of governments with differing objectives. Federalism assumes that a new state is to be created out of autonomous member states. In the federal schema the population has the right to elect members to the central government, thus providing for a direct relationship between individuals and the central government, independent of the people's relationship with the member states. It is a system that delegates political power to other political organs at different levels, usually based on geographic subdivisions. Confederate governments assume that the member states are sovereign, and are only part of a quasi-league. They view the center as solely "an agent of the states." Confederations assume that the political center cannot dictate to the individual governments, as central governments normally do. The confederal government provides a weak central authority with very limited powers, and the member states assume that they may or may not decide to cooperate as is necessary or possible. In this type of government, the sole responsibilities for the central organ are the coordination of foreign and economic policy, and direction of military operations in times of war.[24]

If Monteagudo, who was one of the better educated of his society, did not discern these distinctions, he should not be judged too critically, since political figures in the United States of America, the most successful practitioners of federalism, could not agree as to the exact nature of the relationship between the central government and the states until after the civil war of 1861–1865, when the question was permanently resolved in favor of recognizing the supremacy of the central government.[25] Monteagudo's conceptual problems regarding an integrated state would appear repeatedly in the works of many other writers and political figures who seemed to fear relinquishing a major portion of their state's autonomy to a stronger, more centralized federal form of government, a clear indication that they were not ready for a truly unified state, or that they were unsure as to how to proceed towards establishing a state that would provide the political autonomy many Latin Americans sought. It is significant that most of the early plans for political integration called for confederal forms of government. The continual advocacy of confederation as a mode for integration suggests that the Latin Americans were genuinely unwilling to surrender a major portion of their state autonomy.

The failure to create any type of unified political structure in which Latin Americans could deal with common problems during the early years of the wars for independence and post-revolutionary period proved to be a serious error. This omission meant that the potential of armed conflict would always attend future problems between states. The various new governments would be left to fend for themselves on every problem ranging from slavery to state finance. One of the major problems spawned by this failure was the rise of military figures to take control of the political system in their respective countries. Another problem that arose as a result of the new emerging state system was the many suspicions and jealousies held by political rulers and their client groups, which would eventually be transferred to the governed with the creation of an artificial nationalism. Future generations of Latin American statesmen and writers recognized these problems and sought to rectify them almost from the very beginning of the national period, but they could not envision the difficulties they would encounter in seeking to reverse the fragmentation of the region even in their most unimaginable nightmares. The future efforts of Simón Bolívar and others to create a united Latin America highlight the occlusions of political and economic integration that would bewilder unionists for many years.

III

THE FIRST DIPLOMATIC EFFORT: THE PANAMA CONGRESS

Come now, and let us reason together...—Isaiah 1:18

What we have to do now can be finished in a couple of days.—
Manuel Vidaurre to Pedro Gual, April 5, 1826

Simón Bolívar and the Rationale for Political Integration

The first genuine effort towards creating a politically integrated Latin American polity was a state initiative. It appeared in 1824 when Simón Bolívar, the president of Gran Colombia, called upon the governments of Latin America to send diplomatic representatives to a congress in Panama to arrange the details of such a plan. This was to be a strictly voluntary union without any element of coercion to achieve the proposed objective. It was the first of several diplomatic efforts that sought to promote Latin American political union. The effort would be limited primarily to the Spanish-American states, although not all of these countries demonstrated an interest in the project. This conference remained the most important attempt to achieve that goal until the dawn of the 1960s. Bolívar's clarion call began a slate of state-directed initiatives by diplomats who would seek to create a politically integrated state.

The diplomats assigned to this mission faced the arduous task of considering the needs, dictates and changing instructions of their home governments in order to produce a satisfactory treaty. After agreeing to a treaty, they submitted it to their respective governments. The ensuing political obstacle course proved to be daunting for the supporters of political integration. A review of the historical sources negates the suggestion made by Colombian historian

34

Jorge Pacheco Quintero that activity by the United States derailed the conference.[1] The reasons for the failure of the first attempt to unite Latin America arose from the inability of Ibero-American countries to deal with myriad problems between individual Latin American states, and from the divergent objectives and means sought by the governments.

The 1826 congress had its origins in the problems faced by Latin America immediately after it secured independence, among them threats from Spain and the Holy Alliance to re-impose a monarchy on the region. This was the primary motive for calling the congress, but not the only one. In addition to foreign threats, a major problem facing the region in 1824 was the appearance of rivalries among the Latin American countries that could easily lead to a war more devastating than any foreign threat. Some states had aspirations for enlargement, all had territorial disputes with their neighbors, and all sought to play balance-of-power politics. As a result, political integration was promoted as a means for averting fratricidal war.

The possibility of each society experiencing civil war or internal unrest was also very real in 1824. All the Latin American countries faced problems associated with their political, social and economic development that eventually proved too complex for the young states. Most of them would experience military revolts, and social, regional, ideological, political or class-inspired insurrections. As a result, many Latin Americans began to consider the possibility that a new and distinct political organization could resolve these issues.

Bolívar's propagation of a unified Latin America was based on the supposition that the Ibero-Americans were culturally similar, and that such kinship could provide the basis for an integrated state. His nationalism and ideology were similar to the nationalist, liberal creed pursued years later by Camillo Cavour, Giuseppe Mazzini and Giuseppe Garibaldi, the unifiers of Italy who spoke of universal fraternity. As a traditional nineteenth century nationalist liberal, Bolívar readily accepted parallel notions concerning the right of a people to govern themselves, the protection of private property, and a "civic nationalism" that recognized the rights of the individual irrespective of race or religious background. This attitude was evinced in 1815, when he wrote, "More than anyone, I desire to see America fashioned into the greatest nation in the world, greatest not so much by virtue of area and wealth as by its freedom and glory." The nationalism expressed by Bolívar cannot, however, be equated with the nationalist tribalism of the twentieth century because he did not emphasize bloodline, or articulate a desire for conquest of other peoples and countries, but instead focused on the many cultural ties that bound Latin Americans together.[2]

Bolívar felt that the geography of the region posed a problem to political integration, but he recognized that geography alone did not constitute a legitimate or logical reason for impeding the creation of a new political organization. On the contrary, he asserted, Latin America was "one fatherland." In June 1818 he wrote, "All the Americans should have only one fatherland, now that we have had perfect unity in everything." His long-term plan was to create an "American Pact" encompassing all the American states, once royalist forces were defeated. The new republic would "present America to the world with an aspect of majesty and greatness without example among the ancient nations. America thus united, if heaven may concede us this desired wish, could then call itself the queen of the nations and mother of republics."[3]

Bolívar emphasized that political integration would assist Latin America in dealing with the many problems it would face in the future if "all the states allied themselves in a common law that would settle their external relations and provide them the conserving power of a general and permanent congress." A major objective of integration, according to Bolívar, would be to insure "internal order be conserved intact between the different states and within each one of them." This concern stemmed from the threat to property holders that came from the poorer classes, and from the constant political bickering afflicting the Latin American political landscape, which would continue for decades to come. It was clearly recognized that any state suffering civil war or internal tensions would make a tempting morsel for predatory powers. Thus, in case of foreign attack or internal anarchy, the confederation could quickly provide assistance against "anarchical factions" that might fuel the fires of military adventurism.[4]

Bolívar's plan for a unified Latin America was reinforced by his reading of an essay written by Jean-Jacques Rousseau on the city-state of Geneva and its republican form of government. The essay convinced him that a large state was more likely than a small one to survive upheavals. It is unclear if Bolívar was familiar with the *Federalist Papers*, or with any other treatises dealing with federal or confederal systems of government. As he saw it, the primary purpose of any political entity simply was survival: "The primary substance of all things is existence, the rest is secondary.... In the end it is always better to be, than not to be."[5]

Bolívar envisioned the new state forming along a north-south axis from the California-Oregon border all the way to Tierra del Fuego, and on an east-west path from Puerto Rico to the Galapagos Islands.[6] All member states of the proposed organization would be politically equal. "Not one would be weaker with respect to the others, not one would be stronger."[7] His views are not surprising, as he had commanded troops from Colombia, Venezuela, Ecuador, Peru, Argentina, Chile and Cuba. This experience provided Bolívar with a more sophisticated view of Latin American society than those held by his more myopic contemporaries.

Bolívar's call for political integration was not simply for a joint alliance or for the merging of a particular sub-region of Latin America. His 1824 proposal called for the creation of a political organization that would link the various republics. His writings reveal that he often used differing political terms synonymously in referring to the desired structure for political integration, i.e., confederation, federation, or congress of plenipotentiaries. It seems he discerned no differences between these terms. This failure to differentiate may have been a deliberate effort to maintain flexibility by avoiding specific details that could have alienated various groups. It may be that his use of these sufficiently distinct terms resulted from changing perceptions of political conditions that were in a constant state of flux. The only matter consistent in Bolívar's thinking is that after 1815, he favored a measure of autonomy for the various republics, which he recognized as a necessity if a successful state was to be created. He articulated this political flexibility in his famous Jamaica letter when he wrote, "I say, do not adopt the best system of government, but the one that is most likely to succeed."[8]

Bolívar was consistent on certain fundamental political issues. He energetically supported a pro-independence policy, believed in the need for a politically integrated Latin America, and held a lifelong belief in the alleged inadequacy of the common people to participate in government. He supported an aristocratic type of republic, resembling the early United States, but preferably similar to Great Britain. Bolívar's multi-state government would have granted the executive broad powers while providing representation for competing interests, although the gentry, which was the most influential group in the nineteenth century, would have been the primary beneficiary of his plan. Ironically, Bolívar, a man of political flexibility, originally opposed a federal from of government for Latin America because it was "over-perfect and it demands political virtues and talents far superior to our own."[9]

This change in Bolívar's views resulted from the political factionalism that had evolved in Latin America as competing local and regional elites struggled to accumulate political power. He suggested that diverse and rugged geography, climates, and regional interests could impede the creation of a truly centralized state. Consequently, he favored the creation of a federation or a confederation for the region. This organization would be more than an alliance, but not quite a centralized, unitary state.

There were earlier calls for integration, as already noted, but no other historical figure is so identified with the cause of Latin America political union as Bolívar. On June 3, 1811, in an address to the Patriotic Society (Sociedad

Patriótica) founded by himself and José Miranda of Caracas, Bolívar asked: "Is not our problem that of all the Americans? What then can we discuss if such a confederation that has been proposed now exists, and is so deep, and so profound?" He warned Latin Americans that if they did not unite, they would lose an indispensable opportunity to deal effectively with the many problems they faced, asserting that "to vacillate is to lose it."[10]

Until his death, Bolívar never ceased supporting the idea of a politically re-integrated Latin America. While many historians would attribute the first calls for political integration to other individuals, the historian Ignacio Quiroz wrote, "It is Bolívar who consecrated the great and constant energies to achieve this project that constituted the greatest ideal of his life and which places him above all the liberators."[11] The historian Jorge Pacheco Quintero agreed that Bolívar's name should take pride of place because "the unity of the continent as well as good relations between all the American nations was a constant in the public life of the liberator."[12] Likewise, General Daniel F. O'Leary, Bolívar's highly efficient and articulate aide, wrote that the first genuine initiative for unification of Latin America had to be attributed to the liberator.[13]

Having recognized the need for political integration earlier in the revolutionary struggle, Bolívar sought to link the various states to Gran Colombia through bilateral treaties with each Latin American state. He accomplished this objective with a number of states. It then became his objective to create a Latin-American congress that would be confederative or federative in nature. In an effort to win political support for his idea, Bolívar wrote to Bernardo O'Higgins, the ruler of Chile, stating he was sending a minister plenipotentiary to implement what was in effect his primary foreign policy objective, the political integration of Latin America. The letter reveals a man filled with enthusiasm over the prospect of creating a new political organization in which he claimed that

> the union of the five great states of America is itself so sublime that I do not doubt but that it will come to be the cause of amazement in Europe. The imagination cannot conceive without admiration the magnitude of such a colossus which, like Homer's Jupiter, will cause the earth to quake with a glance. Who shall oppose an America united in heart, subject to one law, and guided by the torch of liberty? Such is the objective which the government of Colombia contemplates in appointing to Your Excellency, as its Minister Plenipotentiary, Senator Joaquín Mosquera.[14]

Unmoved, the Chileans, like the Argentines, failed to attend the congress, and indirectly contributed to its eventual failure by refusing to provide the necessary political support.

From Lima, Bolívar issued his official call for a Latin American congress on December 7, 1824. The invitees included Mexico, Rio de la Plata (Argentina), Gran Colombia (Colombia, Venezuela, and Ecuador united), Chile, Peru, and the United Provinces of Central America (later known as the Federal Republic of Central America). He proposed that an assembly of plenipotentiaries be nominated by their respective governments and meet in Panama. Representing the half-way point between the Latin American countries made Panama a reasonable and symbolic site for a convention which, Bolívar claimed, would surpass the glory that Corinth held for the Greeks.[15] In spite of his admiration for ancient Greek civilization, he cautioned his fellow Latin Americans against following their political path. He feared the same host of problems descending on the Latin Americans as had befallen the Greeks: "Heaven forbid that our future history should be that of the Greek nations, which, it appears, could exist only long enough to witness but brief flashes of freedom, followed by fearful tempests of tyranny, instead of surviving to produce happy men and citizens."[16]

In a letter to all the Spanish-American republics, co-signed by José Sánchez Carrión, his minister for foreign relations in Gran Colombia, Bolívar wrote that after fifteen years of war the Latin American states needed to create a new structure "in order to achieve a system of guarantees that in war and peace will be the shield of our new destiny. It is about time that the interests and relations linking the former Spanish colonies have a foundation, if possible, that perpetuates these governments." Bolívar argued that such authority and guarantees could only be preserved by "an assembly of plenipotentiaries appointed by each of our Republics," and that an assembly was necessary to "maintain a uniformity of principles and whose very name alone should put an end to our quarrels."

Bolívar suggested that the congress convene no later than six months from the date of his invitation. He referred to its attendees as "confederates," probably because it was the least threatening term to those states anxious to preserve their autonomy. He hoped that a permanent capital might be chosen quickly, and the powers of the congress agreed upon. Postponing the conference, he wrote, "would deprive us of the advantages which that assembly will afford from its very beginning."[17]

Prospects for the congress looked good. Moral and political support came from Great Britain. In the United States, Senator Henry Clay spoke enthusiastically about the conference. Europeans also demonstrated their support for the Panama Congress. This was ironic because the main impetus for the congress arose from a perceived military and naval threat from Europe. The most effusive support on the continent came from Paris, where an attack on the Latin American republics was supposedly being coordinated. In 1825, M. De

Pradt, the former archbishop of Malines, France, published a work praising the forthcoming establishment of the Panama Congress while also predicting its failure:

> A congress in America! A congress of communities! A congress to terminate the war between Europe against America and to determine what rights one portion of the globe has with respect to the other parts! O Sovereign God! In what epoch do we live! If we compare these great novelties and grandeur what will the rest of history compare to except, the most ancient times? In what epoch of the world has such a reunion been called forth from the bosom of a territory so vast, and destined to fail despite so many similar interests? Admirable America! If you can elevate yourselves over the world with the luster and beneficence that is signaled by the daily apparition of the heavens which in other times received your culture and whose brilliant image is represented on your flags.... I could contemplate in it and present a great scene of the world, of men equal in majesty to those Romans, whose royal aspect [appearance] imposed respect, and interests whose superiority equals those of the superiority of America over Latium and Epirus.[18]

De Pradt understood that the many difficulties faced by the Latin Americans would need to be overcome, in particular the age-old problems of provincialism, political inexperience and factionalization that he felt emanated from their colonial background. Nevertheless, he argued that Latin America had legitimate interests to secure and positive prospects for the future, if it could consummate such a union. De Pradt's statements provided valuable moral support from abroad for the cause of Latin American cooperation. He observed that the objectives of the congress were to create a confederation or an even weaker structure. De Pradt expressed concern that the growth in the number of armies might lead to war. A reorganization of the region would minimize that possibility.

The situation was ironic, De Pradt argued, because the Latin American states possessed "maritime" attributes and were therefore in a unique position to impede the growth of militarism in their countries.[19] His assertion was based on the assumption that maritime states focus their manpower requirements on producing sailors and merchants. This view promoted the idea that such states forged links of economic interdependence, minimizing the risk of war and the need for armies. Although De Pradt recognized that the congress was meeting for the sole purpose of defeating Spain, he advocated a "perpetual union between all the new states of America" if the former metropolis did not cease its bellicose actions.[20] He failed to realize that the requirements of war were not enough to forge such a union. An effective union required the presence of a political class sophisticated enough to understand the need for economic interdependence.

Invitation Extended to Great Britain

An invitation to attend the Panama Congress was extended to Great Britain. This was logical because of the importance of Britain as the most influential political, economic and military power in the American hemisphere. British foreign secretary Sir George Canning, however, was reluctant to involve his country with the proposed Panama conference. Eventually he agreed to send an observer with strict instructions to maintain neutrality, and to offer any assistance necessary and compatible with Britain's position as a nonparticipant.[21]

Canning's primary concern and objective vis-à-vis Latin America was that the United Kingdom not enter into any agreements that entailed political obligations. At this point in time, the UK wished to avoid any military conflict. The primary foreign policy of London was to enlarge British access to foreign markets, which required a peacetime environment. As far back as October 1823, Canning had informed his various commissioners in the region "that so far is Gt. Britain from looking to any more intimate connection with any of the late Spanish Provinces than that of political and commercial intercourse, that His Majesty could not be induced by any consideration to enter any engagement which might be considered bringing them under His dominion."[22]

Once the congress was scheduled, it became necessary for the Latin Americans to clarify any doubts regarding their goals at the Panama Congress vis-à-vis the British government. In a meeting with the Gran Colombian minister to Great Britain, Manuel José Hurtado, held in London on November 7, 1825, Canning was assured that the objectives of the congress were strictly peaceful.[23] Two months later on January 23, 1826, Canning sent a formal note to Hurtado explaining the objectives of the British mission assigned to the Panama Congress:

> The duty of His Majesty's commissioner at Panama will be, not to interfere in any way in the international concerns of the newly independent American States; but while he watches over the interests of Great Britain in her relations with those States, to afford every assistance that may be required of him, to the deliberations of the Congress, so far as may consist with the neutral position in which Great Britain is placed between the American States and Spain; and to evince by all means in his power, the anxious desire of His Govt. to maintain harmony between the several States of America, to restore peace (if possible) between these countries with Spain, and to preserve their general tranquility of the New World and of the Old.[24]

On March 18, 1826, Canning appointed Edward James Dawkins as commissioner to the Panama Convention and formally notified the Latin Americans of the decision. Dawkins arrived at the Panama Congress on June 22,

1826. His instructions listed three goals: to advance British interests, to promote peace, and to collect information in support of the first two objectives. Canning wrote Dawkins, "His Majesty has no other object in sending you to the Congress than to obtain the most regular and correct information of its proceedings, and to assure the American States collectively of the friendly sentiments and the lively interest in their welfare and tranquility which His Majesty has repeatedly expressed."[25]

In discussing Canning's intentions, R.R. Arragon noted, "Observation and the expression of good-will alone would not have justified the dispatch of an agent and two secretaries to distant and insalubrious Panama." Arragon stressed that there were specific and important goals assigned to the appointment of Dawkins. He argued that the primary objective of Dawkins was to relieve border tensions in the hemisphere that might lead to war, as in the tense dispute between Argentina and Brazil over Uruguay, then known as the Banda Oriental, which nearly led to war between them. Dawkins was also instructed to seek reconciliation between Spain and the newly emerging Latin American states in the hope that peace and tranquility might create a sounder foundation for the expansion of trade between Britain and Ibero-America.[26]

British Concern About the United States

Even before the British government was invited to attend the Panama Congress, Foreign Secretary Canning had anticipated that an invitation would be extended to the United States. He speculated about the possible British response to the United States if it sent diplomats to the congress:

> I have been reflecting a good while on the difficulty in which we are likely to be placed by the intended Congress of American States—more especially if, as is not improbable, the U.S. of North America are invited to send a deputy to it. Shall we send any Minister there, if invited or uninvited, or shall we take no notice of it? Either is embarrassing: but I incline to think the last—though the easiest— the most dangerous course of conduct. Yet if we send to what specific purpose?[27]

Canning was suspicious of any actions taken by Washington. He made it clear he favored the construction of an exclusively Spanish-American political league. He emphatically opposed inclusion of the United States, especially if Washington were to assume a leadership role. Canning informed Dawkins that such an organization "would be viewed by your Government with great jealousy as approaching to that species of league of the Americas as against Europe, which you are already apprised His Majesty could neither acknowledge nor approve." Canning forcefully reiterated his policy in a letter addressed to Dawkins, adamantly stating:

> Any project for putting the U.S. of North America at the head of an American confederacy as against Europe would be left as an ill return for the service which has been rendered to those States, and the dangers which have been averted from them, by the countenance and friendship and publick declaration of Great Britain; and it would too probably at no very distant period endanger the peace of both America and Europe.[28]

Bolívar, too, was apprehensive about inviting the United States because he knew it would antagonize Britain, whom he viewed as the arbiter of world affairs.[29] The position of the British foreign secretary was in part a response to the earlier publication of the Monroe Doctrine in 1824 that directed a warning towards the Holy Alliance prohibiting any further European colonization. Canning let it be known that Britain considered the United States to be in the same legal and political situation as the European states were in.[30]

One British journal was even more blunt about any attempts by the United States to exclude Britain from the American continent when it militantly declared that Britain would maintain pride of place, and continue to maintain a political role in the Western Hemisphere as long as "Canada, Nova Scotia and the West Indies were hers, she would never be the only American power excluded from an American Congress."[31]

Bolívar Seeks British Alliance

Two recurring concerns of Bolívar were the rise of political factionalism and the threat of domestic unrest posed by various groups in Latin America. Both problems were bringing anarchy to the region. Bolívar hoped some sort of alliance with Great Britain would provide a reconstructed Latin America with a foundation for dealing with domestic problems and foreign military threats.[32] Bolívar had great admiration for the United Kingdom. There were two major reasons for his attitude. First, he appreciated the stability British society had achieved during the course of its lengthy political evolution. Second, during the course of the Latin American wars for independence, Bolívar had visited Britain and had received extensive financial and military assistance from its government. His dependency on the British for military and political support was so critical and extensive that in letter dated May 19, 1815, he had suggested turning "the provinces of Panama and Nicaragua over to the British government for the latter to make them the center of commerce by building canals" in return for military supplies.[33] Likewise, his military campaigns included large number of British volunteers. Bolívar's admiration for the United Kingdom was reflected in his observation, "The philosophy of the age is English politics."[34]

At one point Bolívar suggested to a British official that a monarchy might be preferable for Latin America, a suggestion that was leaked to the public and created considerable suspicion of Bolívar. The mere consideration of establishing a throne earned him many enemies. There is no evidence, however, that his primary or ultimate objective was the establishment of a monarchy per se. His rationale for contemplating a monarchy was his belief that the quest for total equality on a political level would bring ruin to the region. Eventually, he suggested the possibility of requesting a protectorate from Great Britain in the summer of 1825.[35] The British Consul general agent, Charles Ricketts, serving in Lima, Peru, was in an excellent position to observe socio-economic-political realities. He suggested Bolívar sought an alliance with Britain because

> Under the protection of Great Britain the South American States would learn the measures most advisable to adapt for the general preservation and tranquility; disagreements would be prevented; the respective governments would be consolidated; wholesome laws and regulations would be established; the colored population would be kept in awe by the union which was formed; the Albocracy would gradually increase in power; and ere the lapse of many years each State would be relieved from all existing apprehensions.[36]

It is clear from the memo that by 1825 events in Latin America had come to a political, economic and social nadir, and Bolívar was desperate. Tensions were rising and new measures were needed to deal with them. Cognizant of these problems and trends, Ricketts wrote Canning that Bolívar was hoping

> Great Britain would not be a silent observer of the discussions which would arise in the Congress, since he was satisfied that they could not terminate any practical good, unless aided by your judicious and impartial counsels. The several states required to be upheld by the power and influence of Great Britain, without which no security could be expected, no consistency preserved, and no social compact maintained. All would be alike subject to destruction by disputes with each other, and by internal anarchy.[37]

Latin Americans rejected Bolívar's ideas about creating an alliance or confederation with Britain. He and the Gran Colombian government were accused of attempting to make separate treaties with foreign governments without consulting the other states. Manuel Lorenzo de Vidaurre, a future Peruvian delegate to the Panama Congress, argued that an alliance with Great Britain would be similar to the Portuguese-British alliance, which he referred to as a model of "true servitude."[38]

Bolívar's fellow Colombians were not well disposed to such a plan either.

The minister of foreign affairs for Gran Colombia, José Rafael Revenga, adamantly opposed Bolívar's proposal. He believed a British–Latin American pact, whether it took the form of an alliance or a protectorate, would only strengthen Great Britain. Revenga cautioned that if Latin Americans ever sought to break away from the supranational organization it would entail a bitter struggle between both societies.[39] Bolívar defended his proposal for an alliance with Britain, assuming, of course, America could be restructured. The proposed alliance with the United Kingdom would assist a reorganized Latin America in developing and strengthening its political institutions and political culture, although he recognized there might be serious problems in cementing an alliance between so many weak countries and the most powerful state on earth:

> It seems to me that we would gather much importance and respectability in an alliance with Great Britain, because under its shadow we could grow, become men, instruct and strengthen ourselves, in order to present ourselves with a level of civilization and strength that are necessary for a great nation. These advantages do not diminish the fears that powerful nation [Britain] will in the future be the arbiter of counsels and decisions of the assembly: that its voice would become the most penetrating, that its will and interests become the soul of the confederation that it should not be crossed or displeased for fear they need to avoid an impossibly strong enemy. This in my opinion is the major danger that exists in mixing a country that is so powerful, with others that are so weak.[40]

Bolívar added, however, that if Britain came to predominate in such an alliance, it would be a healthy domination, because it would produce an "immense mass of power," providing Latin America with the necessary stability for its institutions.[41] Nevertheless, he recognized and anticipated that other serious and intractable problems could result if the proposed alliance between the United Kingdom and the proposed Latin American Confederation ever came to fruition. He was nevertheless cognizant of the territorial ambitions that Britain might possess. Bolívar worried that the British might decide to take possession of the island of Chiloe, off the Chilean coast, because it was the first port after rounding Cape Horn that would provide English merchants with a definite commercial advantage in the Pacific if they possessed it.[42]

In spite of these potential problems, Bolívar deemed it necessary to court the United Kingdom because it was an American power that could serve to counter the influence of Europe and the United States. Britain could also tame the territorial desires of Brazil, which the Spanish-speaking states recognized could be mollified by British pressure. The recommendation by Bolívar died a quick death, because of opposition led by Revenga and the refusal of Britain to enter an alliance.

That the proposed alliance never reached fruition is less significant than the belief by some Spanish-American leaders that British amity and support was required in the Western Hemisphere for any fundamental political initiatives. It would be erroneous to conclude that Bolívar's proposal arose out of docility or a fawning servitude to a foreign power. His policy recommendations must be analyzed and considered in light of the political, social and economic milieu facing Latin America at the time. Latin America's political leaders faced a morass of domestic problems complicated by the diplomatic and military intrigues of the Holy Alliance, in the early and middle 1820s. An objective analysis of his pro–British campaign would acknowledge that Bolívar dealt shrewdly and flexibly with Great Britain (though he did not attain the desired alliance). Latin American leaders had to carefully negotiate with foreign powers utilizing all the diplomatic caution and skill at their disposal because few if any options were available to them. In the midst of this political discussion within Latin America, the British stood firm in their desire to remain aloof from potential Latin American political snares. British objectives remained narrowly focused on maintaining and expanding their commercial markets in the region and minimizing the political influence of Europe and the United States.

Invitation Extended to Other American States

Invitations were extended to almost every country in Latin America, except Paraguay, which was governed as a hermetically sealed state under President Gaspar Francia, a dictator, who sought to isolate his country as much as possible. Bolivia was invited to send delegates, but the two plenipotentiaries, Doctor Mendizábal and Mariano Serrano, never arrived.[43] The Brazilians did not participate because they recognized the incompatibility of their government with the new republics. In fact, Brazil did not demonstrate any interest in integration efforts until 1960. Despite the refusal of the Chilean government to participate in the event, it declared itself fascinated by "the immense advantages of it." Buenos Aires refused any association with the project. According to the Colombian historian Pedro A. Zubieta, Buenos Aires refused to participate because the other states refused to utilize the congress for settling the territorial dispute between Argentina and Brazil over the Cisplatine republic, later to be known as Uruguay. Another reason states refused to participate was the suspicion they held of Simón Bolívar. Both Argentina and Chile erroneously viewed the proposal as an attempt by Bolívar to extend his personal political control over all of Latin America.[44]

The United States was also invited to attend against the wishes of Bolívar, who thought it might offend Great Britain. He referred to Britain as the ruler of the world, and considered it "more capable of deciding everything."[45] Nevertheless an invitation was extended to the North American government and on December 26, 1825, President James Monroe sent a letter to the United States Senate discussing the proposed Panama Congress. He stated that the conference "involved interests of the highest importance for the union." He nominated Richard C. Anderson of Kentucky and John Sergeant of Pennsylvania to serve as envoy extraordinary and plenipotentiary, respectively, to the Panama Congress. Anderson died en route and Sergeant arrived late.[46] Sergeant attended the follow-up conference in Tacubaya, Mexico, but left when it became obvious it would prove fruitless.[47] The letters of political executives and diplomats from the Latin American states attending the Panama conference hardly mention the United States; although they did indicate a distrust of the U.S., they were not alarmed by its proposed presence. This latter development suggests the state system of Latin America is exclusively to blame for the failure of the Panama Congress, as Washington's role was negligible.

Efforts to include Brazil at the conference were extensive. A formal invitation was extended to that country, despite the possibility of war between Brazil and Argentina and the intense suspicion other Latin Americans had of the Brazilians. (In case of such a war, there was the possibility the other states would side with Buenos Aires, which was Bolívar's plan). As early as 1824 the Mexican minister to Great Britain, José Mariano Michelena, met with the Brazilian minister to the United Kingdom regarding the "idea of a plan of union between the new governments of the great American continent." The immediate Brazilian reply to Michelena is unclear, but it is clear the Brazilians never seriously considered the idea of a political union with the rest of Latin America due to fundamental differences in their political structures. Of course, many other Latin Americans viewed the Brazilian system as incompatible with the republican form of government that existed throughout the independent Spanish-speaking countries.[48]

The Brazilian government did, however, eventually agree to attend the conference after noting the extensive Latin American desire to include it in the conference, and officially accepted the invitation. The acceptance was confirmed by the Brazilian minister to London, Manuel Rodrigues Gameiro Pessoa (Gameyro), in a letter dated October 30, 1825, which was addressed to the Colombian minister resident in London, Mr. Hurtado.[49] Gameiro stated that Brazil had accepted the invitation to Panama so his country could associate with the other states of America. Gameiro, who referred to Pedro I as "my master," claimed the acceptance was offered because "the politics of the

Emperor are so generous and beneficial that he is always quick to contribute to the repose, happiness and glory of America." The Brazilian minister's letter was deliberately vague and did not indicate what his government hoped to accomplish at the Panama Congress or why it was sending representatives, save that Brazil's plenipotentiaries would maintain "strict neutrality" between the Spanish-speaking American states and Spain.[50]

The acceptance by Brazil to participate in the conference and the vagueness of Gameiro's letter were undoubtedly the result of pressure put on Brazil by Great Britain. Indeed, Hurtado received assurances from British foreign secretary Canning that Britain had used all of its influence to persuade the Brazilians to attend the Panama Congress.[51] Despite Brazil's formal acceptance, it did not send representatives, nor is it likely it ever intended to do so.

Problems Facing Latin America

One of the problems facing the proponents of political integration was the need to strike a balance regarding the newly proposed political organization. This issue revolved around the proposed duties of the individual governments and their relationship to the proposed central government. A foretaste of the congress's future fortunes may be gleaned from the comments of the Mexican minister to Great Britain, José M. Michelena. While in London, Michelena assiduously solicited the opinions of the various Latin American ministers resident there. After some preliminary discussions with his counterparts, he counseled Mexico City that Latin America should unite "with the objective of accepting the principles of their independence, without intervening in the form of government nor in the internal organization of those states, that will form an offensive and defensive league," but added that the various states first needed to integrate their own societies. He also suggested that political union between the Latin American states should continue to be the ultimate objective of each state.[52]

As the member delegates began to assemble and discuss their agenda in Panama, it became clear that Michelena's assessment of Latin America political reality was accurate. The main question for the attending delegates became how to maintain the independence of their respective states. Their joint solution resulted from extensive compromise that called for creation of a solely defensive military alliance, which would assist them in thwarting the predatory designs of foreign states, yet recognize their sovereignty. It would also assist them in resolving differences amongst themselves. The diplomats soon discovered that their respective national legislatures would not be so generous in agreeing to surrender any political power. Nevertheless, plenipotentiaries from Central America, Colombia, Mexico and Peru eagerly arrived at the appointed rendezvous in Panama and attempted to create a constitution for a reorganized Latin America.

While these efforts were in progress, Bolívar lobbied the Latin American governments to support the cause of political integration, always cognizant of the chaos facing the region. In a letter to Francisco Paula de Santander, the vice president of Gran Colombia and a close political ally, he forcefully emphasized that political restructuring of Latin America was absolutely essential if anarchy was to be prevented. Unless the trend was reversed, he argued, "The malady will be deep routed and it will penetrate to the blood. I return, therefore, to my original plan of federation as the only remedy," which he stated would be "a temple and sanctuary from criminal trends."[53]

In spite of the many dilemmas facing the diplomats, Bolívar was enthusiastic and positive about the prospects of forming a new state and confided to Santander, "Every time I think of this project I am enchanted, for the creation of a colossus is not a common occurrence." The project was of such vital and inestimable importance to Bolívar that he provided the vice president with instructions to allay any offenses or problems that might threaten the congress and the potential union of the various states, stressing the importance of keeping the region from slipping into more serious problems:

> You must order that everything must be overlooked, so that we may have federation. Consideration must be given to any request from whatever quarter, though it may mean tolerating a certain amount of foolishness for some time; what I mean is that the federal union, or the outward appearance of that political system, must be pursued at all costs. Its mere shadow saves us from the abyss, or at least prolongs our existence.[54]

Bolívar insisted that he was exasperated with the state of political factionalization, anarchy and egotism permeating Latin American society. He told Santander, "Only the expectation of this federation will keep me in America a while longer, that is, until the American Congress becomes a reality." Doubts were expressed to the vice president about how long such a congress might last, but it was suggested that even a short-lived assembly would assist Latin Americans through the difficult first years of statehood. "This congress," wrote Bolívar, "must survive us at least for the first ten or twelve years of our infancy, even though it might dissolve forever following that period. It is my feeling that we will live on for centuries if we can only survive the first dozen years of childhood." Bolívar argued that even if the congress resulted in failure, it would nevertheless provide a firm and decisive foundation for political relations between Latin American states in the future. He concluded by adding,

"First impressions last forever. Moreover, the relations that will be established during those years will serve us for years to come."[55]

Bolívar insisted that if the congress succeeded, it could play a positive role by peacefully resolving territorial disputes between the various states. He observed that whenever European countries had depended on their diplomats to solve problems between competing states there had always existed inevitable problems "that kept them apart," but when the various European countries worked within the congress system they had "composed their differences ... and now they are invincible." If such a system had worked successfully for the Europeans, argued Bolívar, it would ensure a smoother road for Latin American development. "It would seem that we being nothing, as we are only in the process of being born, should not hesitate for a moment to follow their example."[56]

Even before the Panama Congress was held, with all its problems, Bolívar let it be known he was only continuing public service until he could see the congress actually convoked. He considered the congress to be Latin America's last best hope. If it failed, there was nothing more he could do but let history run its course. Failure of the congress would be the last straw for him. His correspondence makes it abundantly clear that Bolívar understood it was only his prestige that maintained the effort to create an integrated Latin America. Bolívar's disappointment with the progress of implementing republican institutions in Latin America was reflected in a letter to Santander:

> My heart is set on the Isthmian Congress. If I were to leave, it would never be held, or at best, who knows what it would be like? The one thing that keeps me in America, and particularly in Peru, is this very Congress. If I achieve it fine, if not I shall lose all hope of being of further use to my country. I am thoroughly convinced that if this federation is not formed, there will be nothing to look forward to.[57]

A few days after Santander received Bolívar's letter, he was in receipt of another one dated January 23, 1825. In this memo, Bolívar expressed discomfort with the international situation as it related to Latin America. He reiterated that it was imperative the congress be held, lest the Holy Alliance come to an agreement with Brazil to use it as a base for military and political operations against the fledgling republics. He feared the Brazilian emperor had come to an understanding with the Spanish government for the purpose of reconquering these independent states for the ideological cause of absolutism. Bolívar observed that the Brazilian throne was powerful enough to destroy the armies of all the other Latin American states. He claimed two thousand German soldiers had arrived on Brazilian soil and six thousand Russian troops were en route for the purpose of enforcing legitimacy. The Brazilian monarch could take advantage of the political chaos surrounding the Spanish-American countries to his favor. "He would, of course, begin with Buenos Aires and end with us." The only effective measure that could be taken to offset this problem, claimed Bolívar, would be the immediate convening of the Panama Congress.[58]

A few days later, Bolívar reported the murder of Bernardo Monteagudo, a long-time political ally. The assassination was symptomatic of the habitual political unrest in Latin America. Monteagudo had been a staunch supporter of political integration and a radical political figure; his death only helped fan the flames of enmity between the various political groups. The murderers were apprehended and confessed to the crime. During the interrogation they implicated two members of an opposing political faction known as the *godos* (Goths). Bolívar theorized that he was probably intended as an additional victim and blamed secret agents of the Holy Alliance, in particular France, for carrying out the murder in collusion with local residents of Lima. Bolívar identified the French agent responsible for the murder as the Count de Moges, who was eventually ordered to leave the country. Amidst this crisis, he wrote Santander, "I am weary of serving and of having my mind in constant turmoil."[59] The concern with intrigues launched by the European powers was aggravated by the threat posed by Brazil, which he felt acted as the chief agent of the Holy Alliance in South America, leading him to urgently plead the cause of a common Latin American statehood as a remedy. Of equal importance, he stated that his political authority would be relinquished upon its inception:

> If we the free nations do not form a similar union we are lost. Although I repeatedly speak of this union, I can never mention it often enough.... My current obsession is to send representatives to the Isthmus to establish one great Federal Congress. I again urge you to dispatch representatives because of the urgency and usefulness of this action. This fact is so obvious that every American must be convinced of the need for a general assembly. I believe this to be the last service that we shall be able to render America, and upon its realization I shall relinquish all my authority.[60]

Bolívar's concern with the threat posed by the Holy Alliance cannot be underestimated. From the historical perspective of contemporary times, it may now be dismissed as an unrealistic consideration by the European monarchs, but Bolívar and the Latin Americans took this threat very seriously. Bolívar recommended that once the Panama Congress of Plenipotentiaries met, they needed to adopt measures that would provide them with at least one hundred thousand men, and that this army should be "maintained by the Confederation itself and independent of the constituent nations." He also called for the establishment of the "federal navy," which presumably would be free of any control by the individual republics.[61]

Bolívar expressed hope that the Panama Congress might alleviate domestic problems, such as racial discrimination, and ensure that "domestic control would be preserved untouched among the states and within each of them." He suggested that a symmetrical political balance of power could also be achieved through convocation of the congress and claimed, "mankind will a thousand times bless this league for promoting its general welfare, and will reap from it untold benefits."[62] He wrote that the success of the proposed confederation would be of such benefit that "it is reasonable to expect that, since the advantages of membership in the Confederation are to be great, the penalty involving their loss must be still greater in proportion."[63]

In the meantime, Bolívar expressed disillusion with political conditions in Chile and the United Provinces of the Rio de la Plata (Argentina) because they were in a state of chaos "and practically without government." Bolívar specifically referred to the numerous problems that plagued Argentina. He referred to Buenos Aires as little more than a "Hanseatic City without territory" and pointed out that Brazil had wrested control of Uruguay from Buenos Aires, the Native Americans controlled the rest of the country, and Santa Fe had declared its independence. The desperate situation in Argentina led Bolívar to re-emphasize his earlier proposal for an alliance with Britain, claiming it could provide maximum flexibility to Latin America's political leaders while they wrestled with the morass of problems facing their countries.[64]

Another problem facing a majority of Latin Americans was the desire of Brazil to annex the territory of adjoining Latin American states. This matter had become a vexing concern to Bolívar and the other Spanish-American political leaders. They realized that the primary objective of the Brazilian government was to engage in predatory territorial acquisitions via cooperation with the Holy Alliance. On May 30, 1825, in a letter to Colombian vice president Francisco Paula de Santander, Bolívar expressed concern over a military incursion by Brazilian troops into the region of Chiquitos in Bolivia, which was supposedly a response to pro-royalist factions in Bolivia who had called upon the Brazilian emperor for assistance. Bolívar viewed the Brazilian occupation of Uruguay and the geo-political situation with serious alarm, convinced that "the meeting of the federated states becomes more urgent than ever."[65] Alarmed by events along the Brazilian border, Bolívar stated that even if the proposed isthmian congress served only military purposes, it would be beneficial, though he cautioned against any military action against Brazil until further study, since he was unsure if the order for this military operation was the result of a rogue initiative undertaken by the Brazilian military commander or had come from the emperor himself.[66] Bolívar indignantly complained that the Brazilian emperor continuously exhibited a "haughtiness and insulting attitude" to the other Latin Americans. He wrote that this arrogance stemmed from the monarch's overzealous self-confidence from knowing Brazil had Britain's support, which had been given in return for generous trade privileges from Rio de Janeiro.[67]

Bolívar and the other Spanish American leaders had to tread very carefully, because they knew this multitude of problems could easily explode into multiple and uncontrollable crises. A military conflict with Brazil would only exacerbate problems. By early May 1826, Bolívar expressed a heightened sense of alarm over the situation, noting that Paraguay had formed an alliance with Brazil.[68] The only remedy for the Brazilian situation was to convince and co-opt British officialdom to support the predominantly Spanish American position (in South America) vis-à-vis the Brazilian monarch's bellicose stance. Bolívar and his associates eventually succeeded in accomplishing this task, although they did not say how, save for a letter to General Antonio José de Sucre in which Bolívar stated that an "understanding" with Britain had been reached, whereby the U.K. would maintain the peace between Brazil and the other South American states.[69]

To the many critics who opposed a closer collaboration with the United Kingdom, Bolívar portrayed his position as one of political expediency, survival and a long-term strategy for success: "First the Confederation must be born and grow strong and then the rest will follow.... During its infancy we need help so that in manhood we will be able to defend ourselves. At present the alliance can serve our purpose; the future will take care of itself."[70] He insisted to critics that Latin Americans needed to tie their interests and political system to the prestige of the British Empire, and emphasized that London should not be offended in any manner due to its overawing military power. Bolívar provided the following advice and caution:

> We must take advantage of this annoyance and bind ourselves body and soul to the English in order to preserve at least the forms and advantages of a legal and civil government, for to be governed by the Holy Alliance would mean a rule by conquerors and a military government. To find actual proof that we cannot exist, whether alone or in federation without England's benediction, witness the fall of Napoleon's great empire at the hands of the English.... The entire Holy Alliance quails before Great Britain. How are we to exist if were do not bind ourselves to her? England is rapidly advancing, and woe to him who opposes it. Woe to him who is not her ally and who does not link his future with hers.... For my part, I plead for this policy, loudly and whole heartedly.[71]

These comments clearly demonstrate Bolívar's grasp of reality regarding the complex problems of the day and his ability to compromise cherished ideology in favor of a workable political system. His focus on the need for political stability to preserve the republican revolutions supports the view of Bolívar as a flexible statesman rather than an inflexible firebrand, as portrayed by his enemies.

Prelude to Panama Congress

In a letter to Colombian foreign minister Revenga dated February 17, 1826, Bolívar ironically and curiously articulated a position that may have been responsible for the failure of the Panama Congress. He suggested that the assigned plenipotentiaries be allowed to discuss only preliminary proposals for "treaties of alliances, even if they were strictly defensive," which would be subject to approval by their respective legislatures lest the diplomats be accorded too much power. Eventually this requirement meant that the proposal would be ricocheted by politicians long enough to see the proposal die a slow death. Why this shrewd politician supported such a position is unclear because he was a disciple of the concept that necessity justified less-than-ideal actions. It is possible that he sought to limit discussions that he felt might spawn further factionalism.[72] Perhaps by this date, Bolívar recognized that the outcome of this effort might be nothing more than a defensive alliance.

A few months earlier, on October 31, 1825, he had expressed just the opposite view in a letter to Colombian vice president Santander. The Liberator wanted unlimited powers for the Panama Congress: "I believe that these ought to be enlarged to the infinite and given a vigor and truly sovereign authority." Nevertheless, in another letter of May 7, 1826, reflecting his constantly changing views, he called for "a true federation in place of the Confederation."[73] Less than a month before, in April 1826, Bolívar had been told by Pedro Briceño Méndez, one of the two Colombian delegates to the Panama Conference, that he viewed the Panama Congress with pessimism. Briceño Méndez sarcastically noted that the only foundation for the assembly was the "indifference of the states that considered this great project." Another problem that plagued the congress was the ever-present feeling of mutual suspicion that arose among the attending states. This was to some extent logical, as the first and foremost obligation of any state is the perpetuation and preservation of its own interests and survival, a practice the Latin American diplomats and politicians keenly understood and exercised, although the state system had only recently evolved in Latin America. The attending diplomats and their governments were always cautious about entering into any agreements. Suspicion was bound to fall on Bolívar. He was, after all, hosting the congress on Colombian soil (Panama was then the territory of Colombia).

A major issue of concern was Bolívar's position as ruler of two separate independent countries at the same time: Gran Colombia and Peru. His rule in Peru was a complicated situation. He had come to act as the ruler of Peru by taking control on September 10, 1823, after he had chased the remaining royalist troops out of the country. When Bolívar and his army entered Lima, he found the city immersed in a constitutional crisis, in which the president, Riva-Agüero, was involved in a violent political dispute with the congress.[74] Bolívar sided with the congress, and Riva-Agüero was forced to flee. Bolívar then acted as temporary president, with the consent of the congress. (Some would refer to Bolívar's rule as dictatorial, but he did in fact defer to congress on some matters.) In this capacity he was forced into an awkward situation because he appointed delegates to the Panama Congress for Peru but refused to order them to vote any particular policy. The Peruvian delegates were instructed by Bolívar to follow the instructions of the Peruvian congress and/or council of state.[75] This situation was aggravated because Peru had territorial claims on the territory of Gran Colombia which that government refused to discuss. Bolívar fervently hoped this dispute could be settled peacefully by the congress. Bolívar understood the predicament he was in as he was president of two countries at the same time, and recognized that there would be suspicion of his motives. He had recently authorized establishment of an independent Bolivia, causing even more suspicion.[76] Bolívar viewed himself as a sort of "defender of states" whose goal was to promote self-government for those who desired it. It was not his desire to brutalize people or societies into submission. In fact, he acted in the highest traditions of Sulla, emphasizing that he would provide self-government for each independent political unit, allowing them to follow their own course. Bolívar claimed he "detested authority" and was bothered by affairs of state, yet it fell upon his shoulders to conduct such matters.[77] His actions and integrity were ardently defended by his subordinate, General Daniel F. O'Leary, who wrote that Bolívar was motivated by "disinterest" in personal aggrandizement. O'Leary observed that after Bolívar had given instructions to the delegates of Colombia and Peru, he abstained from further interference in the matter, save to support the union of the participating states.[78] The outcome of the congress confirms the statements of Bolívar and O'Leary that Bolívar did not despotically manipulate delegates, though he could have done so. As president, Bolívar continuously respected the rights of the new states, although he knew before the congress was held that it might prove unsatisfactory. Bolívar had no intention of performing a role similar to that of Otto von Bismarck.

A factor that complicated matters was the suspicions that permeated the congress. Briceño Méndez was especially distrustful of the Peruvian delegates Manuel Pérez de Tudela and Manuel Lorenzo de Vidaurre. He claimed Tudela had made the delegates even more fearful of problems posed by regional rivalries.[79] In a letter dated April 26, 1826, he claimed Peru and Vidaurre were responsible for the creation of the discord and said, "In their hands is the remedy."[80] Briceño Méndez also distrusted the Mexican delegation, which had not arrived as of April 26, 1826. He had not received any information from the Mexican government regarding their delegation, which had departed in March 1826. Concern was expressed that perhaps Mexico City was engaging in some sort of chicanery: "Since they have fooled us before with equal offers, they could ridicule us again." He asserted that if the Mexican delegates did not arrive, the result would be the "ultimate confusion and discredit" of the assembly, although he gladly noted with some irony that the Panama Congress did have the support from foreign governments such as the United Kingdom, although the Latin American states held reservations about the level of integration they favored.[81] Mexican actions and statements eventually confirmed that they had a different agenda from either Colombia or Peru. Manuel Vidaurre confirmed these suspicions in a conversation with Michelena two months later, in which he claimed the nature of the Panama conference was not an "amphitionic council, or a deliberative assembly, but a union of individuals to discuss military measures."[82]

As the date for the congress approached, Bolívar confided that he had little hope that Chile, or that the United Provinces of the Rio de la Plata, would attend the conference. He added that their governments, however weak, would only subject the congress to "ridicule" and "sarcastic" criticism. The mere presence of their delegations would only serve to "benumb and contradict" every effort to achieve stability, which, he noted, stemmed from their disorderly political status. This observation underscored his understanding that a united Latin America would be limited in its unity. He lamented that the invitation to the British government had been made public, because it was still unclear as of February 1826 if the U.K. would attend. Bolívar was concerned that the public announcement would only lower the prestige of the proposed confederation if Britain refused to attend. If the British delegation could have arrived secretly on American soil, its mere prestige, he wrote, would have immediately induced other Latin American states to seek admission to the proposed confederation.[83]

Problems Facing the Congress and the Plenipotentiaries

From the beginning the congress was plagued by a variety of problems such as a growing public animus towards Simón Bolívar, provincial suspicions, the weather, and even charges of treason. As delegates to the Panama Congress arrived, they began to complain bitterly about their new surroundings. They found Panama City to be wanting in any of the comforts of civilization. The Peruvian delegate Manuel Vidaurre complained of the horrid tropical heat and the insects, and claimed, "There was not a single theater or cultural center worthy of the name and merchant vessels are hardly seen in port."[84]

The impact of the climate should not be underestimated. Panama possesses an extremely harsh, humid, tropical climate that is unsuitable except for the most physically robust individuals who can successfully adapt to the climate. In 1825, this grim environment took the lives of several individuals attached to the retinues of the various delegations. The climate was such a negative factor in all considerations that Colombian vice president Francisco Paula de Santander wrote before the congress got underway that the plenipotentiaries should be given free rein to determine the site of any future meetings so they could maintain their health.[85]

The Colombian delegate to the congress, General Pedro Briceño Méndez, who was related to Bolívar, claimed the climate was so severe that he could not think of bringing his wife.[86] He described the ambiance in the most negative terms: "The climate is so cruel, the city so unsightly and so inconvenient, the poverty so widespread, the roads so impassable and all the resources so scarce and so dear that it is not even possible to think."[87] "Black vomit" and yellow fever also existed in the city. Briceño Méndez complained that it was unjust "to sacrifice their men of state in a climate so abominable." He caustically referred to the city as a "desert and a cemetery." Indeed, the climate was so harsh that two servants attached to the Colombian delegation died after having succumbed to the disease-infested environment. Within a month, the British delegation also lost two members of their staff.[88]

Pedro Gual, the other Colombian delegate wrote that the location was inappropriate for carrying out their duties: "This is not the climate for diplomatic negotiations, which demand much meditation and composure of mind. Here one lives in continual alarm."[89] Briceño Méndez stoically added that the climate exacted a heavy sacrifice, though he would dutifully suffer in Panama until Bolívar's anticipated arrival.[90] Bolívar recognized that the unhealthy and undesirable climate in Panama was a problem. He suggested that Quito, Ecuador, then a territory of Gran Colombia, would be a suitable replacement for the isthmus in future negotiations.[91]

Aside from discussing the harsh climate, Briceño Méndez informed his superior that he doubted any viable results could be produced at the congress. He argued that without creating a true federation, the congress would yield little of any positive value.[92] His counterpart for Gran Colombia, Pedro Gual, asserted that unless the congress was successful, the system of states, which had been utilized for the re-organization of Latin America, would lead to regional ruin.[93]

A major problem soon arose for the Peruvian delegation when José Maria Pando, one of the original delegates sent from Lima, found himself the subject of allegations that he was collaborating with Spanish agents, a rumor maliciously circulated by his rivals. He was recalled in 1825, with assurances that he had the full confidence of Bolívar. Indeed, the true reason for his recall was that Bolívar intended to appoint him to the post of minister of foreign relations for Peru. Pando was eventually replaced by Manuel Pérez de Tudela.[94]

The Peruvian delegate, Manuel Vidaurre, who was a strong partisan of centralized government for Latin American, hoped the plenipotentiaries would act as legislators in a federal system. He called for free trade, the elimination of interstate tariffs, one legal system, and the abolition of slavery as a means of ameliorating future problems. He emphasized that failure would have lasting consequences: "This will perhaps be the last attempt that may be made to ascertain whether mankind can be happy." Vidaurre could not envision that the new instructions arriving from his government would alter the outcome of the congress.[95]

Vidaurre was keenly concerned about Latin America's deteriorating political, economic and social conditions. He claimed continual upheavals would eventually produce a "tyranny" in the region and expressed hope (perhaps falsely) that Bolívar might be able to hold the region together via the proposed confederation.[96] These hopes, however, were eventually exacerbated by a major breach that developed between Vidaurre and Bolívar. Vidaurre personally suspected Bolívar of egotistically seeking to secure unlimited political power for himself via the Panama Congress, in spite of the fact that he owed his appointment to Bolívar, who had selected him and Pando as plenipotentiaries before Bolívar left Lima in April 1825.[97] Vidaurre took umbrage at Bolívar because he felt the Liberator had assumed dictatorial powers in Peru. He especially resented Bolívar's written reproach that he (Vidaurre) should not publish his political views in the newspapers. Eventually, the Peruvian began to suspect Bolívar had sent him to Panama so he could be removed as a political obstacle. Prior to arriving in Panama, Vidaurre had been chief justice of the Peruvian Supreme Court, a position that wielded much more influence. The mere contemplation that he might have been duped into assuming his position at Panama no doubt intensified Vidaurre's hatred of Bolívar.[98]

Vidaurre also attributed unscrupulous political intentions to Bolívar's formation of a separate independent Bolivia, which had been detached from Peru. Bolivia had been a territorial bone of contention between Peru and

Argentina. It had formerly been a part of the Viceroyalty of La Plata, but was now claimed by Peru. Consequently, Bolívar decided to create Bolivia as an independent state. This left Vidaurre extremely suspicious of the Liberator's policy, claiming that the new state left Colombia as the strongest country in the region. He observed that a new balance of power existed and caustically added, "It is known for whom the balance favors," though he eventually omitted this phrase from the actual letter sent to Bolívar.[99]

Viduarre's animus towards Bolívar intensified over time, and he was unable to reconcile his desire for a strong unified Latin America state with his opposition to Bolívar. He could not contain his strong dislike for Bolívar and openly criticized him to the Mexican, Central American, British and Dutch agents in attendance.[100] Vidaurre militantly opposed the proposed alliance with Britain and was instrumental in its defeat. He insisted that any foreign alliances be supported by unanimous consent of all the states.[101]

Differences and suspicions arose from interpretations and official proposals among the delegations. These differences deepened after a lengthy private conversation Pedro Gual and his colleague Briceño Méndez had with the Peruvian delegates, Pérez de Tudela and Vidaurre, on April 5, 1826. (Pérez de Tudela had replaced Pando.) In the course of the discussion, Gual revealed that language used by Vidaurre suggested a change of attitude as signaled by his comment that "what we have to do now can be finished in a couple of days." In and of itself, this comment should not have spurred so much suspicion, since it could have been assumed that the Peruvians presupposed the other delegates were in agreement over the details to be worked out; but Gual ascertained that Vidaurre's comments represented an indifference to the negotiating process and its objectives of creating a unified state. Two nights later on April 7, 1826, Gual's suspicions were confirmed when both Colombian delegates had a "lengthy and confidential meeting" with Pérez de Tudela and Vidaurre. At this meeting the Peruvians made the objectives of their government clear. In the course of the dialogue it became evident that the goals of Colombia, Peru and the other states did not coincide and would only serve to impair the success of the congress. As an example, the establishment of a federal navy was a primary goal for the Colombians. Pedro Gual argued that the establishment of a strong navy was so important that other states needed to "forget their geographical locations."[102] The Peruvian delegation emphasized that its government sought only a defensive alliance with other Latin American countries, rather than a centralized political union. The delegates also stipulated that Peru would not sanction the establishment of a federal navy. Oddly, Vidaurre complained that the dilution of the proposed government came from Mexico, which insisted that the navy was to be a "confederated navy" with one of the squadrons under the control of Mexico City. It is unclear, however, if the burden of blame lies with Lima or with Mexico City. It is also unclear if the Peruvian rejection of a federal navy emanated from its own initiatives or the desire to placate Mexico.[103]

Likewise, Lima stipulated that commercial treaties could not be adopted while its congress did not provide instructions on such matters. The Peruvian delegates stated that Lima also reserved the right to determine the boundaries between Peru and Colombia, an issue that added to the tension developing among the representatives.[104] This was particularly disappointing to everyone, since Vidaurre's prior views indicated that he had favored as strong a central government as possible.

Why did this attitude on the part of Vidaurre occur? It is known that Vidaurre had previously articulated the need for a strong central government and was unhappy with the ultimate outcome, which created a weak defensive-military alliance. Vidaurre had been named a plenipotentiary, which meant he had full powers to negotiate a treaty. Unless he received specific instructions directing a new policy, he could not have followed any other course of action. Evidence does not exist to suggest that Vidaurre deliberately or cynically misled the other delegates solely for the purpose of disappointing them. New instructions received by the Peruvian delegation from Lima directed them to follow a complete political reorientation, limiting their options. In fact, the two Peruvians mentioned that they were following the demands of their government.[105] By examining the prior statements of Vidaurre before and after his discussion with Briceño Méndez and Gual, it is evident Vidaurre was left with no choice but to follow the new instructions from Lima. Such a dramatic shift in policy should not be surprising, since the region was a cauldron of political contradictions brought on by the region's shifting alliances. Lima's instructions to the Peruvian delegation were undoubtedly as discouraging to Viduarre as they were to the Colombians.

Gual and Briceño Méndez immediately informed their superior, Foreign Minister Revenga, of the distressing meeting held with the Peruvian delegates. They expressed concern that new instructions issued to the Peruvians would "shrink" the scope of the congress. The two envoys were shocked at the reversal by Vidaurre, who had supported a strong all–Latin-American federation, although they understood this reversal came by way of the Peruvian government. Gual and Briceño Méndez expressed further dismay at the attitude of the Peruvian government, which they asserted ironically owed its existence to the military efforts of Colombia. The two delegates were vociferous in their condemnation of the Peruvian government's conduct, claiming, "They have completely destroyed the foundations of our transactions [work] that consisted

in the perfect unity of the principles and sentiments between the Plenipotentiaries of that republic and ours." In their reports, the Colombian diplomats
asserted that the nature of the problems they faced stemmed from the historical
development of Latin America: "We are suffering insuperable difficulties during the course of these negotiations flowing from local considerations, from
egoism, jealousies and puerile suspicions inherent in our ancient colonial status." They felt the new Peruvian demands threatened the purpose of the congress and concluded that Colombia would be better off maintaining its foreign
policy towards Lima rather than "recasting it, which would only restrict any
advantages we could receive from them." Gual and Briceño Méndez were quick
to qualify their statements by noting that the objective of the Panama Congress
was not to create a system for individual states to take advantage of each other,
but rather to broaden the ties between states. In spite of the obstacles confronting them, the delegates did not allow themselves to despair completely
and expressed hope for the success of the congress.[106]

The next day Gual asserted that all of Peru's objectives were diametrically
opposed to those of the Colombian delegation and questioned the possibility
of reaching an understanding with Lima's representatives.[107] Gual expressed
concern to Bolívar that the proposed assembly would fail, although he fervently hoped for its success. He expressed hope that Bolívar might be able to
convince the Peruvians to change their minds, but this did not transpire. Likewise, Gual sarcastically inquired if the Peruvians would need permission from
their government to deal with Edward Dawkins, the British commissioner to
the congress. Gual lamented the problems the congress faced and warned, "If
this path is not muted many of them [Latin American states] will be the
ridicule or the toy of many, as has been the case with the wise Rivadavia, who
after having managed for a lengthy time the affairs of his country has gone to
London where he has been treated like a child. I see Peru entering into the
same category."[108]

The Colombian asserted that his country fervently "desired" to "identify
its fate with her allies" and stressed that the congress had to succeed in order
to implement the provisions for a strong, centralized defensive military
alliance, which was the first and foremost objective according to Gual. He
concluded that unless this goal was secured, "it would be better to do nothing."
In anticipation of more problems, Gual contemplated a potential explanation
of events in order to avoid embarrassment should the congress fail. He suggested that a "plausible pretext" might read, "This assembly has deferred itself
for such and such a year expecting a concurring plenum of the American states,"
and that this pretext be employed in case of a diplomatic breakdown. This
explanation, he argued, would minimize the negative publicity and embar-

rassment that Latin America would face if the congress reached an impasse. Then, hopefully, he wrote, the world would slowly forget the vexatious debacle of failure and begin focusing on other global issues.[109]

The British representative to the congress, Mr. Dawkins, noted that personal ambitions and provincialism were serious impediments to any fruitful progress. He felt that the Mexican delegate, Michelena, was seeking to lead the rest of the states at the expense of Colombia, and that Mexico was in fact indifferent to the congress. These suspicions may have been correct, though it may have been a mistaken assumption of Dawkins and the Colombians. It is a question that can never be adequately answered, unless one accepts the assumption of Briceño Méndez that Mexico was engaged in a cruel hoax.[110] In assessing this issue it should be noted that one of Mexico's primary foreign policy objectives since the failure of the congress has been the establishment of a politically integrated Latin America. This, of course does not allay the accusations by Dawkins, Gual or Briceño Méndez, since the political priorities of states can change quickly.

Opening Session of Congress and
Treaty of Confederation

In spite of earlier tensions, the congress eventually convened to begin its work with all the delegates in attendance at eleven o'clock on the morning of June 22, 1826, in the municipal hall of Panama City. A matter of concern for the delegates was a speech written by Vidaurre that had been published in the local newspaper, the *Gaceta Extraordinaria*. This publicized manifesto irritated the other plenipotentiaries, who felt it was inappropriate for Vidaurre to have proceeded with his public discussion prior to officially informing them. According to the historian Reginald Arragon, the newspaper claimed that Vidaurre used the writing in a speech to the congress. In fact, the alleged speech was never given.[111] Vidaurre's article discussed the region's problems and identified the colonial heritage as the culprit. Vidaurre then proceeded to outline what the congress needed to accomplish:

> The great American congress, which should be a council in great conflicts, a faithful interpreter of treaties, a mediator in domestic disputes, charged with the formation of our new international law, finds itself invested with all those powers necessary to accomplish the noble, great, and singular object for which it is convoked.... The whole world is going to view our works, and to examine them with deliberation. From the first sovereign to the last inhabitant of the austral regions there is not one individual indifferent to our task.[112]

The Peruvian diplomat took the opportunity to warn his listeners about the task ahead: "With respect to ourselves there are two terrible hidden rocks. One, the desire of aggrandizement by some states at the cost and injury of others; the second, is the danger that an ambitious man aspire to tyranny and enslave his brothers." The statement was probably aimed at Bolívar, although the unstable situation in the region already pointed to the possibility of a dictator coming to power.[113] Vidaurre emphasized the necessity of success for the congress, recognizing that it would be the subject of great controversy by future generations. He warned the attendees:

> The inhabitants of the Americas which were formerly Spanish will cover themselves with infamy in the eyes of all known nations if they fail to promulgate such wise, equitable, and just laws as will insure their present felicity and that of their descendants for many generations.... Our names are to be written either with immortal praise or eternal opprobrium.[114]

As a product of enlightenment philosophy, Vidaurre believed that organized human societies could improve through a restructuring of political, economic and social systems. He argued that the reorganization of commerce would strengthen the bonds between the individual states. Latin Americans, he maintained, could create the appropriate conditions for forming a stronger political union via the elimination of customs duties, which would increase economic dependency between states.

> Above all, let us form one family, let the names which distinguished our respective countries be at an end, and let us adopt the name of brothers. Let us carry on commerce without obstacles and without prohibitions, let American goods pass every custom house unexamined, let us give ourselves continued proofs of confidence, disinterestedness, and sincere friendship, let us form one code of public law, which admires the civilized world; by which an injury to one state is understood to be against all.[115]

Vidaurre commemorated the labors of Spanish American leaders from other states, thus acknowledging his close identification with Latin American civilization: "Fellow laborers, the field of glory has been laid open to us by Bolívar, San Martín, O'Higgins, Guadalupe and many other heroes superior to Hercules and Theseus."[116] The Peruvian plenipotentiary also called for the total elimination of slavery and for the establishment of racial equality by demanding, "Let the sad and despairing countenance of the African, oppressed with the chains of force and power, disappear from our fields. Let him see at his side a man of that color which he thought was a mark of superiority. He will then reasonably perceive that he is no different from other men."[117]

The proposed alliance with Great Britain, however, came under scrutiny by Vidaurre. The Peruvian emphasized that an alliance could only come to fruition via the common consent of all contracting states. He forcefully rebutted Bolívar's claim that it was necessary for the domestic and foreign tranquility of the region. The strength of societies, argued Vidaurre, ultimately emanated from the form of organization they adopted.[118] He warned the congress that Latin America should be distrustful of any person or situation that might result in an individual accumulating too much political power:

> First, let the confederated governments guarantee each other's liberty and independence. Second, never let an individual be entrusted with more power than is necessary to accomplish the purpose for which it was granted. Third, the greater the power the shorter time it ought to be enjoyed, if this is compatible with its intent. Fourth, to whom power is confided be made to depend upon that part of the nation which is disarmed. Fifth, not to maintain permanent armies except in time of war. Sixth, to avoid this frightening evil, irreconcilable with domestic tranquility of society, by every means in our power, and which honor and prudence dictate.[119]

The writing provided an intellectual and political format for the congress to consider. The delegates immediately sat down to work. A total of ten working sessions were held in which the diplomats worked out the details of their plan. Three weeks later and a year-and-a-half after the congress had been called by Bolívar, the diplomats produced a document entitled, Treaty of Union, League and Perpetual Confederation between the Republics of Peru, Colombia, Central America and the United Mexican States. The treaty, which was formally signed July 15, 1826, consisted of thirty-one articles. Article 1 proclaimed the determination of the contracting states to "mutually ally and confederate themselves in peace and war, and contract to this end a perpetual compact of friendship, a firm, inviolable, and intimate union binding each party."[120]

The organization would be empowered to resolve problems between member states and to arrange treaties with foreign nations. The provisions of the treaty demonstrated that the plenipotentiaries were primarily concerned with the ability to "mutually guarantee the integrity of their territories." Article 2 stipulated that the treaty would maintain the "sovereignty and independence" of all its members through a "common defensive and offensive" military alliance against all "foreign domination" of America.[121]

Article 3 obligated member states to defend each other by contributing military and naval forces. Three separate military accords were attached to the article on the same day. Article 10 prohibited the creation of separate peace treaties with enemy states while foreign armies were on the soil of any members of the alliance. Article 11 stated that the congress was to meet every two years and that the appointed plenipotentiaries were to be given adequate powers by their governments to accomplish their tasks. The time and place of future meetings were to be determined by future agreements.[122]

Article 13 called on the signatory powers "to negotiate and conclude, during common wars, with one or more outside powers, treaties of alliance, concert, subsidies and contingents in order to hasten their termination" and for the establishment of mediation between the confederates and foreign powers.[123] Article 14 denied member states the right to permanent or temporary treaties that might create political or military alliances without the approval of all the other member states. Article 16 obligated member states to settle their disputes amicably, which was a major objective of the congress and its supporters. It provided for the resolution of such problems by a vote of the assembled congress. Article 21 stated that member states were obliged to defend their own territory. It also stipulated that they were not obligated to seek authority from the congress in case of invasion. Article 22 obligated member states to defend each other in case of invasion. Articles 23 and 24 guaranteed the citizens of one state the same rights as citizens of the host states with respect to the court system. They were also guaranteed the right to freely practice their professions. These provisions protected property and the right to dispose of it as individuals saw fit, a major tenet of classical liberalism.[124] Article 27 pledged member states to engage in joint actions to eliminate the slave trade. This type of activity was never jointly undertaken, but it is a credit to the Latin American nations that by 1830 most of the individual states had successfully abolished slavery, a course of action to which they had earnestly committed themselves. Article 31 provided for the next assembly meeting to be held in Tacubaya, Mexico.[125]

Early in the congress, the Colombian delegates Briceño Méndez and Pedro Gual had proposed articles that would have banned the use of trade barriers, but the Mexican delegation opposed it because of pressure from foreign entrepreneurs and manufacturers that did not wish to see their investments face competition. When the Colombians suggested renewing the negotiations on this matter (supposedly with modifications), the Mexican delegates José Mariano de Michelena and José Domínguez stated that they had no authority to deal with such issues, as the Congress of Mexico had not provided them with instructions on the matter. The Central American and Peruvian delegates later informed the Colombian representatives that they also needed authority from their legislatures to proceed. R.R. Arragon argued that the opposition to a commercial clause resulted from a reluctance of those countries to provide the generous trading concessions sought by Great Britain and the United States. The Colombian delegates wrote that the reason for the failure to have the commercial clauses included stemmed from the lack of instructions. Article 25 of the treaty attempted to delay consideration of commercial considerations by stipulating that this sensitive and complex issue would be dealt with at the next congress, to be held at Tacubaya, Mexico.[126]

The congress was then, as required, transferred to Tacubaya ostensibly because of the oppressive heat of Panama. The removal to Tacubaya signaled that a serious diplomatic impasse had been reached and that the various parties were ready to cease negotiations. The adjournment to Mexico was less a result of the weather than a product of political intrigue, envy and a lack of genuine interest in the creation of a viable political union. Provincialism had played a major role in the proffering of new sites. Each member state suggested that the next site be situated on its own territory. R.R. Arragon claimed that Tacubaya was selected on the insistence of the Mexicans, who threatened to leave the congress altogether if one of their cities was not selected as the next site.[127] The Mexican position was that the site should be as far removed from Bolívar as possible.[128] Bolívar argued that the congress should not be moved to Mexico for fear it would come under the influence of Mexico City and the United States.[129]

The British representative, Dawkins, observed the acrimony among the competing states and commented, "This arrangement will be far from agreeable to the others, especially to the Colombian Deputies, but they are so anxious to retain the adherence of the Mexicans, that they will rather consent to follow it to Mexico, than expose themselves to the possibility of its dissolution." For his part, Dawkins felt that the next site for the congress should have been on Colombian soil due to what he considered that country's strategic geographical position.[130]

In the meantime, a separate agreement was eventually drawn up on July 15, 1826. Known as the Convention on the Transfer of the Assembly, or the Concert Which Refers to Article Eleven of the Treaty of Union League and Perpetual Confederation, it stated that the purpose for transferring the congress was to maintain the "health, security, and facility of communication with Europe and America." It also stipulated that ensuing meetings would be held in Tacubaya within eight months, unless there was a need to move to another site. The inclusion and development of this special convention was superfluous, as the issue had already been decided in the formal treaty. The ancillary agreement stipulated the formalities to be followed and provided for the continued use of plenipotentiaries. It was agreed that at the next meeting those states that had ratified the treaty would exchange diplomatic notes to that effect.

The ancillary accords that complemented Article 3 of the Treaty of Union dealt with the military and naval obligations of the member states. The first ancillary accord was known as the Agreement on Military and Naval Contingents. It addressed the number of ships, troops and funds that would be required for military undertakings. Mexico would be required to provide 32,750 troops, Central America 6,750, and Peru 5,250. The naval accord stipulated the number of ships and the cannon to be placed on board.[131]

The second ancillary military accord was known as the Convention on Contingents Between the Republics of Peru, Colombia, Central-America and the United Mexican States. It dealt with the employment and use of military and naval forces. In case of a military emergency in which a state was invaded, the other states would be required to provide financial and material assistance as needed by the confederation to carry out its military obligations. The injured state would also receive a subsidy of $200,000 from each of the member states. As part of their obligation to provide naval assistance, the accord stipulated the financial obligations of the member states to support naval projection. Mexico would be required to furnish $4,558,475, Colombia $2,205,714, and Central America $955,811 for that objective.[132] The provisions of the accord meant the treaty would be totally ineffectual. In all probability, if the treaty had gone into effect the member states would not have been able to keep their naval and military commitments due to the high costs and the extreme poverty of the contracting states.

The work of the Panama Congress to strengthen their military position vis-à-vis Europe was negated by the passage of a third accord, intended to compliment the Convention on Contingents Between the Republics of Colombia, Central America, Peru and the United Mexican States. Its purpose was to make modifications and adjustments to the two other military accords. Known as The Agreement referred to in Article Two of the Convention of Contingents of This Date Celebrated Between the Republics of Colombia, Central America, Peru and the United Mexican States, it dismantled the many hours of work the diplomats had engaged in by the insertion of its contradictory provisions. Article 3 stated, "The contingents should not be utilized unless the invasion is serious, that is to say, in excess of five thousand men disembarked, or if they march on, or take possession of a strong point, or fortify themselves along the coast, or that they enter a country as far as thirty leagues."[133] Bolívar was furious at the provision, complaining that it condemned the invaded states to permanent occupation.[134] This last accord confirms how strongly the emergent state system had become rooted in the political culture of Latin America. It demonstrates that the states sought to accumulate privileges for themselves while incurring few if any obligations to their fellow signatories of the treaty. Only a handful of the states were willing to make a genuine commitment to work together, which could only be undertaken by pledging to assist the other states in times of military crisis.

The treaty and its ancillary accords called for the creation of military and naval forces to meet external military threats. Army forces, however, were not to become a federal army and would not fall under the control of a central authority. The armies were to remain under the command of their own governments. Article 4 stated that military commanders intending to aid a member state victimized by a foreign army would be required to take the shortest and most convenient routes to the theater of operations, and were obligated to notify the state authorities that they would be arriving—a puerile requirement not conducive to maintaining the element of surprise necessary for successful military operations.[135] Furthermore, this collection of troops would depend on assigned allotments of troops and monies from the various states, as agreed upon in the ancillary military accords.

There was, however, to be a navy, alternately referred to as a "federated navy" and "confederated navy." In the Convention on Contingents Between the Republics of Colombia, Central America, Peru, and the United Mexican States it was referred to as a "federated navy." In practice, the navy would not be a federal organ. It would be organized around a naval board with representatives selected from Gran Colombia, Mexico and Central America as required in the accord. (Article 21 stipulated that Peru would not be obligated to provide service in the Atlantic, but that its naval forces would remain in the Pacific theater.) The board was to be responsible for directing the Atlantic fleet. The individual states would be responsible for organizing and maintaining their own naval vessels. Article 10 likewise required specific monetary appropriations to be carried out by the various states. Article 12 stated that naval vessels were to carry the flag of their home country. The officers of these vessels were to be judged by the laws of their respective countries until a corpus of rules, regulations and laws could be developed by the naval board.[136]

The position of the Peruvian navy vis-à-vis other participating states was revealed in Article 21 of the Agreement Referred to in Article 2 of the Convention on Contingents of This Date, Concluded Between the Republics of Colombia, Central America, Peru and the United Mexican States. Peru was to maintain its ships in the Pacific, where they would be divided into two squadrons. The first squadron was to patrol the U.S.–Mexican coast all the way to Panama, and the second squadron would patrol to the southern coast of Peru. This accord referred to a "confederated navy," which was a more accurate term. Articles 15 and 16 stated the number of vessels to be maintained by the states and the number of guns their vessels would carry. Articles 17, 18 and 19 discussed the financial obligations of the various states.[137]

The proposed treaty not only had many flaws, it had many critics, including Bolívar, who found many faults with it. His main criticism of the proposed

Treaty of Union, League and Confederation was based on security problems that might eventually face the proposed entity. He objected to publishing the order of battle to be utilized in case of war, since publicity was not conducive to successful operations. He asserted that the treaty would actually provide foreign powers with valuable intelligence information in preparing their military campaigns, rendering the purpose and work of the congress ineffectual.[138] Bolívar again called for a comprehensive treaty that would permanently bind the various states together, and said that he opposed a partial union. At the time the delegates were completing their work at Panama, Bolívar wrote to Briceño Méndez, the Colombian delegate, asking for a delay of the treaty, because he felt some of its provisions might hamper future projects he was contemplating.[139]

Not everyone was so disgruntled by the treaty. As he prepared to depart Panama, Briceño Méndez reflected on the work he and the delegates had engaged in. For the most part, he was satisfied with the treaty and what had been achieved: "It is incredible that so much was accomplished in twenty-three days in such a horrible climate as this."[140] On board the ship *Macedonia* a week after the congress terminated, Briceño Méndez wrote, "With ratification of the treaties, we can think of ourselves as forming one great nation with respect to Europe." He observed that since contributions of troops depended on population size, the greatest burden in time of war would actually fall on Mexico. The strength of the treaty, he argued, was that though troop contributions might be larger or smaller, all states possessed only one vote.[141] The ship eventually brought him to the port of Buenaventura, from which he would commence the long and tedious two-hundred-mile trip back to Bogotá, Colombia. Weary and seasick, Briceño Méndez wrote that the treaty had been the most progressive of its kind to date. He wrote to Bolívar that the work accomplished at Panama was extensive, though it was only the beginning. He expressed enthusiasm that once the treaty was ratified, the prestige of the Latin Americans would be enhanced. Nonetheless, he acknowledged that the treaty was not an ideal instrument.[142] The congratulatory view of Briceño Méndez was premature. The congress adjourned as a dismal failure, because the provisions of the treaty would never be put into operation. Only Colombia ratified the treaty in its senate.[143] From the beginning, the congress and its work were doomed to failure. The signatory states consigned their project to an unsuccessful beginning by pledging themselves to a weak confederation where the almost unlimited sovereignty of each state was formally desired, acknowledged, and maintained. Even if the treaty had been ratified by each of the states, it would have encountered a host of problems. The first of these would undoubtedly have concerned the interpretation of the treaty regarding the exact responsibilities and powers assigned to the congress and the individual states. This would have had devastating repercussions in time of war, with every group pursuing their own interests. The second source of problems would have been the various exceptions provided for in the articles, which could have led to arguments among the states as to what constituted reasonable exceptions to treaty provisions.

The provisions of Article 3 and the separately signed military contributions accord meant that in times of peace and war, the various states would find themselves squabbling over what they considered their appropriate financial obligation. The treaty left the collection of such funds to the good faith of the state governments. Instead of viewing domestic and military expenditures as a national concern, they were treated as matters for local politicians to deal with.

An analysis of the proposed treaty immediately reveals that there were hardly any provisions for the settlement of disputes between the signatory states except articles 11, 12 and 13, which really served as objectives. There was no viable mechanism devised to resolve disputes except through mediation, which was not binding, nor was a method instituted for dealing with domestic issues of an economic or social nature. Indeed, every time the various states discussed their territorial borders, an air of tension arose.[144] Nevertheless, ratification of the treaty could have served a positive purpose. It might have brought the various Latin American states together into a continual dialogue demonstrating to them the necessity of creating a stronger and more efficient organization.

Bolívar was disgusted with the results of the congress and wrote to Vice President Francisco de Paula Santander, "All is lost, neither a general federation nor a local constitution can restrain these unruly slaves; particularly now that everyone pursues his own ends. I regard the Congress of the Isthmus as a theatrical play, and I view our laws as did Solon, who believed that laws only served to burden the weak without restraining the strong."[145] With the end of the congress, Bolívar, left to muse about the many shortcomings of the treaty, wrote, "The congress of Panama, an organization that might have been magnificent if only it had been effective.... Its power will be a shadow, and its decrees mere advice, no more."[146] Manuel Vidaurre was so exasperated by the outcome of events that he refused to go to Tacubaya and wrote that sending a replacement would be a "totally useless waste."[147]

R. R. Arragon argued that the shortcomings of the Panama Congress resulted from its creation as "a diplomatic body, not a sovereign council." He asserted that the congress was limited by the concern of some delegates over the intentions of Spain and the Holy Alliance. With the gradual demise of a foreign threat there was no longer any incentive to consider further political consolidation.[148] Historical analysis of the integration movement up until the mid–nineteenth century reinforces Arragon's analysis. The Latin Americans would repeat these efforts in the future when faced by external military threats to their independence. Whenever Latin American states were faced by military threats throughout most of the nineteenth century, their governments demonstrated a continual willingness to coalesce efforts towards formation of a potential organization that would bind them in a military emergency. When threats evaporated, integration efforts ceased, as if by reflex.

Historically, this situation of political fragmentation is not unique to Latin America or its people. Germany and Italy were also fragmented for many centuries, crippled by internecine warfare and foreign domination. Perhaps the most famous and illustrative parallel would be the example of the Greeks in their struggles against the Persian Empire. Once military emergencies ended, the Latin Americans, like the Greeks, lowered their guard, resulting in political fragmentation that led to wars among themselves and eventual domination by foreign powers.

IV

TRANSFER TO TACUBAYA
AND THE DEFEAT OF THE
TREATY OF CONFEDERATION

If only there were someone to arbitrate between us...—Job 9:33

Meeting at Tacubaya

The Panama Congress was relocated to Tacubaya, Mexico, a small and bustling town roughly three miles from the outskirts of Mexico City. The new site provided the attending diplomats all the benefits of a large city. The plenipotentiaries then split into two groups. One diplomat from each delegation was to attend the Tacubaya conference while the other was to report home for the purpose of providing information to his own government. The Peruvian delegates never arrived in spite of their stated intention to do so.[1] In the meantime, the British delegate, Mr. Dawkins, believing that the congress would be a failure and that nothing more could be gained by his government's presence, sailed back to the United Kingdom.[2]

Pedro Gual was chosen as the Gran Colombian representative to attend the Tacubaya meeting. His ship arrived in Acapulco on October 22, 1826. There he was handed a tube carrying the diplomatic credentials of the Peruvian delegates, Manuel Pérez de Tudela and Manuel Lorenzo de Vidaurre. Curiously, the tube had been opened, although the Peruvian diplomats had not arrived. Why the tube was handed to Gual is unclear, since he was representing the Colombian legation. Gual was not given a satisfactory answer as to why it had been opened and preceded the Peruvian diplomats. He assumed that the secretary of the Peruvian delegation had inadvertently mailed it when the ship left Panama, or that the captain or crew of the *Jóven Corina* had opened the tube out of curiosity. The luggage of the Peruvian delegates arrived, although the two would not be heard from again.[3] Vidaurre had made it clear while in Panama that he was no longer interested in participating in any further conferences, and returned to Lima. The Peruvian diplomat was bitterly disappointed with the treaty because of its many flaws. He informed his superiors, "Nobody knows better than yourself that I am indomitable in my opinions ... my ideas are entirely contrary." He also commented that a replacement would be a waste of time.[4] Pérez de Tudela had been somewhat more optimistic in his assessment of the events at Panama, stressing that they had been "frank, amicable and cordial."[5] However, he was unable to depart for Mexico because his ship was in poor sailing condition.[6]

Nevertheless, Gual did not wait for any other delegates and began his arduous trek eastward towards Tacubaya. He would serve in Mexico for several months, which gave him ample opportunity to observe the slow progress of the ratification process. His unique position also allowed him to scrutinize Mexican politics. Gual's mission was to follow the treaty as it worked its painful way through the Mexican legislature, which would eventually reject the treaty. In the meantime, Gual eagerly awaited news of the treaty and its progress from his Colombian homeland. The diplomat constantly reviewed news of the treaty's progress through the two commissions of the Colombian Chamber of Deputies. He criticized the members of the commissions for their lack of experience in diplomacy and denounced them as being motivated by politics. Gual accused them of currying the favor "of a people that do not know their true interests" and implored the Colombian government to continue its program for integration without bowing to public opinion.[7] In April of 1827, while in Tacubaya, Gual complained that the Mexican Chamber of Deputies had not yet presented its assessment of the Panama treaty, noting that several points were at the heart of the discussion, although he did not specify what these issues were. Gual had by this time informed the Mexican government of Colombia's ratification of the treaty. He noted that a Mexican minister confidentially complained to him that the government in Mexico City was "impotent" to reach a decision on the treaty.[8] In a May 1827 commentary, Gual noted that the entire political life of Latin America had become deplorable:

> It is a complete calamity for the Spanish speaking states of America that at the time they were to have created the most beautiful institution that has ever been seen, an institution that would have consolidated her political existence forever, they [the states] have for the most part fallen into horrible confusion.... How is it possible to establish a confederation from discordant and disorganized parts? Is it possible that the confederation can restore the internal health of each state? Or should the same confederation be the result of established order and profound calculation on the part of each one of them?[9]

Gual emphasized his absolute commitment to the success of the confederation, stating that if the treaty were ratified he would happily retire. On the other hand, if the confederation failed to materialize, it would be a difficult disappointment for him that "would weigh heavily on me for the rest of my life."[10] Aside from Bolívar, perhaps no other figure devoted so much time or energy to the attempt to implement the confederation. The goal of achieving a politically integrated state, however weak and deficient, was so vital to Gual that he implored his superiors not to remove him from Mexico until the successful formation of the confederate congress had been achieved.[11] In the meantime, the plenipotentiaries from the United States and Holland, who had come as observers, decided to leave Tacubaya and return home, believing that nothing of substance would be accomplished there.[12]

A few months later Gual, still working in Mexico, noted that he had been promoting political integration since he had left Bogotá in September of 1825. He admitted that he had miscalculated the possibility of creating a genuinely integrated state, describing his work as a struggle of one against all odds, although he believed the effort had not been wasted. He objected to the claims made by Bolívar's opponents, who viewed him and Colombia as "instruments of tyranny," a criticism Gual viewed as without merit and designed solely to foil the confederation.[13]

Gual found his work in Mexico on behalf of the confederation to be an exasperating experience. He did everything possible to secure the treaty's passage by the Mexican legislature, even to the point of volunteering to attend the Chamber of Representatives in order to answer any questions regarding the proposed integration plan. The situation was so frustrating that he seriously considered resigning his post, thereby reversing his previously written pleas to stay in Mexico. He suggested that even with his resignation, consideration of the treaty might be continued by "leaving negotiations open to renewal when it is thought more convenient.... I am convinced my presence in this country will not prove fruitful.... Our government has given sufficient proof of the desires that animate her."[14]

Opposition to the treaty in Mexico was so intense that on February 8, 1828, Gual notified his superiors that he had irrevocably decided to leave Mexico. He did not believe the treaty would ever pass, yet he would remain in the country for ten more months. The blatant hostility to the ratification of the Treaty of Confederation and the ancillary accords in the Mexican Chamber of Representatives were symptomatic of the myopic provincialism affecting the entire region. Among the arguments that echoed in the Mexican legislature against the Treaty was that "Mexico was itself enough." Other opponents claimed, "Mexico should not unite her fortunes with some republics of little importance where the most frightening anarchy reigns." One representative asserted that the treaty would ally Mexico with Colombia, which was "dominated by a tyrant," which greatly offended Gual.

Gual eventually arranged a meeting with Mexico's president, Guadalupe Victoria, and explained that he was leaving because he felt he could do no more to assure ratification of the treaty. President Victoria asked him to stay, and promised that he would struggle to secure passage of the treaty through the legislature. Gual agreed to remain. He felt it was his obligation to press forward with any possibilities that might prove fruitful. He expressed his gratitude to President Victoria for his support, but privately doubted that any effective measures would or could be taken by the Mexican government to ensure passage of the treaty. Two days later, however, Victoria was able to secure a hearing and a vote on the treaty in the Chamber of Representatives, where it was deliberated in secret and where it passed with minor alterations. The treaty then passed to a commission of the Senate. Gual did not know when that body would conclude with its deliberations, but he decided it would be "prudent" to continue waiting.[15]

Gual believed a more successful moment for the confederation might arrive in the future when the "public interest and the good of America supersedes the spirit of party." After surveying the turbulent political landscape of Mexico, he commented, "This conflict of diametrically opposed interests does not offer any opportunity for negotiation." He blamed the inability to reach any compromises on the ideological fanaticism that was gradually taking hold of Mexican political culture, as it would in the rest of Latin America: "Passions entirely brutalize men and countries rendering them inaccessible to reason and deaf to the clamor for their own well-being. I do not know any remedy that can radically cure this ill except allowing the combustion to consume itself."[16]

A few days later Gual wrote that in spite of its public support for the treaty, the Mexican government did not demonstrate a genuine commitment to ratify the accord. Indeed, the two years that Gual spent in diplomatic circles within Mexico enabled him to become a keen observer of that nation's domestic politics and the foreign intrigue that had become rooted in the country. This condition led him to write: "Today it is the [political] parties that maintain her government in complete inaction, or the perspective that it [Mexico] does not need anyone, or the intrigues of the American Minister Poinsett."[17]

In light of the political acrimony in Mexico, Gual decided to write a note to the Mexican plenipotentiaries Michelena and Dominguez, requesting a meeting with them to determine whether or not the treaty had a chance of passing the legislature. The interview took place on November 25, 1827. Gual told the Mexican diplomats that he had waited through three sessions of the legislature without viewing any positive results on behalf of the treaty. He asked them if the treaty had a realistic chance of passing in the Mexican legislature. If not, it might be appropriate for him to return to Colombia. It appears from the meeting that both Michelena and Dominguez were genuinely in favor of the treaty and concerned over its fate. Gual discovered that they were as perplexed as he was by the attitude and inaction of the legislative branch. Michelena and Dominguez told Gual that they had been assured by the various legislative commissions only two days before that reports had been prepared for presentation to both houses.[18]

This did not prevent Gual from criticizing Mexico's performance on the treaty and exchanging harsh words with the Mexican plenipotentiaries. He told Dominguez and Michelena that Mexico had been negligent in attending to its foreign affairs, pointing out that Mexico City did not maintain a diplomatic agent in Bogotá or even Guatemala. Gual harshly wrote later that such "conduct argues a contempt for the new states, including the Republic of Colombia."[19] Michelena and Dominguez were quick to point out that no other state had ratified the treaty and that it had many enemies in Mexico.[20] One of the fears circulating in Mexico was the possibility that Bolívar sought total political power for himself. The two diplomats said that foreign intrigues in Mexico engineered by the Holy Alliance were seeking to maintain discord in Latin America. According to Gual, Dominguez and Michelena stated that the Europeans were "counting on success because of our inexperience and lack of abundant administrative and diplomatic knowledge." They recognized that there was an implicit danger posed to Latin America if there should be further delays with the treaty. In fact, failure to ratify it might one day lead to a war between Latin Americans that "would furiously consume Colombians, Mexicans, Peruvians, etc., etc., not because of our own appropriate interests which fortunately are identical, but rather as mere auxiliaries or instruments of the policy of other cabinets."[21] Dominguez and Michelena stressed the sensitive nature of the discussion and asked that their conversation remain private. They also asked that Gual limit his discussion of their conversation to his personal writings. Gual felt that the two diplomats had been forthright with him, and lamented that Mexico would one day regret not taking advantage of the opportunity for creating a politically unified state, however weak it might seem: "I know that the government of Mexico will someday regret, in the not too distant future, allowing this opportunity to escape."[22]

In the meantime, Dominguez and Michelena suggested in August 1827 that the Tacubaya congress intervene in the civil war and chaos then prevailing in Central America. The congress, lacking any genuine powers pending ratification of the treaty, allowed the matter to await formal discussion until December 1827, thus showing its total ineffectiveness and allowing Central America to remain mired in chaos. A series of meetings were held, beginning in December of 1827, and lasting through February 1828, to discuss this problem. However, a serious complication arose when Gual claimed there was no legal or political basis for intervention. Furthermore, any intervention would have to follow a written request for military assistance.[23]

On December 8, 1827, Antonio Larrazábal, the Central American plenipotentiary (he also served as the resident bishop of the cathedral in Guatemala City), informed the other plenipotentiaries that his government had accepted the proposal of the Mexican delegation. But in spite of the agreement between Larrazábal and Mexican diplomats, any formal action without ratification of the treaty was premature. As a result, no coordinated political or military action was taken regarding the situation in Central America.[24]

The Central American civil war could have formed the basis for closer links between the states, but the disagreements between Gual and his Mexican counterparts only drew them further apart, to the point that they realized they had nothing in common except their goal of ratification of the Treaty of Confederation. A broad interpretation of the treaty, or some type of agreement between Mexico and Gran Colombia concerning intervention in Central America, would have brought the two states closer together. Notwithstanding Gual's criticism of the Mexican government, an agreement on this issue could have closed the large political gap that had been created by mutual distrust.

In the meantime Gual awaited further action on the treaty. His view that the Mexican government was incapable of forceful action on its behalf eventually proved accurate. A few weeks later there appeared an article in *El Correo de la Federación Mexicana* in which President Victoria indicated his support for ratification. Gual expressed great disappointment with the tone of the article, claiming it confirmed Victoria's ambivalence about supporting the treaty.[25] In August of 1828 (a month later), Gual informed his superiors that the Mexican senate had rejected the Treaty of Confederation, and that it would be useless to consider further action on behalf of the unification program.[26]

The defeat of the Treaty of Confederation in Mexico City left no recourse for Gual except to return home. Despite his frustrations with President Victoria and the Mexican legislature, he absolved Michelena and Dominguez of any blame, asserting that they had always acted in good faith.[27] When he drafted his last letter from Mexico, Gual exhibited mixed feelings about the time and labor he had invested in the confederation program. He was sorry to leave Mexico without having achieved his goal of "realizing the great work of the America confederation after waiting so long to exchange pending ratification." The failure and defeat of the Treaty of Confederation, to which Gual had dedicated so much of his time and energy, must have been a crushing and painful blow to him. He had given up the prestigious post of foreign minister for this cause. Nevertheless, he perceptively recognized the positive results that had been achieved during the previous four-year-long campaign, which "consoled me by assuring that there would be no interruption of the intimate and fraternal relations that happily existed between the republics."[28]

One reason for the defeat of the treaty in Mexico was that it was on the brink of a civil war. The various factions sought only their immediate personal, political and ideological goals. Gual observed that the treaty had been debated under great tensions. The personal and political animus demonstrated by all parties in Mexico City was so intense that by 1829, after Gual had departed, it was described as a "rabble-ridden city" whose government was under the control of "sans-chemises." The suspicions that were awakened by the Panama Congress and the ideological acrimony in Mexico led Bolívar to describe Guadalupe Victoria, whom he intensely disliked, as the "vile issue of a savage Indian woman and a barbaric African" who had taken control of an ochlocracy. In ensuing years, this discord would weaken Mexico even more and complicated her relations with other states.[29]

Defeat in Retrospect and Its Future Implications

The majority of the Latin American leaders never had any intention of framing a strong centralized union. The injection of so many contradictory clauses in the treaty is a clear indication that the Latin American political classes did not consider the creation of a federal or confederal system dedicated to the propagation of a truly unified state to be in their immediate interests. For Bolívar, his pragmatic policy of integration proved a bitter personal failure. The defeat of the treaty demonstrates the degree to which Latin American culture became enamored of the new state system, and how firmly entrenched that system had become in Latin America's political culture in only a few years. Indeed, the number of states in the region would increase within a hundred years, further frustrating unionists.

Another problem facing the Latin Americans was their lack of negotiating and diplomatic experience. Their history of diplomacy was limited to Spain, the United Kingdom and occasionally other Latin American states. In the case of Spain, with which the Latin Americans had been at war for many years, peace treaties had not yet been formulated. During the revolutionary wars and the earliest years of independence, Great Britain had acted as a patron providing financial assistance, political support and mercenaries. Diplomatic relations among the Latin Americans were scarce and limited to the number of years they had been independent.

The Latin American states also lacked extensive negotiating experience. The new republics had little, if any, experience with representative government, which by necessity requires the ability to compromise. By 1826, it was clear that the Latin Americans had become politically polarized over very passionate ideological issues and fundamental public policy matters that had not lent themselves to political flexibility.

To what extent the integration process was defeated by personal animus towards Bolívar, and by petty regional jealousies and suspicions, is debatable, although it is certain that these factors also played a role in the failure of the congress. The Mexican and Peruvian delegates held strong suspicions of Bolívar, who had urged the union of the proposed confederation with the British Empire—a proposal that alienated them as well as many of his allies in Colombia. His flirtation with a possible monarchy for Latin America and his strong support for a republic in which the executive would be elected for life stirred suspicions about his personal ambitions. The very idea of establishing a monarchy or an elected executive for life was anathema to the large republican faction that had waged war against Spain. Bolívar's suggestions were not only premature but clumsy, and they undoubtedly contributed to the failure of the congress.

A careful study of Bolívar's writings will shed light on this matter. On May 20, 1825, in a letter to Vice President Santander, Bolívar claimed that Mexico had proposed that he be selected as a generalissimo of the anticipated union. Bolívar asserted that he was not interested in such a position, but that he was honored and "grateful to the Mexicans for their high opinion of me." In the same note he instructed Santander to warn the Colombian delegates not to nominate a Colombian for the position of generalissimo as it would precipitate jealousy. He was emphatic that under no circumstances should the Colombian delegates in Panama nominate him as director of military operations. These comments give support to the supposition that Bolívar placed the welfare and success of the proposed union above all other matters, including any personal ambition.[30]

Why did Mexican opinion turn so strongly against Bolívar ? The offer by the Mexicans to make Bolívar a generalissimo may have been due solely to the military threat posed by Spain and her allies in the Holy Alliance. As of 1825, he had been the most successful and resourceful general of the entire independence movement in Latin America. Bolívar had a proven track record, and to defeat an invasion from abroad would have required his valuable skills.

When the possibility of a foreign military invasion subsided, his expertise was no longer required, and Bolívar proved unable to maintain his political dominance. It was at this point in time that he needed to engage in more extensive consultations with Latin American leaders. Instead he continued to promote his controversial proposals regarding the political structuring of the proposed executive branch with a monarchy, alienating large segments of the population and making it necessary for him to publicly disavow his proposals due to the intense criticism they aroused. This he did not do. The failure to modify or renounce his political stance contributed in some measure to the failure of the conference, though from the vantage point of history and the written historical record, there is no reason to assume it was the only factor. Nor is there any historical evidence to suggest that Bolívar sought personal political aggrandizement at the expense of the Latin American people.

Writing in 1829, three years after the Panama Congress, Bolívar surveyed the Latin American political landscape and lamented the political divisiveness that had intensified throughout the entire region, a situation that portended future chaos. In an anonymous letter written from Quito, Ecuador, but attributed to Bolívar, he wrote: "Throughout America we shall see but a single trend in public affairs. The cycles are similar, varying at most according to time and conditions but otherwise paralleling the stages and the events in the other newborn states."[31] Likewise, Pedro Gual, a major participant in the Panama Congress negotiations, wrote to Bolívar after leaving Mexico in May of 1829 that he was fed up by the constant vexations "caused by those exaggerated doctrines that our people neither understand nor comprehend.... What a horrible state of affairs!"[32] Gual was, of course, referring to the ideological schisms that had appeared in Latin America. One of these issues concerned the merits of centralized government versus a federal system. Another schismatic political problem that concerned Latin Americans was the role that the church played in the social and economic life of their country, an issue that resulted in several coup d'états that paralyzed orderly representative government throughout most of Latin America.

It is clear from Bolívar's correspondence that he favored an integrated Latin American government with the broad powers necessary for successful governing. This perspective was not held because of politically selfish reasons. It should be remembered that Bolívar allowed the various governments he formed to deal with the treaty as they saw fit. He did not threaten them with armed force, though he could have. Bolívar did not even prevent the political fragmentation of his own Gran Colombia with military action, though he could have done so. He was averse to the possibility of war between the Latin Americans. In fact, Bolívar engineered the creation of Bolivia as a buffer state in order to prevent war between Peru and Argentina. Likewise, the use of armed force would have violated his creed in self-determination. It was the sincere belief of Bolívar and his supporters that a powerful central government was the minimum required for preventing the disintegration of such a state. Even if a strong central government could not be created, an organ with the ability to coordinate solutions to problems was needed if for no other purpose that preventing internecine friction. These powers would be needed in order to maintain any semblance of political control and administrative efficiency for such a large state.

Bolívar and his supporters soberly recognized that the large, geographically diverse regions that were physically isolated but contiguous to each other were prone to petty provincialism and enjoyed their political autonomy. They realized that this problem required a centralized coordination council, preferably an organ that would act as did the Congress of the United States of America in order to achieve its objectives. The unionists were perfectly willing to compromise on supporting home rule for the individual states, an arrangement that they viewed as wholly appropriate for the individual political units, considering the expanse of space and geographical divisions. Bolívar had urged creation of a strong central government because of the many complex social problems that plagued the region—ranging from racial tensions to low educational levels in the various states. Recognizing that the creation of such a government might not be politically feasible, Bolívar repeatedly demonstrated that he was flexible enough to support a confederal form of government, if for no other purpose than to promote further political and economic integration.

The failure of the Treaty of Confederation was a defeat not only for those who sought to create a unified Latin America; it was also a major defeat for political adherents who sought to advance the creation of a society whose tenets would embrace classical liberalism. During the next forty years it appeared that Latin America would never be able to enjoy the fruits of liberal society. Instead it fell into political, social, economic and cultural turmoil, rendering representative government prostrate. This constant volatility would eventually pave the way for a wave of authoritarian governments all over the region. The 1860s and 1870s would bring some tranquility to some states, but eventually the twentieth century would bring back a recurring cycle of disappointing constitutional crises affecting the political evolution of the various states. The appearance of dictatorships in Mexico with Diaz, Perón in Argentina, Vargas in Brazil, Pinochet in Chile and the numerous dictatorships in Central America buttressed by the U.S. military are a testimony to this.

The failure of the Panama Congress and the meeting at Tacubaya also meant that the economic vitality of the area would be sapped by futile military expenditures and ineffectual central governments. Fortunately for Bolívar, he did not live to see the painful appearance of so many new political states in the region. Soon after his death, a surge of sectionalism swept over all of Latin America. This phenomenon was already in the process of incubation as Central America split into various independent states. Gran Colombia would fragment into the independent states of Colombia, Venezuela and Ecuador, and by the early 1900s Panama would be separated from Colombia in a fictitious independence movement financed by the United States in order to secure control of the isthmus for the future canal zone.

The conditions for this disorder were exacerbated by the failure of the states to consolidate into a larger union. Many of the Latin American states of the 1820s were not economically viable at independence or in the decades that followed. The populations of the new states were too small to facilitate the type of foreign economic investment experienced by the First World. All of the states were self-sufficient in terms of food production and most needs could be met by local producers. When local demands could not be met, they utilized overseas suppliers from Europe or the United States. Indeed, Latin American governments eventually sought to protect their primary exports from each other. As a result there was little incentive to facilitate trade between the new Latin American states. Eventually the interests between elites of Europe, the United States and Latin America grew closer, while economic relations between Latin Americans stagnated, in the new system of states.

Ratification of the treaty would have created a new balance of power against the gentry and their ability to control the economic markets of the time by creating a larger internal market. This in turn would have facilitated the strengthening of new domestic commercial and industrial groups that could have counteracted gentry interests. For their part, the landed oligarchy had little interest in forming reciprocal interests within Latin America through the Treaty of Confederation. A local problem could be more effectively dealt with in a known environment than in one with new actors. Failure to ratify the treaty meant that the economic development of Latin America would be postponed.

Perhaps no group in Latin America suffered more from this economic situation than the nascent middle classes, the primary source of support for classical liberal societies. This group would have to await political and social gratification for many years. The members of this class were frustrated by their small numbers for many decades, and would have to await their turn to secure advantages they felt belonged to them.

In the decades to come the middle classes would consummate shifting political alliances with both authoritarian and liberal regimes in order to obtain and maintain these benefits. They would clamor perennially at various ideologies as if they were divinities, with the expectation that they would provide them with the economic security and comfort they desperately sought. These middle classes of the various states would elect presidents and legislatures, only to see them replaced with civilian or military dictators. In many instances the U.S. government via the military or some other U.S. agency would intervene to restore order. In many instance the middle classes supported these coup d'états. Insofar as political and/or economic integration remained unlikely, the middle classes would continue to vacillate between these opposing political alliances. Their goals could have been secured through the creation of stable political and economic institutions, if a viable integration program had been adopted.

In spite of the serious setback of the Panama Congress and Bolívar's bitter personal disappointment, a pro-unification agenda would continue to be enthusiastically promoted by some Latin American diplomats and individuals who felt that their problems could be addressed through the political and/or economic integration of the region in the decades to follow.

Was anything of any value achieved by the Panama Congress? Irrespective of the disappointing failure to reach its immediate objective, the conference did yield positive results. It initiated a dynamic process of inter–American cooperation among the Latin American nations that has never been abandoned. This cooperation had contributed to the development of relatively peaceful relations among the Latin American states. The Panama Congress became the first significant effort towards multilateralism practiced by the independent Latin American states. This multi-state diplomacy recognizes that Latin Americans possess a common heritage and common problems that need to be addressed by the group. In the realm of foreign affairs, this consciousness has not been shared with other cultures. Hemispheric affairs require attention; Latin American affairs remain fraternal matters.

V

OTHER STATE-DIRECTED INITIATIVES IN THE NINETEENTH CENTURY

Oh foolish people... What magician has hypnotized you and cast an evil spell upon you?—Galatians 3:3

An evil spell must have been cast on Latin America.—Guillermo Matta, *Unión Americana*, 1867

Mexico and the Integration Effort

Throughout the nineteenth century the Mexican government proved to be an ardent supporter of diplomatic efforts to create a politically integrated Latin America. Ironically, the Mexican government had originally rejected Bolívar's unionist proposal. Mexico City nevertheless continued to pursue the issue with new diplomatic initiatives. These endeavors paralleled efforts to maintain its physical survival as a nation in the midst of internal turmoil and continual political, military and economic pressure from the United States, and later France.

A perfunctory review of Mexico's role in the Panama Congress will shed light on Mexican efforts. On February 23, 1825, the president of Mexico, Guadalupe Victoria, replied in the affirmative to Bolívar's circular. Victoria claimed his country supported the Panama Congress, "which would serve as a base for the interests and relations that reciprocally unite them."[1] Lucas Alamán, Mexico's minister of foreign affairs, concurred, claiming that Panama was a wise choice because it "appeared to be the site which offers the most advantages." He supported Bolívar's efforts to coordinate attendance of the other Latin American states.[2] The Mexican legislature later refused to ratify the treaty.

With historical hindsight it may be recognized that no other country in the region would have benefited so much from the formation of an integrated Latin American state as Mexico. The benefits would have been tremendous, especially with regard to its relations with foreign countries, particularly the United States. As of 1827, relations between the two states had not yet flared into mutual hostility, although Mexico was, at this early date, trepidatious about its northern neighbor. This wariness towards the United States can be corroborated by the private suspicions that both Mexican and Latin American diplomats voiced regarding the United States, long before the U.S. intervention in Texas. The adoption and implementation of the Treaty of Confederation would have provided Mexico with a modicum of diplomatic flexibility in dealing with the United States and later France. Because of Mexico's size and population density, approval of the treaty would have provided her with sufficient influence within the integrated state to create any alliances necessary to thwart the alleged excessive influence of Bolívar.

Nevertheless, political and economic integration of Latin America became a key foreign policy objective of the Mexican government in the nineteenth century. Some efforts were the result of Mexican initiatives, while some were proposed by other Latin American governments. Mexican efforts at promoting integration since the 1826–27 isthmian debacle have been prodigious and indicate a demonstrable consistency within some quarters of its foreign ministry. These efforts indicate that the Mexicans came to view legislative rejection of the Treaty of Confederation as a serious error. Subsequent Mexican initiatives for integration ultimately proved disappointing. Some were noteworthy, while others merit only passing attention.

Mexico's initial efforts at promoting political integration began with the Panama Congress, when José Dominguez and Brigadier General José Mariano Michelena, formerly Mexico's representative to Great Britain, were appointed as plenipotentiaries to the assembly. Mexico's appreciation of the approaching political rendezvous can be gleaned from the correspondence that emanated from the president of the Council of Ministers. They were provided a list of objectives for their mission. The instructions they were given were as follows:

(1) To jointly sustain the independence of all nations from foreign powers;

(2) To sustain domestic peace of each state and its respective integrity;

(3) To sustain republican governments;

(4) To deny colonization by foreign states on the territory of contracting states;

(5) To determine the general principle that American public law will be based on respect for the new states as well as foreign powers; and

(6) To form a plan for the common defense of every state threatened by a foreign power: to form general budgets, assign contingents, and to designate the other means appropriate for fulfilling these objectives.[3]

Additional instructions given to Michelena and Dominguez concerned the length of the congress and potential military alliances. The government instructed them to seek a three-month-long conference, with the provision that they could extend the meeting time by an additional two months if necessary. In addition, the two delegates were empowered to arrange preliminary and concluding arrangements concerning (1) the time and manner in which future congresses would meet, (2) the place of any reunion, (3) the rules and regulation that should be observed in case of an extension of the meeting or for extraordinary sessions, and (4) the enforcement mechanism for contracted obligations assuming the final ratification of these negotiations was concluded.[4]

Michelena emphasized that issues of common concern to all attending republics should be given priority at the congress. While residing in Mexico City, the two envoys expressed concerns regarding several issues, which they forwarded to their government for advice. Among the matters for which they sought guidance were whether a military alliance should be offensive or defensive and which country, if any, should lead such an organization.[5] They were instructed that an alliance should have both qualities and come under the direction of all states in an offensive military agreement. The two envoys were informed that regardless of any majority votes in the Panama Congress, the Mexican government would finalize any treaties.[6]

An issue of keen importance for all Latin American societies beginning in 1830s was the development of authoritarian dictatorial regimes that came to power via military coup, or that after being elected refused to leave office. Even at this early date, this problem had become a matter of deep concern to the region. Both Dominguez and Michelena inquired from their government as to how they should treat countries that had "perpetual executive power" or a "supreme military chief."[7] They were informed that they should negotiate with any government, but that they should "advance the policy that no state in any confederation would be allowed to possess a perpetual government of one or more persons"—an obvious reference to Bolívar.[8]

With respect to Brazil, the Mexicans made it clear in 1825 that they supported its active participation at the Panama Congress, although Lucas Alamán indicated that he was distressed by the incursion of Brazilian troops in the Chiquitos area of Bolivia, attributing it to an overzealous commander. This concern was tempered by the hope that a united Latin America would be able to present a united front to the Holy Alliance.[9] In March of 1826, the changing political reality obligated both Michelena and Dominguez to formally ask Mexico City if Brazil and the United States should be admitted to such a federation as proposed by Bolívar. The Mexican government replied: "If they appear admit them, if they have the power to enter into an offensive and defensive alliance." Brazil never showed any genuine interests in the Panama Congress, and its lack of interest in participating never became an issue for the rest of the Latin Americans, although there was strong disappointment that Argentina and Chile did not send representatives to congress.[10] In analyzing Mexican efforts, it is important to understand the international situation as it existed in the 1820s, 1830s and 1840s. During the 1820s the Mexicans, like the rest of the Latin Americans, feared European encroachments on their territory. At this point, relations with the United States were relatively amicable, and Washington was widely admired throughout Latin America for its economic vitality and stable representative government and for ideological reasons. There had always been disagreements and suspicions between Mexico City and Washington, but these did not rise to the level of animosity that would come in later years. By the 1830s the Latin Americans, especially the Mexicans, realized they had no reason to fear Spain or the Holy Alliance. They soon learned that their new antagonist was to be the United States and that they could not depend on British support. In 1831, Mexican diplomats in Guatemala acknowledged that the interests of the United States and Great Britain were not identical to theirs.[11] This recognition was usually limited to diplomats or political leaders in direct contact with the United States or Britain. There were many other Latin Americans who were slow to realize the changing reality of international relations in the Western Hemisphere and the impact that such changes would have on their own countries.

The first indications that serious problems were evolving came with the dawn of the 1830s, when the Mexican government found itself embroiled in a complex dilemma related to its political control of Texas, which was being challenged by Anglo-American colonists in that province. This would be the first war in which a Latin American country would lose territory to an external force. The problem would grow as the momentum of U.S. chauvinists and their program of territorial expansion gathered extensive political support in both their home press and their government. The situation would finally explode into the Mexican-American War of 1846–48, which poisoned relations between the countries for many years. In this conflict Mexico lost one-half of its territory as a result of the harsh surrender terms imposed by the United States. Because of this war with the United States, the Mexican government eagerly sought to form a new balance of power in the Western Hemisphere as a way of maneuvering out of any future military predicaments.[12]

Despite the failure of the Panama Congress, Mexico City proceeded to adopt a pro-integration policy. On March 13, 1831, the Mexican government sent a circular to the various Latin American states requesting them to consider another Latin American congress to be held in Tacubaya, Lima or Panama. This conference was never convened.[13] Another attempt came on November 2, 1831, when Manuel Diez de Bonilla, the Mexican minister to the Federal Republic of Central America, residing in Guatemala City, informed that government that Mexico City was interested in sending representatives to all the Latin American countries in the hope of creating a political union of the "former Spanish colonies" for the purpose of "standardizing the political interests of all," which Diez de Bonilla asserted was "absolutely necessary." He called for a new meeting to complement the Panama Congress and suggested it to be in Tacubaya, Mexico. Diez de Bonilla further suggested that energy should not be wasted on inviting the United States or Great Britain, "whose interests are so contrary to ours."[14]

The purpose of the new proposal would be to consider the measures necessary "to eliminate disagreements between the various Latin American states and to remedy them once they occur via an amicable intervention" as well as to take steps "to determine the territory that belongs to each republic and to ensure the integrity with respect to the new republics." Any such assembly, he asserted, needed to adopt a uniform standard of citizenship to be provided to each national citizen in all the Spanish-speaking countries, and a uniform code that would recognize the registration of maritime vessels by every member of the proposed state. Diez de Bonilla also advised that any invitation to Brazil should be extended by a Spanish-American assembly if it should ever meet, rather than by the Mexican government alone.[15]

The Mexican government eventually approved the plan of Diez de Bonilla. Meanwhile, the Mexican minister in Lima, Peru, following the instructions of his government, sent copies of the proposal to the various Latin American governments. The diplomatic note asked the governments to consider where they might wish to convene—Lima, Panama or Tacubaya, Mexico. The purpose of the meeting would be to create

> The union and close alliance of the new states for the purposes of defense in case of foreign invasion, the friendly mediation of the neutral states for the settlement of disagreements that arise between two or more sister republics, a code of public

law stating their mutual obligations are real and achievable objectives for the common good, and possible.[16]

The plan proposed by Diez de Bonilla failed to materialize. Nevertheless, Mexico persisted with its efforts. On August 6, 1839, and April 2, 1840, the Mexican foreign minister, Juan de Dios Cañedo, asked the Venezuelan government for its thoughts on convoking a new congress, but the proposal proved fruitless. All efforts of Dios Cañedo to reconvene a new conference were exasperated by the chronic internal chaos that Latin America experienced during the ensuing years.[17] The offers made by the Mexican government sought either a defensive alliance or a confederated state. As weak as this form of government would have been, Mexican initiatives for a new congress fell on deaf ears.[18] The Venezuelan historian J.M. Torres Caicedo explained that these failures arose because in this time period, the Latin American states followed a policy predicated on the theory of "cada uno para si [every man for himself]."[19]

By 1857, the Mexican government reinitiated its efforts to initiate some form of political unification. In that year, the Mexican envoy extraordinaire and plenipotentiary to Guatemala, Juan Nepomuceno de Pereda, wrote a lengthy note to the Mexican Foreign Ministry regarding the advisability of reconstituting a congress of Spanish-American representatives, dated March 27, 1857. Nepomuceno wrote at a time when continuous American political and military pressure on Mexico and Central America was being applied. From his diplomatic position he could view the intrigues of both American and British agents seeking to gain political influence in the region. The highly articulate envoy wrote with a sense of urgency, imploring his readers to consider the "entire existence and conservation of the race." Nepomuceno argued that closer political unification was not just a matter of principle but of survival. "To be or not to be," he wrote, was the crux of the matter. He argued that the only way Mexico and Latin America could avert political and national annihilation would be to reconstitute a congress of plenipotentiaries representing all the Spanish-American states for the purpose of forming a political and military alliance.

Nepomuceno detailed the following propositions in his discussion of a new political union: First, he perceived a threat to the Latin American people that he asserted came from the Anglo-Saxon race represented by the United States. Second, it "was necessary to create an offensive and defensive alliance between the Hispanic-American states, reunited in effect with a Congress of Plenipotentiaries." Third, it would be "convenient to extend the alliance to other states of the Latin race, or at least the Spanish nation."[20] Nepomuceno wrote with a sense of keen urgency that "the existence of the Latin-Iberian race on the American continent is entangled in the web of a trial." He added,

"This is the most important and serious question that should absorb the attention of the governments and of statesmen; that they should be jealous of the
nationality of the Hispanic-American nations." Though these concerns had
been voiced before by the Mexicans, the intensity of de Pereda's comments
demonstrates the genuine fear he felt for his country's physical survival.[21]

Nepomuceno acknowledged that it would be difficult for some of the
Spanish-American governments to enter into any form of an alliance. He suggested that formation of a unified congress might give way to the creation of
jealousies "that are inherent with small states." Another problem he anticipated
was how adequately the various states could utilize their resources in a military
emergency. Likewise, he regarded the various levels of social and political
development of the various Latin American states as an impediment to integration. He even considered the possibility of allowing Spain into a confederated state, but informed his superiors of the many outstanding problems
posed by such a union, including the fact that Spain did not yet recognize the
independence of El Salvador, Guatemala, Honduras or New Granada. Considering the problems of creating a confederated state, de Pereda shied away
from taking a strong stance either way with respect to any integration proposal,
but indicated his pro-integration sentiments by concluding that any instructions that might be provided to a Mexican diplomat carry the provision to
"make as extensive an alliance with the Spanish nation" as possible.[22]

It was impossible for Nepomuceno's proposal to come to fruition. Mexico
was in a state of anarchy and confusion. Mexican society had become polarized
between conservatives and reforming liberals. After adoption of a new constitution in 1857, Mexico exploded into a conflict known as the War of the Reform
that lasted from 1858 to 1861. The political chaos became so unbearable that
some individuals began to reconsider the republican form of government.
Eventually some Mexicans invited the Austrian prince Maximilian to rule in
place of politicians and ideologues that were tearing at their society. Due to
this chaos Nepomuceno's plan could never receive serious consideration, but
Mexico continued to pursue political integration as a foreign policy objective.

In 1886 the Mexican government undertook consideration of another
integration project initiated by the Bolivian Embassy in Paris. On October 8,
1886, Aniceto Arce, the Bolivian minister to France, sent a circular inviting
the various members of the Spanish-American diplomatic corps to the resi-
dence of the Bolivian legation, which was located at forty-four Avenue des
Champs-Élysées. The meeting took place at 2:30 in the afternoon and was
attended by Arce and the ministers of Argentina, Colombia, Guatemala and
Uruguay. The ministers from Chile and Nicaragua were absent, the former
suffering from ill health.[23]

Upon arrival at the gathering, the diplomats settled to discuss various matters. The most important issue was initiated by the Colombian minister to France, Francisco de P. Mateus, who informed the delegates that his government had directed him to determine if another Panama Congress could be convened for the purpose of creating a Spanish-American league. Ramon Fernandez, the Mexican minister to France, observed that an effort to guarantee the neutrality of the Panama isthmus was of particular concern to the Colombians because "according to Mr. Mateus, the Colombian government does not believe that its neutrality is well guaranteed by virtue of the dominating tendencies of the United States."[24]

The Colombian minister, Mr. Mateus, invoked the name of Bolívar in his call for the creation of such a congress, stating that the proposed conference was to be held for the primary purpose of establishing "the bases of a perfect union between its respective countries and an offensive and defensive alliance against the absorbing tendencies of other governments." The second purpose, according to Ramon Fernandez, was to "develop the bases for international Hispanic-American legislation," which was to be implemented as a means for dealing with and eliminating the claims of European states seeking to expand their influence in Latin America. Fernandez emphasized that at that very moment, the Colombian government was embroiled in such a conflict with the Italian government, which was claiming damages for the merchant vessel *Flavio Gioia* under threat of military intervention in Colombia. He explained that the problem between the nations would never have occurred if "a confederation of all the Hispanic-American countries existed."[25]

The diplomatic ministers in attendance at the Paris meeting decided it would be best for any proposals for a confederation or a new Panama Congress be referred to their respective governments for consideration. Apprehension about publicly calling a new congress was aired by the Argentine minister, Mr. Paz, who suggested planning such a conference without inviting the United States might offend that country, since it claimed an interest in the Panamanian isthmus. Paz suggested that failure to consult the United States might result in a more bellicose policy by Washington. The Mexican minister, who supported the proposal, suggested that the Colombian government take charge of any attempt for a new congress since the initiative had come from Colombia. Mr. Mateus replied that it was the "desire of his government to do so, but that it wished to ascertain the plausibility of such a venture via the opinion of the other Hispanic-American governments" prior to making its goals publicly known, lest his government "suffer ridicule" in the event of another failure at political integration.[26]

At the conclusion of the meeting all the attending diplomats unanimously affirmed the Mexican proposal to allow the Colombian government to rekindle the pursuit of a new isthmian conference. It does not appear, however, from the information available, that these diplomats or their governments took any further action regarding the discussions of October 11, 1886, in Paris. The negative outcome of this proposal proved disappointing for the unionists, as the various Spanish-American states proved unwilling or unable to unable to reunite their diplomats in a new congress.[27]

Several years later, in 1895–96, a new proposal for a politically integrated state was proposed to the Mexican government by Ecuador, but it too proved futile. The Ecuadorian plan was a well-designed document that identified problematic issues for consideration and resolution by the Latin American states. The new project reiterated many of the previous concerns voiced by other governments. The proposal called for the elaboration of a new international law for America, which gained immediate and enthusiastic approval by the Mexican government. The Ecuadorians responded by requesting that the conference be scheduled for August 10, 1896, in Mexico City. It met as scheduled but was quickly terminated after it failed to reach a quorum. This was the last major effort and conference for an integrated Latin America to be attended by the Mexican government during the nineteenth century.[28]

Federal Republic of Central America: Francisco Morazán and J. Cecilio del Valle

Even before Bolívar and the Mexican government were attempting to form an integration program for the Latin Americans, the Federal Republic of Central America had been formed in 1823. It is notable because it is the only truly multi-state federation to have been created in Latin American. The history of this political unit can be traced to the peaceful separation of Guatemala from Mexico. Guatemala was at that time a part of the newly independent Mexican state. As a Spanish colony it constituted a separate administrative body, known as the Captaincy of Guatemala or alternatively as the Kingdom of Guatemala, which was divided into administrative units known as intendancies.[29] After the separation from Spain the various intendancies became independent and formed a loosely organized group of states known as the United Provinces of Central America, which included Costa Rica, El Salvador, Guatemala, Honduras and Nicaragua. The United Provinces were the forerunner of the Federal Republic of Central America. It was decided early in their independent political history that these political units should unify into a stronger, more cohesive state.

A constitution was soon drawn up in November 1824 by a group designated the National Constituent Assembly and was ratified after the first elected
congress discussed its merits. Conservative forces favored a unitary form of
government, while liberals favored a federal system. The constitution that was
approved in August 1825 provided for a federal structure. The newly unified
government became officially known as the Federal Republic of Central America; it lasted until 1838. The new government quickly floundered amidst political and constitutional problems arising from various interpretations of
election laws, partisan politics, and provincial and local jealousies. Incredibly,
an example of this jealousy was the relative importance of Guatemala City
and the resentment that arose when that city received a bishopric over other
cities.

One of the principal leaders of the Federal Republic of Central America
was Francisco Morazán. He was a staunch supporter of Central American Federation and hoped for a further union of all the Latin American states. On
September 16, 1830, he wrote: "The alliance of the American nation, though
frustrated up to now, is certain ... when this admirable combination shall be
put into practice. She will appear to all the New World with all the power that
it is capable of, because of its advantageous geographic position and immense
riches, the justice of its governments, the same laws, its growing numbers of
inhabitants, and above all the common interests that unite them."[30]

The story of the doomed Federal Republic of Central America can be
told largely through a study of Morazán's life. Indeed, the political history of
the union paralleled his life. Morazán was born in Tegucigalpa, Honduras, on
October 3, 1792, and died in defense of the federation before a firing squad
on September 15, 1842. He was president of the Federal Republic of Central
America from 1830 to 1834 and from 1835 to 1839. Morazán, like all other
Latin American political leaders of his time, found himself dealing with devastating political schisms wrought by liberal and conservative ideologues.

The conservative faction favored the maintaining of traditional Hispanic
values, traditions and political policies of the Spanish empire. They supported
the conservative Roman Catholic Church as the official religion. The conservatives favored policies conducive to the export of their agricultural products
and to maintaining the communal lands of the Indian peasantry. The conservatives staunchly rejected the massive reforms supported by the liberals, and
pursued states' rights as a mechanism for upholding their immediate interests.
On the other hand, the liberals favored elimination of communal lands, free
trade, foreign investment, religious toleration, and rejection of corporate privileges.

The new country had a promising but ominous beginning. Simón Bolívar looked upon its development with great enthusiasm. He viewed the new union as having great potential for the future. In a letter to Vice President Francisco Paula de Santander of Colombia, Bolívar suggested that the new country attend the Panama Congress. Bolívar's optimism was predicated on the assumption that Guatemala (Central America) was the "most federally disposed country in all America.... We should therefore throw wide open the doors to admit her."[31] Soon after its first president took office, the Federal Republic sent delegates to the Panama Congress, but its presence at the congress was marred by internal political divisiveness within its own borders.

The problems began in 1825 when the first president of the Federal Republic of Central America was elected. He was Manuel José Arce, a liberal who defeated the moderate José Cecilio del Valle from Honduras. Both sides were disaffected with the victory, which had involved all sorts of arguments and differing interpretations of the electoral laws. In order to secure political victory Arce made concessions to the conservatives to win the votes needed in the electoral college to achieve victory.

Ideologues from both sides cried foul play and gave way to their unreasonable passions. The various political factions refused to provide the young republic with a chance to begin its infancy with a clean slate. The liberal supporters of Arce accused him of cynical opportunism for making political concessions to the conservative forces. The conservatives never failed to criticize his agenda and were always suspicious of him. When Arce decided to eliminate the liberal governor of Guatemala, Juan Barrundia, in 1826, the government of El Salvador, which was also liberal, decided to provide military aid against Arce, thus initiating a bitter legacy throughout the region.

In 1829, a new president, the liberal Francisco Morazán, took office as the executive of the federation. He inherited a morass of problems and proceeded to deal with them in a decisive but counter-productive manner, causing rancor and rebellion among the conservative elements. The most controversial of these policies was his anti-clericalism, which resulted in the exiling of various high clergy as well as his conservative political enemies. Nevertheless, he instituted the jury system and moved the capital in 1834 to San Salvador, which aroused strong resentment in the old capital of Guatemala City. Throughout his term as president, Morazán faced various types of armed insurrection. In 1833 an Indian rebellion led by Anastasio Aquino began in El Salvador, which only added additional volatility to the unstable political and social environment. In addition to this problem, Guatemala faced serious secession movements within its borders. In Nicaragua, civil war broke out between the two cities of León and Granada. In Costa Rica, warfare broke out between various cities before San José emerged as the victorious municipality. These petty, irrational and fruitless struggles reduced the Central American municipalities and their citizens to the condition of quasi-feudal baronies.

In 1833 Morazán ran for president again but was defeated by José Cecilio del Valle, who died before being inaugurated. This allowed Morazán to become president again, because he was the candidate with the second-most votes, thus making him eligible for the office. In February 1835, a special election was held that secured Morazán's victory. His presidency was soon beset by more violence. In 1837 a massive outbreak of cholera broke out in Guatemala with disastrous consequences for the population. The clergy claimed the disease was God's punishment of Guatemala and the liberals. The punishment came, according to the clergy, because of mistreatment the church had suffered at the hands of Morazán's supporters.

In response to the epidemic, a rebellion against the liberal governor of Guatemala was launched by the Indian leader Rafael Carrera, a charismatic figure who supported the church and the conservatives. Carrera succeeded in using the outbreak as a rallying cry to oust the liberals, with the assistance of the Indian masses. Carrera's revolt against the liberal governor proved successful. By 1838 the entire Central American union was in tatters. In that year, Costa Rica, Honduras and Nicaragua left the union and began their independent political existences. Shortly thereafter the western portion of Guatemala broke away to form the new state of Los Altos. In 1840, Morazán led troops into Guatemala to reclaim that land for the union, although by that time, it was too late to revive the Federal Republic. In the ensuing military campaign he was quickly defeated by the shrewd Carrera. Morazán escaped to Colombia (Gran Colombia) and entered Costa Rica in 1842 with plans to recreate the union, but was captured, declared a tyrant and executed.

It is in this state of anarchy that the Federal Republic of Central America ended. The local political figures of Central America succeeded in fragmenting the federation into a number of ostensible countries that could really be considered nothing more than city-states or even mere appanages. It would be many decades before Central Americans could overcome their narrow localisms and integrate their own respective countries. The Central American states degenerated into five weak states unable to sustain stable political systems or economies. It was only with great difficulty that they were able to maintain their political independence.

Nicaragua, for example, remained an independent state only with great difficulty as it faced a serious ordeal with the arrival of the U.S. agent William Walker, who sought to create a pro–United States government that would facilitate Washington's control of a possible canal in that country. The Mexican plenipotentiary to Guatemala, Juan Nepomuceno de Pereda, wrote in 1857 that it had been an arduous task for the Nicaraguans "to defeat the hordes of the usurper Walker."[32] The ability of the Central American states to maintain their independence is mainly attributable to international political rivalry, rather than any farsighted policy from the local leaders of the isthmus. It is only because the United States and Great Britain competed and feared each other in their efforts to construct a canal across the Colombian state of Panama or Nicaragua that these regions remained politically and territorially intact.

Another prominent leader in the quest for Central American integration and a forceful supporter for the political integration of all of Latin America was José Cecilio del Valle. He was born in Honduras in 1776 and received his degree as an attorney in 1803 while residing in Guatemala. Del Valle served briefly in the Mexican government during Guatemala's brief period as a province of Mexico during the monarchical period. With Guatemala's decision to separate from Mexico, he left his post to serve his new country in its efforts to unite with the rest of Central America. He eventually became the conservative candidate for the presidency of the Federal Republic of Central America. When he lost that campaign due to shrewd political maneuvering on the part of the liberal candidate, del Valle published a book condemning the victory of Manuel José Arce and thereby contributed to the political acrimony that ensued.

Throughout his political career, del Valle proved an ardent supporter of unionism. He urged the summoning of an all–Latin-American congress in which the representatives of the various countries would be given full powers to deal with important issues. He recognized that the new nation-states of Latin America were not true nations but rather elements of the same civilization, and referred to them as "provinces." As a hard-nosed pragmatist, he asserted that Latin Americans needed to adopt the most utilitarian plan so that "no province of America would suffer foreign invasions, nor be victim to internal divisions." Del Valle observed that a need existed to "form a more efficient plan to elevate the provinces of America to the level of prosperity and power that they should rise to."[33]

Del Valle proposed that with political integration, an economic program could be initiated that would assist every state but which, at the same time, would provide each member the autonomy needed to deal with its own problems. He argued such a political organization would "obligate other states to respect such a decision." His economic program called for establishment of a commercial treaty among all Latin American states and the formation of a merchant marine. The intention of such plans was to create a state capable of withstanding any external aggression.[34]

On February 23, 1822, in an article written for one of the major Central

American periodicals, del Valle wrote: "America expands through all the zones; but it forms one sole continent. The Americans are disseminated throughout all the climates; but they should form one family." He referred to Latin America as the "face of our fatherland." He wrote that if Europe could unite itself in a congress on matters of major importance then surely the Latin Americans could be united in a "cortes [parliamentary body] when it was necessary to do so."[35]

Del Valle called for a general congress to be convoked and for representatives to be sent to said congress with "enough powers to deal with major issues that should be the object of her reunion." His call was similar to Bolívar's plan and preceded the Liberator's plan by a few months, although such a proposal was hardly an original idea since it had been openly but informally discussed for many years. He suggested that a major problem confronting such a union would be to insure that "not a single province of America should become prisoner of foreign invaders or victim of internal divisions." Likewise, he called for a general treaty on commerce that would facilitate inter-regional trade. Del Valle did not envision a strong federal state in the mold of the United States. Instead, true to the traditions of the Latin Americans, he favored a loose confederation, as evinced by his suggestion that the proposed congress should determine how many troops and money each state should contribute to the defense of Latin America. In other words, his scheme envisioned individual states determining matters of national security, rather than a central government determining policies and strategies for a common defense. This approach would have condemned the confederation to internal political friction in case of a war with a foreign power, and consigned it to military defeat. To ensure that the individual states would remain politically supreme at the expense of any centralized political power, he suggested that in case internal chaos affected any state, the rest of the states should send troops to quell the disturbance for the sole purpose of allowing the state legislatures the opportunity to resolve critical issues and restore order.[36]

Del Valle spent considerable time soliciting support for the constitution of the Federal Republic of Central America. In November 1824, the year the federal constitution was drafted, he wrote that without such a document the various administrative units (countries) would find themselves "poor, degraded and miserable." He warned the people they would have to "swear to defend the integrity of your territory, swear to throw back from your land any foreigners that come to invade or create treason; swear to be independent or to not be at all." He implored the population not to allow the states to forget they were part of a federal union. Del Valle also asked his audience to "respect the constitutional authorities." More important, he targeted as his audience those individuals who would serve in public life and declared, "No discourses should exit our lips solely from mouths that have not been formed by education, or from men who do not see liberty except in revolutions and trouble."[37]

Del Valle died in 1834 amidst the floundering and destructive tendencies of both the Federal Republic of Central America and the failed Panama Congress. Like Morazán's work, del Valle's efforts inspired countless Central Americans to argue for the reunification of the region. Unfortunately, del Valle warnings were ignored and problems became unavoidable. Eventually, the federation sank into a morass of acrimony, secession and ultimately failure. Simón Bolívar, who observed these events from Quito, Ecuador, wrote in 1829, when it became apparent the union was in serious trouble: "The lawful authorities have been removed; the provinces have rebelled against the capital; brother wars upon brother, a horror which the Spaniards prevented, and this war is to the death. Town fights town, city stands against city, each with its own government, and every street is a self-constituted nation. In Central America all is bloodshed and terror."[38]

The result of these problems was that the union was never rebuilt in spite of many fervent efforts by Central Americans. These efforts continued into the twentieth century but failed. Considering the rampant provincialism that has plagued Central America, this failure is not surprising. The idea of re-unification has remained popular among educated groups of people, but obstacles posed by politicians and various political considerations have prevented its realization. Likewise, the idea of unifying with the rest of the Latin American states has remained popular in Central America. If the Federal Republic of Central America had succeeded, a larger Latin American political union might have been possible. The effects would have been salutary. A larger unified group of states might have made it more difficult for political ideologues to amalgamate so much power, by forcing them to contend with other political alliances at the state and union level.

Long after the demise of the Federal Republic of Central America, the historians D. Ramón Rosa and Rómulo E. Durón acknowledged that the continuing and alluring power of political integration as an aspiration for Latin America was predicated on the "desideratum for patriotism in order to regulate the international relations of the Latin American people, constructing a permanent peace and increasing her moral, political and industrial progress. The disastrous War of the Pacific is proving the necessity of a league of salvation for the greatest and most expensive interests of the Americans."[39]

According to Rosa and Durón, the Central American union failed because it utilized a federal form of government rather than a unitary system. They maintained that a centralized unitary structure would have provided a cohesive political system that the Central Americans could have used to deal with their problems. Federalism, they contended, caused more problems than anticipated and was responsible for destroying "our historical unity." The two writers argued that the federalist system had proven too complex for Central America because it had required a population with a high level of education and was thus unsuitable for a population with little if any education. Federalism was condemned as "a system of government that is the most difficult to practice." Likewise they asserted that the federalist system had created an uneconomical political unit for a "people lacking communication and resources." Rosa and Durón lambasted the adoption of the federalist system as the catalyst for the constant outbreaks of insurrection and civil war. With respect to the ideological struggles that arose within the Central American state, they portrayed the conservatives positively, and as "having reason" for their views, while the liberals were described as having "good intentions." They acknowledged that such factionalization cost the Central Americans dearly and noted that future generations of Central Americans would be condemned to deal with the same problems.[40]

The efforts to reconstruct a unified Central America have been so numerous as to be exasperating to even the most dissimulating diplomat. A few scholarly studies of these attempts have been made, but any lengthy discussion of these efforts is beyond the scope of this study, with the exception of Salvador Mendieta's strivings, which will be discussed later in this work.

The Peru-Bolivian Confederation: Rivalry and War with Chile

Since this study will not deal at length with any attempt at political union that did not include at least four member states, the Peru-Bolivian Confederation will be dealt with only briefly in order to highlight certain points. The confederation was formed in 1836 and lasted effectively until 1838. This organization was put together by General Andres Santa Cruz, who had served as an officer under José de San Martín. Santa Cruz was eventually elected president of Bolivia and, taking advantage of the strife in Peru, was able to intervene in the politics of that country and effectively create the new confederated state. The purpose of the confederation was to bring together two states that were very similar in terms of their political, economic and social structures. Both Peru and Bolivia had large Native American populations in which Quechua or Aymara was spoken. A significant number of these Native Americans did not speak Spanish. Large numbers of the Native American population lived in isolated mountain villages. Many did not even participate in the money economy, living in their self-contained common lands. During the independence movement both states were strongly pro-royalist and were the last states to secure independence. Upon securing statehood, they came under the political control of the conservative factions.

Both Argentina and Peru had sought control of Bolivia. Their claims were based on the old administrative claims of the viceroyalties of Peru and the Rio de la Plata. Bolivia's territory had been a part of both viceroyalties. With the demise of the imperial system of viceroyalties and the beginning of the independence period, Bolivia became a point of contention between Peru and Argentina. In an effort to eliminate this problem, Simón Bolívar deemed it best to create Bolivia as an independent state.

In order to bring their mutual interests together, General Andres Santa Cruz created the Peru-Bolivian Confederation. It fell short of the integration program that Bolívar had called for but had the potential of dealing with the intractable problems facing the new state. The confederation was an attempt to bring some order to the region via the construction of a strong conservative government. Santa Cruz presided over the government as the "protector," to which office he was elected for a ten-year term. Argentina and Chile feared the new Peru-Bolivian Confederation and sought to maintain a balance of power. Eventually the political and economic problems that flared between the confederation, Chile and Argentina led to war. The result of this unnecessary war was the defeat and failure of the confederation. It was the first serious war to break out between Latin America states. Chile emerged victorious from the war after the battle of Yungay in 1839, by which time the confederation had ceased to exist. The war served no useful purpose for the Latin American people, serving to only fan the flames of an artificial and petty nationalism that evolved in Latin America. The conflict was the logical outcome of the state system in Latin America and the utilization of the Western European geo-political policy of balance-of-power politics, which proved unsuitable for Latin America and its development.

In retrospect, the most significant outcome of the war was that the three countries did not harbor grudges for very long. In the 1860s the countries allied themselves in a war against Spain when Madrid ordered the occupation of the Chincha Islands off the coast of Peru. This alliance eventually included Bolivia, Chile, Ecuador and Peru. These states found themselves unofficially allied with the Dominican Republic, which was being temporarily occupied by Spanish forces during the 1860s. Eventually the Spanish government recognized the futility of pursuing its interventionist policy and abandoned its efforts in these conflicts. Nevertheless, the threat posed by the old imperial center brought the Latin Americans closer together. These conflicts in South America demonstrate the high degree of Latin American national consciousness and solidarity in times of military crisis, regardless of the violent fratricidal conflicts they had previously engaged in. This consciousness continued to provide the unionist kernel needed to advance a new form of state organization required for the promotion of mutual interests.

The Peruvian Diplomatic Initiative: The Lima Conference of 1847–48

In 1847 the Peruvian government decided to undertake its own diplomatic initiative for creating a politically integrated Latin America. The impetus for this project was to some extent the result of the Flores affair, an attempt by the caudillo of Ecuador, Juan José Flores, to reintroduce a monarch into his country via Spanish military assistance. The invasion plan would have been extended to Peru and perhaps even Bolivia and Argentina. The Flores plan failed miserably. As a result of the conspiracy, Peru called upon the other nations of the region to protect their independence via joint efforts in November of 1846. The favorable response led the Peruvian government to conclude that perhaps a new diplomatic overture could secure an integrated state in Latin America.

The government in Lima sent invitations to Bolivia, Chile, Colombia, and Ecuador to join the Peruvian government in sending diplomats to meet in Lima, for the purpose of enacting a series of agreements to strengthen American cooperation. The primary objective of the meeting, however, was to draft a treaty establishing a confederate government that would be operated by a congress of plenipotentiaries. The diplomats were directed to specifically discuss issues concerning territorial disputes among themselves. They were also to establish agreements dealing with commerce and postal carriage. The representatives assembled in Lima between December 11, 1847, and March 1, 1848, convening for a total of nineteen sessions. In attendance were José Ballivian (Bolivia), José Benavente (Chile), Pablo Merino (Ecuador), Juan Francisco Martín (Colombia), and Manuel Ferreirós (Peru).[41]

The treaty that was drafted in Lima recognized that each of the represented states had experienced a difficult political evolution founded on "sweetened hopes." It claimed that "in a similar situation there was nothing more natural and necessary" than for the Spanish-American states to "leave their state of isolation" for the purpose of creating a viable political union that would maintain their sovereignty and independence along with their "institutions, dignity and interests." According to the proposed treaty these links were possible because of the common origin, language, customs and religion. It negated the belief that geography was a problem for political union, asserting instead that bordering each other and sharing a common geography were logical enough reasons for unification. The treaty articulated the belief that the countries shared a common cause, "common necessities, and reciprocal interest." It affirmed that the Latin American states should not view themselves as simply individual states, but as part of a nation or a civilization.[42]

In many respects the provisions of the treaty were similar to those of the Panama Congress. The proposed confederation treaty was known as the Tratado de Confederación (Treaty of Confederation). Article 1 of the treaty stated that the purpose of the accord was to maintain the independence and sovereignty of the signatory states and to protect their territorial limits. Article 2, section 4, recognized the chronic problem posed by "adventurers and individuals who were unauthorized" to invade with foreign troops, sought to unseat governments, or "establish colonies," a reference to the work of the Flores conspiracy. The provision was intimately linked to the acquisition of Texas by the United States and to Washington's employment of filibusters, although there is no evidence that any of the signatory states considered plans for action against the United States, despite a clear will to oppose Flores. Article 7 confirmed the territorial limits each state had possessed on the date of its independence, recognizing that such borders corresponded to the old Spanish administrative units in place as of 1810, although the Peruvian delegate had been instructed by his government on November 30, 1847, to call for the recognition of territorial demarcations as of 1824 (the year of the Battle of Ayacucho), based on the principle of *uti possedetis*.[43]

Article 9 required differences between the member states to be settled amicably via mediation by the proposed confederation. It stated that member states would never employ force against each other. Article 12 asserted that the confederation would preserve the independence and sovereignty of each state, and that it could not intervene in the internal affairs of individual member states. The article stipulated that the confederation could send troops to any state if that government failed in any way to comply with its obligations incurred with signature of the treaty. Article 14 dealt with the problem of extradition. Article 15 stated that each state would contribute naval and military forces, or their equivalent in monetary compensation, in proportion to the size of its population. Article 16 stipulated that troops responding to a military crisis could pass freely through confederate territory in order to achieve their objectives. This article effectively repudiated a centralized military command, leaving security concerns in the hands of local leaders. Military direction of confederation troops was to be carried out by the "Jefe Supremo" (political ruler) of each state or his designee. In time of war, these leaders would have been unable to effectively coordinate military efforts without confusion or rancor. However, hope for the future of the organization was indicated by the inclusion of article 19, which established a coat of arms for the confederation. It was to be an emblem picturing the American continent; the names of the member states would be inscribed in the featured engraving of America. The top of the seal would carry the inscription *Confederación Americana.*[44]

The treaty required the member states to refuse recognition of any territories that might be annexed by enemy armies.[45] Article 21, section 2, stipulated that the confederate congress would have the exclusive right to interpret treaties and laws. Section 3 of the same article required a plurality vote by plenipotentiaries to implement laws. Likewise, section 3 stipulated that laws passed by congress did not require ratification by the individual home governments. This clause was the most significant portion of the treaty because it attempted to create a secure foundation for the permanent maintenance of the organization by attempting to avoid future problems regarding political interpretations by the individual states. Allocation of this responsibility to the central government would ensure the possibility of its survival in times of constitutional dilemmas, thus avoiding the fratricidal problems of Mexico and Central America. Article 22 stipulated that the Congress of Plenipotentiaries could negotiate as representatives of the confederation with respect to foreign affairs, as well as other matters pertaining to the interests of the member states, or in conflicts between the individual members. The Tratado de Confederación was formally signed in Lima by the attending plenipotentiaries on February 8, 1848.[46]

The diplomats met again to attempt modifications to the treaty on December 16, 1848. The plenipotentiary from Bolivia suggested a proposal intended to strengthen the treaty. His recommendation was based on the need to remove any confusing interpretation of the treaty regarding the relationship between the Congress of Plenipotentiaries and the individual states. He also sought to create a socio-economic-political order that would promote stability within Latin American society. The plenipotentiary suggested incorporating a fifth section into article 2 that would have explicitly allowed the confederacy to intervene in the internal affairs of member states if coup d'états were undertaken in any state. The delegate made clear the necessity of removing these "unconstitutional" states "in order to arrest the cancer." Nevertheless, the majority of the plenipotentiaries rejected the proposal.[47]

One reason the modification was rejected was that many of the delegates saw any form of intervention as a denial of their political sovereignty. Some of the plenipotentiaries feared that legitimate revolutions might be interpreted as being instigated at the behest of foreign powers. There was concern that the term "legitimate revolution" might be dangerously interpreted in any manner by any political group or faction. In view of Latin America's intense and highly passionate political atmosphere, charged with intrigue, ideology and egotism, many things could go wrong for the elite. They saw no reason to add an unknown quantity such as a Congress of Plenipotentiaries into the equation. They recognized that they could deal with internal groups and problems within their borders, although they might not be able to deal with groups within another political entity. The attempted revision was introduced in recognition of the military revolts and separatists movements appearing in numerous countries. Although Mexico did not participate in the Lima Congress (presumably because of logistical problems associated with the Mexican-American War), its government was a glaring portent of Latin America's political future, which was to be chaotic.

Details of the Tratado de Confederación were known before the diplomats had concluded their work. Almost immediately, government officials back home began criticizing the proposed organization. In Peru there was discord within the government about what the objectives and responsibilities of the confederation should be. The minister of hacienda (public finance), J. Manuel del Rio, wrote the minister of foreign relations on January 3, 1848, that the proposed congress should not deal with commercial issues because "in the realm of international relations consideration of prior agreements could not be omitted." He asserted that the interests of the various states were distinct and that no two interests were the same and suggested it would be difficult for a Congress of Plenipotentiaries to pass resolutions "without favoring some states while causing damage to others."[48] As an example, del Rio cited Peruvian trade with Great Britain and the United States, which he claimed were given "most favored nation status" and whose commerce, he argued, should continue to be treated equally with that of the future confederation.[49] He insisted that only a complete "agreement to abolish prior treaties and rights on commercial matters" would be acceptable.

The Chilean plenipotentiary to the congress, Don José Benavente, was adamantly opposed to the objectives of the conference, and constantly functioned as an obstructionist on order from his government. The Chilean government had informed Benavente that his mission was to form a defensive alliance that was "convenient for the common security of the South American republics, for the adoption of measures to repel the invasion of Don Juan José Flores begun in Spain against one, or some of them, with a common agreement."

These instructions permeated his every word and action at the Lima meeting.[50]

Benavente outlined some of his objections to Manuel Ferreirós, the Peruvian plenipotentiary. He lambasted the provision that each state should come to the aid of any other state involved in a war with a foreign nation. Benavante argued that this requirement might place some states in untenable diplomatic positions: "Let us suppose that Buenos Aires ... would invoke the aid of other states to dislodge Great Britain from the Malvinas Islands. What would they do?" He sought to intimidate the other delegates by pointing to the continual tension between the Central American states and the British government. "What would we do to help one of these states if they were members of the league?"[51] He also objected to powers that would be given to the proposed Congress of Plenipotentiaries as "anti-constitutional" because such a congress would usurp the powers given the individual states and eventually render that group of diplomats "sovereign."[52]

Benavente criticized article 21, which stipulated that the Congress of Plenipotentiaries could enact laws binding on all member states without requiring ratification by the individual governments. He cautioned his political supporters that the powers elaborated in the treaty were a danger to their liberty and frighteningly resembled "nothing more than the federal form of government of the United States."[53] What kinds of problems would this create? Benavente did not specify what types of problems he had in mind. He dealt with this political issue only on the broadest and most theoretical plane. It may be surmised, however, that he was concerned with legislation that might attempt to usurp the socio-economic order that in 1848 comprised a small elite, a small middle class, many peasants and large numbers of the unemployed crowding the cities and countryside. What would happen if reformers of Jacobin persuasion actually succeeded in organizing the nascent working class and a large lumpenproletariat?

Some of the Latin American states had already experienced the trauma of attempted reforms that threatened the interests of the elite. For Benavente and the Chilean elite, Mexico probably stood as a glaring example of a country attempting to recognize the socio-economic base of society, a process that had inadvertently but irreversibly led that nation into abysmal chaos and factionalization, eventually contributing to its military defeat at the hands of the United States. Could this chaos filter into Chile via the creation of a new political entity? He clearly believed that the gentry and commercial elite of his country were better off with a government system they understood and could direct. Benavente also expressed concern that an invasion of one state by a foreign state would automatically involve Chile in a war, bypassing the Chilean congress and its prerogative to declare war. The treaty, he argued, "confers such authority to a foreign power that it deprives itself of a precious portion of state sovereignty."[54] Benavente claimed that the obstacles affecting a confederation such as proposed in Lima would be like a "waterfall of fecundity" that would render the organization "inefficient." Another concern was that nations that had nothing to do with the initial conflict might be hurt much more by ceasing commerce with potential adversaries than the most likely antagonists, which probably would have been the United States, Britain or France.[55] Benavente warned his fellow anti-unionists that it was likely a Congress of Plenipotentiaries would itself become a federal state, because any laws would have to be administered and enforced by newly created government organs. This would eventually lead to the establishment of "distinct departments of government over which it would plant a union." He seemed to satisfy himself when he smugly asserted that the "germ of federalism would probably not live long enough to evolve."[56] For Benavente the ideal government was a confederation that would allow individual governments the ability to follow their own interests without fear of coercion by other states, whereas in a federal system all states would be required to obey laws passed by central authorities. The compromise and limits required by a centralized system were anathema to many political elites accustomed to the political prerogatives they enjoyed within the spheres of localism and independence.

Why did the Chilean government agree to attend the conference in the first place if it was implacably opposed to any viable program of political integration? It is known that Benavente scrupulously followed the instructions of his government by insisting on a military alliance that would repel a possible monarchist coup d'état by Juan J. Flores if he were backed by Spanish forces. Perhaps the Chilean government sent Benavente as more than simply a representative. His fervent opposition to the confederation, which would have been a decentralized and extremely weak union, suggests that Chile sent him to destroy the proposed organization as an idea. Historically the Chilean political leaders have pursued a successful but unproductive "balance of power" foreign policy. They have consistently sought total political autonomy for themselves and clearly did not wish to see a stronger, more effective political unit arise on Chilean borders as demonstrated by its war with the Peru-Bolivian Confederation.

For the most part, the Tratado de Confederación was a well-written, well-thought-out document, considering its limited objectives. The treaty, however weak, could have served as a vehicle for further centralization of political power, enabling it to clarify the responsibilities of both the center and the individual states. The treaty would have provided the minimum powers needed by any government to maintain order and its existence, while concurrently providing for home rule. The exception was article 16, which would have led to further divisions and impotence in times of war, but this provision could nevertheless have been modified to fit political needs.

As it was written, the treaty attempted to eliminate some of the problems identified by Bolívar and his supporters as flaws in the previous Panama Congress. In framing their proposals, the delegates to the Lima Congress demonstrated that they had studied and learned some lessons from the previous isthmian debacle, and clearly exhibited a desire to avoid the same problems and snares that had plagued the Panama meeting. Their failure was not for lack of effort or dedication. From the wording of the treaty, it appears that the diplomats and the presidents who had sent them were genuinely committed to the accord (with the exception of the Chilean government), only to see their work rejected by their governments several months after the treaty was signed.

Rejection of the treaty resulted from two factors. First, there was a lack of commitment on the part of the individual Latin American governments because they had grown complacent with the demise of foreign threats to their governments. When the threat of a foreign invasion from Europe had dissipated and they had become convinced the United States did not pose a direct physical threat to the individual South American states, they decided to ignore the treaty. Second, most Latin American leaders refused to consider any proposal that threatened to minimize their influence in society. As of 1848, a majority of the various Latin American leaders had decided to support most of Benavente's objections. Indeed, the only part of the treaty that was ratified was the consular section.[57]

The 1855 Proposal

In the mid–1800s Latin Americans found themselves receiving moral and political encouragement in their quest for political integration from the Spanish government. Ironically, the government they had feared so much in the 1820s was turning out to be their steadfast ally. In 1855 the Spanish chargé d'affaires in Santiago de Chile, Eduardo Asquerino, wrote a letter to the Spanish Ministry of State calling for Spain to assist the Latin Americans with their integration plans. This plan never evolved into an international conference, but its origin and course warrant discussion.[58] Asquerino's plan was particularly novel for two reasons: first, because of its request for the assistance of the Spanish crown, and, second, because it called for Brazil to be an integral member of the organization.[59]

Asquerino's motives for his program were similar to those expressed in the previous Lima and Panama proposals. His concerns were fueled while assigned to Mexico, where he came to believe that Spanish-speaking civilization was in peril of becoming extinct, because of the Mexican-American War. He was later transferred to Santiago de Chile, which had become a bastion of popular pro-integration sentiment. There he came in contact with the Sociedad de la Unión Americana. It was in the 1840s and 1850s that this organization was formed for the purpose of promoting citizen involvement in unionist goals. The organization was extremely active in Santiago, and Asquerino soon found himself surrounded by such integration activists as Miguel Luis Amunátegui, José Victorino Lastarria, Benjamín Vicuña Mackenna and Guillermo Matta.

Asquerino was also heavily influenced by a lecture given at the University of Chile Law School by Juan Manuel Carrasco Albano, who spoke at length on the need for a South American assembly. In his address, Carrasco insisted that the march of civilization demanded that its "various factions draw nearer to one another." He lamented that in "the cradle of nations we see nothing more than isolated tribes."[60] Carrasco suggested that only an assembly representing all the Latin America countries could adequately deal with the many problems facing the region. He called for standardization of the legal system, removal of tariff systems, and more importantly, the establishment of a single monetary system. Carrasco suggested an assembly of diplomats from each of the different Latin American countries manage the congress.[61] Carrasco expressed alarm concerning the physical and cultural survival of the Latin Americans, claiming Texas and California demonstrated that Latin American nationality was in danger of disappearing from America, unless various trends were reversed. He warned his audience, "Hannibal is at the gates."[62]

Although both Carrasco and Asquerino believed Latin American civilization was in danger of extinction, there were distinct differences between the two men. As a diplomat, Asquerino held the initiative because of his access to diplomatic and political leaders. His efforts were limited to creating a system that would coordinate national security matters for the Latin Americans. As a private individual, Carrasco was restricted to the speaker's circuit. Asquerino, however, held the ear of both the Spanish and Chilean governments. Asquerino proposed a military alliance with a coordinating council to protect the Latin Americans from the United States, in particular to "prevent the United States from increasing its power and influence." Asquerino was especially concerned with eliminating the threat posed by filibusters. The alliance members would also oppose the creation of any protectorates in Latin America, and were to dispute the sale or the cession of any national lands.[63]

Asquerino suggested that the Spanish government should provide the initial guidance for the creation of such an alliance, but because of old Latin American suspicions of Madrid, he proffered that Spain should ask the Chileans or Brazilians to undertake the initiative. If such an alliance could be formed, then Britain and France could be invited to join as members for the purpose of keeping the United States at bay. Asquerino's idea was eventually rejected by the Spanish government. Asquerino eventually began a periodical known as *La América, Crónica Hispano-Americana,* which has been described as "the most influential organ of Pan-Hispanism in the nineteenth century." Though Asquerino's proposal never came to fruition, his enthusiasm continued to be propagated by his publication.[64]

The topic of potential political unification soon found its way into the public ears of unionists around Latin America. One writer, Manuel Ancízar (Colombia), suggested the proposed government might resemble that of the United States. Ancízar 's concern mainly emanated from his preoccupation with the possibility of future European colonization efforts. He proposed a constitution for the new union that essentially outlined its future responsibilities and urged that the new government should have the right to create new states and provinces. Ancízar cautioned that the success of such a proposal depended on respecting the geographical borders that already existed. He also added that there was a distinct danger that the various Latin American states might, in fact, end up as part of several sub-regional organizations, which could lead to new rivalries.[65] In spite of the many problems facing a repeated effort to construct a political union, the urge to regain such an initiative proved irresistible, and efforts were soon underway to resume the elusive dream.

1856 Hispanic Ambassadors' Conference in Washington

One of the ironies of the Hispanic-American quest for political integration came in 1856, when the various ambassadors of the Spanish-speaking countries of Latin America met informally in Washington, D.C., to attempt to work out their differences and to consider some form of unification. This effort proved fruitless and did not expand beyond discussions, but the initiative merits brief consideration. The concern of these diplomats stemmed from Washington's pressure on the various Latin Americans states as U.S. interests began expanding from Mexico and the circum–Caribbean, southwards to the rest of Latin America. The two recent wars between Mexican and American forces in 1836 and 1846–1848 had left Mexico exhausted and bankrupt.

If perchance any Latin American diplomats continued to naively perceive the two wars as simply border disputes, the unabated American pressure on Latin American civilization would soon dispel these views. Shortly after the war, in 1853, the United States negotiated the Gadsden Purchase, in which it bought a large piece of Mexican territory, under the not-so-subtle threat of a renewed war against Mexico. With the Mexican War concluded in favor of the United States, the balance of power was unalterably shifted in favor of Washington. American foreign policy then turned its glances towards other Latin American territories. The post–Mexican War diplomacy of the United States called for the control of the Central American isthmus as necessary for establishing communications and transportation links between the east and west coasts of the U.S. This new development found Washington, D.C., competing with London for influence in Central America, especially Nicaragua and Panama. In particular, both countries harbored the desire to construct and operate a canal in the isthmus or one that flanked Lake Nicaragua. Both sites were of as much commercial and strategic importance as any river, lake, sea or road ever contested by any government in human history. Whoever controlled this region would control trade between the Americas, Europe and Asia. It had been a dream to construct such a canal for four centuries. The construction of a canal would shorten travel by months, reduce freight charges and produce enormous profits.

The possibility of constructing a canal was so credible that by 1846, the United States, recognizing that its superior military apparatus would be victorious in the Mexican war, began planning for the new postwar political and economic order. In order to secure access and control of the isthmus for a canal, some mantle of legal and political legitimacy in the area was necessary. Thus, the United States and Colombia signed an agreement known as the Mallarino-Bidlack Treaty. This treaty stipulated that the United States would assist Colombia to protect the unrestricted passage of people and goods across the isthmus of Panama, by employing military force if necessary. The treaty made Colombia the very first protectorate of the United States. The presence of U.S. troops could then legitimize a permanent U.S. presence in Panama. The Colombian senate eagerly approved the treaty. Bogotá perceived that it would benefit from such a canal, and from an American promise to protect transit rights. The treaty never provided Colombia with the benefits it sought.[66]

With the end of the Mexican-American War, the boundaries of the United States extended from the Atlantic to the Pacific Ocean. The ensuing rivalry between the American and British governments over control of a future canal convinced them they would have to agree to a compromise if a potential war was to be avoided. In 1850 the Clayton-Bulwer Treaty was signed and approved by both governments. The treaty stipulated that both parties would share control of any future canal. They agreed not to occupy any portion of Central America. To avoid future misunderstandings, they also agreed that if the canal should be built, their governments would not fortify the site. The United States gave evidence of its willingness to challenge the Latin Americans and Britain with its continued attempts to control the circum–Caribbean in 1853, when Washington, under the direction of President Franklin Pierce, issued the Ostend Manifesto, which stated that the United States intended to acquire Cuba irrespective of the wishes of the Spanish government.

The policies of the United States led Justo Arosemena, a Colombian diplomat and essayist, to write with alarm that the "daring stares" of the United States had turned Nicaragua and Cuba into its hostages as of 1856. He perceived a dangerous situation for Latin Americans in which the "eagle sought to grasp the collar of the condor." Arosemena wrote that as a result of their problems, the "prize of universal trade that the genius of Isabella and Columbus had gained for our people" had passed from Latin Americans to the United States. He referred to the North American concept of "manifest destiny" as "disproportionate ambition." He nevertheless assured his readers that if Colombia and the other Latin Americans awoke to the challenge they faced, it was still possible to save "our race and our nationality." Arosemena argued that if Colombia and the other Latin American republics awakened to the menace and readied themselves for the challenges from Washington, D.C., or any threat to their independence, they would triumph. This triumph was to be accomplished by a political union.

The Colombian claimed that in order for Latin America to survive it was necessary for the Latin Americans to imitate the form of government utilized by the United States: "What calculation did for the Confederation of the North, time, experience and danger should do for the Confederation of the South." Arosemena added that such a confederation should be built from "Panama to Cape Horn" and that the Latin Americans would then "be one family with only one name, and a common government, and one purpose." There was no mention of Mexico or Central America in his plan. Why this occurred is unclear. Perhaps it was an oversight, or perhaps Arosemena believed it was impossible to redeem the political situation of those states.

The end result for Latin Americans in achieving a political union, claimed Arosemena, would be a society that was "the same nation, great, free, wise and magnanimous, rich and powerful." In the future Arosemena would actually have the opportunity to attempt implementing such a policy, when he was chosen to represent the Colombian government at the future 1864 Congress

Plenipotentiaries, which met in Lima for the purpose of creating such a union.[67]

In the meantime the 1856 ambassadors' conference worked to arrange for a more permanent arrangement of continuous consultation. The consideration given to Washington, D.C., by the 1856 meeting underscores the fragmentation of the Latin Americans caused by their political differences. Ironically, the various Latin American ambassadors resident in the United States approached the Spanish ambassador posted in Washington, Alfonso de Escalante, with a proposal for a defensive alliance with confederate overtones. Escalante was to act solely as an intermediary for this new Latin American effort. It is uncertain to what extent if any this proposal came out of Asquerino's ardent proposals in Chile, although it would be reasonable to assume that his efforts carried considerable intellectual weight. The plan was similar to the prior Panama and Lima proposals. The main difference between the former schemes and the new proposal was that Brazil was to be included in the plan. It was proposed at the Washington meeting that the plenipotentiaries meet in Rio de Janeiro for future political conferences. The Spanish minister of state, Juan de Zavala, showed support for the proposal and encouraged the inclusion of Brazil in the plan. The proposed program would have forbidden the individual states to cede any territory to a foreign state. It would also have made it illegal for the various states to provide foreign corporations with special concessions with regard to the construction of public works. This proposal was suggested because the Latin Americans were fearful that concessions to foreign companies would inevitably provide foreign states with an excuse for armed intervention on the grounds of protecting the special interests of either the government or a foreign corporation.[68]

The Spanish ambassador's role as intermediary and coordinator is significant because it highlights the difficulties and frustrations the Latin Americans had in promoting such projects. Ironically, Washington, D.C., which was feared by the Latin Americans, was the only place where a sizable number of Ibero-American state representatives could meet without having to engage in lengthy preliminaries for designating a meeting place that would host a pro-integration dialogue. The Latin Americans also used the Spanish government to sound out how other European governments might view the formation of such a confederation, with the objective of procuring approval from both Britain and France. The enthusiasm of the Spanish government was strong until Madrid consulted with Britain and France, which refused to support the plan. The historian Mark Van Aken theorized that Britain and France were too preoccupied with the problem of the Crimean War to be concerned with matters in America.[69] As for the Spaniards, Van Aken claimed that they could not afford to offend the United States without the aid of the British or French governments, lest Madrid find itself losing Cuba.[70]

The 1864 Initiative of Peru

In 1863 conflict broke out between Spain and Peru when several Spaniards and Peruvians were involved in a violent incident on a hacienda in Talambó, Peru. The event was followed by the arrival of a Spanish naval squadron in Callao. An attempt was made to settle the dispute. When these efforts proved unsuccessful, the Spanish admiral, Vicente Yáñez Pinzón, seized the Chincha Islands, on April 14, 1864, claiming they would be returned to Peru when Spanish claims were satisfactorily dealt with. The Peruvians refused and war broke out. This struggle was the impetus for a new regional integration congress initiated by Peru.

The Peruvians called for a new congress to seek the integration of Latin America on January 11, 1864, in recognition of this problem with Spain. A diplomatic circular sent by Peru called for an "American fusion."[71] This was to be achieved by calling together a new Latin American congress that was to consider forming an alliance.[72] The exact nature and structure of the new organization was not discussed, but the document expressed concern over the continued independence of the various Latin American governments that were being harassed by European governments seeking some type of advantage. The Peruvian foreign minister, Juan Antonio Ribeyro, stated that the century had provided "costly and prolonged" tribulations for the Latin Americans in their efforts to promote integration. He emphasized that these efforts had not been in vain. Ribeyro stated that Peru's foreign policy was to work for the union of Latin America as a principle of "civilization of justice, progress, and common well-being." He called on the Latin Americans to accept and follow a foreign policy that would "broaden a cordial friendship among all of them, facilitate commercial relations," and allow them to settle territorial differences in a conciliatory manner. Achieving the goal of working together would make the Latin Americans "strong and respectable."[73]

Ribeyro claimed that political and economic integration was a priority desired by many governments: "American fusion is so necessary, that there is not a government from the continent that does not desire it, that has not had the same inspiration; but unfounded fears have contained these plausible starts of patriotism, believing it a practical possibility whose execution can save all the republics, which would provide conditions of true independence." Aware of the vagueness in previous treaties that had plagued past integration conferences,

Ribeyro suggested that governments "simplify the works of the congress, reducing the bases to a few articles." The new organization he envisioned would "conserve peace ... fortify indispensable institutions ... and reject hateful pretensions that produce envy and malevolence."[74]

The note from the Peruvian Foreign Ministry stated that the congress should be held in Lima, or anywhere considered beneficial by a "majority of governments." The invitation required the governments to provide plenipotentiaries for the task "without delay" and with full "respective powers and full discretion" to carry out their charge. Among the most important points elaborated in the invitation was the statement that the Latin Americans "formed one nation." There were six articles stipulating the agenda for the congress. Articles 1, 2 and 3 concerned the maintenance of Latin American independence, a major concern of the Peruvians who were at war with Spain. The articles also reflected their concern over the Spanish takeover of the Dominican Republic and the conquest of Mexico by French troops. Articles 4 and 5 dealt with the perennial quarrels over territorial limits that plagued the Latin Americans. These articles explicitly recognized war and boundary disputes as serious problems for Ibero-America. They stipulated arbitration as the only means for settling such matters. Article 6 dealt with the issue of treason to any Latin American state. This matter was given specific attention because in all cases, Latin American nationals had invited, aided, participated, and provided moral and political support to the invading forces. Ribeyro's notes, although elaborating many of the same points made in earlier unification attempts, are noteworthy for their consistency with previous invitations and objectives. The various articles demonstrated the Latin American desire to solve a number of problems that remained constant and vexatious over time. The Peruvian circular expressed the following intentions:

(1) To declare that the American nations represented at this congress form solely one family, linked together by the same principles and by the same identical interest to sustain their independence, their autonomous rights, and their national existence.

(2) To adjust an international treaty to facilitate epistolary correspondence, in order to facilitate mercantile operations and the progress of civilization, that shall have all the securities, guaranties, and immunities necessary to the promotion of public and private interests on behalf of the American communities.

(3) To commit the governments, in consideration of the union to be established, to furnish each other all the statistical data that shall afford a perfect idea of their wealth, population, natural and artificial means at their

command to defend each other, to form a homogeneous whole, which shall serve as a guaranty of general peace and of respect for fundamental institutions.

(4) To dictate all the measures and accept all the principles that are conducive to the settlement of questions regarding boundary disputes, which are, in nearly all the American states, the cause of international quarrels, animosities, and wars, disastrous to the honor and prosperity of the nations.

(5) To irrevocably abolish war, substituting it with arbitration as the only means to settle all the failings of intelligence and motives for discord between any of the South America republics.

(6) To remove all pretexts that serve as a foundation for treason to the American cause, prescribing the moral punishments on those who because of petty passions enter arrangements against the independence of any state, its institutions, or the stability of peace.[75]

Several Latin American countries responded enthusiastically.[76] The Chilean government, represented by Manuel A. Tocornal, stated that his government was genuinely interested in "realizing the ancient thinking on American union" and asserted that perhaps the internal problems suffered by the many Latin American states might be resolved with membership in a "superior order," a clear reference to the need for political coordination among the Latin American states.[77]

Tocornal referred to the new attempt as "eminently national and American." Nonetheless, he sounded a negative and divisive note when he raised the question of whether it was wise to proceed with the conference without the "assistance" of other Spanish-American states that might not attend. The diplomat also questioned the wisdom of proceeding without the United States and Brazil. Tocornal felt that the results of any conference would be diluted in proportion to the number of states that did not participate. He felt that a second congress would eventually be required to take the interests of any absentee states into account, thus complicating matters. The Chilean representative asserted that these two states would not view events with "indifference" and that their interests had to be respected. His concerns over the United States and Brazil were not impressive enough for the rest of the governments to pay any attention to him. It was an unrealistic assessment of the requirements for a successful congress. The states did not need the approval of the United States or Brazil. They needed an agreement to unify, a task that had always eluded them.[78]

The government of Colombia also stated it would attend the conference. That government appointed Antonio María Pradilla to represent the Foreign Ministry. He suggested that the "object of the reunion be modified" so that only the interests of the Spanish-American countries be discussed and that only the "American republics of exclusively of Spanish origin" attend. Brazil was excluded because its monarchical form of government was seen as incompatible with republican political systems. It was not left out for cultural reasons. Historically the Spanish-American states had claimed a cultural bond to Brazil. Likewise, a political connection existed between both societies dating to 1580–1640, when the king of Spain ruled Portugal and Brazil. This view has been accepted by most Brazilians.

Significantly, Pradilla mentioned that the Colombian government opposed an invitation to the United States of America because "it is well known of which there is abundant testimony, the correspondence of the Secretary of State in the last year that the government of that republic professes and practices an absolute non-involvement in the business of the Hispanic American republics, rejecting as a general principle all types of alliances."[79]

Pradilla added that his government would seek to deal with a host of problems, including the rights of citizens, uniform postal and telegraph regulations, the abolition of passports, the expanded use of arbitration to deal with the potentially explosive issue of boundary disputes, free navigation on mutually held rivers, a uniform system of weights and measurements, and the establishment of general principles for conducting trade and industry.[80]

The Bolivian Foreign Ministry, represented by Rafael Bustillo, wrote that it was necessary for such a reunion, since all the Latin Americans shared the same territories and because the rivers they shared all "flowed into the territory of each other to the sea." He cited the growth in commerce between them as a reason for seeking a new mode of relations. This basis for a political union was the "same religion, identical language, and similar customs."[81] His eloquent note asserted that although there might be "distinct groups ... they constitute and cannot stop constituting one sole and great family in which eminently appear the feature typical of their common origin, with small variations that are not enough to erase their general physiognomy." He went on to add, "Nationalities of this type cannot leave recognizing that union between them ... is an indispensable condition for their prosperity." Bustillo believed that although union might seem strict or difficult for some countries, it was the "appropriate instinct for the weak to unite in order to become strong." He observed that as isolated countries they lived in a condition in which their existence had been "minimized." Unification, he asserted, would provide a "great national existence, impressive and great" for all humanity to admire and "minimize their evil tendencies."[82]

Bustillo suggested that the conference turn its attention to the issue of free navigation upon the rivers of the South American continent that were shared by various states. This problem was a serious concern to all nations in the River Plate region. He suggested that the Latin America states adopt the principles established at the Congress of Vienna in 1815 permitting freedom of navigation on Europe's rivers for their own navigation. Equally significant was Bustillo's urging that the congress adopt a single monetary system and a uniform system of weights and measures.

The Venezuelan minister of foreign relations, General D.A. Guzmán Blanco, sent a note to Lima confirming his government's support for the Peruvian proposal. In a note dated January 23, 1864, he stated:

> Different American governments are convinced, not only in the present, but from many years back, of the convenience and even necessity, perhaps urgent, in which the nations of this continent should reunite in some central point a Congress of Plenipotentiaries, that have as their object a positive law, so that quarrels between them can be harmonized reciprocally.[83]

Guzmán Blanco also indicated concern for a plethora of other sensitive issues that had to be settled among the Latin Americans, such as matters of international law regarding war and peace, maritime limits and jurisdictions, the registry of maritime vessels, river navigation, contraband and blockades, the award of indemnifications, limits on reprisals, the rights of foreigners living in Latin America, and the appropriate use of "bellicose resources."[84]

Justo Arosemena, who had previously represented Colombia at the Lima Congress, observed that these issues had all been discussed but required resolution by formal treaties. (He would represent Colombia again.) The Colombian expressed hope that diplomatic solutions could be quickly found. Arosemena also lobbied for treaties dealing with professional credentials, which would have allowed the certification and free practice by individuals of their professions in a number of Latin American states. Likewise, he supported a treaty to strengthen postal and telegraph links.[85]

Arosemena was an ardent unionist. He enthusiastically lobbied for the cause of political union with the appearance of his work *Estudio Sobre la idea de una Liga Americana,* published in 1864 immediately after he returned from Lima. His study asserted that it was realistically possible to affect a political union in Latin America, although he recognized it would be difficult since previous unification initiatives had been failures. Indeed, in the year 1864, the European region known as Germany was not yet a fully unified state. The Germanic states, which were much more economically developed than all of Latin America, were still struggling towards unity. Arosemena wrote that if unification was not a possibility for Europe, it was a pragmatic and "possible acquisition" for Latin America, which he viewed as one civilization.[86]

The beginning of the congress was anticipated with enthusiasm by the

Peruvian public. The local newspaper *El Tiempo* editorialized: "May reason and calm direct our debates and wisdom and justice preside over our resolutions. Instruments of Providence do not forget the lessons that she has given you in history, and think about that wisdom that regulates the universe, respecting the liberty of man; his agent, that drives so many nations to their destinies without diminishing their liberty."[87] The comment was directed towards the diplomats who would conduct the negotiations and indicated what elite Peruvian society desired: the ability to maintain as much political autonomy as possible (a goal all the other states sought) while still benefiting from a loose type of confederation that would be conducive for warding off any foreign military threats—in this case Spain, which was still involved in military activity against Peru in the Chincha Islands. The passage, nevertheless, provided the necessary moral and political support for the idea of some type of Latin American league, however loose, and demonstrated the heightened sense of awareness by Latin Americans that they formed one civilization.

On November 15, 1864, the conference met at two o'clock in the afternoon, in the beautiful Torre-Tagle palace with its splendid colonial–Churrigueresque-style architecture. In attendance were Juan de la Cruz Benavente (Bolivia), Manuel Mont (Chile), Vicente Piedrahita (Ecuador), Justo Arosemena (Colombia), P.A. Herrán (Guatemala), José G. Paz Soldán (Peru), Antonio L.A. Guzmán (Venezuela), and Faustino Sarmiento (Argentina).[88]

The opening session was attended by the diplomatic corps, the Council of Ministers and a military color guard, which saw the emergence of a huge crowd of spectators that blocked many of the nearby streets. The Peruvian minister of foreign affairs, Mr. Calderon, addressed the assembled plenipotentiaries. He greeted them by noting that their assignments were to "consult the interests of the continent." He was followed by José G. Paz Soldán, the Peruvian plenipotentiary and the designated president of the congress, who asserted that their objectives represented the will of the Latin America people. Paz asserted, "The people of America owe a vote of gratitude to their governments, who have faithfully interpreted their desires." He added that these goals were based on the necessity of expanding relations between the various countries based on "union and fraternity." Calderon asserted that the development of human relations required the creation of intimate bonds between the Latin Americans, in which the beneficiaries would be "justice and law." The diplomat recognized the impact that modern day developments could have on the integration goal, when he noted that this objective could be enhanced via "the medium of commerce and the telegraph." He called for the maintenance of domestic peace as the basis for economic development, which was obligated to coincide with liberty, independence and justice.[89]

Soon after the plenipotentiaries met to discuss the proposed union, negotiations bogged down over the issue of the Chincha Islands dispute between Peru and Spain. Justo Arosemena, the Colombian delegate, lamented this turn of events, since it meant that discussion of other issues necessary for implementing a political union would have to be postponed or ignored. Arosemena recognized, however, that he had to defer to the will of the other diplomats. This was very difficult for him, as he had been a militant and tireless unionist his entire life and believed that the congress might allow him to see his dreams come to fruition, but this vision would not be realized.[90]

The congress did however succeed in drafting a treaty, which contained 20 articles. One of the most important provisions was article 1, which reiterated prior declarations that the contracting parties were bound in a league that would be "intimate and fraternal" so as to form "one family in its aspirations and measures of progress." It asserted that the maintenance of Latin American "independence, sovereignty, and territorial integrity" was the principle objective of the agreement. Likewise, it stated that the political autonomy of the various contracting governments was to be scrupulously observed. Article 2 stipulated that governments appearing in Latin America that did not represent the people were not to be recognized by the member states, a clear reference to any governments that might be imposed by foreign armies. Articles 3 and 5 discussed the problem of border disputes between the respective member states, requiring them to submit territorial problems for arbitration. The rest of the articles dealt with how the military alliance would be operated, and numerous other details requiring cooperation.[91]

The treaty was never implemented. The purpose of the congress had been to seek a political union. The conclusion of the Spanish military occupation of the Chincha Islands meant there was no necessity for a military alliance. Without an enemy poised at their homeland, there was no incentive for coordinated activity by Latin Americans; thus negotiations floundered into ineffectuality. The political class and the groups it represented were again able to foil further attempts at integration, leading Guillermo Matta to quote and expand on the scriptural passage of Galations 3:3, "Oh foolish people.... What magician has hypnotized you and cast an evil spell upon you? An evil spell must have been cast on Latin America."[92] Although unionists suffered another disappointing round of diplomatic efforts, they were not totally discouraged. The latter half of the nineteenth century would spawn a resurgence of pro-unionist activities by idealists who abandoned their hope in diplomacy and utilized the pen to bring new ideas and new approaches to the long-sought dream of unification.

VI

IDEALISTS TAKE
THE INITIATIVE

New Approaches to Integration

With the demise of the 1864 Lima Congress of Plenipotentiaries, the last major diplomatic initiative for the political integration of Latin American died out. There would be other diplomatic attempts to foment political union throughout the nineteenth century, but they proved insignificant and produced the same disappointing results. It became clear to unionists that new strategies and tactics were needed if they were ever to achieve their goals. The new mechanisms that would be utilized for reaching this objective would be the written word and the non-profit organization created for the sole purpose of arousing interest and support for Latin American political union.

The new approaches appeared in the middle of the nineteenth century with a group of idealists. Their weapons of choice were the pen, the book and the essay. These individuals believed that unification might be achieved if a massive effort to persuade large numbers of people could be undertaken. It was the specific intention of these unionists to target the educated middle classes as their audience. Their efforts were prodigious and herculean, but in the end their works proved disappointing because of the strength, the inertia, and the logic (or the lack of logic) imposed by the nation-state system. These efforts underestimated the resilience of the state system. Their failure was also due to the indifference shown by political leaders. Since most Latin Americans lived in isolation from each other and received little education or news about the other Latin America states, it was easy for this narrow provincialism to prevail.

In spite of their failure, the work of the unionists was not in vain. The writings of these idealists constitute an intellectual strain running through

Latin American history that forcefully argues Latin American society is one civilization—a trend that continues to this day. Their works demonstrate the continuous efforts made by a dedicated nucleus of Latin Americans who have appeared in every generation and who have tirelessly sought to convince their fellow Latin Americans of the desirability of closer political bonds.

José María Samper and Integration

In 1859, the Colombian writer and intellectual José María Samper wrote an article calling for the unification of Latin America. He proposed that the new organization be called the Colombian Confederation. Samper did not explain why this name should be adopted, but in the nineteenth century the name "Columbia" was frequently used as a synonym for "liberty" and "America." Samper wrote that the newly unified republic should consist of "Bolivia, Buenos Aires, Chile, Confederación Granadina, Costa Rica, Ecuador, Guatemala, Honduras, Mexico, Nicaragua, Paraguay, Peru, San Salvador, Santo Domingo, Uruguay and Venezuela."[1] His nationalism extended far beyond Gran Colombia's borders: "The cause of Colombia is solely one, from the northern borders of Mexico to the mouth of the Orinoco and from the River Plate. It is the cause of the democratic republic."[2]

Samper's plan included only the Spanish-speaking countries. He excluded Brazil because of its political structure, emphasizing that its monarchical form of government was incompatible with the republican system. Samper also stressed that the continued presence of slavery in Brazil made it incompatible with the policies pursued by the Spanish-speaking countries. Brazil, he argued, would never accept a "reformed and liberal" democracy. He criticized Brazilian foreign policy for its "pretensions to intervene in the domestic affairs of Argentina, Paraguay and Uruguay," a foreign policy pursued with "a cunning spirit."[3] Samper nevertheless recognized that because the large Portuguese-speaking state bordered six of the Spanish-speaking countries, it was especially important to maintain cordial relationships with Brazil for reasons of trade and commerce, including all the rivers they shared. Most importantly, Samper acknowledged that Brazil shared "homogeneous aspects" with the rest of Latin America, thus recognizing Brazil as a member of Latin American civilization.

Samper's plan excluded the United States because he felt that country was playing an improper role in the Western Hemisphere by seeking to expand its territory and political influence. At that time, the United States was attempting to establish a protectorate over Mexico with the McLane-Ocampo treaty. Also, various expansionist groups, mainly from the Southern slave states, were calling for the annexation of Cuba. Samper, like many other Latin Americans, was concerned about the use of the filibuster "as a measure of certain expansion without responsibility by any foreign government," which he correctly attributed to the foreign policy of the United States. His remarks were a reference to soldiers of fortune, such as William Walker and others, who were particularly active in the 1850s. These men and their financial backers were seeking to foment insurrections in Mexico and Nicaragua for the purpose of creating separate states, or as a prelude to future annexation by the United States.

Samper's concern over foreign designs on Latin American territories led him to promote some form of political integration. He lobbied specifically for a confederation that would be based on the propagation of "liberal institutions and general progress." By pursuing these goals, Latin America would have the strength to "develop our resources ... repel all foreign violence, protect ourselves from vices of the antagonist nation, dealing as equals with each other, and later tie our luck to the same Americans." He pointed out that "separated and weak we cannot do anything; united and strong we could easily settle our differences." Samper concluded that an alliance between governments would be chimerical. The only viable integration program would be a unification of the entire Spanish-American people.[4]

The Unión Americana and Benjamín Vicuña Mackenna

In the 1860s a new initiative for Latin American integration appeared from a non-governmental source. It was a completely private undertaking led by a number of prominent Chilean citizens, which included Benjamín Vicuña Mackenna, José Victorino Lastarria, Pedro F. Vicuña, Miguel Luis Amunátegui, Manuel Antonio and Guillermo Matta, Álvaro Covarrubias, Domingo Santa María, Juan N. Espejo, Francisco Echaurren Huidobro, and Isidoro Errázuriz.[5] The name of the organization was the Sociedad de la Unión Americana. It was initiated at the behest of the Comisión Directiva de la Unión Liberal, a Chilean organization. It established chapters in Valparaíso and Santiago. The 1860s would be the most productive period for the new organization. In 1862 the Valparaíso chapter, under the direction of Juan Gregorio de Las-Heras, was asked to establish a new branch in Santiago, which would temporarily be placed under his leadership.[6] The proceedings and resolutions of this organization reveal an institution whose membership demonstrated a high level of culture and commitment, as evinced by their activities, publications, and business-like orderliness.

The objectives of the Unión Americana were, first, to preserve the independence of the Latin American states vis-à-vis foreign territorial expansion; second, to insure the continuation of republican governments, which had become an ideological hallmark and intellectual underpinning of Spanish-American political culture; and third, and most important, to spur interest and support for a supranational government (either federal or confederal) that would bind the Latin Americans into a closer political union. The Unión Americana would seek to accomplish its goals by "studying, discussing and formulating the conditions and methods by which this great idea can be realized."[7]

The Unión Americana called for a politically integrated Latin America that would stretch from "Montevideo to Mexico."[8] The organization explicitly expressed its desire for political union based on common interests emanating from a single distinct civilization. They elaborated their support as being the "common cause of the great Hispanic-Latin nationality of the new world" and referred to the other Spanish-speaking states as "sister republics."[9] The unionist perspective echoed by the organization's members demonstrates the extent to which such views emanated from a continuous historical and cultural consciousness. They presented a militant but dignified statement against the state system as it had evolved in Latin America. They blamed the state system for all the ills of Latin America, claiming that it was the bedrock of "pusillanimousness, treason and complicity between the governments." What was required was a genuine interest in securing the goal of political unification in order for it to become a reality.[10] They further stated that their mission was not a new one, and that it was neither subversive nor demagogic, but was rather the work of Latin America's greatest men. Anticipating criticism from defenders of the state system, the organization pledged that it was in fact free from any "stain of treason or apostasy." Their cause was a "principle incarnated in the hearts of the people, and in the hearts of the popular masses."[11]

The founders of the Unión Americana believed that the political unification of Latin America could not be achieved by the numerous state governments; only an organization representing the people from the individual states would be able to unify the region. The directors of the Unión Americana in Valparaíso wrote to the Santiago chapter that the purpose of the organization would be achieved by, "not the governments, but the people to whom the initiative and accomplishment of this work falls to for opening barriers and to fill the abyss that today divides the various nationalities that populate the soil of America, in order to reunite them as a whole and to create one great and powerful family strongly united by ties of blood, and historical memories."[12] The leadership enthusiastically added: "Once the promotion of these generous ideas ... revives the sentiment of love and fraternity ... no other name except American or brothers" would ever exist.[13]

The Unión Americana of Santiago had the moral and political support of a number of counterparts. Branch organizations of the Unión Americana were created in La Serena and Quillota, both in Chile, as well as in Lima, Peru. Soon after the organization expanded into the rest of Latin America, a local Unión Americana was founded in Sucre, Bolivia, in February 1863, with 454 signatures supporting its inauguration. Another Unión Americana in South America opened up affiliates in San Luis de Potosí, Mexico, and formed links with the Junta Patriótica del Distrito Federal de México, while that country was under French control. The objective of these branches was to create an all–Spanish-American state.[14] The links with organizations that supported liberalism and a republican state establishment were extensive and included the Defensores de la Independencia in La Serena, Chile, and Lima, Peru. The Union also maintained extensive contact with the Club Libertad and the Club Progreso in Buenos Aires. Eventually invitations to form Union organizations were extended to all the provinces of Chile.

The membership of the Unión Americana expressed the concern that the political independence and liberty of Latin America was beset by foreign occupation. In 1864, Spanish forces occupied the Chincha Islands, which belonged to Peru, pending the settlement of claims made by Spanish citizens. In 1861, the Dominican Republic had been temporarily reconquered by Spain at the request of its own ruling caudillo, Pedro Santana, who had invited Spanish forces under Isabella II to rule his country for protection against Haiti, and as a means of preventing political opponents from assuming political power. In 1862, Napoleon III of France appointed Archduke Maximilian, brother of the Austrian emperor Franz Joseph, emperor of Mexico. Foreign rule came to Mexico based largely on the arguments of conservative monarchists who felt that only a strong government could give the country the stability it needed to resist further U.S. territorial expansion into Mexico. The conservatives also saw monarchy as a means of maintaining traditional conservative elite privileges. Archduke Maximilian would rule Mexico until 1867, when French forces were withdrawn.

The members of the organization were as enthusiastic about their cause as they were confident of victory and encouraged others to join. In a note to potential recruits they argued that in spite of "mean-spirited ambitions that were trumpeted by equally mean spirited-interests," those diligently seeking to unify Latin America would "consecrate their efforts with the realization of such a noble enterprise." They maintained that Latin American union would open the "doors to commerce, industry, the arts, and become the refuge of those fleeing persecution by traditional despotism."[15] In an effort to increase membership, the Unión Americana opened its membership to all social classes. It was emphasized that the organization excluded no one, and that all were welcome to participate actively in its work from the "honored artisan to the wealthy proprietor ... irrespective of political party membership."[16]

In June of 1862, the president of the Valparaíso chapter, Ramón A. Dehesa, and his three secretaries, José A. Torres, Ricardo Palma and Juan R. Muñoz, signed a letter elaborating their views on political integration. The political fragmentation of the American republics, they wrote, was to the "discredit, debility and ruin of this beautiful portion of our globe," and the enlargement and increased power of Latin America would serve as a bulwark "for the great social principles and a secure camp and sanctuary for human dignity." The authors argued that "alleged obstacles, exaggerated by the imagination and promoted by selfishness, bad intentioned local interests and other ruinous passions were the daughters of ignorance" and had made the integration quest look impossible, when in reality "it could be done with the support of the public and the governments."[17]

One of the founding members of the Unión Americana was the well-known and highly respected Benjamín Vicuña Mackenna. His membership in the Union served to enhance the prestige and legitimacy of the organization. Vicuña Mackenna's pro-integration stance was inculcated in him by his father, Pedro Félix Vicuña. Benjamín Vicuña Mackenna was born on August 25, 1831, and educated at the University of Chile as a lawyer. In 1856 he began to write for a new journal entitled *El Ferrocarril*, which was published for the next thirty years. This work allowed him to detail the political, cultural and economic development of Chile. In 1868 he became editor of the prestigious work, which he undertook with "moderation and level-headedness."[18] During his lifetime he wrote several influential and respectable scholarly works, including a historical treatise of the integration movement that was eventually published by the Unión Americana as *Estudios Históricos Sobre la Federación Americana*. This essay was a summary of integration efforts. In his essay Vicuña Mackenna sought to persuade the public that it was possible to achieve integration. He argued that a total political union of Latin America had been possible as far back as 1810, but because the two prominent Spanish-American military leaders, Bolívar and San Martín, had viewed each other with envy, they had forestalled any possibility of union.[19] He wrote that Chile had an obligation to repair the damage done by its government with respect to previous congresses. Vicuña Mackenna asserted that it had been a mistake for Chile not to attend the 1826 Panama conference, and he blamed it for the unraveling of the 1848 Lima Congress of Plenipotentiaries. He also lambasted

Chile's role in the war against the Peru-Bolivian Confederation, which had been destroyed by "Chilean bayonets."[20]

Vicuña Mackenna argued that in spite of the many obstacles and repeated failures to create a unified Latin America, the fervor for the idea remained intensely vigorous, "without any decline in its faith and its work since the first years of independence until today," and he referred to the continuing effort as a uniquely "American agitation." He insisted that the possibility of attaining the goal of Ibero-American political unification could be reached with the support of the Latin American people if Latin America could avail itself of "prudent" leaders.[21]

The Unión Americana continued its efforts to persuade and influence Chileans and Latin Americans for a number of years, but its membership remained limited to intellectuals and idealists. Only these groups were interested in regional integration. In 1861, the organization began a compilation of documents and pamphlets written in favor of political integration since the beginning of the independence period. The compilation was subsequently published in 1862. For the most part, the general public, which was the intended audience of the organization, remained preoccupied with its everyday quest for material survival and did not respond as hoped for. As for the Chilean government, it remained content to ignore the goals of the Unión Americana and instead continued its counter-productive policy of balance-of-power politics in Latin America. Nevertheless, the Unión Americana left a rich legacy of documentation for scholarly review and analysis. The collection demonstrates the concern expressed by the adherents of this organization and sheds extensive light on the most significant endeavors of nineteenth century Latin Americans for political unification.

In spite of the efforts of the Unión Americana, the Latin American states remained fragmented, even with the ominous threat of foreign invasions. This political fragmentation suffered by the Ibero-Americans testifies to the poor political judgment and skills possessed by the early Latin American political leaders as well as to the limited resources available to them. Indeed, this political fragmentation was partly due to the limited economic links between the various countries. The fragile, resource-exporting economies of Latin America actually served to foster closer relations with Europe and the United States rather than with the other Latin American states. Nevertheless, the organization played a major role in continuing to propagate the belief that the Spanish-Americans were not only one civilization, but also one people. This served as a counterweight to the artificial nationalism that was then being formed.

Pedro Felix Vicuña

Pedro Felix Vicuña (1806–1874), the father of the famous Benjamín Vicuña, was one of the earliest intellectual essayists to support a politically integrated Latin America. He wrote a small booklet in support political integration entitled "Único Asilo de las Repúblicas Hispano-Americanas." His essay was written sometime between 1836 and 1839 during the war between Chile and the Peru-Bolivian Confederation. Vicuña wrote, "A great congress of all the Spanish-American republics with the sole objective of intervening in the differences that may arise between them and to assure domestic tranquility of each one of them appears to be the specific medicine for so many pains." Such an approach would alleviate Latin America's many domestic and security problems.[22]

In a historical analysis of Latin America's woes, Vicuña blamed the Spanish throne, which had been occupied by the Austrian Hapsburgs, for many of the problems that Latin America suffered. He recognized, however, that Spanish control had provided the Latin Americans with an important common heritage, and that the Spaniards had created numerous "indissoluble" links between Latin American countries. He argued that the interests of the Latin Americans were the same as those of any brothers. Time was not enough to "cool their fraternal sentiments," which emanated from their Hispanic heritage, which could be found in the same customs, norms, values, and beliefs anywhere in Latin America. Vicuña noted that religion was one of the major links bonding the people of the different states together, and he reminded his readers that historically people of the same nationality, even when divided by numerous states, often maintained a collective consciousness as members of the same family. Of all the bonds between the Latin Americans, Vicuña considered language to be the most powerful and influential link. Language, he argued, was the greatest agent of political and cultural socialization: "How many advantages would come to all the Americans with this sole point of contact? Of course, it would facilitate the maximum communication between them, the most expensive protection for the sciences and the arts, a much vaster field for literature, the advanced facilitation of commerce—in one word, what person is not linked by this principal mechanism of our civilization?"[23]

Like other unionists, Vicuña lamented the fratricidal wars that had occurred between the Latin Americans. He urged political integration as a mode of settling divisive territorial questions in a peaceful manner. He lamented the Chilean war against Peru, and regretted that an alliance had been completed between Chile and Ecuador against Peru, a "fellow nation" in spite of the fact that Lima professed friendship towards Santiago. Vicuña claimed that all of Latin America was a tinderbox waiting to explode into war. The possibility of such a conflict spreading beyond two countries, he argued, was very real. He urged Latin American policy makers to take the issue of war seriously. War, he argued, would seriously undermine Latin American civilization. He characterized this dangerous scenario as a situation that would entail "an expansive war that would consume our wealth and paralyze the march of our regeneration, which requires an unalterable peace for progress."[24] Political unification, on the other hand, would allow the different states to take their grievances to a central government for mediation and resolution.[25]

Vicuña also examined the state of domestic affairs in the region and viewed with alarm the political chaos that was quelled in bloody government reprisals. He deplored the state of "vandalism" that permeated the political scene in neighboring Argentina. Vicuña also speculated about the possibility that Chile and Argentina might one day coordinate military activity in case of a foreign action threatening their security, thus ending their rivalry, but recognized that "lack of unity and a system" prevented any viable joint action on the part of the two states. Vicuña asserted that because of this problem, European states did not take Latin America seriously: "they only give us the importance in concluding commercial treaties with us under the pretext of reciprocity." Such a situation was as unacceptable for Vicuña as it was for other unionists.[26]

Vicuña argued that Latin Americans needed a moral force to deal with these complex problems, but where was this moral force to be found? "The union of all America [Spanish America] is the only power that can provide this force," he suggested. Such a union needed to be as binding as possible, so that no state would be able to secede. A unified state would embrace the central tenets of nineteenth century classical liberalism. A political union, Vicuña insisted, was the only basis for improving Latin American society. The establishment of such a state would allow the greatest virtues of mankind to flourish. He enthusiastically declared, "Only there could truth finally triumph; and ambition, tyranny and despotism would encounter the hand of vengeance from oppressed liberty." With this union, domestic tranquility would finally be attained. He issued a firm warning to the politically acrimonious who would dare challenge the stability sought by classical liberalism, believing that in a unified state, "just and legal governments would find firm support in their patriotic endeavors while revolutionaries and anarchists will find their pretensions in a sepulcher."[27]

Vicuña's essay reveals an individual who shrewdly anticipated objections to his program and hoped to compromise with his ideological opponents and assuage their fears. He understood all too well that opponents of integration had consistently denounced political unification as the forerunner of political tyranny; therefore, he energetically sought to grapple with this accusation. He acknowledged that the Latin American governments cherished their political autonomy and were not likely to surrender it without resistance. He recognized that they feared forming a government similar to the federal system of the United States of America, which Vicuña viewed as a successful model to be imitated.[28] The government he propagated was similar in structure to that of the United States. He was willing to concede to his ideological opponents that their objections to a federal system were legitimate, but he countered such concerns by asserting that the problems associated with federalism could be surmounted by a well designed constitution, one that was similar to that of the North Americans.[29]

Vicuña wrote that the central government required sufficient authority to exercise its responsibilities. Its purpose would be to propagate the maintenance of classical liberal tenets as the foundation for Latin American society, and it could best be preserved by establishing a "Great Congress" to oversee the establishment of a political union. Liberty would be maintained by a separation of political powers possessed by the central government. Vicuña called for a constitution to regulate the affairs of the individual states, although he did not use the term *constitution* but instead used the expressions *legal code* and *pact*. This pact would have defined relations between the individual states and the central government. Vicuña suggested that this code would determine the number of representatives each state would have in the legislature; residency requirements; and salaries and responsibilities for representatives, who would serve only three-year terms in order to minimize "venality." In order to minimize fears regarding the autonomy of the individual governments he called for an "international code" to regulate affairs among the states.[30] To assuage opponents' fears of integration, Vicuña's proposal reserved the right of the states to try their representatives in their own individual courts. He cautioned his readers that such a legal code or pact needed to be drafted carefully, always paying attention to the interests of the various states by taking into account their concerns and avoiding "thorny questions" that might arise and lead to political acrimony.[31]

The provisions of the pact proposed by Vicuña suggest the establishment of a confederacy. He proposed that security needs be met by the use of military contingents supplied by the individual states. While it may be argued that Vicuña sought a weak central government, his writings contradict the implications of the term "international code." The use of the term "international" suggests that this organization would function as a supranational organization, with the implication that the states were to retain their political sovereignty. Such a system would have been nothing more than an alliance, which was not the objective of Vicuña. The use of such a term would have led to all sorts of acrimonious political interpretations. It may be concluded that Vicuña's suggestions were based on ideological and political expediency, in order to alleviate fears about the creation of a strong central government for Latin America. His admiration for the federalized United States and his belief that it should serve as model clearly indicates he preferred a federal Latin American system.

Vicuña cautioned his readers that if political union were not achieved, Latin America would suffer the same dismal fate as the European states, which were always engaging or preparing for war in spite of their numerous diplomatic exchanges and treaties of amity. His proposal and observations clearly indicate his belief that the state system was as calamitous for the Latin Americans as it had been for Europeans, especially those nationalities that were divided by numerous political units, such as the Italians and the Germans, who had still not created unified nation-states. Vicuña died in 1874, aware that the goal he had worked for had not been realized by the Latin Americans.[32]

Juan Bautista Alberdi

Another essayist intellectual who championed the cause of political integration was the famous and influential Argentine diplomat Juan Bautista Alberdi, born on August 29, 1810. He wrote the 1853 Argentine constitution in the hope that the fratricidal chaos that had plagued his homeland would abate. He recognized that the problems Argentina faced were not unique but rather endemic to the region. His remedy was to form a continental congress that would represent all Latin American states.

Alberdi acknowledged that such a plan, proposed many times before, had always met with rebuff and ridicule. Nevertheless, he adamantly rejected the notion that attempting to create a continental congress was based on utopianism. If this idea had been proposed by poets it could be viewed as a dream; but Bolívar's efforts were not utopian, he observed. Bolívar's proposal certainly merited more respect that the usual response to another proposed congress.[33] Alberdi argued that the rejection of the Panama Congress by Latin American governments was only a rejection of the 1826 congress and did not represent a permanent rejection of future congresses.[34]

Alberdi claimed that political union was the pragmatic answer to Latin America's discord. His call for yet another congress recognized that a foreign threat was not an adequate motivation for political unification.[35] His primary purpose was to settle various territorial disputes between Latin American states.[36] He especially emphasized the importance of ameliorating problems relating to riverine navigation.[37]

Alberdi maintained that Latin America had been "poorly constructed" and that it was vitally "important to reconstitute" its political divisions, which were relics of the "doddering" Spanish empire. The entire region would benefit from closer political coordination among the states. Alberdi used the example of Bolivia before and after as an example of the political and commercial coordination that had been provided by the Spanish authorities. Bolivia, he argued, had provided precious metals to the Spanish empire prior to its independence, but with the dawn of the national period that country could no longer do so due to control of waterways by other states. Alberdi suggested that a new congress be formed to deal with these structural problems, and that the individual states provide the congress with enough powers to adequately fulfill its mission. He expressed hope that a congress could act as arbiter of territorial disputes between Latin American governments.[38]

Latin America's enemies were not foreign military threats but the poverty that pestered the region, and so Alberdi called for a program of economic development to be directed by the congress. This new government would provide a single economic policy, adopt a single currency and abolish the myriad customs duties imposed by all Latin American states. He pointed to the German Zollverein as a successful prototype. Alberdi added that such a congress would allow technical and literary advances to blossom.[39]

Alberdi believed that the existence of the individual governments in no way impeded the existence of a single nation: "There is a more profound unity that is more powerful; it is not the identity of governments or destiny." The most important identity came from possessing the same nationality, which emanated from the "same customs, social institutions, sentiments and language."[40] According to his proposal, the congress would have been composed specifically of the Spanish-American republics. He rejected any proposal to include the United States in such a project, or that the congress only be a military alliance between the Latin Americans.[41] Alberdi never saw his objective come to fruition, but his ideals had the intellectual vigor needed to attain legitimacy with the educated segment of society. He died in 1884 while residing in France.

Francisco Bilbao

Francisco Barquín Bilbao, one of the early and preeminent members of Chilean liberalism, was also a prolific writer. He utilized his prominence to propagate the importance and pragmatism of political integration. Like other writers before him, he viewed political integration as the appropriate mechanism for improving both the political and economic status of Latin America. His biographer claimed that Bilbao was "a propagandist of noble impulses" and that his work reflected the "doctrines of liberty and democracy." As a young man Bilbao resided in Europe from 1844 to 1850, which allowed him to witness the liberal and nationalist uprisings of 1848. The campaigns for national unification in both Italy and Germany had a profound impact on the young Bilbao. The defeat of the German liberals and their failed attempt to unify Germany at the 1848 Frankfurt Convention did not dissuade him from seeking the same objective for Latin America. When he returned to Chile, he helped form a liberal political opposition to the conservative Chilean oligarchy, whose primacy had been engineered by Diego Portales, the architect of Chile's political system.[42]

Bilbao later returned to Paris, keeping close contact with the South American community there. On June 22, 1856, he discussed the necessity of political integration before a crowd of over thirty people, mainly South Americans. The speech and its later printed format were composed in the traditional rodomontade of nineteenth century liberalism. He noted that previous attempts to achieve this objective had failed, a failure that had left Latin America fragmented, but he reiterated—in the parlance of liberal nationalism typical of Garibaldi—that unification needed to be achieved, and that the ultimate goal of this objective was the attainment of universal liberty and justice for all humanity throughout the world:

> The idea of a confederation of South America, proposed by Bolívar ... has not resulted. The states have remained disunited. Today we are again seeking a congress. We have surmounted many difficulties and we ask much more than we had previously imagined. This is not only an alliance to ensure the foundation of independence against initiatives from Europe, nor only looking towards commercial benefits. Our objective is more elevated and transcendental. To unify is the soul of America. To identify its destiny with that of the republic ... to save territorial independence and the initiative of the American world, threatened by invasion, by Europe and by the division of the states, to unify its thinking, to unify its heart, to unify the will of America, to unify the ideal of universal liberty, universal fraternity and the practice of sovereignty.[43]

Bilbao spent considerable effort refuting objections to political integration. His suggestion that Latin America needed a capital raised objections among the opponents of political union. He recognized that the term *capital* had become synonymous with *centralization*, a term used by his adversaries, who sought to identify it with monarchy and conquest. Bilbao asserted that a capital and some level of centralization were needed for mankind to progress.

"Peace is the unity of liberty," he responded to his critics.[44] He implored his fellow Latin Americans to consider the future of the region and their relationship to that future with respect to political integration:

> Is there ... such little faith in the destiny of the Latin American people that we expect a foreign will or a different genius to organize and disperse our luck? Have we been born so disinherited of the gifts of personality that we renounce our own appropriate initiatives and solely create a foreign, hostile and even dominating initiation of individualism? I do not think so.... The historic moment for the unification of South America opened with independence conquered.[45]

Bilboa cautioned his readers that Latin America was parading "headless" through its political development with the world looking on. Latin America, he wrote, had gained its independence "by reason and by force." The region needed to keep the autonomy gained at such a heavy price. In particular, he cautioned that if the Latin American countries did not unify they would fall prey to the United States, which grew stronger with every passing year.[46] He referred to the Walker filibustering expedition in Nicaragua as a threat to all of Latin America's liberty: "Walker is the invasion, Walker is the conquest, Walker is the United States."[47] Bilbao compared and contrasted the United States with Russia. Like others of his day he recognized that the world would one day be dominated by these two superpowers. He suggested, "Russia is absolutist barbarism, but the United States, leaving behind the tradition of Washington and Jefferson, is demagogic barbarism."[48] He regretted that the North Americans had left the Latin Americans so far behind in terms of economic and political development. Bilbao lamented that the United States, which "should have been our star, our model and our force, converts itself everyday into a threat to the autonomy of Southern America."[49]

In spite of his warnings and concerns about the United States, Bilbao articulated his admiration for its federal republic, as well as its historical and ideological foundations. He implored his fellow Latin Americans not to fear employing the political practices of the North American federal union, and reminded Latin Americans that their cultural ancestors, the Romans, had frequently adopted the practices of their enemies and subjects.[50] He pleaded with his readers to consider the purposes for pursuing a political union similar to the United States:

> Permit me to insist. We must develop [our] independence to conserve our natural borders and the morals of our fatherland. We have to perpetuate our nationality, American and Latin, and the development of the republic, to dissipate the small nationalities so we may elevate the great American nation, the Confederation of the South. We must prepare the camp with our institutions and books for future generations. We should prepare this revelation of liberty so that we may

produce a more homogeneous nation, newer and purer, extending into the pampas, the plains, and savannas irrigated by the Amazon, the Plate and given shade by the Andes. None of these can be procured without union, without unity, without association.[51]

Bilbao was adamant in his call for a political union of Latin America. When the congress met it needed to deal with specific matters. The congress should establish a universal Latin American citizenship, create a common code for Latin America, form a pact to cement a federal and commercial alliance, abolish inter–American customs duties, adopt a system of uniform weights and measurements, and act as a tribunal to adjudicate territorial tensions between individual Latin American states. Bilbao also called for the establishment of an American University for Latin America. His desire for such an institution was based on the recognition that many sons and daughters of Latin America's upper-class families were poorly informed about their own countries and largely unfamiliar with the regions surrounding the cities they lived in.

Bilbao suggested that the cost of maintaining the new government be determined by the congress, and that it be paid by the individual states. This prorated system seems to be a method of financing that many unionists proffered until about the 1860s. Why this method was preferred and suggested so many times by the proponents of Latin American integration is unclear. The reason may have been simply a lack of experience with a federal system, or perhaps they did not envision the enormous political, administrative and legal complications that would have arisen between the central government's revenue collection agency and the many individual state governments. It may be assumed that Bilbao and others recognized that this form of revenue collection was unsuitable for a politically integrated state, and that it was suggested as a compromise to those with political objections.

In addition to this program, Bilbao articulated a classical liberal political structure and program for the proposed state. He called for a separation of church and state, European immigration, and universal education, all of which were objectives of Latin American liberals in the nineteenth century. Bilbao also articulated the need to support and develop a distinct Latin American literature, although he did not suggest how this goal was to be achieved.[52]

"Our fathers," he wrote, "had the soul and the word [honor] to create nations; let us also have the soul to form the American nation, the confederation of the Republics of the South ... victory over fatalism, victory over deeds. Victory over the wicked! What do we want? Liberty and Union." Bilbao emphasized, "Liberty without union is anarchy. Union without liberty is despotism. Liberty and union will be the Confederation of the Republics."[53] He proudly boasted that just as Cato the Elder had ended all his speeches with the phrase "Delenda est Cartago," he [Bilbao] would end his writing with the phrase "the necessity of the American Union."[54]

Francisco de P. G. Vigil

Francisco de Paula González Vigil was another supporter of Latin American political integration. His career was unusual in that he served as a priest, a politician and an essayist. He was a creole born in Peru on September 13, 1792, and lived and worked there his entire life. Vigil served a total of eight terms in the national legislature. Beginning in 1845, he directed the National Library of Peru, writing profusely on the issues of national reform and church-state relations. He was as dauntless as he was pragmatic, taking it upon himself to condemn the right of the Vatican to control the policies of the individual church organizations in independent states.

The exact date of his pro-integration writing is unclear. The extracts that were published by the Unión Americana give the dates as 1848 and 1855. Vigil viewed political integration as the most suitable means for the political and economic evolution of Latin America. His essay "Paz Perpetua en América o Confederación Americana" was a treatise on various historical efforts to promote political integration, using Europe as a reference point for the study of these efforts.

Vigil noted the major differences between the English colonies that were to become the United States and the Spanish-American colonies integrated under the Spanish crown and under one law, the Code of the Indies. He observed that the thirteen English colonies were able to reconcile their differences and unite under the aegis of a federal system, whereas the Latin American states took separate political routes to independence. Upon independence from Spain the new Spanish-American states subdivided in an effort to create federal systems within their own countries, a factor that Vigil viewed negatively, claiming that this "spiritual indiscretion" resulted in the division of the Latin Americans instead of facilitating their union and reconciliation.[55]

Vigil maintained that one of the problems the Latin Americans had encountered in their failed unification efforts before 1848 was they could not determine the exact nature of a "confederation," often associating this term with an alliance or league. Vigil argued that it was mistake to convoke congresses attended by plenipotentiaries. The only effective remedy for the acrimony that followed the 1826 Panama Congress, the Tacubaya Summit and the 1848 Lima Congress, he argued, would be a constitutional convention that would have representatives from all the Latin American states. His proposal was novel; no other Latin American writer or politician had ever proposed a constitutional assembly for the purpose of pursuing a political union.[56] Vigil died in 1875, never seeing a unified Latin America or even a more liberal and prosperous Peru. He is considered one of the more progressive writers of early Peru, and indeed of Latin America. While his quest for political union never materialized, the tradition of espousing a unified Latin American state would continue after him. His efforts would be the last major undertaking for many years as Latin Americans began to realize that creating a political union would require more than a strong determination on the part of individuals or organizations.

    With the demise of the Unión Americana, the quest of idealists to implement a politically integrated Latin American state entered a dormant phase. The state system stubbornly refused to hear their initiatives. The idealists had proven unable to motivate the mass of people into pressuring political figures into reconfiguring Latin America. With the exception of minor diplomatic initiatives, the unionist movement remained inactive until the beginning of the twentieth century, when the region began to undergo development of new social, economic and political conditions.

VII

INTELLECTUAL AND POLITICAL PARTISANS OF THE TWENTIETH CENTURY

The unionist movement, which had exhausted itself during the nineteenth century, began to renew itself with feverish energy at the beginning of the twentieth century. The new century saw ardent champions of political integration who formed a tradition of their own. Most of them were South Americans, with many hailing from the River Plate basin, a bastion of Pan-Hispanic and pro-unionist thought in the twentieth century. There were two categories of advocates: the traditional intellectuals and the political activists. The intellectuals limited their efforts to essays and books. They took advantage of the advancements in communications that came from urbanization and industrialization. This intelligentsia was from the middle class, and though they were usually prominent before their unionist writings, they lacked the political and economic power to influence the course of events. The writings of José Enrique Rodó and Manuel Ugarte, who wrote in the early twentieth century, reveal the essential concerns of their time. Their enthusiasm eventually extended into the student community, which eventually participated in the quest for political union.

The political activists are represented by Salvador Mendieta, Víctor Raúl Haya de la Torre, Gabriel del Mazo and Servando Cuadro. Both Mendieta and Haya de La Torre were men of inexhaustible energy and enthusiasm, writing articles and books to accelerate political integration. In addition to their writings, they created political parties for which political integration was a major objective. Both men and the parties they founded failed to attain any viable power or political union. Likewise, both had to face political exile, and only Haya de la Torre ever held public office (towards the end of his life). In the

137

case of Servando Cuadro, his political activities were limited to agitating for labor unions and serving on the executive committee of the Uruguayan Socialist Party. Nonetheless, he was fervently active in the political sphere and wrote profusely on behalf of his objective until he died. Likewise, the twentieth century saw a mantle of student idealism at work for unionism. One of these activists was Gabriel del Mazo, who was active in the University Reform Movement, which sought to restructure Argentine education. A brief student unionist movement also appeared at the end of World War II in Uruguay before it fizzled out.

Both Mendieta and Haya de la Torre were able to attract considerable political support, but they were denied political power by state authorities who viewed their activities as subversive, thus denying them any possibility of achieving their ultimate objectives. The efforts of both Haya de la Torre and Cuadro represent a unionist turn to the political left, which was unusual, because most pro-integration activity had historically stemmed from classical liberal ideology. These partisans had their origins in the nineteenth century but found their widest articulation, circulation and acceptance in the twentieth, due to the new developments that facilitated the renewed propagation of political unification. The two great unionist intellectuals of the latter twentieth century were Andrés Townsend Ezcurra, from Peru, and Alberto Methol Ferré of Uruguay. Both men were heavily influenced by the work of their respective countrymen. Only Methol Ferré lived to see the creation of a viable economic trade bloc for Latin America, currently known as MERCOSUR, with genuine unionist potential.

Twentieth century Latin America had new concerns and problems. It also possessed a vibrant and dynamic intelligentsia backed by a middle class fully committed to economic development and the emergent nationalism that permeated the individual states. These groups enjoyed prestige within their own lands and resented efforts by foreign states, primarily the United States, to intervene in Latin America. The concerns of the intelligentsia and the middle class were not limited to their own country, but encompassed all Latin American states, which they identified as one nation and civilization.

With the onset of modernity, various regions of Latin America began the process of industrialization. Those countries that did not experience some modicum of foreign investment and industrialization desperately yearned for it. Cries for measures to increase industrialization were heard all over Latin America. Some countries were more successful in this endeavor than others, due to various factors. Mexico was one country that experienced a massive influx of capital, benefiting primarily its mining and oil sectors. Argentina also received massive infusions of foreign capital, mainly from the United Kingdom. This investment was directed primarily towards Buenos Aires, where massive refrigerator warehouses were developed for the purpose of exporting beef to the United Kingdom, its largest customer. The British also invested large sums of capital into the Argentine railroad system that brought the cattle from the countryside to Buenos Aires for slaughter, and thence to Britain. The heavy British demand for beef to supply its large middle class accelerated the development of Buenos Aires into an influential and prosperous port city.

By this time a widespread social consciousness had developed in Latin America, made possible by urbanity and extensive distribution of newspapers. Latin American society became acutely concerned about the large pockets of poverty within its boundaries and came to view industrialization as the appropriate method of alleviating such blight. Industrialization, however, came slowly to Latin America. It began with the growth of the mining, oil, coffee, sugar and cattle industries, which eventually led to the development of railroads and smaller industries controlled by foreign interests. It was these foreign investors with their surplus capital who, in collaboration with domestic elites, launched Latin America onto the path of industrialization.

The onset of World War I spurred further industrialization in Latin America, as it became cut off from its traditional buyers and manufacturers. This situation arose due to the naval campaigns of Britain, Germany and the United States that were aimed at choking the supply lines of their enemies. The war induced recognition among Latin Americans that they needed to become more economically self-sufficient in times of world crises. However, industrialization proceeded at a pace that was not commensurate with that recognition. Still, it changed the political, social and economic landscape of the region irrevocably.

By the turn of the century, the lengthy tradition of the pro-unionist ideal had been taken up by individuals operating in a distinct social, economic, and political milieu that promised not only material advancement but also inspired a renewed hope that political union might be achieved. The year 1900 had brought important changes to the Western Hemisphere. The United States had recently wrested control of Spain's colonies. Cuba and Puerto Rico were separated from Madrid and became protectorates. With these possessions, the United States had gained total military supremacy in the circum–Caribbean basin, which had effectively become an American lake. By 1901, the British Empire recognized the new balance of power and acquiesced to the new state of affairs by signing the Hay-Pauncefote Treaty, which granted the United States the exclusive right to own and fortify a canal on the Central American isthmus. With this treaty, the United Kingdom implicitly recognized the region as Washington's sphere of influence and thereby created an enduring rapprochement with the United States.

José Enrique Rodó

The turn of the century saw the publication of a book of great cultural and literary significance for Latin American society. In the year 1900, the Uruguayan essayist and professor of literature José Enrique Rodó published his famous *Ariel*. The book, a comparison of ideal cultural values, served to promote a Latin American consciousness. To make his point, Rodó utilized the concept of national character. He argued that the Anglo-Saxon and Latin American civilizations each possessed distinct cultural traits, which he failed to identify with the level of socio-economic development existing in the respective societies. To a large extent, Rodó's work was a reaction to the recent turn of events in the Spanish Caribbean. He asserted that the United States represented the spirit of William Shakespeare's Caliban, a rude, aggressive, grasping character, incapable of appreciating the nobler aspects of life. Not so *Ariel*, the epitome of Latin American culture, the spirit of heroism, nobility, idealism, genteelness, and intellectual appreciation. *Ariel* represented a quasi-aristocratic yearning for the eighteenth and nineteenth century, when gentility and nobility of spirit ostensibly permeated social circles.

Rodó rejected the rise of the scientific concept of positivism that had become the methodology of the new social sciences in the Western world. This concept posited the use of empirical research as the foundation for the acquisition of all true knowledge. Rodó objected to positivism, because he viewed it as a dehumanizing perspective that had risen to prominence over the older system of philosophical inquiry and speculation on social issues. Rodó's book did not specifically call for the unification of Latin America, but it did promote the idea of one Latin American nationality fragmented by various states. This was of course, the primary intellectual prerequisite needed for political unionism. The importance of his work lay in his ability to successfully promote the notion of Latin America as one civilization on a vast scale. The idea itself was not original per se. It was a perspective already held by many people, but one which was intellectually reinforced by *Ariel*. Rodó asserted that the main task facing young Latin Americans was to create a *gemeinschaft*:

> If you ask me in the present hour what our mission is that comes to us from above; if a youthful willingness directed me to indicate the pursuit that would be the most fertile, and which efforts most promising of glory and good, I would answer; to form a Hispanic-American sentiment. I would seek to strengthen the consciousness in our countries of the idea of our America as a common force, as an invisible soul, as the only fatherland. Our entire future is virtually in this work.[1]

Rodó's work strengthened the bonds of group solidarity among a people that were overwhelmed by the material, economic and military disparity between themselves and the United States. Although his analysis and conclusions were erroneous and outdated, the book functioned as an inspiration for reaffirming the traditions and values of Latin American culture at a time when many in the region were questioning its values and ideals in the face of challenges from the United States.

Manuel Ugarte

Another notable intellectual supporter of Latin American unity in the twentieth century was Manuel Ugarte, an Argentine journalist who traveled widely throughout Latin America and the United States. Born in 1878, Ugarte became a member of the Socialist Party in his early youth, yet remained a firm believer in Christianity. He founded the periodicals *La Patria* and *Vida de Hoy*. His most influential writings were *Mi Campaña Hispanoamericana, El Porvenir de la América Latina*, published in 1911, and *El destino de un continente (The Destiny of a Continent)*, written in 1923. The impact of his ideas was felt all over Latin America.

Ugarte began his pro-integration efforts in 1910 after a long period of reflecting on the future and potential of Latin America. He was disheartened by the negative turn of events resulting from Washington's military and political intervention in Latin America. Grimly aware of past failures at achieving political integration, Ugarte recognized that no single individual could ever unify the region. Nonetheless, he hoped intellectual activities would move the cause forward by inspiring "superior impulses and noble idealisms."[2] He gave his first lecture on the problem of Latin American fragmentation to a favorable audience in Barcelona, Spain, on May 25, 1910. This was followed by another major address to an audience at the Sorbonne on October 14, 1911, a presentation organized by the France-Amérique Committee and the Groupment de Universités. M. Paul Appell, dean of the Faculty of Science and rector of the Sorbonne, introduced Ugarte as a supporter of "an independent union of the Latin republics of America, for the purpose of developing a common future of civilization and progress." That same year, Ugarte published his *El Porvenir de la América Latina*.[3]

Ugarte viewed Latin America as an integral whole, both geographically and culturally, and referred to it as a nation and, more specifically, as "La Patria Grande," which translates as "the Great Fatherland." Throughout his life, Ugarte called for the social, economic and political "reconstruction of America."

He argued that political unification for Latin America presented a viable means of solving the myriad problems facing it as a "developing society," including problems posed by the proximity of the United States.[4] Ugarte defined Latin American culture as being Iberian in origin. For him the common cultural bond uniting Latin Americans was Spain. He argued that Spain represented for Latin Americans what England represented for the United States: "our antecedents, our honorable origin, the strong root whence flows the life-giving sap of the tree.... It is fitting, we should not lose sight of this glorious starting point, this backbone of our memories.... In this historic past lies the central point of our common history in Latin America."[5] He viewed the rest of Latin America as a cultural extension of his own country:

> For Spanish Americans the fatherland means Spanish America. The sentiment of patriotism means that no natural sentiment of attachment to one's province, region, or territory of that great fatherland of ours belong to any one state into which she is politically divided. For my part, I have always understood it this way. The political unity of Bolívar's dream should consecrate and make incarnate this moral unity. Bolívar's dream is still a dream, the realization of which will perhaps, not be seen by the generations now living. What does it matter? Italy, before it had been turned into a political expression by the sword of Garibaldi and the apostle Mazzini, was only the geographical expression of Metternich. It was the genius of the idea that created the fatherland itself.[6]

Ugarte insisted on the inclusion of Brazil in any political union claiming its culture hailed from the Iberian peninsula, giving it a cultural affinity with Spanish America. He warned his readers about a "partial Latin Americanism," claiming that any country isolated by such a policy would eventually become an enemy. Brazil, he wrote, ought to be "kept within the bounds of our grasp and treated like a brother within one great family."[7] For the most part the Brazilian press reacted favorably to Ugarte's appearance in Rio de Janeiro, but some papers expressed disapproval of what they viewed as an anti–Washington stance. This attitude is not surprising in view of Brazil's ineffectual efforts in the past to gain influence and prestige in Latin America via a close relationship with the United States.[8]

Ugarte called on Latin Americans to divorce themselves from their myopic view of the region by "combating in each country the limited vision ... and supporting a broader vision of nationality ... which will supersede any political or racial perspective ... which would be in reality nothing more than to remain loyal to the tradition of the initiators of independence who did not seek to govern over only factions or localities, but who sought to govern a powerful entity capable of having an impact on the world."[9] The issue of Latin American union proved a constant theme throughout his life. He never formally proffered a particular political structure or program for political unification, but sought instead to keep the integration ideal alive by continually discussing its merits. He implored his readers to consider the possibility and benefits of political integration:

> Work towards the ideal of a Continent morally united, so as to recreate at least by diplomatic means the homogeneous community dreamt of by the pioneers of independence; retrieve by means of this union the honor and security of our territories, and make each republic stronger and more prosperous within a higher organization which should be the supreme guaranty of their regional autonomy.[10]

Ugarte not only sought a Pan-Hispanic agenda; he also articulated his opposition to the imperialism then being practiced by Washington. He viewed the United States as a threat to genuine democratic rule in Latin America and regarded U.S. policy in that region as being no different than the policies of the European imperial powers in Africa and Asia. He referred to North American policy vis-à-vis Latin America as "delinquent" and argued that the United States had substituted brute force for moral authority and that, because of this, Latin American unity was necessary to offset the pressures coming from Washington.[11] Ugarte argued that Latin America's losses to Anglo-Saxon America were due to

> a lack of dexterity in diplomatic contests, absence of foresight and order, and in discipline accompanied by paralysis ... lack of character and will ... isolating the ancient Spanish metropolis on the summits of memory, and abandoning it in mid–ocean ... twenty republics that had lost all idea of steering a course.[12]

Ugarte admitted that as a young man he had been unconcerned with the causes and consequences of imperialism, in particular the 1898 Spanish-American War, which had profound consequences for Latin America and the United States. At the time of the war he had been only eighteen years old. He first became aware of U.S. imperialism when he visited New York. Before that Ugarte insisted he had been unaware of North American history and its expansionist course at the expense of Hispanic civilization. He attributed his ignorance to the "incomplete and desultory instruction of South American schools." Prior to his visit to the United States he had no access to this information and wrote that he had been taken completely by surprise by the bombastic and neurotic claims of the United States that it would rule over the entire hemisphere.[13] He described Latin American scholarship and its educational system as totally inadequate and unsuited to the region's needs. The educational system, he wrote, presented only

> a local and mutilated interpretation of history that focused on the separation of the colonies from Spain. History as it was practiced was ... a local chronicle in which anecdote predominated and no higher conception, no analytical judgment, no clear perception of the significance of this phenomenon for America

and for the world, succeeded in emerging from the names and dates. With the knowledge of our common history came the bitter grief of understanding that our ills were far more the work of our own incapacity to struggle, of our lack of knowledge of the laws of sociology, our narrow vision and self absorption, of our dispersion and forgetfulness of higher interests, than of the greed of outsiders.[14]

Ugarte recognized that his lack of knowledge about Latin America was a serious deficiency in his own background, so he eventually began a tour of the region. The purpose of this grand tour was "to establish a contact with each of the republics whose cause I had defended en block; to get to know them directly, to observe their true situation at close quarters, and complete my general impression of the Latin America territories by traveling right to them." The trip proved as fruitful as it was an invigorating educational experience, because it allowed him to acquaint himself with the people of those lands on a firsthand basis. The voyage provided Ugarte with the opportunity to rectify any negative opinions he might have had of the lands or the inhabitants. During the journey he made it a point to interview businessmen, publicists, writers and political figures for the purpose of determining the true political, economic and social conditions of these countries. Wherever he travelled, Ugarte wrote that he could feel "the pulse of young people whose sympathies I could feel from a distance." With this trip the young man became aware of the tremendous problem of geographical isolation posed by the harsh territory of Latin America. The countries through which he visited possessed geography completely different from his native Argentina, which is a relatively flat land. However, Ugarte came to the erroneous conclusion that the harsh topography of the region had made unification difficult. He completely ignored the political unity proved by the Spanish crown. Nevertheless, the trip did not dampen his spirits or his belief in political integration. It also convinced him of the need to overhaul the educational systems in Latin America, which he viewed as "deficient" because they did not prepare students for contact with other Latin Americans. Ugarte regretted that "an Argentine can talk with more propriety about Korea than Guatemala and a Paraguayan knows more about Alaska that Cuba."[15]

Ugarte also urged Latin Americans to view Simón Bolívar's attempt at political union as a viable model that could still be implemented. He credited both Bolívar and San Martín for seeking to turn the ex-viceroyalties into a "coherent union, and a vigorous nation" that "might have aspired to balance the weight of the United States." Ugarte wrote that the work of these two figures who sought to keep Latin America united had been heroic, but acknowledged that their efforts had fallen to venal and inept leadership—a reference to the individual states and the leaders who killed Bolívar's plan:

For the great patriots of the days of independence, who were always inclined towards federation, had been succeeded by weak or ambitious bosses, who after a generation of multiplying subdivisions found themselves enmeshed in past mistakes struggling without solidarity.[16]

As a result of this chaos, Ugarte argued, the future of the region had resulted in

petty rivalries, local narrowness, violent ambitions, base envy, all these meaner instincts ... frustrated the action of these heroes by multiplying artificial dismemberments, and transforming Latin America into a huge nursery of small republics, some of which had fewer inhabitants than a city ward in New York.[17]

Ugarte sought to compare the logic and reality of Latin America's situation with the example of the thirteen English colonies. He observed that the thirteen English colonies had been able to successfully unite, but lamented that the Latin American states, which were already united and tied by language, religion and custom, had fragmented. Ugarte noted that if the English colonies had not united each would have been a separate country. "What type of history book would have been written," he rhetorically asked, if the thirteen entities had developed separate diplomacies, armies, histories and customs barriers? In the case of Latin America's development, he argued that the proliferation of states was due to a selfish "anxiety to multiply public offices" in order to satisfy "personal aims," with devastating results for Latin America.[18] An equally curious question could be echoed today. What type of history book would have been written if the Latin American states had remained united?

What might have been a great and noble force, intervening effectively in world discussions, and defending the interests and ideals of a really solid group created by history, was reduced to a dismal, clamorous collection of feeble units, fighting among themselves and exhausting each other in absurd revolution, without possessing sufficient material or moral force to win as a united whole the respect of the great nations.[19]

Ugarte's pro-unionist lectures and writings earned him widespread recognition that was both positive and negative. The *New York Evening Mail* viewed his work with enthusiasm and sympathy, claiming his writing was "excellent logical and complete." His work was praised by French intellectuals who feared for the future of Latin America and were sympathetic to Ugarte's plan for some form of political union. The *Le Siècle* of Paris stated on March 1, 1911, that Ugarte's work demonstrated that "the Latins of the new world understand the danger, as is shown by M. Manuel Ugarte." Likewise, the *Época de Madrid*, an influential conservative newspaper in Spain, applauded his efforts, as did the *Le Revue Mondial* and the *Paris Revue*. *El País* of Buenos Aires, which was edited by Dr. Carlos Pellegrini (who later became the president of Argentina), stated that Ugarte's work demonstrated the Latin world was not completely oblivious and indifferent to U.S. encroachments and that a school of thought actually existed among the Latin American intelligentsia that opposed the predatory policies of Washington on moral, political, ideological and cultural grounds. The most frequent criticism of Ugarte came from his fellow Argentines, who complained that he took too much interest in foreign countries. He was quick to respond to such criticism by replying that this "narrow local conception which had done us so much damage" needed to be ameliorated and that only the fear of individual governments who sought to maintain their power limited the Latin Americans from achieving the goal of political integration.[20]

Ugarte eventually visited every Latin America capital between 1912 and 1914 in order to popularize both the unionist and the anti-imperialist cause. The various newspapers that covered his activities noted that he was greeted with great enthusiasm and that throngs of people followed him wherever he went. While he was travelling through Mexico in 1912, efforts were made to stifle him by President Madero, who was concerned by Ugarte's criticisms of the United States. Madero later relented, but Ugarte did not forget the president's obsequiousness to Washington. Ugarte had harsh words for Madero, whom he described as an "idealistic demagogue" and as a "bookworm demagogue."[21] Madero, he claimed, had made promises he could not keep, especially with respect to land reform, even though he knew it "could not be carried out."[22] Ugarte described Madero as a dupe of the United States who had been disposed of after he "had served his purpose for an hour."[23] His words had an immediate impact on U.S. leaders in Mexico. The editor of the *Anglo-American* objected to the fact that the Mexican government allowed Ugarte to speak: "It would seem a strange thing to me that Mexico, a friendly nation, with which the United States have cultivated the most cordial relations, should go so far as to permit the public expression of ideas such as those put forth by this gentleman." One author, Charles F. Yaeger, was furious with Ugarte, claiming he was seeking to poison relations between the United States and Mexico. The *Nueva Era*, a newspaper that entertained opinions of the most influential North Americans, was also critical of Ugarte. As a free society Mexico could not silence Ugarte as influential North Americans had hoped. Perhaps Mexican society had not perfected representative government, but it was not a despotism where dissent could easily be stifled. Mexico's tradition of supporting free speech and extensive popular support for Ugarte was evinced by the massive political support he received from Mexican legislators in the Chamber of Deputies.[24]

On February 3, 1912, Ugarte gave his lecture to an estimated three thousand people in Mexico City. The event was described as one in which people's struggle for entry led to a riot and "pandemonium." Ugarte refused to speak until everybody outside had been seated.[25] Exactly one year later in February 3, 1913, he gave a speech to an estimated ten thousand people in Buenos Aires, believed to be mainly students. After the lecture, he informed an enthusiastic crowd that escorted him home that they needed to establish a "center of propaganda for Latin-American ideals."[26]

Ugarte's enthusiasm for political unity envisioned a democratic political structure for the region. Like other intellectuals of his day he foresaw the building of a socially just society. He had become a socialist of the Christian Democratic variety early in his youth, thereby ideologically rejecting Marxism. By 1939, he described himself as a socialist who was "serene and reasonable." He felt that a socialist program involving nationalization of private assets for Argentina and Latin America was premature and undesirable in a society with an advanced level of economic development. Ugarte referred to such a program as being "utopianist even for Europe."[27] He began to question socialism by 1923–24, the very year he began work on *The Destiny of a Continent*. In it, he expressed a distrust of popular politics, which he identified as being the source of much of Latin America's problems. He saw the discord and the constant political clashes in the history of the region as being the product of second-rate men who had managed to come to power by appealing to the masses. Ugarte explained that Latin America's political evolution and its relationship to the rise of demagoguery and the masses was a logical outcome. He wrote:

> Evil always has the advantage over virtue; not that the national character inclines to favor injustice, but because the instinct of discontent and opposition adopts and applauds in good faith whatever may be harmful to a third party. Lacking in that calm and discernment which are necessary to see through intrigues, make a mock of plots, and confine envy or vengeance within their own limited and proper sphere, our democracies fell from the very outset into an orgy of destruction. Accusations of treason, dictatorship and breach of faith, not to speak of direct attacks on person, always found the masses greedy to back them up and repeat them. Thus was created the atmosphere which made possible the triumph of this malady of chronic revolution, and the triumph of interior abilities.[28]

Ugarte undoubtedly recognized that his Pan-Hispanic campaign would not bear fruit. Nevertheless, he never doubted that a politically integrated Latin America was the most appropriate means for establishing enduring peace and the economic development of the region. He placed his hope for a unified and just Latin America in the hands of its young people: "We have faith in the youth of Latin America. We are confident that the younger generations will endeavor to unify their aims and their common course."[29]

Ugarte eventually utilized his numerous talents by serving his country in the Argentine Foreign Ministry. His fervent Pan-Hispanic perspective made him uniquely suited for supporting solidarity between Argentina and the rest of Latin America. Furthermore, his extensive knowledge and interest in the region provided him with many connections with diplomats, intellectuals, political figures and other socialists. These contacts would prove beneficial in his new career. Ugarte served as the Argentine ambassador (under the first administration of Juan Perón) to Mexico from 1946 to 1948. In 1949 he was appointed ambassador to Nicaragua, and in 1950 he represented his country in Cuba. He died in 1951 while in France. His body was eventually returned and buried in the La Recoleta cemetery of Buenos Aires, where many of Argentina's most illustrious citizens are entombed.

Salvador Mendieta: Militant Unionist of Central America

While most efforts promoting political integration came from South America in the early twentieth century, particularly from Argentina, a notable endeavor was being carried out in the Central American isthmus. In this portion of the Hispanic world an idealistic commitment to political unity provided the foundation for the life's work of Salvador Mendieta. Attempts to recreate the Federal Republic of Central America were nothing new. Indeed, the efforts had been prodigious. The activities of Salvador Mendieta, however, are the most notable.

Mendieta was born in Nicaragua in 1882. As a young boy he dreamed of re-establishing the unified Central American state, and he remained an enthusiastic supporter of integration his entire life. It is uncertain when he became enamored of this cause, but his dedication certainly crystallized by the time he had entered the university. As a university student, Mendieta was fascinated by the fact that the Central Americans had once been unified into one state. Why had it fragmented? What could be more logical that to recreate this state? What mechanism could do more for alleviating the massive problems affecting the area than to reconstitute this state? These questions led him to undertake the writing of major essays. In 1896 he wrote a baccalaureate thesis entitled, "The Constituents and the Federal Constituent Assembly of 1824." In 1900 he completed his doctoral dissertation while studying in Honduras, in the field of law entitled "Organization of Executive Power in Central America."

The young Mendieta became active in the cause of political unification and formed an organization in 1895 known as the Minerva Society while he was still in college. Later in 1899, he helped to found another organization known as El Derecho (The Law), which published a journal with the same title. Both were discussion groups and did little practical work towards creating union, although they served to keep interest in the theme alive among young people, the intelligentsia and those seeking to remedy the problems of Central America.

In the year 1899 Mendieta finally took pragmatic action towards fulfilling his objective by creating a political party dedicated to reunification, which he called the Central American Unionist Party.[30] His political agenda earned him the animus of Manuel Estrada Cabrera, the dictator of Guatemala, who in 1900 forced Mendieta into exile in Honduras. Mendieta stubbornly and energetically attempted to form Unionist Party branches all over Central America. In 1903 the Nicaraguan dictator José Santos Zelaya incarcerated Mendieta. He was soon released and traveled throughout Central America to keep unionist ideology alive. Mendieta wrote profusely on the topic, eventually writing seven books in the hope of fomenting a groundswell of support for his cause. In 1955, after learning that the Nicaraguan dictator Anastasio Somoza had ordered him jailed, Mendieta went into exile in El Salvador, where he lived until his death.[31]

Mendieta had long believed that integration was essential to Latin American social and economic development. His last major book, *La Enfermedad de Centro-América* (*The Illness of Central America*), became his best known work. Here he analyzed the many problems of Central America such as poverty, malnutrition and an inadequate educational system, asserting that the squalid poverty in which most Central Americans lived was an impediment to the formation of a higher political system as embodied by political integration. Mendieta poignantly recognized the minuscule role that Central America played in international relations, which he viewed as regrettable. Few if any of the isthmian states had embassies, legations or even consulates until after the beginning of the twentieth century. He observed that the region was viewed with "disdain" by other states around the world. According to Mendieta the German statesman Ahrens considered Central America to be "located in the lower scale of states that are ungovernable and anarchic." President Theodore Roosevelt referred to the various Central American states as being "incoherent and lacking in any great ideas or sentiments." The Brazilian foreign minister, Rio Branco, who had delusions of rivaling the United States as a great power by allying his country with Washington, crudely insulted the Central Americans by saying "in front of our own representatives that we are worthless countries incapable and unworthy of independence." Mendieta pointed out that wherever Central America's representatives appeared they were constantly offended and humiliated. He argued that the economic viability and existence of some Central American states was so tenuous that, in the case of El Salvador, the Presidential Palace had been mortgaged. As of 1910 that debt had not been repaid.[32]

Mendieta's work was primarily concerned with the unification of Central America rather than the political integration of all Latin America. Nevertheless, his endeavors proved fruitful in promoting stronger cultural bonds between Central Americans and the rest of Latin American civilization. This cultural awareness has been the seminal foundation for all integration movements in Ibero-America. The quest of Mendieta has lived on in the implementation of the Central American Common Market (CACM), which is the closest the isthmians have come to reintegration. CACM is considered a very limited success. It has not brought the high levels of prosperity that its enthusiasts desired, but this may be attributed to the weakness of CACM and its failure to integrate with the rest of Latin America, as well as to the small internal market that the region possesses. To this day, few if any Central Americans desire to speak of political integration, which they view as an embarrassing topic because of the many failed attempts that have occurred over many decades, but they do appear to support the current policies of economic integration that are embodied in the Central American Common Market. Mendieta's work and the limited success of CACM may yet prove to be fertile ground for future integration efforts with the rest of Latin America.

Gabriel del Mazo

The integration movement continued to maintain momentum and gained a wider following towards the end of the First World War with the beginning of the Argentine University Reform Movement, begun in 1918. One of the founders of the University Reform Movement was Gabriel del Mazo. He was born in 1892 and was educated as an engineer. With the gradual growth of this student-led initiative, he soon became one of their chief spokesmen. The movement sponsored a pro–Latin American agenda and sought a greater cultural awareness by all Latin Americans. This view was absolutely essential for any group seeking to create a politically unified state. He vigorously promoted and continued the tradition of seeing Latin America as one civilization. Del Mazo explicitly called for expanding his agenda to all of Latin American society. His plan was to include those who were not of European ancestry, as were the Argentines, by incorporating the Native American masses from the rest of Latin America into the definitive consciousness of Latin American society. Del Mazo called for a program directed towards a "vast undertaking aimed at organizing and unifying Indo-Spanish America on ethical social bases, transforming its states through the inspiration and effort of the genius of its soil and people."[33] His dream of a united Latin America recognized the many problems that would impede such a development, including geography, a factor that he argued could be overcome. Indeed, Del Mazo proposed the construction of a canal through the Amazon region that would extend from Buenos Aires to Panama and would span the River Plate and the Amazon and Orinoco rivers.[34]

The reform movement in the universities called for cultural independence from both Europe and the United States, rooted in the Córdoba Manifesto of 1918. It was a pro-democratic undertaking with both liberal and socialist adherents, and occurred at a historically and culturally significant moment in Latin American history when intellectuals all over the region began to call for a new cultural awareness and pride in the diversity of Latin American society that set it apart from the Iberian peninsula. In Mexico, for example, the intelligentsia militantly called for the celebration and rediscovery of the Native American past in history, art, and music, and in the educational system. Modernity had produced new perspectives, expectations and goals. The development of this new and dynamic nationalism was ironic, because to some extent it impeded the further acceleration of the integration process by focusing on the uniqueness of each country, but it also spawned closer bonds with other Latin Americans via a vigorous encouragement of interest in the other states of the region and through the recognition that the bonds between Latin Americans could not be negated through political or territorial divisions.

Del Mazo's integration program envisioned a Latin America that would rid itself of some of the new developments that had appeared in the region, especially in the universities, whose faculties had come to embrace positivist social science doctrines under the various liberal governments that had come to power in the late 1800s. The University Reform Movement articulated a strong contempt for the rise of positivism on the university campuses of Argentina and the rest of Latin America, just as José Enrique Rodó had expressed earlier. Del Mazo wrote that the movement was dedicated to removing the "liberal oligarchy, positivist and scientific, that scorned ethical and aesthetic values and considered material progress, without preoccupation for justice—the superior ideal of the Argentines." It was his hope that these goals could be exported to the rest of the area so that the movement's objectives might be realized on a regional scale.[35]

Del Mazo also sought to create a student alliance with other Latin American students. He claimed his reform movement was "pro–American." Later in the 1940s he sponsored a similar organization for the University of La Plata, Argentina, which promoted an "affirmation of the American character of the university." He called for the establishment of a Council of Latin American Studies and urged closer links with other Latin American universities for the purpose of seeking to "create with American youth the bonds of our common fraternity." Indeed, the Argentine university system already matriculated a large quantity of students from South America, with a substantial number of alumni who eventually returned to assume important positions of responsibility in their home countries.[36] Thus, Gabriel del Mazo and the University Reform Movement which he nurtured succeeded in expanding the sentiments of fraternal consciousness among many Latin Americans, and this served as a necessary first step in creating stronger and more cohesive links between Latin Americans.

Víctor Raúl Haya de la Torre

One of the most important and innovative initiatives for political integration originated with Víctor Raúl Haya de la Torre. The uniqueness of his approach came from the fact that he blended a vigorous personal emphasis on political unification with numerous speeches, essays and books in addition to the creation of an international political party dedicated to the political integration of Latin America.

Although Haya de la Torre never held public office until the last year of his life, he was one of the most well-known political figures in Latin America. Born February 22, 1895, in Trujillo, Peru, he came from a family that was moderately wealthy and recognized throughout the region. His father's work as a journalist inspired the young man's interest in political affairs. Young Victor attended the universities at Trujillo and Lima, where he studied law. While at the university, he came under the influence of the University Reform Movement in Argentina, which had been initiated by his good friend Gabriel del Mazo. Another major influence on Haya de la Torre was the Mexican revolution, which promoted the inclusion of the Native American masses into the political process. Both movements and the parallel growth of foreign economic influence in Peru stimulated his political views, which embraced elements of both nationalism and Marxism. The success of the University Reform Movement in Argentina encouraged him to engage in militant student activity and to become involved with the emerging workers' movement in Peru that was demanding an eight-hour work day. Haya de la Torre, like other Latin Americans, could not escape the widespread influence of the Mexican revolution, which propagated a new intellectual reappraisal of the Native American in Latin American societies. His political ideas were further stimulated by his travels in Mexico, which included a meeting with the Mexican minister of education, José Vasconcelos, a major figure in the indigenous movement. These political influences had a profound influence on Haya de la Torre's future thinking, and he eventually formed the American Popular Revolutionary Alliance (APRA).[37] In 1919 he became president of a student group that became the nucleus of other student clubs that eventually formed the core of APRA.

APRA was founded in May 1924 while Haya de la Torre was living in Mexico. This organization was the first all–Latin American political move-ment, and found adherents all over the region. The primary reason that APRA was formed, according to Haya de la Torre, was to respond to the "aggressive manifestations" of the United States.[38] The movement also had as its objective the spawning of a new cultural and political awareness in Latin America. The party stressed the inclusion of the Native American into society and called for a greater appreciation of the various indigenous cultures that existed through-out the region. On a political level the movement propagated socialism as an alternative to the then-dominant classical liberal political and economic sys-tems of Latin America. Haya de la Torre's party was active in supporting polit-ical movements and rebellions that were viewed as anti-colonial. In February 1925, he offered aid and assistance to General Sandino of Nicaragua, who was engaged in a war against the United States Marines operating in that country.[39] In June 1925, in a public address to a Paris audience, he asserted, "One of the most important projects of imperialism is to maintain our America divided. Latin America united, federal, would make one of the world's most powerful countries and would be regarded as a danger for the imperialist Yankees."[40]

APRA's integration agenda attracted the Argentine political leader José Ingenieros in 1927. The membership of Ingenieros in APRA was a significant boost to the prestige of APRA, because the well-known Ingenieros was also one of the founders of the Argentine Socialist Party. His participation in APRA helped to bridge the gulf between various ideological groups who favored political integration in conformity with a federal form of government and a pluralistic (democratic) political system.[41]

Because of the continental perspective offered by the APRA perspective, it was only logical that Haya de la Torre would embrace an all-encompassing view of Latin America. He personally took part in designing a flag that repre-sented the "Continental Fatherland." The flag displayed all of Latin America, extending from the U.S.–Mexican border at the Rio Grande to Tierra del Fuego at the southernmost tip of Argentina. The flag was referred to as the "flag of Indo-American unity."[42] Haya de la Torre envisioned a state that would not only be an all–Latin American state, but an Indo-American society, a term that according to him was conceived by Jiménez de Asúa in a casual conversation. Haya de la Torre claimed that the term *Indo* was utilized to denote the languages spoken in Latin America of Indo-European origin, i.e., Spanish and Portuguese. The expression *American* recognized the contribution and role of the Native American and the autonomous development of the various states of Iberian origin in Latin America. Whereas all the other integrationists had praised the Iberian foundations of Latin America, Haya de la Torre was the first unionist to boldly include the Native American background into the mainstream of the region, claiming that "the new revolution in our America will have a base and feeling that is Indian."[43] His writing emphasized that the "primary work" of the Indo-American was "to think and work for the unity of our countries."[44] He asserted that one of the main goals of Latin Americans had to be the education of their people regarding the other states in the region. The Peruvian caustically observed that the ruins of Egypt were better known to Latin Americans than were those of Machu-Picchu, a situation that arose from the "absurd nationalism" that had gripped the region.[45]

Of significance was Haya de la Torre's blatant hostility to the Spanish heritage. He saw nothing positive about the role of the Spanish government in America, denouncing it as "decadent and sanguinary." The disparagement of Spain's legacy was not original; indeed, other unionists, such as Bolívar, had also viewed the Spanish past negatively, but this was within the context of the liberal revolutionary tradition that needed to demonize Spanish rule in order to legitimize the republican separation from Spain. Haya de la Torre's anti–Spanish denunciations developed within the framework of the modern world and the new ideologies that had arisen. He castigated the expression "Hispanoamericanismo" as a term embraced by the conservative General Francisco Franco of Spain.[46] Haya de la Torre also confronted the usual charge against the unionists that decried them as hopeless romantics. He believed the very opposite, that unionists were hard-nosed pragmatists, and lamented that the various national political figures were viewed as "practical."[47]

Haya de la Torre stated that the political agenda of APRA "incorporated in its great primary program the ideal of the economic, political and cultural unity of these countries as its principle and fundamental objectives," as well as an anti-imperialist platform.[48] Likewise he claimed, "For APRA the primary anti-imperialist policy is the federation of the twenty republics of Indo-America. It is not feasible to resist imperialism without working for a united Indo-America; it is not even worth calling oneself anti-imperialist if one is not a sincere and militant unionist."[49] Haya de la Torre stated that there were numerous reasons for pursuing the objective of political integration: "Our republics require economic solutions under a unitary concept of technical collective action with which is required analysis and understanding.... Our problem is not only development and monoculture, but also transportation, markets and culture." He called for the formulation of a constitution for all of Latin America that would serve to "impede the predominance of the dollar and to place democracy in a new world." Haya de la Torre also suggested that the new constitution be based on the general democratic principles of the various twenty constitutions of Latin America. This constitution would contain the "minimum liberties, rights and obligations" for all Latin Americans. His suggestion included the creation of a Permanent Assembly of the Americas and the establishment of an Inter-American Court of Justice that would act as a balancing force against violations of the proposed constitution.[50]

Haya de la Torre recognized that the Latin American states were considered insignificant around the world, and that these countries were in fact viewed with disdain by the industrialized nations. He wrote that if even just four or five Indo-American states unified, they "would be viewed with respect and without doubt, jealousy." He lamented that the quest for unity was seen by many as "beautiful idealism." Likewise, Haya de la Torre was particularly bothered by the treatment accorded to the supporters of political integration, who were often ridiculed as "loudmouths or Bolsheviks" or "piously applauded as lawyers for lost causes."[51] Nevertheless he realized how disillusioned Latin Americans had become by the many previous failures to create a politically unified state. He quoted the anti-unionist Froilán Turcios at a congress in Honduras as claiming that unionism was "the dream of Quixotic America." Turcios caustically referred to "*Hispanoamericanismo*" as a useless effort that would have to await an end to the hostile regionalism confronting the region.[52] An acquaintance of Haya de la Torre residing in France sent him a disillusioned letter that stated, "Poor dream of Bolívar ... poor dream of us all! Poor dream also of Ugarte! Illusory dream of all the Hispanic American youth! ... Our America escapes from our hands. Poor miserable page of history that we leave to the men of tomorrow. Who knows how many generations will pay for our crime against the spirit!"[53]

Haya de la Torre was keenly aware that in the smaller and more isolated countries of Latin America, regional localisms were very intense. It was in these smaller states that "the patriotism was more hostile and selfish and much more primitively inflamed." Further, he observed that the larger countries with more advanced economies were much more receptive to the idea of Latin American unity, because of the superior "education of that development."[54] Haya de la Torre theorized that potential moves towards integration in Latin

America could take two paths. One road was the "imperialist" path, and the other was an "anti-imperialist" approach. The imperialist path would be a "product of the political economy of the United States, similar to the project for a European Federation." This imperialist maneuver was made necessary, he argued, by the fact that modern capitalism needed to expand and develop in as many countries as possible in order to fuel its growth. On the other hand, the anti-imperialist approach would require a socialist federation to defend the economic interests of the masses. He argued that if the Europeans were successful in forming a United States of Europe as proposed by the French foreign minister Aristide Briand in the late 1920s, the United States of America would then seek to support a unified Latin America "under the control" of Washington. Haya de la Torre suggested that both the United States and the Latin Americans would eventually seek to form their own bloc in order to defend Latin America from the economic policies of a potentially unified Europe. He argued that the United States would be obligated to support Latin American integration under its own control in order to create a balance of power against a unified Europe should that entity ever come to exist and seek to implement policies inimical to the United States. The prospect of a unified Latin America coming under North American control was disturbing to Haya de la Torre, who suggested that such a situation would be no better than the "dominions of the British Empire," which he referred to as a "colonial federation."[55]

A unified Latin America, he pointed out, would form a "vast country of eight million square miles, with ninety million inhabitants" and with great economic potential. According to Haya de la Torre, this unity had always been impeded by the United States, which he believed promoted petty nationalism among the various states.[56] Likewise, he charged that the governing classes of the various Latin American states served the interests of Washington with their constant antagonisms. As examples, he cited Peru's struggles against Chile, and Brazilian rivalry with Argentina.[57] Thus, Haya de la Torre urged warfare against "our governing classes," which he viewed as "auxiliaries and accomplices of imperialism."[58] He regarded revolution as the only viable method of overturning these alleged U.S. sponsored governments. He applauded APRA as being in the forefront of leading workers, intellectuals, peasants, Native Americans, students and teachers in defending the "sovereignty of our countries." In response to charges that APRA was a tool of international communism, Haya de la Torre replied that it was an "autonomous Latin America movement without any intervention or influence by foreigners" formed by a "spontaneous yearning by our countries to defend their liberty by defeating their internal and external enemies united."[59]

The year 1936 found Haya de la Torre as energetic as ever, seeking to convince his readers that the pursuit of political integration was becoming more urgent with the passage of time: "Every day makes it more indispensable that anti-imperialism and unionism, two aspirations required by the necessities of life and justice, to organize and scourge politically."[60]

Haya de la Torre's career was an exceptionally lengthy one that lasted until his death in 1979. His work to bring about a socialist government failed, as did his pro-unionist efforts, because he was unable to secure enough support. Indeed, throughout his career he was constantly finding himself in political exile. It was not until 1979 that he held a political position when he appointed as honorary president of the Constituent Assembly. Although Haya de la Torre's pursuit of political unification did not see fruition, this did not stop or hinder his enthusiasm for striving towards this objective. In spite of the fact that he sought political power, he was also an idealist. Only an individual with a high level of idealism could have continued such struggles in the face of overwhelming opposition and continual defeat. Eventually, he became one of the most influential Latin Americans of the twentieth century, due to his unceasing work and altruism. Haya de la Torre's legacy remains to this day because his political objectives represented and continue to reflect the views of many Latin Americans.

Andrés Townsend Ezcurra

Andrés Townsend Ezcurra was a contemporary and disciple of Haya de la Torre. He was born in Peru on March 23, 1915. Heavily influenced by the political program of APRA, the young, idealistic Townsend Ezcurra joined the party in April 1931. He rose quickly in the ranks, working very closely with Haya de la Torre in the Central Committee, serving the party until 1981 when APRA purged him from its ranks for "ideological deviation." He asserted that though he had been removed from the party he remained a "convinced Aprista, militant Hayista, in the faith, but not in the church."[61] Due to his political activities he was deported to Chile in February 1935. Townsend Ezcurra then relocated to the Universidad de la Plata in Argentina, where he obtained his doctorate in 1942. He returned to his natal land, where became a professor of history at the Universidad Mayor de San Marcos in Peru. In December 1948 he was exiled again. While outside of Peru, he taught in Argentina, Panama and Guatemala. Living in Central America, his curiosity became piqued by the development of unionism in that region, and he eventually wrote a scholarly account of Central American unification in the 1820s and 1830s. The book underwent publication in 1958 and 1973.[62] Unlike his mentor, Townsend Ezcurra did achieve political power, when he was elected as a legislator for the Lambayeque district in 1963. In 1968 he was elected speaker of the Chamber of Deputies. Concurrently he pursued his unionist efforts. His great unionist achievement was the organization of the Latin American Parliament, which was established in Lima on December 7, 1964. He was elected unanimously as its first secretary general and was continuously re-elected to that position until 1991. His role as secretary general of the Latin American Parliament was largely symbolic as that organization has no enforcement capability, nor could it create law. Eighteen countries eventually joined the organization. The parliament limits itself to drafting and adopting resolutions promoting peace, fraternity and closer ties. Although Townsend Ezcurra's career as an elected political figure did little to effectively promote Latin American unification, his stellar and tireless work served to fuel the imagination of countless unionists. He died in 1994. Both the Peruvian legislature and the Latin American Parliament have placed busts of Townsend Ezcurra in their public foyers.

Student Unionism Post–1945

The activities of student unionists were rather limited after World War II. Their activities were heavily influenced by the feverish intellectual dynamism of the first half of the twentieth century. This enthusiasm was particularly pronounced in Montevideo, Uruguay, where a group of students at the Universidad Nacional formed an organization known as La Asociación Juvenil Americana. In order to have their voices heard the students organized their own newspaper, entitled *Crisol*, which appeared at the end of the Second World War.[63]

The young writers intended to promote political union for Latin American as a format for discussing the many problems facing Latin America and the world. They called for an end to the "zones of influence" policy promoted by the great powers. They viewed this policy as the source of future friction and supported self-determination for all peoples, a common sentiment at the end of the war, which reverberated with great idealism and hope. The statement was directed primarily at the United States, which had long acted as the policeman of the Western Hemisphere. True to the influence of the French revolution on Latin America, *Crisol's* staff promoted the concepts of "Liberty, Fraternity and Justice." In addition, their objective was to save young Americans from "deception" and to turn America into "an example for all the world."[64] Likewise, the university students emphasized their commitment to "peace, democracy, republicanism, self-determination for all peoples and liberty." In addition, they sought to stimulate discourse between the citizens of the many states so that there would be a "comprehension of mutual problems." Such discussion would create an ambiance whereby people from any Latin American state "might feel at home."[65] It was believed that this discourse would enable the mass of people to sympathize "with each other's problems as if they were their own."[66]

The students recognized that the objective of supporting closer links between the Latin American states was not new, but was a "current distributed throughout all the latitudes of the America." *Crisol* was "not content to be simply a part of it, but also wishes to give it a new impetus," wrote one student.[67] Closer bonds were to be achieved by promoting the political unification of the entire region from Mexico to Tierra del Fuego: "Our liberators gave us to understand that the separation from the metropolis was not the culmination of their work." The pursuit of Bolívar's dream of peaceful political unification was in fact, forever "incarnated in every good American, seeking to obtain that peaceful victory," wrote the students. The writers utilized Haya de la Torre's phrase of "union Iberoamericana." Although the students declared their support for the socialist party of Haya de la Torre, their work remained liberal in tone.[68]

Luis D. Schinca, a former writer for the paper, reminisced that the periodical represented the "bountiness of youthful enthusiasm as is exemplified throughout time."[69] The young writers were determined to pursue their goal with success. "Our task is arduous and long; we do not expect to fail. If someone wishes to join us, and we expect that there will be many who desire to collaborate with us, we will receive them with the sincere embrace of a brother. Forward America!"[70] With such zeal it would have been preposterous, as well as useless, to tell the students they might not succeed. Eventually, the newspaper was forced to cease its activities. As with so many other student organizations, the paper competed for the time and resources of students. Thus, the many obligations of university life forced the young docents to cease their writings.[71]

The writings in *Crisol* serve as a reminder to adults in the political class that although youth is not very sophisticated, it is not naïve. It has questioned and continues to query the state system as the most appropriate form of organization for Latin Americans. The articles of *Crisol* are an eternal testimony to the boundless energy, idealism and inquisitiveness that excites every rising generation.

Servando Cuadro

In the late 1940s and early 1950s another important intellectual espousing political integration was the fiery Servando Cuadro. He may be considered the last of the Latin American idealists to publicly call for political union prior to the appearance of the technocrats who would come to pioneer economic integration in the 1950s and 60s. Cuadro had little formal schooling, but was instead self-taught.[72] He was heavily influenced by the works of José Enrique Rodó and Manuel Ugarte. As an intellectual, he was intrigued by the possibility of re-organizing Latin American society.

Cuadro began espousing the pro-unionist cause long after it was clear that efforts by more prominent Latin Americans to convince their fellow citizens about the necessity of political unification had failed. In the face of much ridicule, Cuadro bravely reiterated the policy prescriptions made by others before him. Cuadro was not, however, the type of individual to be intimidated by what the public might think of him. He firmly believed in his cause and felt that the issue of political integration needed to be openly discussed by the broad public. Indeed, he saw his role in life as that of an "agitator" and "*campanista*" (partisan), a role for which he was ably and uniquely suited. Throughout his life he proved no stranger to controversy or challenges, which seemed to actually energize him. Nonetheless, Cuadro was considered an "affable and correct" man by his colleagues within the Socialist party.[73]

Cuadro was born on October 23, 1896, in the Uruguayan province of Florida. His father was a yeoman farmer who dealt in cattle and lumber products. The young Servando later worked at the Cervecería Montevideana (the Montevideo Brewery). A colleague of Cuadro referred to his life as "one of chance and wandering."[74] When he was dismissed from the brewery, Cuadro proved his mettle by leading a strike against the plant. He had originally been a member of the Blanco Party, the traditional and conservative party of small farmers, the gentry, ethnic Spaniards and those who were staunchly Roman Catholic. His experiences as a laborer induced Cuadro to join the Socialist Party in 1915; he remained a member until 1939 when he was thrown out because he was so combative and obstreperous. At that point, in a reversal of political allegiance, he initiated a virulent campaign against the leadership of the socialists. He remained however, a committed leftist of the nationalist Latin American variety. Although he rejected Marxism and continued his belief in Christianity, Cuadro continued to affiliate himself with socialist ideology until his death.[75]

Cuadro's commitment to the all–Latin American perspective was as absolute as it was all-consuming. He participated in the founding of the

Alianza Universitario pro Federación Latinoamericana. In order to popularize the idea of political integration he wrote a total of 148 short articles for the weekly journal MARCHA based in Montevideo, Uruguay. These articles appeared between February 27, 1948, and November 14, 1952, under the column title "Los Trabajos y Los Días" (The Works and the Days). Some of these articles were eventually published in a book under the same title in 1960.[76] These articles were compiled after Cuadro's death by Ariel B. Collazo, a fellow unionist and socialist.[77]

Cuadro asserted that he wrote to "create an ambiance for the ideas of the Hispanic-American Federation." He argued that the political unification of Latin America was a logical proposition and noted that all the great countries of the world were the products of political union: the United States, Britain, Germany, Russia, Italy, and Spain. If Latin Americans proposed to create a great civilization, they needed to pursue political unification, for "only the great nations count in history" and "only the great nations are owners of their destinies." He reminded Latin Americans about European efforts to promote political integration that had been instigated by Eduard Herriot, and suggested that if the Europeans who had distinct languages and histories were actively promoting their own unification, then certainly the Latin Americans who had more in common could easily achieve this objective.[78]

Cuadro implored his readers to think about the political unification of Latin America in a logical and historical perspective. Unification would ultimately occur, he argued, leaving future historians of Latin America to determine why the process had been so lengthy: "Historians of the future will be strained to comprehend not how Spanish America came to constitute one sole and great nation, but why it did not become one from the moment of her emancipation; why it did not know how to avoid these separatist vicissitudes at the beginning of her history and why it took such a long time to achieve its unification and national identity."[79]

Cuadro's proposal explicitly left the United States out of any integration scheme. He considered the United States as a negative factor in the hemisphere that needed to be opposed. For him political integration would provide Latin Americans with a mechanism with which to resist U.S. hegemony. He did, however, openly embrace the entry of Brazil into such a union. His rational for this proposal was that Brazil, like Portugal, was an offshoot of Iberian civilization. This view was accepted by most other Latin Americans. This was in stark contrast to the nineteenth century perception that Brazil would not make a viable partner because of its monarchy; the monarchy had been replaced by a republican state as of 1889.[80]

Cuadro's unionist struggle came to an end with his death on February

27, 1953. He was buried in the Cemetery of the North in Montevideo, Uruguay. Few people attended his funeral or graveside. Likewise few words were spoken on his behalf; perhaps it was the logical end "of an existence that did not know spectacular success and mundanity, or the easy victories of fame," according to his friend Roberto Ares Pons. Pons pointed out that for men like Cuadro, the rewards of life were "more intimate and arduous," coming from the "hallowed values within the spirit." If he was not successful, argued Pons, it was because Cuadro did not serve "moral malleability ... mimicry, or serve as a don of likeability."[81]

Cuadro's writing represented the culmination of a series of unproductive efforts undertaken by politically motivated intellectual activists, a fact not lost on sympathetic observers who, while recognizing the benefits of integration, also understood the many impediments that stood in the way of Latin American union. The works of Cuadro and his fellow unionists who campaigned for unionism in the twentieth century were not in vain. Their unionist writings continued to militantly and defiantly promote a cultural and political tradition that hailed back to the 1820s. Indeed, few Latin Americans would have disagreed with them. The evidence suggests that many people agreed with them, but the common man has always believed that a major restructuring of the state system will require initiatives from political elites. In fact, it would be difficult to find anyone bold enough to argue that a political-economic merger is a bad idea. The work of twentieth century unionists paralleled that of European unionists who were actively struggling to create a United States of Europe. Indeed, at the time of Cuadro's death, European elites were working to create the European Common Market (European Union).

Alberto Methol Ferré

A close friend of Servando Cuadro who was heavily influenced by him was Alberto Methol Ferré, who was a prolific writer. As a boy he stuttered, making him rather shy, but he excelled in writing. After graduating from the university, Methol Ferré took a position as a journalist where he met Cuadro and befriended him. As a reporter he was one of the few individuals able to attend Cuadro's funeral. By the 1960s he had become a prominent citizen of Uruguay and was appointed director of the Port of Montevideo. He was later appointed by the Catholic Church to serve as its lay liaison to Rome. Originally, he had belonged to the Blanco Party, a traditional conservative and Catholic organ, and then moved progressively towards the ranks of the center-left Christian Democratic party. After Cuadro's death he became interested in the efforts of Juan Perón to integrate the two economies of Argentina and Brazil via unification of their labor unions. This plan never materialized, but the works of Cuadro and Perón left an impression on Methol Ferré. His work took a historical approach, citing the region's Catholicism and Iberian heritage as the natural bond between the people. As with previous unionists he cited the vitality of the region and implored readers to consider the extended possibilities available to Latin Americans should they unify. Methol Ferré accepted Cuadro's thesis that only continental-size states could effectively compete in the modern global economy and cited the United States, the European Union, China and India as modern-day examples.[82]

One of his favorite topics was the role of youth in unionist activities, which led him to write a short paper on the topic.[83] Affectionately known as Tucho, he was one of the few ardent unionists to see the creation of a genuinely viable economic trade bloc with the potential to advance to a political level, with the creation of MERCOSUR. Methol Ferré warned his readers that unless Latin Americans became firmly committed to integration, their countries would remain economic dwarfs. Prior to his death on November 15, 2009, he remained confident that Venezuela would accede to the union followed by other states. He regretted that Mexico might be the very last state to join the union because its association with NAFTA complicated negotiations.[84]

Why did most of these Latin American unionists fail to see a viable integration? They were unable to achieve their goals because the concept of the contemporary state and the loyalty it required had been inculcated in the common man over several generations, making it almost impossible for all save the most independent-minded individuals to conceive of an alternative political structure. The common man recognized that any viable unionist efforts would have to come from elites. Lethargy would have to be overcome by the political class. Nevertheless, unionist writers of the twentieth century continued to inspire and to provide intellectual respectability for unionism through their efforts. By the 1950s, a new approach was clearly needed. But what approach might prove successful or have any potential for achieving its objective? The economists of the 1950s and 1960s, operating at the behest of their political leaders, thought they had the answer with the creation of the Latin American Free Trade Association (LAFTA), created by the Treaty of Montevideo in 1960.

VIII

1948–1960:
THE AGE OF THE ECLA
AND THE TECHNOCRATS

By the 1950s diplomatic and idealistic initiatives for political union had withered away. No one wished to be associated with the idea. However, integration per se would not be rejected if it could be associated with a strictly economic agenda. The United Nations Economic Commission for Latin America (ECLA) became the progenitor of the modern movement that exclusively sought economic union. It was also the first time that economic union became an objective of the Latin Americans. The appearance of the ECLA marked the beginning of the technocratic phase of the integration movement in Latin America. The model of integration proposed by the United Nations was the first modern economic development program elaborated for Third World states. The organization had its origin in the crisis of economic development facing the region as a result of the 1929 depression and World War II. The termination of the Second World War meant Latin America lost its U.S. markets. The decrease in trade with the United States demonstrated to Latin Americans that their dangerous dependence on foreign markets had returned to haunt them. These unstable economic cycles had serious consequences for Latin American societies, affecting such areas as adequate housing, education and employment.[1]

How were Latin Americans to deal with these problems? They were quick to understand that they could expect no help from the outside world, especially the United States. This irritated them, because Washington soon embarked on a vigorous program to reconstruct the devastated European economy via the Marshall Plan. While providing billions of dollars in assistance to Europe, the United States explicitly demonstrated that it was not interested in assisting

Latin America with financial aid programs necessary for economic development. At the Chapultepec, Mexico Conference held in 1945, the United States
informed Latin America that the key to their economic development would
be determined by their adherence to free trade policies.[2] Latin Americans
found to their dismay that they were on their own. Indeed, it was not until
Fidel Castro established the first communist state in Latin America that the
United States demonstrated any interest in advancing development projects
for the region.

During the years between the two world wars, Latin Americans had succeeded in implementing a modicum of industrialization, mainly in the realm
of consumer goods. Countries such as Brazil and Mexico had been able to successfully inaugurate the construction of steel mills, but the growth of heavy
industries was hampered by a lack of capital. Most of the Latin American
economies were too limited to take advantage of the economies of scale needed
for industrialization.[3] Many of these countries had populations that were too
small or too poor to support industrialization.[4] In many states large numbers
of Native American peasants remained outside the market economy. Consequently, Latin America had to depend exclusively on its own initiatives.

One option that had been advocated for many years by the pro-unionists
was the possibility of regional integration. Political unification was out of the
question, but economic integration was a possibility. It offered the potential
for larger markets, a wider range of resources, and lower transportation costs
without cumbersome tariffs on imported goods. Such an arrangement might
make it plausible to deal with a wider number of problems. A student of the
integration process, Gustavo Lagos, noted that the United States and the Soviet
Union were not only great powers, but were also continental powers that were
in effect "continental confederations" and large common markets.[5]

Development of the ECLA

In spite of all the discussions on economic development carried on in the
press and among various government officials, the Latin American states were
unable to agree upon the necessity of integration or what mechanisms needed
to be implemented. Popular groups proved unable to gather enough support
for political or economic integration by their own efforts. This meant that
the initiative would have to come from an outside source. It was hoped that
the United Nations would serve as a neutral medium in dealing with the highly
complex and political problem of development. Ironically, the move towards
Latin American integration would result from preliminary studies conducted

by this external organization, although the initiatives for the discussion and creation of integration plans would come from the Latin Americans themselves.

The United States opposed any U.N. involvement, suggesting that such a committee might be better situated within the Organization of American States (OAS). This was bitterly opposed by Latin Americans, who wanted a committee that could be as neutral and free of U.S. influence as possible.[6] Eventually Latin Americans were able to garner substantial support for the creation of a special U.N. Committee for Latin America, which first met in 1948 and had headquarters in Santiago de Chile. This committee became known as the Economic Commission for Latin America (ECLA), identified in Latin America as the Comisión Economica Para América Latina (CEPAL). Although numerous countries belonged to this commission, the membership consisted overwhelmingly of Latin American states.

The ECLA was specifically charged with devising a means of accelerating the industrialization of Latin America. It was headed by Raúl Prebisch (1901–1986), a prominent Argentine economist who was professionally well-known throughout Latin America. It has been observed that he was probably more influential than Fidel Castro, though not as well known.[7] Prebisch was personally asked by Trygvie Lie of the United Nations to lead the commission.[8] Under the direction of Prebisch the ECLA conducted various studies concluding that economic regional integration would provide the means of achieving economies of scale. His views on integration were heavily influenced by the two world wars and the Great Depression. These events demonstrated to him that Latin America was in a precarious trading position with respect to the rest of the world.

Prebisch hailed from a patrician family and was related to other influential families, as well. His uncle had been José Félix Uriburu, president of Argentina from 1930–32. With these connections and his extraordinary abilities, he was appointed the director of the research office of the Bank of the Argentine Nation, in 1931. While there he helped draft the charter for creating a central bank. Finally, in 1935, he was asked by Roberto Ortiz, the economics minister under President Augustin Pedro Justo, to become the first director-general of Argentina's Central Bank. He held the position until 1945, when Juan Perón replaced Prebisch with a member of "his team."[9]

Prebisch and his ECLA colleagues argued that in order for viable economic and industrial development to occur there had to be a significant increase in production along with access to a market large enough for its consumption. Like many other Latin American economists, he recognized that industrialization was dependent on capital input, which would be available according to the perceived disposability of such output (anticipated market demand). When an increase in both production and consumption occurred, the result would be an accompanying increase in income and employment.[10] The dependence on primary exports subjected countries to unfavorable terms-of-trade. Thus, protection had to be provided to the nascent industries of Latin America. This structuralist view became known as the Prebisch-Singer thesis and dominated Latin American economic development theory for many years. This perspective rejected the concept of comparative advantage promoted by classical liberal economists as a retrograde policy that subjected Latin America to servitude. It was a concept that Latin Americans loathed and considered absurd.

The Prebisch-Singer school of thought soon became a central tenet of ECLA economists and the supporters of economic integration.[11] The theory promoted import-substitution industrialization (ISI) within each Latin American state. ISI was promoted via private and state intervention in the economies of all Latin American states to varying degrees. Generally speaking, structuralists supported state intervention when private initiative could not provide goods and services. Many economists came to favor the application of the model on a larger scale, which could be achieved by economic integration.[12] With the "easy stage of ISI" complete by the 1950s, it became clear that the prevailing system of fragmented states offered only limited opportunities for economic expansion; thus, the glimmer of economic integration seemed brighter amidst a number of stagnant economies.[13]

The ECLA theory of economic development was characterized as socialist by some of its critics, but, in fact, this doctrine did not seek to eliminate free enterprise.[14] It is significant that Prebisch and his disciples never discussed or intended to create an autarkic Latin America via economic integration. ECLA doctrine did not reject trade with the rest of the world. Prebisch and his followers viewed excessive protection as negative.[15] The ECLA proposal sought only to expand the manufacturing base of the region, via minimal tariffs within the framework of the global economy. Protection would be granted until domestic manufacturers could compete with First World states. ECLA documentation concerning economic integration repeatedly stipulated that private initiative was to be both the primary goal and the mechanism for achieving economic integration.

ECLA Initiative for Economic Integration

The ECLA's recommendation for initiating economic integration in Latin America was first proposed in 1949.[16] Two years later in 1951, such a plan was specifically suggested for Central America. In 1953, the ECLA studied the possibility of integrating the economies of Argentina, Brazil, Chile and Uruguay, but the governments of these states did not heed its advice. Enthusiasm for such a plan was limited to a few economists and technocrats. Indeed, consideration of economic integration was limited to a few economists.

In 1955, the ECLA proposed the creation of a Latin American Free Trade Area for South America and Mexico. In May of 1957, the ECLA recommended that its secretariat should "expedite the implementation, within the shortest possible time" of a Latin American common market. It suggested that this be done in collaboration with the Organization of American States. The objective would be to gradually "establish a Latin American regional market on multilateral and competitive bases."[17] A designated "working group" was formed to work out the details of the plan. The group met in Santiago de Chile, in February 1958. It included a large number of technocrats, most of whom were economists, and several respected Latin American businessmen and development experts. Among the latter were Enrique Méndez Delfino, president of the Buenos Aires Stock Exchange, who represented the investor class and the interests of finance capital. At the Santiago meeting the ECLA issued a report explaining its rational for a common market. Cognizant of the report's historical significance, the committee observed: "There is no need to stress the importance of the document, since it has already produced wide repercussions ... and provides a new guide."[18]

The Santiago report stressed that there was also a "social need" for development in the Latin American states. It cited the growing potential of technology for empowerment and asked: "Will Latin America be able to take full advantage of this potential?" The report continued: "Industrialization calls for an extensive market without which the countries of the region will be unable to achieve the high level of productivity characteristic of the great industrial centers. Such a market could be available to Latin America, but it has been broken up into twenty watertight compartments." The report was optimistic that Latin America could meet the challenge. It cited the examples of the European Common Market, the European Free Trade Association, and the Soviet bloc Council for Mutual Economic Assistance (COMECON) as successful endeavors in economic integration. The working group keenly observed that the "only large population group in the world" not associated with an economic integration program was Latin America, and emphasized that the poor economic condition of the population was not an inevitability. The report poignantly noted that Latin America "is wasting for want of economic integration the immense potential represented by modern technology." The situation could be reversed if a common market were implemented. Such a program could be realized when the intellectual acceptance of a common market "that some years ago might have been considered utopian quickly gains ground when enlightened statesmen give it the support of their prestige and define it with conviction." The alternative was a Latin America that would come under increasing economic pressure from the new European Common Market.[19]

The ECLA report urged that membership in the recommended common market be open to all the states of Latin America., and that a single tariff system be adopted "vis-à-vis the rest of the world." Governments would be required to take an active role in the economic integration process, although private enterprise was to be the leader and ultimate result of such an undertaking. Within the liberal market system "specialization in industries ... must be the outcome of the free interplay of economic forces." The economically liberal report added, "It is inconsistent with this principle to accord specific countries the exclusive right to install certain industries or activities or to impose restriction on free competition." The report added that Central America should be treated as "single unit" if so desired.[20] The committee further noted that the "smallness of the market in Latin America" would continue to provide adverse economic "readjustments."[21]

At a second meeting of the ECLA working group held in Mexico City in February 1959. A general structure for the proposed new free trade area organization was recommended. The composition of the committee membership was almost identical, although additional members from various governments were invited. The working group stipulated that it never "had any intention of formulating a specific agreement," but it advised that "member governments give their general approval" to their recommendations. The group noted that any undertaking by them would be prepared only in conjunction with the individual governments. The final outcome was to be "an initial common market draft agreement" that could "bring together those countries interested in putting the idea into immediate effect."[22]

The working group agreed that the purpose of its efforts was to create a common market with the goal of promoting the "balanced economic development of Latin America, its progressive industrialization" and "establishment of a system of preferential system of trade between Latin American countries." This trade bloc was intended to evolve gradually. The working group concluded that member countries should be classified according to their level of economic development, and that preference be given to less developed countries so that their economies would have sufficient time to adjust to any negative fluctuations that might arise from the new economic organization. All Latin American countries were invited to join. If this could not occur, the "greatest possible number" would suffice. The report emphasized that if any country refused to join, the common market would proceed without them. This was a clear warning that any country distancing itself from the common market would risk jeopardizing its trade and industrialization through isolation. All states were "invited to initial negotiations," but those that rejected the invitation were allowed to reconsider.[23] The working group also recommended that special agreements with regard to customs duties be allowed among countries that were "linked by geographical proximity or common economic interests."[24]

Raymond F. Mikesell, professor of economics at the University of Oregon, warned that free market mechanisms would be threatened by the committee's acceptance of "bilateral negotiations" that might lead to trade discrimination. He criticized the committee's recommendations as being "too broad" and for failing to establish a specific deadline for the completion of trade liberalization. Such an omission, he claimed, might result in the appearance "that the principal objective of the common market agreement is to establish a preferential trading area instead of a true free trade area or customs union."[25]

Further consultation was continued at ECLA headquarters in Santiago de Chile, in April 1959. At this meeting, the working group expressed concern about the impact the recently formed European Economic Community would have on Latin America.[26] The European Community responded by issuing a memorandum stating that "misgivings" held by the Latin American countries were unfounded. It expressed confidence that other countries might benefit from the European experience. Economic integration was identified as "synonymous with economic progress and higher standards of living" and as a "source of progress for the free world as a whole."[27]

A special ECLA meeting was held May 11–19, 1959, in Panama City, Panama, at the Palacio Justo Arosemena to discuss the proposed common market. All Latin American countries were invited to send representatives. Not all delegates at the conference were sympathetic to facilitating economic integration. The chief Argentine representative, Arnaldo Tomás Musich, sensed that the conference would not prove productive. He perceived that political and economic integration did "not constitute a fundamental theme in the thinking of the majority of Latin American countries in the 50s or in the first years of the 60s." Likewise, he added, "In those years, the vision with respect to economic integration did not include political integration."[28]

Nonetheless, the Mexican representative supported the proposal and considered the recommended ECLA structure to be "prudent, ingenious and practical."[29] The chairman of the Panama City session, José Garrido Torres of Brazil, emphasized that the project "was an attempt to introduce into economic affairs the same *esprit de corps* which pervaded the political and juridical life of Latin America, in other words, to give Pan-Americanism an economic connotation."[30] Raúl Prebisch informed the delegates that the proposed common market "responded" to the economic needs of Latin America. Referring to the work of the ECLA as "technically excellent," he urged that states supporting the ECLA proposal be flexible enough to openly declare their "willingness to renegotiate the instrument" in order to accommodate other states, so as to ensure the success of the proposed common market.[31] Nevertheless, Prebisch recognized that the prevailing provincialism and lack of trade between states posed a threat to the proposed common market:

> It is not—happily—[*sic*] for Latin America—that I have observed the slightest tendency towards exclusiveness. But what I have noted, on the other hand, is a certain doubt, a persistent doubt in some cases, as to whether the common market could or should be extended to the whole of Latin America. Such misgivings are engendered by a static conception of the common market problem. What is the point, it is often asked, of forming a common market in which the southern-zone countries join with others like Mexico, when there is no trade between them? But the very reason why there is little or no trade is that in Latin America the outmoded patterns of the nineteenth century still prevail.[32]

Prebisch assured his audience that the remedy was to be found in economic integration, which he argued would break up "those outmoded patterns by creating trade where it did not exist. This was possible because Latin America was now entering a period of "energetic industrialization."[33]

Criticism of the ECLA plan came from the United States and Cuba. The U.S. representative, Harold M. Randall, claimed that the effort to go forward with a new regional economic bloc suffered from design flaws because the organizational structure was too loose. Randall stated that the establishment of a free-trade area could not replace a sound program. He expressed concern over the complexity of the classification system used to designate various countries and products, and suggested that a simplified system would be more likely to succeed.[34] The Cuban delegate also found flaws with the ECLA proposal. He was concerned that subregional agreements might appear that would, if implemented, eventually prove an impediment to the creation of an all-inclusive Latin American Common Market. Such arrangements, he argued, would impede "the desired reconciliation and collaboration of different forces throughout the region."[35]

On May 19, 1959, the Panama City session formally adopted Resolution 6 (II), which officially called for the establishment of a Latin American Common Market. The resolution stipulated that the common market was to proceed in "a multilateral and competitive form," as quickly as possible. The objective was to promote a "rise in the standard of living of its people." The resolution recommended that the individual Latin American governments immediately establish commissions to "co-ordinate all national activities that are related to the possible future" common market. Likewise, it advised these national experts to complete their formal proposals for an integrated economy no later than February 1960.[36] In addition, Resolution 10 (II) proposed that the common market be given maximum publicity in order to inform all economic sectors and the general public. It called on the United Nations, the Secretariat of the ECLA, and signatory governments to actively inform the public about the benefits of economic integration.[37]

Though the ECLA promoted the market economy as the primary mode of utilizing economic resources in the proposed free-trade zone, the idea was not universally accepted. Jan Tinbergen, a professor of economics at the Netherlands Economic Institute, provided a socialist alternative. In 1960, he suggested that the ECLA act as a central economic coordinating agency for the member countries of the newly proposed organization. His views were the exception to the classical liberal model proposed by the ECLA, the U.S.A. and most Latin Americans, who supported the idea of economic integration. Tinbergen, who later won the 1969 Nobel Prize for Economics, was an ardent and lifelong socialist. He was no newcomer to public policy planning. During the 1930s Tinbergen served on the council of the research bureau of the Dutch Labor Party and helped draft its political platform. He also served as an adviser to the League of Nations from 1936 to 1938.

Tinbergen argued that "various distributive aspects" had to be taken into consideration so that both the poor and more advanced states would benefit. Likewise, he argued, that there needed to be "a satisfactory distribution between classes of the population." Tinbergen asserted that "market forces are no longer a clear and unambiguous guide" for the promotion of heavy industrialization and economic development. The benefits of "positive intervention" would provide "harmony in the geographical distribution of industrialization." Such an approach would rid Latin America of the "less desirable consequences of a completely free-enterprise" economy. Tinbergen did not, however, advocate a Marxist-style economy as was being developed in Cuba. His models were the United States and Europe. He accepted and advanced the "take-off heavy industry" theory utilized by W.W. Rostow. Consequently, Tinbergen argued, Latin America could avoid the social problems that Europe and the United States had experienced. He cited the creation of the European Investment Bank as an example of an agency devised to deal with the problems affecting European integration.[38]

Despite Tinbergen's suggestions, the market economy would continue to be promoted as the only viable mechanism for ensuring economic integration in Latin America. No deviation from this norm was to be accepted. Meanwhile, the next few months bristled with anxiety and enthusiasm as observers awaited the results of the recommendations made by the Economic Commission for Latin America and the groundwork laid by the United Nations.

IX

THE AGE OF LAFTA

Appearance of LAFTA

The recommendations of the United Nations Economic Commission for Latin America found fruition in the Latin American Free Trade Association (LAFTA), also known by the Spanish acronym ALALC, or Asociación Latino-americana de Libre Comercio. LAFTA's purpose was to foster the reduction of tariff barriers among member states in order to promote national economic development and industrialization, rather than political integration per se as an immediate objective. Its supporters argued that the organization would provide Latin America with more flexibility, gaining trading concessions from the United States and the European Common Market in commercial negotiations. The more enthusiastic supporters of LAFTA hoped it would eventually form a common market. If this occurred, perhaps political unity might be achieved, though few individuals wished to be publicly identified with that objective.

At its inception in 1960, LAFTA had enormous potential. The first seven states to join were Argentina, Brazil, Chile, Mexico, Paraguay, Peru and Uruguay. Four others states followed: Colombia in 1961, Ecuador in 1962, Venezuela in 1966 and Bolivia in 1967. The organization eventually comprised a total area of 19,293,000 square kilometers and included 83 percent of the total population of Latin America.[1] The problem facing supporters of the new trade zone was the method by which LAFTA would achieve this objective. The very nature of LAFTA's charter and the political interests of the home governments meant that the road to a potential common market was fraught with obstacles.

The creation of LAFTA marked the decline of both the politician and the idealist as viable promoters of political integration. LAFTA was to be propagated and administered by the new generation of elite technocrats then coming to prominence in Latin America. Most of these *tecnicos*, as they were called, were economists who had been involved with state policy-making concerning the economies of the region. By the late 1950s, the technocrats had taken firm control of the integration process, although they were divided among themselves as to how far they should pursue their goal. Discussion of political integration was avoided at all cost. The theme had left embarrassing memories and was best left to alleged dreamers. Any talk concerning integration was relegated to the "experts." Some, like Gustavo Magariños, who supported transitioning to a full common market, referred to LAFTA's group of experts as a "conspiracy of technocrats."[2] Perhaps the technocrats could succeed where others had failed.

The LAFTA hierarchy stated: "The idea of an economic integration in Latin America is as old as the life of the nations that form part of it; it is wished, with the creation of LAFTA, to mold that old ambition, creating economic mechanisms for the integration of the regional economies."[3] LAFTA was given the juridical status of an international organization, with the right to enter into contracts, initiate "legal proceedings" and utilize funds in any national currency.[4]

LAFTA was officially established by the Treaty of Montevideo, which was signed on February 18, 1960. The treaty called for the operation of LAFTA to begin on June 1, 1961. The treaty proposed to achieve "the expansion of present national markets, through the gradual elimination of barriers to intraregional trade" for the purpose of "accelerating" the economic development of Latin America, necessary for improving the material quality of life for the people of the region.[5] The treaty made it clear that the ultimate objective was to create a Latin American common market within twelve years by integrating the various national economies.[6]

LAFTA's charter required it to pursue policies conducive to the interests of those nations "which are at a relatively less advanced stage of economic development," especially Bolivia and Paraguay. The Treaty of Montevideo specifically stated, "Economic development should be attained through the maximum utilization of available production factors and the more effective coordination of the development programs." The signatories also agreed that the "strengthening of national economies" would accelerate the expansion of trade within Latin America and with the rest of the world."[7] The Treaty of Montevideo also included the following provisions:

(1) LAFTA headquarters were to be located in Montevideo, Uruguay.
(2) A program of trade liberalization would be implemented over 12 years.

(3) The goal of expanded trade and "diversification of reciprocal" among member states was established.

(4) Most favored nation status would be in effect for member states.

(5) "Taxes ... and other internal duties" would be "no less favorable than that accorded to similar national products."

(6) Numerous "escape clauses" permitted the individual member nations to restrict the importation of member products when and if such goods threatened the "national economy."

(7) Special provisions were decreed for the agricultural industry and the "coordination of agricultural development and agricultural commodity trade policies" were called for.

In order to achieve these objectives, LAFTA and the various national governments sponsored the establishment of the Inter-American Development Bank (IADB) in 1961. Its purpose was to sponsor the financing of infrastructure projects between two or more states as a means of promoting development and regional integration. The IADB was funded by the World Bank, the United States and associated member states. Its first president was Felipe Herrera, a prominent Chilean supporter of expanded regional economic and political integration.

The Treaty of Montevideo also called for negotiations to remove duties on individual items rather than on groups of items. This was to cause serious problems for the negotiations on tariff reductions, because every product had to be dealt with separately. This was a lengthy, tedious and time consuming process. This made it easier for member countries to stall as political and economic conditions changed greatly in the unstable conditions of the 1960s and 1970s.[8]

The treaty called for the establishment of annual negotiations to discuss the reduction of tariff duties by no less than 8 percent of "the weighted average applicable to countries outside the free trade area." Two schedules were drawn up for the categorization of products: the national schedule and the common schedule. The national schedule included items unique or vital to a particular nation's economy. The common schedule was a list of products deemed basic or essential for tariff negotiations. The two schedules would pose problems for LAFTA, because agreement among the member states was predicated on determining what products would be placed in these categories.

Although many Latin American states failed to take advantage of LAFTA, Cuba was anxious to join the group. The Cuban economy had been seriously undermined by American economic sanctions after Havana adopted a Marxist government. The appearance of such a government only ninety miles from the United States during the last two years of the conservative Eisenhower administration set alarm bells ringing throughout the U.S. Washington became anxious to isolate the government of Fidel Castro and by 1961 had fielded an anti–Castro Cuban invasion force at the Bay of Pigs, which ended in abject failure. The United States then began applying political and economic pressure on Cuba. In order to escape the grip of a U.S. trade embargo, Cuba applied for LAFTA membership in 1962. Except for Brazil and Mexico, the member states, influenced by Washington's warning that any regional organization that "included Cuba" would be denied economic assistance, rejected Havana's application.[9] As a result of this pressure LAFTA announced that membership was open to states "whose technical or economic systems are compatible with the treaty of Montevideo."[10]

Internal Problems of LAFTA

From its inception LAFTA faced a series of problems that hindered its ability to meet the objective of creating a Latin American common market. These problems were of an internal as well as an external nature. One problem was that the competing interpretations of LAFTA's charter ensured it would face serious impediments. Another was the recurring issue of individual state interests, which continued unabated. This problem manifested itself around the role of the states, and their perceived relationship to each other and to LAFTA.

Many political, academic and business elites in Latin American made it clear that the ultimate objective of LAFTA was neither total immersion into economic integration nor any form of political union, but merely the gradual elimination of trade and tariff barriers. Representatives of the member countries and other Latin American experts in early January 1961 expressed their views on this matter before the prestigious and influential Council on Foreign Relations (COFR) in New York City, which was seeking to obtain a firm understanding of developments in Latin America. Víctor Urquidi, a prominent Mexican economist, a former director of the ECLA in Mexico City, and an ardent proponent of economic integration, heartily applauded the establishment of LAFTA, arguing that it would serve to ameliorate many of the region's problems. He expressed contentment that the region was moving towards an "all-inclusive Latin American common market" and considered the enlargement of the community to be desirable. Urquidi maintained that the participation of Mexico, Colombia and Ecuador would be bolstered by the probable entry of the Central American states.[11]

Gilbert J. Huber, Jr., who served as director-president of Listas Telefonicas Brasileiras, S.A., informed the session that he believed the rest of the Latin American states would enter LAFTA, but cautioned that there was still great resistance, especially in his own country. Many groups in Brazil favored joining LAFTA only as a "means of stifling it." Huber accused Brazilian nationalists of pursuing a policy of "Brazil first and foremost." He claimed they would destroy it by "suffocating it with kindness." Opponents would "impede progress toward integration" through the utilization of "delaying and stalling tactics." The Brazilian executive claimed that one reason for opposition to the economic bloc was because there was little trade between Brazil and the rest of Latin American. Furthermore, Brazilian industry "was not looking for markets, nor does it know the economic conditions and opportunities in the other member countries." Significantly, Huber informed the committee that because Brazilian industry did not suffer from the problem of excess capacity, opposition to LAFTA could be expected to be intense.[12]

Mexico, on the other hand, was looking for further markets and additional foreign capital, according to Urquidi. His government no longer viewed "geographical proximity" as an impediment to integration. Urquidi added one distressing point for integrationists by emphasizing that LAFTA was viewed in Mexico and in Latin America as a tool for economic development rather than for "attempting perfection" (complete economic integration). This was a clear warning that the public and the international community need not wait for LAFTA to attempt a genuine form of economic integration based "on the U.S. model" or in the mold of the European Common Market.[13]

Rómulo A. Ferrero, the former Peruvian minister of finance and commerce, supported Urquidi, claiming, "There was no thought of a political federation in Latin America," a view echoed by Huber, who claimed, "Regional political federation is not in anyone's mind at present."[14] In opposition, Francisco Lima, vice president of Jerome Barnum Associates and a former official of the El Salvadoran government, said that economic integration could not deal with the problems of the region unless it were accompanied by political union. Roberto Alemann, financial counselor at the Argentine Embassy in Washington, D.C., said his government was adamantly opposed to a common market, and that any attempt to create one would be rejected by the Latin American legislatures. For Argentina, LAFTA was only a means for creating a dialogue with the other Latin American states. Alemann added that a genuine common market would have to await the future.[15]

The problems LAFTA faced were accentuated by the fact that it lacked mechanisms for binding any member state to abide by its economic policy decisions. Nowhere was this lack of enforcement more apparent than in the implementation of tariff removal schedules, a subject of much concern to the individual states and local industries, whether they were public or private in their structure. To a large extent, the problem with tariff removals revolved around the differing levels of economic development of the member countries, and their fears that whatever level they had attained might be jeopardized by a new commercial order. Those countries that were relatively less developed and dependent on one or two primary resources for export proved the most reluctant to cooperate, though the more industrialized states also demonstrated fear of the unknown.

Several articles of the Treaty of Montevideo contained generous exemption (escape) clauses that allowed the member states to remove themselves freely from what they perceived to be harmful economic decisions. These provisions undermined the effectiveness of LAFTA. The treaty also provided for special consideration of the least developed countries, such as Ecuador, Bolivia and Paraguay. Resolutions were adopted by LAFTA that provided special funds to compensate countries that suffered severe economic losses as a result of LAFTA initiatives. It is unclear how many states were actually compensated for alleged economic losses.[16] Nevertheless, the majority of member states, in keeping with the spirit of the integration process, and within their limits, made concessions to the lesser developed states when possible, most frequently by not requiring the lesser developed nations to adhere strictly to the gradual 8 percent reduction per year on their tariffs.

LAFTA experienced substantial problems in dealing with tariff reductions because of the difficulties caused by these negotiations. Most vexing was the issue of reciprocity with regard to tariff agreements among member nations. This was not only an economic issue but a political matter as well, complicated by the fact that LAFTA required its members to deal with tariff negotiations on a country-by-country and product-by-product basis. LAFTA had at one time considered the possibility of dealing with whole categories of products and groups of countries in order to deal with the complexities of their negotiations, but was unable to reach a consensus on the matter.[17]

The matter of commodities tariff reduction was never dealt with satisfactorily. According to George Jackson Eder, the first sign of problems occurred when the number of tariff reductions declined from 7,600 items during 1961–1962 to only about 500 items per year thereafter. Echoing the view of the Colombian ambassador to LAFTA, Eder claimed that these concessions were "phony reductions" and "paper concessions on items not produced in the countries granting them or irrelevant to intraregional trade."[18] The reason for this inability to grapple with tariff reductions stemmed from the aspiration of each country to protect its own industries.

To a certain extent the desire for economic protection arose out of a concern that the LAFTA treaty, which called for economic planning by LAFTA authorities, could lead to a planned economy and create unpleasant choices for all countries involved. Another problem was posed by large corporations seeking to protect their "territory." These corporations lobbied hard to maintain their markets. They feared that free market intrusion by competitors via a common market into their realms would hurt their profit margins. Gustavo Magariños asserted that the large multinational corporations were particularly active in lobbying the governments of their host countries against integration. He cited efforts of both the Gillette and Xerox Corporations of Mexico as examples of big businesses lobbying governments to protect their business interests.[19] It is ironic that many of these corporations based in the United States opposed further economic integration, even as the U.S. government publicly supported the expansion of the integration process.

LAFTA's requirement for special consideration to be accorded to the less developed states also served to complicate the integration process. The task of attempting to regulate equilibrium in economic development failed because attempts at generating an economic equity in the realm of industrial development would have required solving an infinite number of complex questions that could not be dealt with satisfactorily. These problems revolved around basic fundamental issues that were too politically and ideologically charged. For example, decisions pertaining to the desirability of promoting private capital and/or state enterprises had to be made. The location of various industries and their ancillary facilities would also have to be considered. The settlement of these matters would have required the creation of policy-making groups and bureaucracies that would have had to engage in the construction of extremely complex economic planning and regulations, which would have neglected the concerns of a market economy.

If Latin America had become a politically unified state, such economic regulation and planning might have been moderately effective, but without political integration, the individual states continued to flounder economically as they sought to maintain their advantages. This meant that other states would suffer corresponding disadvantages, thus allowing suspicions among the various member states to persist. Ernst B. Hass and Philippe C. Schmitter pointed out in 1965 that LAFTA could be expected to fail "due to an inherent contradiction between the method agreed upon to reach those objectives and the political necessity for ensuring an equal distribution of benefits among such disparate members."[20]

The abundance of political problems, bolstered by an unrealistic and futile quest for economic equity, ensured that the poor states would remain undeveloped. The inability to grapple with the issue of tariff reduction meant LAFTA's objectives would be further undermined by its own membership.

LAFTA and Subregional Organizations

A major factor contributing to the eventual decline of LAFTA was the existence of two subregional organizations. These organizations arose out of concerns over tariff adjustments, in particular from the Latin American countries that were relatively underdeveloped. It was decided by several states that subregional organizations could compete more effectively with countries that had a relatively similar level of development. The first subregional organization was the Central American Common Market (CACM), which appeared in 1960.[21] It was the intention of the ECLA that CACM join LAFTA when the Central American states developed enough confidence in their economies to join the other Latin American states.[22] The second and most important subregional group was formed in 1969 and became known as the Andean Pact or the Andean Group, known in Spanish as the Grupo Regional Andino (GRAN), later renamed the Andean Community (CAN). As early as August 1966, Chilean president Eduardo Frei and Colombian president Carlos Lleras Restrepo were working to promote this group while at the same time claiming they supported LAFTA and a Latin American Common Market. Their chief concern was protecting enterprises in Chile and Colombia from competition by the larger states. Frei wrote Lleras Restrepo that a "hard battle" could be expected in Santiago, but that his support for CAN was the result of extensive consultation with the Chilean Senate and the Chamber of Deputies. One of Frei's concerns was that few of the countries in the new group had democratically elected presidents. Most of them were ruled by military leaders. In many instance only delegates were sent to integration conferences. Frei asked, "How can we work with people that do not have a direct mandate from their countries except as personal representatives?"[23]

The group was nominally under the jurisdiction of LAFTA but retained a considerable degree of independence. It has been compared to the BENELUX subgroup within the European Economic Community.[24] The Andean Group (Community) was formed by the Treaty of Cartagena, signed on May 26, 1969. Its members were Bolivia, Chile, Colombia, Ecuador and Peru. In February of 1973 Venezuela became a member. The objective of this organization was to promote economic integration via the gradual elimination of tariff barriers and to coordinate the planning of industrial projects. The member states have claimed that since joining the pact, trade among them has shown a substantial increase.

Since its inception, the organization has been plagued by a host of problems. Chile withdrew on January 21, 1977, because its government claimed that it was opposed to heavy foreign investment, although in reality its withdrawal was induced by the opposition of the Andean Pact states to the harsh military dictatorship of Augusto Pinochet.[25] Bolivia also left the organization temporarily during 1980–1981 because of the disruption caused by the coup d'état launched by army general Garcia Meza. This was followed by Ecuador's temporary withdrawal from the pact following a military confrontation with Peru.[26] Peru abandoned the pact when President Fujimori launched a coup d'état against the Peruvian government. On May 18, 1991, the presidents of the five governments agreed to terms and objectives of the Declaration of Caracas, which committed the signatories to the creation by 1995 of a common market, which never materialized.

The arguments of those in favor of subregional integration reflected a nationalist perspective. They argued that as the more developed Latin American states were unable to compete with industry and technology from the United States and Europe, so too were the lesser developed states of Latin America incapable of competing with the more developed countries in LAFTA. Hence, it was necessary for them to coordinate their affairs collectively in these smaller groupings to prevent their economies from being devastated. This rationale viewed the nation-state as the ultimate raison d'être by assuming it was possible for individual countries to succeed and compete with one another, despite the fact that most of these states had not fully integrated their own societies and possessed only limited resources. This logic dealt a serious blow to economic integration.

For proponents of an economic integration program that might one day lead to political integration, subregional groups have posed the threat that Latin America itself might be divided into rival blocs impeding the integration process. A regional economic subdivision is a direct rejection of the concept of political and economic unity. The supporters of political unification or of a genuine common market had to contend with the fact that many countries were not seeking genuine political or economic integration. The most ardent supporters of economic integration such as Raúl Prebisch and Gustavo Magariños were unhappy with the trend, but their efforts to ameliorate the matter failed.[27]

LAFTA and State Ownership of Industry

A major problem facing LAFTA negotiators was the existence of so many state enterprises that only served to complicate tariffs negotiations. The problem concerned the relationship between private international corporations and state enterprises; specifically, the role that both sectors would play in the economy. It was hoped that a large number of state-operated economic enterprises would be active in promoting regional planning schemes, but this proved to be a disappointment.[28] The root of this problem was, and continues to be, that many Latin American governments have collected revenues from state enterprises in order to meet the most basic needs of their societies. For example, Petróleos Mexicanos (PEMEX) has contributed a substantial portion of its revenues to education in Mexico. Thus, any tariff reductions that might produce a negative effect on such operations were always viewed warily. As a rule, state enterprises usually functioned as monopolies, which raised concern in Latin America about their efficiency. However, a cut in revenue might result in higher unemployment or a higher balance-of-payments problem.

Public enterprises allowed politicians the opportunity to dispense favors and rewards to their supporters in the form of state employment (political patronage). Consequently, politicians were not enthusiastic about the prospect of state-run enterprises (such as oil companies) competing with one another. This would have depleted profits and probably raised operating costs. Since these funds were often used for programs such as housing construction and education, governments were hesitant about jeopardizing revenues whose elimination might bring about a coup d'état or, even worse, a leftist insurgency. These state-run enterprises often had to compete with private corporations, which could be foreign or domestic. In a few instances, large economic enterprises might consist of private and state capital with representatives from both sectors serving on the governing board.

Latin American society as a whole accepted the prevailing wisdom of the era that economic growth should be directed via state intervention and ownership of key industries. Loss of control over public ownership was viewed as unacceptable by most people and political figures. This economic system, which was prevalent throughout Latin America, was the result of its peculiar historical and economic development rooted in the European experience, where state intervention had proven successful. The Latin Americans recognized early in the twentieth century the dilemma of operating with a paucity of capital necessary for commercial and industrial expansion. In order to deal with this problem, most of the nations initiated state-managed enterprises to deal with the lack of capital vital to modern economies. Among these industries were petroleum, railroads, banking, airlines, the merchant marine, steel, and communications. The profundity of state-operated economic enterprises meant that their elimination or any loss of revenue would threaten the ability of governments to meet their daily expenses of maintaining schools, army, police, roads, and the payment of civil servants. Therefore any proposal for economic development within LAFTA that might erode these precious sources of state revenues were looked at suspiciously by governments forced by rising expectations to act as catalysts for economic development.[29]

The interests of these state-operated industries were not propitious to the objective of economic rationalization given pride of place in LAFTA's charter. For example, state-owned oil companies proved reluctant to engage in any large-scale planning that would facilitate LAFTA's advancement to a full common market. Their cooperation was limited to the exchange of technical information, the construction of pipeline connections, and the use of oil tankers. Nevertheless, state-owned oil enterprises, so vital to the economics of the various countries, created an organization of state-operated petroleum enterprises known as the Asociación de Asistencia Recíproca Petrolero Estatal Latinoamericana (ARPEL) to discuss more effective means of dealing with shared problems and future projects. This organization, established in 1964, included the nine state-operated oil companies in Latin America. It is considered the most successful organization of its type to have engaged in any form of planning, and one that made it difficult for LAFTA to succeed.[30]

The concern over the fate of both state-owned and private enterprises was nowhere as pervasive as in the petrochemical industry. The problem facing this industry was the control and coordination of resources, especially oil and natural gas, as well as the production and distribution of these vital assets. The issue was particularly important for the three big states of Argentina, Brazil and Mexico. Any economic integration would have involved a dispute among these three countries regarding which state's industry would play a preeminent role if integration were to advance the goal of a more rational, efficient and cost-effective system. In a 1972 study conducted by the Committee for Economic Development in New York City, Dr. Jack Behrman, a professor of economics at the University of North Carolina, concluded that in an economically integrated Latin America, Mexico would become the primary producer of "basic and intermediate chemicals." He theorized that if the petrochemical industry remained in the hands of the Mexican government, it would become more powerful and influential than it had previously been. This would result in a decline of the Argentine and Brazilian state petrochemical industries and, of course, their relative political and economic influence.[31]

Cooperation between the member states of ARPEL was limited, because all decisions had to be unanimous. In addition, there was the ever-present problem of concerns reflected by the member states, as well as the internal concerns of the individual state enterprises. It has been observed that "state owned industries in Latin America, as elsewhere, tend to function autonomously and sometimes in disregard of general policy. They are preoccupied with internal problems of management and development and have not yet found it possible to enlarge their focus to include the problems of their opposite numbers elsewhere in the zone."[32] This trend continues to the present day and must be taken into account by those promoting economic integration.

LAFTA and the Establishment of Regional Industrial Study Groups

With the establishment of LAFTA, it was decided that the organization needed the input of industrial and commercial leaders from the private sector whose expertise could illuminate potential solutions for meeting LAFTA's objectives. Accordingly, LAFTA invited industrial associations with all-regional interests to establish offices at LAFTA headquarters in Montevideo in order to advise LAFTA officials on matters of pertinence to both organizations. This was the first time in history that professional, trade and industrial organizations were organized on an all–Latin-American basis. These groups were intended to allow LAFTA officials to plan on a broad scale for various industries. In particular, it was hoped that the study groups would permit national governments, industry, labor unions and the Latin American public to become familiar with various problems and the potential for growth.

The most important meetings were the sectorial commissions that began work in 1963. These commissions had to be certified by their respective governments as being qualified to represent their industries before LAFTA. The committees were to report the effects that LAFTA policies would have on their industries and make recommendations. The sectorial commissions were also intended to provide the Permanent Executive Committee of LAFTA with any concerns or proposals regarding the integration agenda.[33]

One of the most influential industrial study groups was the Institute for Latin American integration (INTAL). It functioned as a research institute, engaging economists to report their findings on some of the more complex and technical aspects of economic integration. Several other new study groups included the Inter-American Bar Association (IABA), the Institute for Economic Integration (IDEI), the Inter-American Institute for Juridical Studies, the Institute of Iron and Steel (ILAFA), and the Latin American Association of Shipowners (ALAMAR). These organizations allowed the members of various industries and professions to become aware of the work and concerns of others working within those fields elsewhere in Latin America.[34] In addition to the sectorial commissions, LAFTA provided the medium for various central banks in Latin America to reach and maintain various technical agreements.[35]

Efforts to Accelerate LAFTA

It was clear by 1964 that efforts to move the LAFTA zone towards a common market similar to that of the European Common Market were lagging. The squabbles over tariff reductions had slowed the integration process. The objective of promoting equity among the larger, medium and smaller economies had proven as elusive as it had been irresponsible and self-defeating. Since its inception, LAFTA had received criticisms from numerous sectors of Latin American society who were dissatisfied because of its lack of progress. In 1965 President Eduardo Frei of Chile, who was himself frustrated with the slow pace of the integration initiative, decided to spur the process by inviting some of Latin America's most prominent economists to a meeting in Santiago de Chile. The purpose of the meeting was to discuss new approaches to creating a stronger organization to implement the economic integration of Latin America. In a letter addressed to the economists José Antonio Mayobre, Felipe Herrera, Carlos Sanz de Santamaría and Raúl Prebisch in early 1965, President Frei asked them to undertake a study that could provide some guidance for the acceleration of the integration process. It was Frei's expectation that the prestige of the four economists would serve to foment further progress towards a common market.[36] Frei stated in his letter that it was necessary to provide a dynamic impetus to the integration process. He noted it was necessary to "surpass anachronistic formulas" concerning integration in order to maintain a place "on the most advanced borders of thinking." For Frei the integration process had become "slow and embarrassing." One of the main problems affecting LAFTA was its lack of a "superior authority" and organs that lacked "dynamic elements." He played to the sentiments of the smaller and weaker economies by asserting that all states, irrespective of the size of their economies, needed to benefit from industrialization.[37] Frei cited the "acute incapacity" of the various states to realize their goals for economic development as the major reason for seeking to promote economic integration. He rhetorically asked them:

> Is it possible to continue to organize the development of our economies in stagnant compartments, condemning our continent to a state of deterioration always more pronounced, without organizing a collective effort between related countries indissolubly united by geography and culture against vast conglomerates that multiply their progress precisely because of their spiritual union?[38]

In April 1965, President Frei received a reply signed by the four economists. It was also addressed to the other Latin American presidents. The four reiterated their commitment to a continuation of an integration agenda that would lead to LAFTA's stated goal of creating a common market. Frei was informed that they had commissioned a study by the ECLA to respond to his concerns. Their opinions expressed a unanimous opinion. Integration was not only urgent, it "required unpostponeable political decisions at the very highest levels" in order to succeed. They made it explicitly clear that their study would not proffer any ideas or propositions that had not been articulated before.[39]

Indeed, the study echoed the main points made by earlier ECLA reports. It was a compendium of the technical (economic) studies that had been previously undertaken. The authors' analyses expressed the logic and rationale of liberal economists concerning the establishment and functioning of modern market economies. They reiterated the argument that extensive industrialization in the region would require larger internal markets, specialization, comparative economic advantage, and economic efficiency. Concern was expressed that the Latin American states continued to spur industries irrespective of their efficiency, a clear reference to the multitude of state enterprises, which often held exclusive monopolies, and the many private establishments that had been induced via lucrative concessions to establish sites in their respective territories.

The study argued that if industrialization continued without expanding integration, economic inefficiency would only become further "accentuated before it corrected itself."[40] The four economists noted that the establishment of a common market was solely dependent on "national efforts." Significantly, they emphasized that it would be futile to conduct any further technical studies unless the states were firmly committed to the expansion of the integration process. They wrote, "Nevertheless, our countries pretend to develop in arbitrarily segregated territories ... and to disseminate their efforts in isolated actions." Latin America, they argued, was not "capable of confronting" the multitude of problems faced by the region alone.[41] They highlighted two major points: first, the "need to learn to work in a community" and, second, the "need to form the community of Latin America." Likewise, the authors cited the need to attract foreign capital in order to advance the economic potential of Latin America.[42]

In their study, the economists cited what they perceived to be the faulty logic of the Latin American states in seeking to promote economic development in an "arbitrarily segregated territory" by "disseminating their efforts in isolated actions" in a global society where "economic blocs of considerable significance had arisen." The slowdown in the integration process was not the result of flaws in the Montevideo Treaty, but the failure of political leaders to establish and "articulate a clear and distinct set of objectives to be pursued." Policy decisions would need to be sustained by a viable institutional frame-work.[43] It was suggested that the Latin Americans begin the trend towards closer association via LAFTA's sponsorship of sectoral accords that would deal with specific industries such as chemicals, autos and steel. It was stressed that import substitution facilities were "colliding" with the newer and more complex industries, and that no country in the region was capable of "embarking or continuing" its development under conditions of efficiency if they remained isolated.[44] In order to satisfy the concerns of the lesser developed states it was suggested that tariff arrangements be utilized to assist states that suffered an inordinate economic hardship from the adjustment to free trade. They also issued a cautionary note in response to the complaints and efforts of the less developed Latin American states to partition the scarce resources of the region, arguing that "no country could consistently derive major advantages that belong to others."[45]

While Frei and the four prominent economists carried on their correspondence, the Economic Commission for Latin America prepared and presented a report to LAFTA. The ECLA report expressed the same enthusiasm for foreign investment, saying that such investment, "in its diverse forms, is the complimentary fountain of resources that are available to countries in development stages." The ECLA study also emphasized the importance of strengthening national income and savings so as to invigorate the economy of each state.[46]

The commission decried the continual deficit experienced by all Latin American economies, and implied that only in times of global military conflict could this trend actually be expected to reverse itself. The study reiterated the ECLA argument (and that of the four economists) that the high cost-per-unit of manufacturing (lacking economies of scale) due to the small internal markets existing in most countries, mitigated against the development of their own economies. Also cited was the opposition of the industrialized First World states against imports of Latin American manufacturers.[47]

The ECLA report concluded by calling for the establishment of a stronger and more centralized structure for the purpose of coordinating a common economic policy for Latin America. Any new institutional reorganization needed to strike a balance between national interests and the proliferation of economic integration. Economic integration in Latin America could "not advance satisfactorily without strong and adequate institutions in a new stage" of development. Integration was viewed as central to the development of the Latin American economy and should be considered a parallel objective with other economic and social goals.[48] According to the ECLA report, the Treaty of Montevideo did "not prevent the gradual and progressive perfecting" of efforts aimed at fostering economic integration, "but aspired that this common market consist of all the countries of Latin America."[49]

In spite of the ECLA report and the letter of support for Frei's political agenda by the four economists, the remaining Latin American states showed little interest in pursuing policies that would strengthen the road to economic integration. The pace of implementing the LAFTA agenda continued to slow down in spite of the 1965 correspondence. It was clear that LAFTA was in serious trouble. All the prestige of the ECLA, President Frei and the four distinguished economists was insufficient to remedy the situation. It became clear to observers that only political initiatives undertaken at the highest levels could resolve the continuing dilemma and move the integration process forward. A very serious obstacle loomed—Eduardo Frei himself. While calling for expanded economic integration, Frei worked behind the scenes to create a subregional Andean organization that would represent the interests of the weaker economies before the stronger states.

In the meantime it was decided that a summit meeting of all the major heads of state from Latin America and the United States be convoked. Subsequently, after a year of preparation, a meeting of all the presidents in the Western Hemisphere was scheduled at the resort town of Punta del Este in Uruguay. The meeting took place on April 12–14, 1967, attended by twenty heads of state amidst heavy security because of the perennial threat of the leftist Tupamaro guerrillas. The convening presidents, including Lyndon B. Johnson of the United States, signed a provision calling for closer cooperation in the field of integration. This "Declaration of the Presidents" pledged the presidents of the Latin American countries to initiate measures for implementing a common market by 1970 that would be completed by 1985.

The presidents agreed to instruct their foreign ministers to institute the policies needed for the creation of a common market program. In addition, the declaration called on the participating states to advance their efforts in support of representative government, along with the promotion of economic, political and social progress. Significantly, it called for the "progressive convergence" of LAFTA and CACM into one organization that would promote the free movement of goods and people throughout the envisioned economic bloc. The document also pledged an expansion of the physical infrastructure of the region that would create communications, transportation, and energy systems to strengthen the bonds among all the Latin American states.[50] A call for the creation of an educational system in Latin America that would stress the importance of integration was included. This represented a clear acknowledgment that Latin American awareness of the other Ibero-American states was a key ingredient in fostering a sentiment of solidarity and was a necessary tool if commercial intercourse between the many states was to expand.[51]

The declaration also emphasized that economic integration was intended as a "collective instrument for accelerating Latin America development" and "should constitute one of the policy goals" of each attending state "as a necessary complement to national development plants." It was imperative to "adopt all measures that will lead to the completion of Latin American integration ... in the shortest time possible." LAFTA states were to be "instructed" by their own governments "to adopt measures necessary" for implementing new integration policies. Likewise, it called on the signatory presidents to work for the harmonization of "national laws to the extent required for integration."[52]

As a concession to the lesser developed states and their demands for preferential treatment, the presidents' declaration asserted that these states were to be "accorded the right to participate and obtain preferential conditions in the sub-regional agreements in which they have an interest." It also called for the establishment of "temporary sub-regional agreements," a clear and dangerous indication that the Latin American presidents approved of the fragmentation.[53]

The presidents also declared their desire to limit military expenditures. While their statement emphasized the need for security, it also recognized the need to reorient their financial resources towards socio-economic projects. Integration needed to be at the "service of Latin America" and was necessary in order to "fortify the Latin American enterprise." The comuniqué demonstrated the commitment of the presidents to the promotion of free trade, and its importance in reaching their objective.[54]

In spite of all the positive fanfare accompanying the summit, President Arosemena of Ecuador refused to sign the declaration, claiming that not enough consideration was given to the lesser developed states. He claimed that the presidents' declaration was nothing more than a "prefabricated and unsatisfactory" statement. On April 13, 1967, Arosemena met with both U.S. and Latin American officials, who sought to change his mind. President Gustavo Díaz Ordaz of Mexico told Arosemena that the document was a necessary compromise agreement, and that it was impossible to devise a totally satisfactory one. Nevertheless Arosemena remained negative, and he was the only president who refused to endorse an otherwise continental resolution.[55]

Reaction to the summit varied. U.S. officials were less than enthusiastic, but were unwilling to label it a failure. Peru's president, Fernando Belaunde Terry, sounded a rather polite but cynical rejoinder: "The documents of this conference are like the score of a symphony—it all depends on how it is played." One unidentified source in a U.S. periodical wrote that the summit had displayed a "let's get moving" agenda, but observed that nothing important had emanated from the meeting.[56]

Hostility to the Punta del Este summit came from the far left, whose chief spokesman in democratic Latin America was Salvador Allende, the leader of the Socialist Party and secretary of the Chilean senate. He was also the primary political foe of Eduardo Frei. Allende's comments were intended to cripple mass support for the meeting. Since he was a major political-ideological figure not only in his native Chile but throughout Latin America, his views carried considerable weight with the large leftist movement that had spawned in the region. Allende portrayed the integration movement as a manifestation of U.S. imperialism. He completely ignored the previous historical tradition of unionism, which had existed for one hundred and forty years. Less than one month after the conference, Allende published a book entitled *Punta del Este: La Nueva Estrategia del Imperialismo*—a clear indication he had long been preparing for the conference. In the work every aspect of the historic meeting was criticized. Allende claimed that efforts to promote economic integration for Latin America bore the "fingerprints of the United States government." The Chilean asserted he had "secret documents" written by Sol Linowitz and the Organization of American States that provided "instructions" to the presidents. Such commands were to be the "whip with which to flog our weak economies."[57] Likewise, Allende complained that Washington's plans for the Alliance for Progress proved it was insincere. He claimed the United States spent ten years' worth of Latin American economic aid every month to fight the Vietnam War.[58] U.S. support for integration, he asserted, was simply "another manipulation."[59] Allende argued that the nationalism that was the basis for Latin American economic integration had to become a "people's nationalism" that would evolve into an "internationalism without national leaders or national satellites." Only then, argued Allende, would true justice prevail.[60]

By this time there were few prospects for further advances in the integration process. The fact that the declaration stated its policies would not begin until 1970 raised questions as to how serious the presidents were to their commitment. LAFTA eventually came come to a grinding halt during the 1970s, and it was officially dismantled in 1980.

Reflections on LAFTA

LAFTA was not the ideal integration the followers of Bolívar and Haya de la Torre had envisioned, but it was the most that could be accomplished at that time. When LAFTA was created there was a great deal of comparison with the European Economic Community (EEC) because it was believed that LAFTA would eventually evolve into a full-fledged common market. Upon closer examination, there existed major qualitative differences between the EEC and LAFTA. The EEC was formed to attain economic efficiency and the political unification of Europe via the integration of its economy. Indeed, Walter Hallstein, president of the EEC Commission, declared in a public appearance at the Massachusetts Institute of Technology on May 22, 1961, "We are not in business at all: We are in politics."[61] This objective was not supported by Latin American political figures.

LAFTA was formed to accelerate the industrialization process in Third World countries with wide disparities in their economic development. Why did the approach in the two geographical zones differ? The answer lies in the economic development of the member organizations. Third World states such as Argentina, Brazil and Mexico were grouped with even weaker economies such as Bolivia, Ecuador and Paraguay, which meant that competing interests had to be balanced. Trade between these states was often minimal. In contrast, the EEC was created by countries considered to be fully developed and industrialized, although they would eventually invite the lesser developed European states into their union. This was possible because of the interdependency that had been forged between the industrialized and lesser developed states of Europe. In actual practice, LAFTA was closer to the ineffectual European Free Trade Association (EFTA), which was formed to deal exclusively with the elimination of tariff barriers.[62]

Despite its failure, the fact cannot be overlooked that LAFTA was the first serious effort at promoting viable integration with any possibility of success since the 1826 Panama Congress. The very formation of LAFTA was a major feat in and of itself. It signified a limited recognition by public officials that Latin American economic integration could create the conditions for alleviating the crisis of economic development and address mutual concerns shared by all Latin American states. LAFTA functioned for twenty years and provided valuable experience to technocrats and economists grappling with the many complex issues of the integration process. The dialog continued far beyond LAFTA's life span.

X

THE UNITED STATES
AND LATIN AMERICAN
INTEGRATION

Your cooperation in promoting a common regional market is highly
encouraging.—President Eisenhower in a toast to Chilean president Alessandri, March 1, 1960

Washington's Early Interest

The United States has always been recognized as a major power in the
Western Hemisphere; thus, the views and policies of Washington concerning
the proposed economic integration of Latin America merit discussion. By the
1950s, the overwhelming influence of the United States had become three-
dimensional in scope: political, economic and military. In the area of economics, the U.S. presence in Latin America was overwhelming. The massive infusion of capital from the United States affected every facet of Latin American
life. American business was cited as Washington's "most conspicuous and most
important presence in Ibero-America today." In spite of much anti–U.S. feeling
in Latin America, elites from the region (especially those in government) dared
not offend the United States, or U.S. capital, so dependent were they on investment from North America. As of 1967, U.S. business employed over one-and-
a-half million people in Latin America. It was estimated that these investments
were responsible for "one-tenth of the total output of goods" and one-third
of exports sent from Latin America. By the middle of the 1960s Latin American
governments had become excessively dependent on U.S. corporations to
finance their governments. It was estimated that one-fifth of the tax revenues
collected by Ibero-American governments came from U.S. enterprises operating in the region.[1]

According to available documents, the United States government con-sistently supported the economic integration of Latin America during the 1960s, as long it followed a free-trade orientation. Questions regarding the wisdom of such support, however, were raised. Nevertheless, opposition in Washington appears to have been slight; suffice to say that any documentation from the U.S. government that explicitly sought to frustrate economic inte-gration per se in Latin America has not been detected, although it may exist in some unreleased group of documents.

The available documentation suggests that U.S. support for economic integration in Latin America was attributed to two factors: first, the alarming security concerns posed by economic instability accentuated by the prolifer-ation of Marxist political parties and the experience of leftist-communist forces in Guatemala and Cuba, and, second, the fear that U.S. economic interests in Latin America might be adversely affected by the appearance of new regional trade blocs (i.e., the European Economic Community), lending credence to Haya de la Torre's prophetic explanation that the level of support the United States would provide to Latin American integration would be in relation to the economic threat posed to Washington by Europe. There was concern in the United States that Latin America, a bastion of U.S. investment, might suffer extensive economic discrimination at the hands of other regional trading blocs. If this were to occur it would eventually have a devastating impact on the Latin American ability to purchase U.S. goods.

Historically, the United States has shown little interest in Latin America except in times of territorial expansion and potential interloping by rival pow-ers such as Britain, Germany, or the former Soviet Union. In the post–World War II years, when economic development became an issue of paramount importance for Latin American political leaders, the U.S. response was one of apathy and neglect. Indeed, diplomats posted to Latin America were often sent there because they were perceived as less capable than their counterparts in Europe, the Far East, or potential trouble spots around the world.

An indication of Washington's attitude towards Latin America in the 1940s and 1950s can be gleaned from the words of George F. Kennan, the early Cold War diplomat who made a trip to Latin America in 1950. His encounter with the Third World did not go well; indeed it smacked of culture shock, as evinced by his comments. His observations on Latin America and its culture were viewed as so excessively harsh that the State Department under Dean Acheson ordered them locked away. Kennan's views were as racist as they were appallingly chauvinistic. While he recognized that Latin America had made impressive material advances, he also held that society in contempt. He wrote that Latin American cities were nothing but bastions of "inordinate splendor and pretense" and had only contemptuous statements to make about the various capitals he visited. Likewise, Kennan could not conceal his deep visceral scorn for the people, claiming that they were victims of their cultural and geographical heritage.[2] Nevertheless, many years later he wrote that it was very possible that Latin America would emerge "as perhaps humanity's best hope for the future," becoming the last bastion of "humane Christian values" emanating from Western civilization.[3]

In the realm of foreign policy, Kennan bluntly stated that the United States should make it clear to the Latin Americans that they depended on Washington. He asserted that the region was not important even for the use of military bases. The United States, argued Kennan, only required access to Latin American resources in time of war. The communists were a problem, but he did not feel it was likely that they would emerge as a military threat. While other diplomats were certainly more circumspect in expressing their views, Kennan's comments provide an accurate appraisal of power relations between Washington and Latin America during the 1940s and 1950s.[4]

As a policy analyst, Kennan never had to concern himself with the issue of Latin American economic integration, but it is inferred from his writing that he would have opposed the concept. He made it clear in his memoirs that he did not approve of state-building based on the premise of linguistic affinity, a concept he denounced in his discussion of European politics.[5]

Concern over communist activities in Latin America during the 1940s and 1950s was relatively mild. Indeed, during this period the United States did not express any real interest in the region. Kennan had been correct in his earlier assessment of communist movements in the region. Communism would not be an open threat until 1959, the year Fidel Castro came to power. His ascension to political leadership also brought numerous attempts to export revolution to other Latin American countries. The appearance of a communist government less than one hundred miles away demonstrated to Washington that it could not afford to take Latin America's loyalty for granted. Marxist ideology could have a very potent appeal for its mass of people. The growing concern over the Soviet-Cuban alliance prompted the United States to seriously contemplate the creation of economic development projects to assist the Latin American governments as a means of resisting communist encroachments.

In light of this growing sense of urgency in the late 1950s, the United States began to view regional economic integration in Latin America as a potentially viable system for economic development. This orientation changed beginning in the 1960s when the United States government and foreign policy experts came to realize the Latin Americans were seriously committed to holding

discussions on the topic of pursuing economic integration as represented by
the signing of the Treaty of Montevideo which created LAFTA.

President Eisenhower, in a discussion with his cabinet on July 3, 1953,
called for unity among the Latin American countries.[6] He argued that as
a means of promoting the new internationalism, the United States needed
to support regionalist policies that were designed to stimulate global trade
through the elimination of tariffs and barriers. Regionalism was also
viewed as a means of promoting economic development and the rights of
free men.[7]

Eisenhower understood the precarious nature of economic monoculture
that plagued Latin America and its relationship to unstable political systems.
He recognized that with respect to economic aid, the United States did not
provide the same level of support to Latin America that it merited. Washington, he complained, was much more concerned with Europe. The president
argued, "You know ... when we speak of the affairs of Europe, we talk on a
totally different level. Unity, unity, unity ... we say it over and over ... we try
to plan or lead ahead toward something better and stronger for Europe as a
whole.... What is true for one continent should be just as true for another."
The United States, emphasized Eisenhower, needed a new approach to the
much-neglected area. With large numbers of its people anxious for the United
States to take on an international campaign for political and economic reform,
perhaps the time was right to promote economic integration for Latin America. "We have to begin and look at all of Latin America—and look at it as a
whole. With all our urgings to the nations of Europe to achieve some kind of
unity, I don't know why they have not chided us long ago about this Western
Hemisphere," stated the president. Eisenhower encouraged his cabinet and
closest advisers to consider and adopt innovative, bold and dynamic measures
to deal with Latin American problems, especially their weak economies,
through a voluntary re-organization of the state system. "Why are we not
thinking and planning a design of unity here?"[8]

Several years later, on a two-week trip to Latin America, Eisenhower
addressed the Chilean congress on March 1, 1960. In the message he referred
to the United States as a common market rather than as a nation. His speech
underscored that it was not nationality that bound the people of the United
States together, it was a common interest as manifested and created by a federation that had successfully served political and economic matters. The structure of the United States was a design that had overcome innumerable
problems; thus he implored the Chilean legislators to look to the United States
as a political and economic model for re-organization of their own state, and
pledged U.S. support for such a restructuring:

The United States, as the largest common market in the world, could not but look with favor on the efforts of other free nations—in Europe, Latin America, or elsewhere—to enhance their prosperity through the reduction of barriers to trade and the maximum use of their resources. We feel that a common market must be designed not only to increase trade with the region but to raise the level of world trade generally.[9]

In a dinner toast to President Alessandri of Chile later that evening, Eisenhower expressed the view that a common market was the most desirable form of re-organization for Chileans. Such a restructuring would serve to augment capital flows into the country. He encouraged them to continue with their progress, claiming, "Your cooperation in promoting a common regional market is highly encouraging, for it promises greater intra-regional trade and once realized will create conditions attractive to foreign development capital."[10] After returning from his trip, President Eisenhower reiterated on March 8, 1960, that Washington was "encouraged by the progress being made toward the creation of common markets," which, he added, promoted global trade and increased economic efficiency.[11]

A year later the new president, John F. Kennedy, told a group of Latin American diplomats at a White House reception that the United States supported integration and that the nation-state system was an economically unviable structure that served as an impediment to the economic advancement of the Latin American people. "The fragmentation of Latin American economies is a serious barrier to industrial growth," said Kennedy. He expressed confidence that a common market would remedy the problems that stemmed from this arrangement.[12] In agreement with his predecessors, Lyndon B. Johnson wrote in his memoirs that the economic integration in Latin America was a principal objective of U.S. foreign policy: "My goal ... was to promote a new sense of regionalism in Latin America."[13] U.S. policy, said Johnson, was dedicated to helping "build those associations of nations which reflect the opportunities and the necessities of the modern world." This was to be achieved by strengthening "the regional organization of developing continents. Thus the concept of regionalism in areas outside Europe emerged as one of my administration's most serious commitments in its efforts to build a stable world order." Likewise, Johnson's secretary of state, Dean Rusk, submitted a draft proposal in 1965 that secured approval from the White House. It cited nationalism and the state system as an outmoded modus operandi: "Old fashioned nationalism is proving an unsatisfactory basis for dealing with the real problems that we all confront. No nation, including the United States can guarantee its security, its prosperity ... by pursuing narrow policies of nationalism."[14]

Johnson reflected the views of American foreign policy elites that argued economic integration in either Europe or Latin America posed no threat to U.S. interests as long as U.S. business interests could continue to trade in those areas. Historically, the United States has supported regional trading blocs on numerous occasions, as evinced by attempts to resuscitate the Central American Federation, the Pan-American program of the 1880s developed by Secretary of State James G. Blaine, and most significantly the twentieth century effort to promote the European Economic Community (EEC, or European Common Market). There was, however, a qualitative difference between Washington's objectives and support for European and Latin American integration. This divergence centered around the mechanisms for promoting economic growth. In the case of European integration, American policy makers insisted on an organization that would utilize extensive economic planning executed by the various governments and the EEC. With respect to Latin American economic integration, the United States was opposed to governmental involvement. The United States insisted that economic integration in Latin America was to be implemented via private initiative, primarily through foreign and domestic investment. The U.S. integration plan was to utilize Latin America as a vast funnel for the infusion of foreign capital, especially surplus U.S. capital. Latin Americans, for the most part, did not reject foreign capital, in fact they welcomed it. They viewed it as a necessary resource. There was concern, however, that their societies might be totally subordinated to foreign financial interests. These fears were reinforced by past political policies employed by both Europe and the United States that had included military interventions, political coups and even employment discrimination in Latin America. Elbio C. Pezzati, former senator from Uruguay, recounted how even in the 1940s hotels or housing complexes controlled by North Americans would not hire locals to serve as porters. Such discriminatory policies left strong suspicions and antipathies toward the United States.[15]

Early U.S. support for Latin American economic integration was based on the premise that any program for economic integration would promote and embrace free trade both within the region and with the United States. Most U.S. policy makers assumed that the economic integration of Latin America would prove a boom to U.S. producers. If, on the other hand, the Latin Americans had sought to create an autarkic Latin American economy, such a policy would have created hostility on the part of the United States.[16] In spite of enthusiastic support for other regional trading blocs, the United States was not originally a warm supporter of the Economic Commission for Latin America (ECLA) when it first appeared, because (1) it was feared its leaders would favor high tariffs against foreign producers, and (2) because Washington might not be able to control future outcomes from the ECLA.

Once the organization was established, talk of a potential integration program became the subject of discussion in ECLA studies by academic and international organizations. Consequently the U.S. government became more interested in the idea.

Non-Governmental Studies

One of the earliest studies on Latin American economic integration was conducted by Raymond F. Mikesell, a professor of economics at the University of Oregon. His study was undertaken on behalf of the Inter-American Economic and Social Council of the Organization of American States in 1957. Mikesell observed that trade among the individual Latin American states formed only a fraction of their international commerce. Most of this intra-regional trade in Latin America was relegated to the southern cone, which to a large extent was facilitated by the existence of the River Plate as a great highway. He cited several reasons for this phenomenon: the profundity of currency and commercial restrictions; the geographic isolation of trade entrepots; the existence of an inadequate transportation infrastructure; the lack of foresight on the part of political figures; inadequate policies; and the ability to recognize existence of regional markets. As a result of these problems, he concluded that Latin Americans had "not taken full advantage of the complementarity of their resources and of existing production." He argued that great benefits would accrue to the region if it adopted a policy of economic integration, in particular if it allowed for "free mobility of labor, capital ... goods and services throughout the region." Mikesell proffered that such a program would "facilitate regional development planning and programming at both the governmental and the business levels."[17]

The author recognized that prior Latin American efforts to achieve integration had failed, but it was "significant that regional economic integration is an ideal which is deeply rooted in the history of the Latin American republics." This indicated to him that the eternal quest might be transformed into a reality.[18] He surmised that a free-trade zone would be a probable prelude to any genuine economic integration because it did "not require a common trading policy on the part of members of the area with the outside world." Mikesell reluctantly observed that the political conditions in Latin America did not portend favorably for the creation of a customs union.[19] Nonetheless, he thought that economic integration might very well lead to political union due to complexities arising from the need to make decisions affecting all parties.[20]

Mikesell emphasized that Latin America could not be considered one exclusive economic zone; instead he argued that Latin America consisted of three economic zones. These zones consisted of the northern South American states, the southern-cone states, and Central America and Mexico together. In spite of this division, Mikesell argued, "The advantages of propinquity include not only lower transportation costs, but also greater facility in establishing distribution channels in nearby countries." He believed that Latin American enterprises would be able to effectively withstand foreign competition.[21]

Mikesell refuted the argument that countries at different levels of economic development could not effectively work together or that weaker states would suffer at the hands of the wealthier states of Latin America. He cited the massive infusion of U.S. capital into Puerto Rico as "a classic example of the advantages of integration between a low-income underdeveloped country and a highly industrialized area." Indeed, he asserted that it was much more likely that capital would flow into the poorer states from wealthier Latin American economies. In anticipation of Latin American concerns that states of similar economic position should be grouped according to their own level of development, he noted, "Puerto Rico's integration with the U.S. economy is far more valuable to her than any program of integration with her Caribbean neighbors."[22]

An intense curiosity about the potential of Latin American integration as a new factor in the world economy soon grew within elite circles of the United States. In 1960 the Council on Foreign Relations (COFR), a nonprofit organization whose purpose was undertaking foreign policy studies and recommendations, commissioned a series of confidential reports to investigate Latin American economic integration. The specific purpose of the COFR reports was to deliberate various questions for its select audience, in particular the impact any formal economic coordination in Latin America might have on U.S.–Latin American economic relations. The meetings that COFR conducted were held in the evening at the Harold Pratt house in New York City, and usually lasted four to five hours interrupted only by dinner.[23]

The diverse members of the committee commissioned to study Latin American integration included Spruille Braden, former assistant secretary of state; William F. Butler of Chase Manhattan Bank; W. Rogers Herod, formerly of the International General Electric Company; Albert O. Hirschman of Columbia University; Edward G. Miller, Jr., from the law firm of Paul Weiss, Rifkind, Wharton and Garrison; Albert Post, of the U.S. State Department; Joshua B. Powers; James H. Stebbins of W.R. Grace and Company; Simon D. Strauss of the American Smelting and Refining Company; and the renowned economist Henry C. Wallich of Yale University. The commission was chaired by Stacy May, an economic consultant to the Rockefeller brothers and their extensive business interests in Latin America. The several reports that were issued by COFR were prepared by Walter J. Sedwitz, an economist on leave from the Federal Reserve Bank in New York City, where he served as the acting chief for the Foreign Research Department. Prior to that time he had been an adviser to the Central Bank of El Salvador. Sedwitz proved to be an excellent choice for the position and was uniquely qualified to conduct the studies, having accumulated years of experience working on Latin American economic problems.

In the first report issued for the meeting of December 7, 1960, Sedwitz noted that the incentive of a foreign threat to stimulate the Latin Americans towards implementing a coordinated program was missing; nevertheless, he asserted, Latin American progress towards the goal of achieving economic integration "had been swift and beyond expectations." It was observed that the goal of achieving a common market had "strong historical roots" that were "firmly entrenched in Latin American thinking" and that the process was gaining strong support among "statesmen and intellectuals" in Latin America.[24] Sedwitz noted that the Latin Americans were considering two regional integration zones, LAFTA and CACM. He noted that the former was far more important, embracing two-thirds of the region's population and four-fifths of inter–Latin American trade.[25] The report reiterated the view articulated by Raymond Mikesell that the region did not form a true economic zone. Likewise, Sedwitz emphasized that the Latin American preoccupation with the categorization of countries according to their level of economic development was untenable. The study estimated that LAFTA's policy for dealing with tariff reductions was "unworkable."[26]

Sedwitz was equally distressed about potential U.S.–Latin American economic relations in any impending integration program. He viewed the economic foundations of integration as being too dependent on ECLA analyses, which were criticized for failing to adhere to classical liberal economic policies such as free trade and a totally free domestic market. Disappointment with ECLA doctrine was expressed for two major reasons: first, ECLA was committed to pursuing "import substitution" and, second, it was seeking to maintain protection for various industries (presumably both private and state enterprises). Although, he stated, many of the ECLA proposals were "reasonable," Sedwitz emphasized that a "conflict" between United States and ECLA objectives existed. He was confident that in spite of these differences ECLA doctrine "could be brought into line with U.S. principles of economic and commercial policy." Sedwitz maintained that the situation existed because Washington had remained ambivalent about Latin American affairs, but he remained confident that the trend could be corrected, as the United States had expressed a keener interest in economic integration over the preceding three years. He also pointed out that the United States had made a firm commitment to support the Central American Common Market.

Support for LAFTA, wrote Sedwitz, was conditioned on its acceptance of GATT free trade standards and the level of "discrimination" that member states would utilize. The possibility of compromise between both U.S. and Latin American negotiators was urgently suggested. Sedwitz argued, "Full U.S. approval of Latin American integration objectives might enhance materially ... the prestige and influence" of the United States and its economic interests with respect to any new organizations created in the region. He cautioned that failure to achieve economic growth in Latin America, which could only be achieved via some form of integration, might result in a repetition of the Castroite experience. Sedwitz urged the committee to recognize that economic matters should not be viewed as the sole criteria. Psychological, political and security matters, he warned, were intimately linked to the success of economic expansion and integration.[27]

COFR was particularly interested in the recurring problem of provincialism that had plagued Latin America. Most U.S. observers viewed Latin American integration as a utopian proposition, citing the traditional inability of the Latin Americans to work together. Sedwitz was cognizant of this view, but he insisted that the United States could not afford to ignore any potential members of a new world system, no matter how "weak or nebulous" they might be. He added that the United States needed to support and "promote the movement" so as to "influence" its future.[28]

Among the concerns expressed in the CORF studies under the leadership of Sedwitz was the possibility that Latin America might become "uncommitted" in the Cold War conflict between the Soviets and the United States—a tension so profound that many observers in the United States and the world believed throughout the 1950s and 1960s that the Soviets were actually winning the political, ideological and military struggle between the armed camps. The possibility that Latin America might become neutral in the struggle was mentioned as a likelihood if a successful integration policy were to be enacted.[29] Sedwitz suggested that competing interests in a democratic Latin America and the United States might not coincide in the future. He speculated that there might come a point in time when the Latin Americans might adopt a pro–Soviet or neutralist position, and argued, "There is no direct relation between effective democracy and peaceful international attitudes." According to his report, the dilemma for the United States was that it could not afford to refrain from supporting economic integration because of the dangers that economic stagnation posed to the security of the region. Invoking national and regional security concerns, Sedwitz argued that "the stake in an expansion of income levels in the developing countries has outweighed competitive considerations."

Sedwitz was adamant in his belief that Washington was firmly committed to the propagation of free trade in the strongest traditions of economic liberalism. The United States, he maintained, had "never entertained any strong fears" that the industrialization of Third World states would adversely affect the economic position of the United States. He acknowledged that some industries might be negatively affected, "but these considerations have always been outweighed by the conviction that the over-all trading position of the United States would benefit from the growth of manufacturing abroad since the industrialized countries are, after all, each other's best customers." This expanded industrialization around the world would be a benefit to the United States by creating demands for further cooperation with the United States.[30]

Stacy May, chairman of the committee, articulated the position of the group regarding the objectives of U.S. policy as being motivated by "the desirability of freeing world trade and reducing international barriers and equality of treatment and non-discrimination." Of even more significance, May noted that GATT free trade policies permitted "such discrimination if it is a step toward complete liberalization of trade" within free trade areas or customs unions, and "if the barriers erected" to protect the new organizations were "not higher than the average of the former national barriers."[31] May cited the European Common Market as an example of an integration program that had been allowed to maintain protectionist ties with its former colonies, especially in Africa, which was considered an economic threat to Latin American commodities traditionally shipped to Europe or the U.S.A. He asserted that U.S. support for "regional accords" in Latin America would thus constitute no larger violation of GATT than that of integrated Europe.[32]

Other matters also came to the attention of committee members. Edward G. Miller, Jr., added that for any regional accord to be successful it was imperative for Washington to provide its fullest support.[33] Spruille Braden, famous for his verbal-political duel with Argentine president Juan Perón, suggested that if a viable customs union were to be implemented it would have to create a "sound currency as a foundation." Braden claimed that this required "a currency redeemable in gold," otherwise the effort would prove unproductive. William May argued that in any integration project, Latin Americans would be forced to endure the strictest financial discipline possible in order to control inflation. Sedwitz asserted that the establishment of a common market might provide the impetus for creating "financial discipline" and "sounder currency practices." Joshua B. Powers rejoined that the difficulty of pursuing financial discipline would be a difficult objective because Latin America could not "control the factors that control its well being." He blamed what he perceived to be the political egotism of the Latin American governments for the predicament in which Latin America found itself. Sedwitz agreed but emphasized that a "political rapprochement" was possible.[34]

The tax structure of the region was also examined for its impact on the integration process. Alfred Neal of the Committee for Economic Development stated that the Brazilian tax system indicated "that country does not have a free trade area within its own boundary," leading to an assessment by Mr. May that the Latin American tax structures were "foolish ... if judged by the requirements of development." Henry C. Wallich suggested that the United States needed to treat LAFTA as one tax zone because it was difficult for the U.S. government to tax U.S. corporations doing business in Latin America. Roy Blough of Columbia University cited the perennial problem of money transfers from Brazil to Argentina as an example of a practice he claimed was "violently abused by U.S. business."[35]

James H. Stebbins inquired if the initiative for integration originated with the Latin American government or with private individuals. No answer was apparently afforded Stebbins, and it appears from the documentation that no effort was made to provide him with that information. Simon D. Strauss commented that even if the Latin Americans signed an integration treaty, there was always the problem of whether or not they intended to comply with the agreement.[36]

W. Rogers Herod questioned the sincerity of the Latin Americans concerning the creation of a common market, which required the free flow of labor and capital. Was Latin America ready for this? He assumed Latin Americans would not readily adjust to the realities of such a change in lifestyle, any more than the residents of New Orleans were ready for racial integration in their own city. Likewise, Herod argued that his former employer, International General Electric, assumed "that the advantages of economic union have been overrated." He claimed that most businessmen ignored it and were totally unaffected by it. Herod stated that in a serious economic crisis the Latin Americans would simply refuse to implement any treaty provisions that inconvenienced them.

Albert Post from the State Department suggested that the success of Latin American integration depended solely on the Latin Americans themselves, irrespective of U.S. support, which he felt was not a critical factor in the matter. It was problematic whether any form of integration could compete with the prevailing nationalisms that he blamed on university professors and students.[37]

Murray Ryss astutely observed that the Latin American integration movement lacked a "dynamic personality" to lead it, as did the European Common Market. He was particularly inspired by the role of Konrad Adenauer and his efforts to promote integration in Europe. On the other hand, William Butler of the Chase Manhattan Bank was not so concerned with integration per se. He preferred to consider free trade rather than economic integration to be the primary goal of U.S. foreign policy in the region. Roy Blough of Columbia University felt that some members of the commission were being too hard on the Latin Americans. He asserted they were being reasonable and that the Treaty of Montevideo, which created LAFTA, was a flexible document that would enable the region to deal with the problems that might arise. He did express surprise at Herod's comments that economic integration did not enjoy greater support from the Latin American business community. William Diebold, a permanent staff researcher with COFR who had engaged in pioneering studies on European economic integration for the organization, suggested that business opposition to Latin American economic union was to be expected, but it should not be considered a deterrent to success. He recalled that Europe had also faced the same problem, but proceeded anyway with the 1957 Treaty of Rome, which created the European Common Market. COFR members noted that regionalism was "advancing" throughout the area, a fact that the committee appears to have lamented.[38] Sedwitz maintained that if Latin America did achieve integration, the accumulated gains could not be parceled out equally to each state, but he added the poorer states would nevertheless benefit. He claimed that if integration were to be achieved, the region would enjoy an "epidemic" of economic expansion.[39]

The COFR study also gave considerable attention to the Central American Common Market (CACM), which was viewed as an organization whose implementation would serve to eradicate the "physical and institution impediments" that had preceded its formation. It was noted that the Central America of 1961 constituted a region that was "little more than an agglomeration of small communities and population clusters" and that the individual Central American states were not fully integrated units.[40] It was hoped that the perennial problem of exaggerated nationalism that historically plagued the region had been surpassed. This obstacle was portrayed as a "negative and is expressed in mistrust and petty jealousies ... rather than in terms of positive national destiny," although it was suggested that the long history of promoting integration in that area augured well for CACM.[41]

The COFR committee also discussed the creation of the Regime for Central American Integration Industries, a technocratic arm of CACM designed to promote equity among the various states through economic planning that would involve determining where industries would be located. This policy was viewed by COFR as promoting rancor and corruption because it gave the governments too much discretion in the economy by fostering discriminatory and arbitrary actions towards the business community, thus providing an opportunity to stifle competition, a situation considered unacceptable and untenable by advocates of competitive market policies.[42]

COFR also discussed the impact that the Pan-American Highway had on trade among CACM members. It was noted that as of 1961, no provisions had been made for assigning maintenance of the road and no plans had been articulated for the creation of ancillary highways.[43]

The COFR committee members expressed some alarm at what they viewed as the "drift toward the formation of impure regional blocs" in the global economy, specifically the appearance of discriminatory practices that had been implemented against other regions. It was feared that such discrimination might create serious problems if it went unchecked, although no one was able to suggest a policy on how to end the situation. Examples of such regional trade blocs abounded. There was the British Commonwealth, the Soviet Bloc trade zone (COMECON), the Benelux states, the European Economic Community (EEC) and the European Free Trade Association.

The two latter organizations had provided special trading privileges to their ex-colonies. These trading preferences ensured price stability for the export and import of foodstuffs and raw resources from the Third World (especially Africa) into Europe. As a result of these trading blocs and the preferential treatment accorded to their members, Latin America had "been pushed further to the periphery of world trade." It was estimated that in the period from 1928 to 1958, the Latin American percentage of world exports had fallen from eleven percent to eight percent. It was feared that if Latin American exports continued to shrink, the region's stability would be imperiled, thus presenting a security risk for the entire hemisphere. U.S. economic interests dictated that the Latin Americans find a viable market for their products created by U.S. capital and using Latin American employees. The many mines, natural resources and agricultural products of Latin America depended on U.S. distribution or transportation systems. Although it was impossible to determine to what extent, if any, damage had been done to the Latin American economy by the EEC, it was clearly indicated that the economy of the region needed some form of protection if the hemisphere were to advance.[44]

The COFR committee's concluding analyses of Latin American economic integration issued on December 12, 1961, stated that CACM actually had greater potential to "establish the basis for a genuine common market." The outlook for LAFTA was not as positive. LAFTA was intended as an association to be utilized solely for economic development. "It is not, nor is it meant to be, an instrument for creating a common market, within which ... certain aspects of economic policy are fully synchronized or unified," wrote Sedwitz.[45]

Sedwitz also had harsh criticisms of U.S. policy with respect to economic integration. He accused Washington of following a double standard with respect to Europe and Latin America. On the one hand, the United States supported discriminatory European trading practices in granting preferential trading concessions to Europe's ex-colonies, yet on the other hand the U.S. inflexibly demanded a free trade policy be implemented by the Latin Americans. Sedwitz surmised that this inconsistency existed because the United States had articulated a clear policy for Europe "which permitted the reconciliation of commercial policy consideration with political expediency." On the other hand, Washington's policy in Latin America had developed as a "commercial policy and little more." The Cold War had changed the world and the region. According to Sedwitz the region "had become an element in the cold war" as of 1959. A new world demanded new, bold and realistic policies. In other words, strategic matters demanded consideration of political, economic and social factors. In order to satisfactorily deal with these pressing issues, Sedwitz recommended that the United States cease its inflexible efforts to apply GATT free trade provisions on Latin America, since their implementation was impractical due to the low level of economic development; the region could not be "judged by the same criteria as those applied to more developed countries." He urged Washington to provide full political and moral support for the economic integration of Latin America and argued that a more energetic promotion was needed to stimulate economic growth and badly needed industrialization. Such efforts could "possibly divert anti–Americanism and discourage subversion."

Sedwitz concluded by providing two major recommendations for U.S. policy makers should they wish to further the integration process: first, that American directors appointed to regional lending organizations that financed economic development be instructed by Washington to promote projects that would stimulate economic integration, and second, that the Organization of American States should take a stronger role in promoting economic integration. These goals, he argued, should be seen by the United States as "basic criteria on which national development plans are to be judged." According to Sedwitz, the OAS needed to play a bigger role in such issues as taxation and land reform, two very sensitive issues in Latin America.[46] Though Sedwitz appears to have enjoyed wide support from his committee peers, there is no evidence that his suggestions were ever seriously considered by U.S. government policy makers or their counterparts in Latin America.

Another private study was begun in 1961 by the Committee for Economic Development (CED), an organization whose elite membership consisted of over two hundred businessmen and academics. CED published its own assessment of Latin America's economic condition after two years of research. Some of the members also had served on the Council of Foreign Relations. Indeed, several Latin Americans who testified during the 1960–61 COFR research study appeared before the CED committee. The CED report did not elaborate any new policies or recommendations that had not been made before, but it is significant in that it strongly advocated U.S. support for Latin American economic integration via the various organizations "on a fair and economic basis" in order to create viable and more competitive markets for the region.[47]

The CED report argued that the economic development of Latin America was vital if leftist insurgencies were to be stifled. Economic integration could serve to reach that objective. The CED committee reiterated concerns previously published in a 1957 document about the worldwide threat posed by communism to the United States via political ideologues actively seeking support among the poverty-stricken masses:

> In the short run it is all too good a possibility that more than one underdeveloped country will embrace communism in the hope of finding a short cut through the difficulties and frustrations of modernizing a backward society. While communism cannot hope to gain its ends in the underdeveloped world by overt military aggression without bringing on World War III, it can hope to triumph by political means if its false promises and panaceas are believed by enough people.[48]

Prior to Castro's Cuba, the security problem posed by militant Marxist states appeared "remote, and the chain of events by which we might be affected long and speculative." By 1961, however, when a communist government allied with the Soviet Union appeared off the coast of the United States only ninety miles away in Cuba, the region was immediately put under intense surveillance by American intelligence agencies. Eventually the dreaded news was brought to the White House that offensive missile systems capable of delivering nuclear warheads to almost anywhere in the United States had been installed by the Soviet military. In addition to the military threat, the Castro government was denounced by the CED report as a system that destroyed basic human rights, promoted "civil war, drives out talent and frightens away capital."[49]

The CED report noted that it had called for action as far back as 1957, when it articulated the view that the allure of communism for Third World peoples was a genuine threat, meriting constant vigilance. It could only be precluded by actively promoting Third World social and economic advancement. The report repeated its prior statement that sounded an urgent warning that the world was at an important crossroads from which there might not be any return:

It has become clear that this demand of the underdeveloped areas for a better way of life is one of the most important facts of present world conditions, and that its importance will grow. It is a demand strong enough to shape world history in desirable or undesirable ways, because the efforts of leaders in underdeveloped countries to bring about economic progress can take the way of peaceful development and growing freedom, or can lead, through frustration, to violence, communist subversion or other forms of regimentation.[50]

The CED report concluded its position on economic integration by supporting remedies offered by earlier studies. It gave full support to both CACM and LAFTA and urged Washington to foster elimination of internal Latin American trade barriers and allow economic protection to industries by their home governments or those regional trade organizations that had the potential of becoming efficient economic entities. It cautioned that although integration would probably prove advantageous to Latin America, it could also turn counterproductive. The report speculated that the Latin Americans might limit competition from foreign capital, resulting in a new economy that would be "self-sufficient but inefficient." Although this was a genuine possibility it was "by no means necessary." The analysis argued that the final outcome depended solely on Latin American initiatives.[51]

Examination by the U.S. Executive and Legislature

By 1963 the economic integration of Latin America had become so important an issue for U.S. policy makers that the Central Intelligence Agency was called upon to issue an assessment. The CIA reported that integration was being propagated as a mechanism for the prestige and influence of Latin America all over the world. The effort had spurred the "imagination of politicians, businessmen and economists" consumed with integration efforts so that LAFTA could become a "vital force for extending Latin American influence in world councils." Noting that LAFTA was founded to take advantage of the economic rationalization available "on the American scale," the CIA maintained its primary goal was the proliferation of increased trade between the Latin American states instead of further industrialization. This was an erroneous conclusion, since ECLA and LAFTA officials had repeatedly emphasized the need for additional industrialization.[52]

LAFTA was also criticized by the CIA for not taking sufficient measures "towards completing the customs union." In addition, it was observed that tariffs continued to exist against the imports of other Latin American states.

The major problem was the propensity of individual republics to continue the practice of negotiating "item per item," thus endangering LAFTA's success. Only Mexico had made any promising economic progress which might be attributed to LAFTA, according to CIA analysts.[53] As for the political implication of U.S.–Latin American relations, the study noted that Washington was publicly "on record" as supporting economic integration. The report further noted that if LAFTA were to succeed, the United States would probably lose a measure of its political and economic leverage in the area. It cited as an example the Mexican efforts to push forth a proposal "keeping ownership of new industries in the hands of member states." The study asserted that this feeling was extensive throughout the area and that it "reflects a widespread chauvinism" that viewed LAFTA "as a potentially strong bargainer against the U.S., the EEC, and other continental systems." Likewise, it noted that in spite of such views, that U.S. trade with the region would increase, as would intra-regional trade if LAFTA succeeded.[54] The CIA study concluded that the objectives of LAFTA were an "aspiration" rather than a "record of achievement." Its strength was solely in its potential, which was seen as unlimited if the member states focused on LAFTA's goal. The attractive benefits of economic integration were so strong, according to the CIA, that eventually Panama would join CACM, which in turn would inevitably join LAFTA.[55]

By early 1965 the executive branch of the United States government, which is solely responsible for the implementation of foreign policy, began taking a more visible public position on integration. In April 1965, President Johnson addressed a large number of Latin American ambassadors accredited to the United States on the anniversary of the Alliance for Progress. At the conference, Johnson stated: "We should support the closer unification of the Latin American economies. The experience of Central America reaffirms the experience of Europe." He added that the advantages of such a Latin American regional organization required "enlarging markets and the elimination of tariff barriers," which he asserted would "be conducive to the increase of commerce and more efficient production, and as such to a greater prosperity."[56] In August 1965, Johnson went on to suggest the creation of a sectoral program similar to the European Coal and Steel Community for Latin America. It was proposed that such a program revolve around chemical and agricultural products, though his idea never came to fruition.[57]

By 1965 other members of the American elite who were involved with political and economic issues began to publicly support Latin American integration as a step toward fostering a larger Western Hemispheric free-trade zone. Senator Jacob Javits of New York had long been interested in Latin American economic progress. On April 5, 1965, the senator spoke before the American

Chamber of Commerce in Mexico at the University Club in Mexico City, expressing his full support for the economic integration of Latin America as a positive step for the region.[58]

Javits was intrigued by the dynamic possibilities integration offered Latin America at a very difficult time in its history and worked diligently to help attain that goal. It was a theme that absorbed his ceaseless energy.[59] He was the founder of the Atlantic Community Development Group for Latin America (ADELA), which was established at the 1961 Parliamentarian's Conference of the North Atlantic Treaty Organization. The purpose of the organization was to be the promotion of economic integration via investment in development projects. Javits believed that regional integration for Latin America had reached a high level of reality, and assistance was needed to facilitate its final goal. ADELA was a "multinational investment company" composed of over 140 banks and industrial firms from the First World states.[60] In spite of the influence of these corporations, the organization floundered because Javits could not find a suitable chairman to provide leadership.[61]

Javits suggested that if the Latin American Common Market could be implemented, further arrangements with the European Economic Community could be established as a basis for promoting free trade. He firmly subscribed to the classical doctrine that free trade fosters international cooperation. This doctrine was to be the foundation of American support for European and Latin American integration, although the United States would insist on its utilization by Latin America much more than with Europe. Javits asserted that if economic integration were to succeed, it would require the Latin American states to "improve the climate for private initiative, while at the same time providing for social justice." He stressed that that these two goals were not incompatible. These objectives were fully in line with the goals of Raúl Prebisch of the ECLA and the many other supporters of Latin American integration. Javits was realistic and astute enough to point out that these objectives would be difficult to achieve. He stated, "We must realize that Latin America would be trying to achieve in a decade what we in the United States, after a century of trying, have not perfected—the operation of private business in the public interests."[62]

By September 1965, interest in the economic integration of Latin America came under intense scrutiny from the legislative branch of the U.S. government. A joint subcommittee of the Senate and the House of Representatives was convened to deal with issues related to economic integration in Latin America and their relationship to the United States. Formally known as the Subcommittee on Inter-American Economic Relationships of the Joint Economic Committee, it was chaired by Senator John Sparkman and began its three-day hearings on September 8, 1965. Its members demonstrated a keen grasp of the many complex issues involved in economic integration. Senator Javits became a key figure in the hearings, and in fact guided the hearings. He applauded President Johnson's commitment to support integration and offered the president his support. In response to criticisms and concerns regarding a Latin American Common market, Javits asserted that unless economic integration was implemented the economic development of the region would be stymied. He recognized that Latin America's bargaining leverage would be enhanced with Europe and the United States but did not view this as negative, rather as positive. The objectives of free competition and economic development would both be advanced via this organization.[63]

The subcommittee interviewed numerous experts in order to assess new trends for the region. Dr. Isaiah Frank, a professor of international economic relations at Johns Hopkins University, adamantly supported integration as a means of achieving free trade on a worldwide basis through economic coordination based on geography. Frank argued, "Ultimately the goal should be a customs union that would exclude only the moon."[64] He was frustrated by the slow pace of LAFTA negotiations and cited several reasons for this: misunderstandings among the Latin Americans, a lack of political will to form a genuine common market, and opposition from vested interests. Frank correctly pointed out that the integration process had been deliberately slowed by the Latin Americans. This was "not a reflection of the ignorance of the drafters ... nor do the numerous escape clauses reflect a lack of understanding as to the importance for successful integration." Frank questioned the sincerity of Latin American and U.S. leaders who claimed to support integration. "I doubt the value of ringing statements from political leaders in Latin America, or, indeed, the United States, exhorting the members of LAFTA to remedy deficiencies of the [Montevideo] treaty." Third World integration, he argued, was simply a more complex undertaking than the European experience because of widely divergent historical conditions.[65]

Dr. Joseph Grunwald, the director of the Brookings Institute for Economic and Social Development Studies, expressed his encouragement for the integration process in Latin America. He argued that the "U.S. common market has been the greatest success story in history." It was an example of dynamic possibilities such a union would hold for the Latin American people. He believed that "long run benefits can enormously outweigh short run losses." Most importantly, he argued that economic integration would lead to political unification.[66]

Concern about competing national ambitions was expressed because this might impede the integration process, especially the chronic rivalry between

Argentina and Brazil. Both countries imported substantial arms. These purchases included expensive naval hardware for the purpose of protecting and or destroying each other's commerce, a far cry from the traditional task of the Latin American military, which was to act as a national guard in times of crisis.[67] Indeed, as far back as 1960, State Department cables indicated that support for economic integration was being stifled by the perennial arms race between these two countries. Congressman Henry S. Reuss cited this nationalism as a continuing problem in the region and worried that it might be "transferred" if the new regional organization (LAFTA) grew in power, with the danger that it might lead to the adoption of autarkic policies.[68]

Emilio G. Collado, vice president and director of the Standard Oil Co. (New Jersey), spoke to the committee as an unofficial representative of America's multinational corporations. He expressed the almost obligatory statement that he favored economic integration but argued that the United States needed to proceed with caution. For Collado economic integration could be "either destructive or constructive depending on its orientation and implementation." He feared U.S. business interests might be subjected to discrimination in any new scheme. Collado argued that the only foundation for economic growth was free trade. Restraints and irrational demands on the market, according to Collado, had led the Central American and Caribbean states to operate oil refineries within their borders in order to "support expensive monuments to national pride" in spite of CACM's existence. The United States, he cautioned, needed to carefully monitor the individuals responsible for developing integration proposals in order to prevent discrimination against American economic interests. These concerns were not surprising, since his corporation had been nationalized by Peronist Argentina and Revolutionary Mexico during the 1930s.[69]

The subcommittee also sought the advice and guidance of George S. Moore, one of the most important figures in corporate America, who was uniquely qualified to explain matters affecting economic integration. Moore was president of the First National Bank of New York, which had more branch offices in Latin America than any other bank, and his involvement with Latin American banking spanned thirty years. He possessed the additional credential of being the president of the Inter-American Council of Commerce and Production, an organization described by Senator Javits as the "equivalent of our U.S. Chamber of Commerce for Latin America."[70] Moore was as familiar with the economic realities of the region as he was with the problems of various industries represented by domestic and foreign interests. Moore was much more confident than Collado regarding the impact integration would have but reiterated that the ultimate objective of U.S. foreign policy must be to

support free trade and pro-markets policies.[71] He observed that the consequences of Latin America's fragmentation had been catastrophic. "Centuries
of mistrust and national political rivalries and conflicts have impeded political
stability, retarded the development of managerial and administrative compe-
tence and weakened confidence in the security of person, savings, and investments," said Moore.[72]

According to Moore, one of the practical problems facing Latin American
businessmen in the 1960s was the "scarcity of marketing information" resulting
from the region's compartmentalization. He blamed the lack of political will
to forge ahead with LAFTA's objectives as the source of all that organization's
problems, and he noted, "Economists, the political leaders, and the businessman share the responsibility for formulating the ideas, making the decisions
and implementing the policies that will ultimately bring economic integration."
Moore argued that the future of LAFTA depended on its success in promoting
trade among the Latin American states. He urged businessmen to put continuous pressure on political leaders in an effort to advance integration and called
for the ideological acceptance of free-market competition in order to achieve
the objectives of LAFTA.[73] Moore observed that if the business community
failed to promote that goal, it was not due to a lack of influence. The bourgeoisie was now sufficiently strong that its interests had to be taken into
account.[74] Moore credited CACM with improving the economic position of
the Central American states and was encouraged that it had "initiated contacts"
with LAFTA in the hope that the two organizations would eventually unite.
He called for the establishment of a council of ministers for LAFTA that
would be empowered to deal with complicated trade issues.[75] Moore also urged
the United States to provide "patient, sympathetic interest" for the integration
process, but he cautioned that LAFTA needed to quickly move forward on
its pledge to relieve tariff barriers and thus "provide the proper environment
for private enterprise."[76]

Moore was explicit in his opposition to any integration scheme that
would implement high tariff barriers against any outside parties. He was referring, of course, to the United States. He emphasized, "We must urge that this
instrumentality not be discriminatory against anyone."[77] Moore's concerns
were quintessentially those of economic liberals. He represented a U.S. business
community that sought further expansion of its capital markets within Latin
America by attempting to create a new economic system in the region that
would primarily be more efficient for the movement of capital throughout
Latin America. Moore stressed that U.S. goals vis-à-vis Latin American integration were based solely on amicable intentions. He pointed to the U.S. relationship with the European Economic Community, to which the United States

had provided substantial moral and political support. "I think the whole world has had enough evidence of our post-war European progress to accept the good intention of this country [the U.S.] in Latin America. I think the deliberations of your committee, and we in private industry, want to contribute all we can," said Moore.[78]

Felipe Herrera, president of the Inter-American Development Bank and the only Latin American to address the committee, stated that economic development was the impetus and rationale for integration rather than any "historical-cultural background of the Latin American nations," although he admitted it was a useful conduit. The ECLA rationale was reiterated: the region's industries needed expanded production of goods and more capital. Competition and efficiency were necessary to correct the contemporary trade system. This was to be achieved by integration, which Herrera claimed was being discussed by all segments of Latin American society.[79] He claimed that "disintegrated Latin America" was simply incapable of absorbing "benefits from modern technologies." Likewise, the pursuit of economic development per se was not enough to remedy the region's maladies "unless Latin America organizes itself as a creative community, brought together by a common cultural heritage and definite political historical objectives." He attributed the present condition of Latin America to its "hesitancy or refusal" to support economic union. Although the region had previously lacked the conditions necessary for achieving integration, "the moment had been reached for fashioning the institutions required" to foment a genuinely integrated Latin America.[80]

At the request of the Johnson administration, Jack Hood Vaughn, the under secretary of state for Inter-American Affairs, and U.S. coordinator for the Alliance for Progress, appeared before the Joint Congressional Subcommittee on Inter-American Affairs. Vaughn had previously served as Washington's ambassador to Panama and as regional director of Latin American Programs for the Peace Corps. He asserted that the United States fully supported the economic integration of Latin America. As an example Vaughn cited the speech given by Vice President Hubert H. Humphrey in April 1965 during ceremonies held to commemorate Pan-American Week. The following month the U.S. delegation posted to the United Nations Economic Commission for Latin America called for expanded "economic cooperation" as soon as possible.[81] According to Vaughn, the ultimate objective of economic union was the "integration of societies and economies.... The objective is to bring all the people of Latin America within their societies, so that they will actively participate in the civic, social, economic, and political affairs of their countries."[82] He cited the U.S. government's commitment to the Central America Common market (CACM), for which Washington had provided sixty million dollars in aid for a variety of regional projects that would come under the jurisdiction of CACM. He asserted that CACM and its success offered positive prospects for further amplification of the integration process throughout the rest of Latin America.[83]

Vaughn emphasized that the United States actively sought the integration of Latin America. He assured the subcommittee that the United States was actively pursuing integration as one of its major foreign policy objectives. In his testimony, Vaughn sought to identify the interests of the Latin American states with those of the United States, arguing that they were mutual. He stressed that the United States was seeking the elimination of tariff barriers as a means of spurring the industrialization of Latin America. With respect to the multitude of external tariffs, he stated: "It is this barrier to more advanced industrialization that we, along with many Latin Americans, hope to see broken down through the removal of the import barriers which now surround the limited national markets." With the elimination of external tariffs, the Latin American states would in one stroke "select optimum locations and produce quality goods for sale at competitive prices," and this would be followed by the establishment of a corresponding infrastructure and the creation of ancillary industries.[84]

Vaughn expressed the belief that eventually a new shift in relations between the United States and Latin America would occur as the result of changing trade patterns. While his comments were general and restricted to the macroeconomic rather than the specific, he informed the committee that the nature of this traditional economic character would include the disappearance of traditional U.S. exports, as Latin America could produce those goods with increased economies of scale. Nevertheless Vaughn acknowledged that the United States had ulterior motives in supporting Latin American economic integration, explaining that these motives were to increase the export of U.S. products to the region. He observed that in this changing trade pattern, Latin Americans would be able to purchase more U.S. goods.[85]

Vaughn also articulated other goals that the Johnson administration sought to achieve; namely, the alleviation of some of the more appalling economic and social problems affecting the region such as malnutrition, housing shortages, illiteracy, inadequate medical facilities and widespread poverty. He maintained that the Johnson administration considered economic integration the first step towards the realistic alleviation of these problems. "We in the executive are convinced that this integration is one of those changes which must take place if the growing aspirations of the Latin American peoples for vastly improved economic and social conditions are to be satisfactorily met," said Vaughn.[86]

Vaughn addressed the recurring problem of changing political systems in Latin America which frequently alternated between democratic states and authoritarian governments based on the power of the military. The specter of having to deal with a potential proliferation of Marxist states such as Cuba was of major concern to the administration. He reiterated the view that the integration process could strengthen the democratic political systems then in existence in Latin America. Likewise it was asserted that the political vitality of democracies was dependent on their economic strength and that this economic health could best be achieved via economic integration:

> This is why the United States has so often and so clearly expressed its support for economic integration in Latin America; nor have we only paid lip service to the principle while remaining otherwise aloof or hostile toward efforts to accomplish this admittedly difficult task.[87]

Vaughn expressed concern about leftist activities that had plagued the area and acknowledged that unless the region sustained sufficient economic growth the area would be consumed in a sea of revolutionary flames. During the exchange between Vaughn and Javits at the subcommittee meeting, the senator expressed deep concern about this possibility and inquired about the significance of recent visits to Moscow by Latin American politicians. He dismissed the trips as efforts to secure additional trade agreements.[88] He pointed to the U.S. commitment of sixty million dollars to the five members of CACM as proof of U.S. solidarity with the integration process.

The Punta del Este Summit

By 1966, some Latin Americans had become concerned that the integration process had become stalled. It was decided that LAFTA needed a further impetus from Latin America's heads of state. In 1966 a call was issued for the presidents of the various countries of the region to meet in Punta del Este, Uruguay, for a discussion on how to accelerate economic integration and to determine what goals should be attempted. The president of the United States, Lyndon Baines Johnson, was duly invited with the expectation that Washington might provide some leadership that the other states might follow. As a prelude to the meeting, President Johnson held a party for Latin American ambassadors at his ranch in Texas, which he described as a "family affair." One White House official dubbed the proposed summit as the "conference of the decade." It was hoped by Johnson and the Latin Americans that the United States would make a decision to provide additional financial aid to help facilitate the integration agenda through the Alliance for Progress. This money was not explicitly for integration per se but was referred to as an economic assistance program. President Johnson asked Congress on March 13, 1967, for 1.5 billion dollars in aid to be distributed via the organs of the Alliance. The money was to be parceled out over a five-year period, but Congress, led by Johnson's erstwhile opponent Senator J. William Fulbright (Democrat-Arkansas), whom Johnson despised, successfully led a campaign against the bill in the Senate Foreign Relations Committee, which voted 9–0 against the proposal, effectively dismantling it. The bill that passed in its place claimed it would provide "due consideration to cooperation in such agreements." Johnson was so aggravated by the vote that his special assistant for national security affairs, Walter W. Rostow, told a group of reporters that the new endorsement articulated by Fulbright was described by the president as "worse than useless." It was a quote that received widespread publicity so as to ensure Johnson's displeasure would make the public headlines.[89]

Behind the scenes, Fulbright supporters claimed that opposition to the appropriations bill was an effort to force President Johnson to actively consult with Congress. In reality, the bill failed because it lacked an internal constituency in the United States. What legislator would support such a bill without a multitude of proactive supporters campaigning on its behalf? It was not an issue that was given much attention by the press. Only a few academics had shown any interest in the matter. It did not generate excitement on college campuses, nor amongst the general public. This was largely because the media paid scarcely any attention to the issue until only a few days before the conference. In retrospect, it is not surprising that the funds were denied, since it was well known that the various Ibero-American governments had difficulty in agreeing on a meaningful strategy for integration.

For his part, Johnson had fulfilled a promise to support integration, but he did not seriously believe economic integration would develop any further than LAFTA's 1967 condition, nor did he express enthusiasm for the project to his advisers. Indeed, while en route to Punta del Este, Johnson complained to his retinue: "What the hell are we going down here for?"[90] It was clear from the beginning that the United States would stress policies at the Punta del Este conference that had been previously articulated by COFR, CED, and the 1965 congressional hearings, which stressed the need for initiatives to originate from the Latin Americans in fomenting economic integration and accelerating economic development. Sol Linowitz, the U.S. ambassador to the Organization of American States and a high ranking official of the U.S. delegation to the summit, stated that U.S. policy at the conference was to let the Latin Americans work out their own problems "for Latin Americans in the Latin American way."[91] To emphasize the point, Washington officialdom asserted that President Johnson had attempted to keep a low profile at the conference, where he repeatedly stressed that any initiatives for economic integration or economic development would have to come solely from Latin America, although the United States would be willing to stand by with political support and economic assistance, provided of course that Congress felt the same sense of urgency. Nonetheless, U.S. government officials wrote that a recurring problem at the summit meeting was the widespread assumption that initiatives were coming from the United States, ideas that Johnson and his government did not wish to perpetuate. Though this may have been a U.S. objective, it was perhaps not a realistic one considering the overwhelming influence of the United States, which had historically seated and unseated governments in Latin America, especially in the circum–Caribbean area.[92]

In spite of his reluctance to attend the summit meeting, Johnson had sought advice from some of the foremost experts on the region who possessed practical experience with the everyday workings of the area, such as David Rockefeller, Lincoln Gordon, Douglas Dillon, Father Hesburgh of Notre Dame University, and Adolf Berle. The president also consulted every agency of the United States government that was involved with Latin America. Johnson reviewed as many briefings and reports as he could from the State Department, overseas U.S. embassies, AID directors, the U.S.–based Council for Latin America, businessmen, trade union representatives and academia.[93] Washington's expectations were shared by Secretary of State Dean Rusk, who said, "The achievement of a Latin American Common Market would make possible a more rapid rate of economic growth and would thereby contribute to the social and political stability of the hemisphere."[94]

When Johnson's plane landed at the Carrasco Airport in Montevideo, Uruguay, he stepped into the flaming cauldron of a leftist insurgency that was plaguing the country. This movement was undertaken by the Tupamaros, who were young, upper-middle-class, urban guerrillas. The intensity and unpredictability of the Tupamaros forced the cancellation of the motorcade that would have taken LBJ through Montevideo. He was instead whisked away to Punta del Este, ninety miles away via helicopter, where security was so heavy that only the residents were allowed to enter the city.[95] Security and administrative details concerning the meeting were handled by the Organization of American States, the government of Uruguay, and U.S. security personnel. When the conference opened on April 12, 1967, the attending presidents gave ten-minute speeches in which "no surprises" were heard. On April 13, 1967, Johnson addressed the assembly of dignitaries pledging Washington's support "to the growing unity of our hemisphere." He stressed the importance of integration and economic development, which would ultimately affect the lives of millions of unborn citizens of the region:

We no longer inhabit a new world. We cannot escape our problems as the first Americans could, in the vastness of an uncharted hemisphere.... If our rhetoric is not followed by action, we shall fail not only the Americans of this generation but hundreds of millions to come. In unity, and only in unity, is our strength. The barriers that deny the dream of a new America are stronger than the strongest among us acting alone, but they cannot stand against our combined will and our common effort.[96]

Johnson added that if the process of economic integration continued, he would ask Congress to appropriate financial aid that would "ease the transition to an integrated regional economy." He also encouraged the Latin Americans to continue with the construction of physical projects that would serve to strengthen the bonds between the various states.[97]

Meanwhile, in a private session held the same day, Ecuadorian president Otto Arosemena stated he would not sign the Declaration of the Presidents. He claimed the entire meeting was "prefabricated." He was in fact, the only president who refused to sign the document. President Gustavo Díaz Ordaz of Mexico attempted to convince the Ecuadorian that a compromise agreement was required to propel Latin American interests forward and that it was impossible to produce a totally satisfactory document. Other Latin American presidents also sought to convince Arosemena to change his mind, but he remained unconvinced.[98] The U.S. government responded by characterizing the decision by the Ecuadorian government to criticize the Alliance for Progress and the Johnson government as "aggressive and negative."[99]

The U.S. press was well briefed by Washington officialdom as to what was expected at the conference, and echoed the same skepticism that emanated from their government, as if on cue. The summit was described as "jinxed from the start" due to nationalist concerns and the common belief in Latin America that each country could become self sufficient. The conference was also labeled as "one of the most productive experiments in the history of international summitry" because of its potential.[100]

The U.S. State Department eventually judged the summit meeting a success, though it noted that implementation of the recommendations needed to be undertaken. A report issued in mid–1967 claimed that the presidents had maintained favorable personal relationships and that important "decisions were reached with a maximum of involvement of all governments."[101] According to the State Department, U.S. foreign policy goals in Latin America were fourfold:

(1) Avoidance of Latin American recourse to extremes in terms of communism, nationalism or Latin American regional exclusivity.

(2) Strengthening of U.S.–Latin American political relationships.

(3) Maintenance of mutually advantageous economic relationships with Latin America.

(4) Evolutionary economic, social and political progress in Latin America, leading toward more cohesive societies; more stable, responsible and democratic governments; and stronger nations.[102]

The State Department viewed Latin American interests as being parallel with those of the United States. These interests were identified as increased political representation for all segments of the population; the protection of "cultural and national identities"; expanding economic and social opportunities; and increase in trade on a global scale.[103] It was stressed that the United States needed to continuously monitor the situation in support of its economic interests especially with regards to any potential common market. At the same time the State Department cautioned that any activity that took place within the confines of the Organization of America States could not expect confidentiality regarding its activities. The report stated that several pieces of sensitive material had been leaked "almost as soon as it was introduced" within the OAS, a clear warning that any sensitive communications regarding U.S. policy on integration or any other matter would have to be cleared with Washington, or risk the chance of exposure.[104]

After the conference U.S. envoy Sol Linowitz sought to enlist support for Latin American economic integration in an address he made to a convention of American businessmen, although he was cautious about making any assessments about the outcome of the conference. He nevertheless repeated that any initiatives for a Latin American Common Market would have to come exclusively from the region. He emphasized the sense of danger that was acutely shared by many people in 1967 concerning the future of Ibero-America, which he feared contained the seeds of a tinderbox. The ambassador urged American business to consider the "needs of the people" as a step toward creating amicable relations, and he implored his audience to imagine the almost unlimited economic opportunities of efficiency and expansion that would arise from economic integration, particularly the airlines, railroads and steamship companies that might benefit tremendously by joint ventures (presumably with the U.S. multinationals) as a result of new forms of organization. Such steps, he argued, would bring mankind closer together.[105]

Although Senator Javits did not attend the Punta del Este summit (the conference was reserved for the U.S. executive), he was working feverishly behind the scenes to bolster the integration process. In an article for *Foreign Affairs* he stressed the urgency of the summit meeting, imploring his audience that it might be the last opportunity to achieve effective economic coordination for the region. Failure to do so could lead to further economic instability. Economic integration required support from the most important political figures in the Western Hemisphere and needed to "include the creation of a genuine Latin American Common Market." In order to achieve this task, Javits reiterated his goal of forming an Action Committee for a Latin American Common Market, which he had called for in 1965, when he invited various Latin American leaders who would champion "democratic reform and unity" to collaborate with him in establishing such an organization. By 1967, Javits began forming this organization. His collaborator was Dr. Alberto Llera Camargo, who was instrumental in organizing leaders from Europe, the United States and Latin America to serve on the committee. The eventual demise of LAFTA and political indifference from Latin American leaders (presidents and military rulers) doomed the project.[106] Javits endeavored to convince the educated and enlightened U.S. audience that such a committee would augment the work of politicians and diplomats in fomenting economic integration, so that it would serve "as the focal point for those working toward the same goal." The committee was designed to "solicit" the active support of key leaders of non-communist political parties, business groups, labor unions, academia, and the Latin American press who "agreed on the principle of economic integration and who are prepared to build up the necessary political support" required for the success of a viable common market.[107]

Javits explained that the most important segments of Latin American society, i.e., business and political leaders, had publicly supported economic integration, but noted political action was lacking and as a result LAFTA had stagnated. In order to expedite the matter, Javits called for the executive branches of the Latin American states to make an immediate decision to start negotiations that would provide for a definite time period for the heads of state to draft a new accord and name a special committee to oversee implementation of its provisions.[108] Javits correctly asserted that although the problems of a poor system of transportation networks, geography and the low level of inter–Latin American trade existed, these were not sufficient grounds for assuming economic integration was not feasible. These, he argued, were the traditional arguments made by the enemies "who would oppose or delay economic integration." The true reason for faltering efforts, he claimed, lay with the ever-present problems of "inertia and a provincial nationalism ... which are blocking economic change," not with topography or economics.[109] Javits urgently pleaded with his readers to consider the consequences of failing to act, reminding them that this could be the last opportunity to reach new possibilities.[110]

In the meantime, the Johnson administration conducted its own post-

Punta del Este public debriefing. On his return to the United States, Dean Rusk provided an interview to the National Broadcasting Network's *Meet the Press*. The secretary of state explained that the summit had proven productive because the Latin American presidents had formally "committed themselves to move toward a common market for Latin America.... Everyone, I think recognized that time is running short," although he cautioned that it would not be until 1970 that a determination about the success of the conference could be made. The secretary added that the Latin Americans had agreed not to impose additional tariffs on each other, though he noted it would be difficult to coordinate the economic policy for so many states, especially because they were at varying levels of development. When asked by John Hightower of the Associated Press, "Are you merging strength, or are you merging weakness?" Rusk explained that the creation of an internal market of two hundred and fifty million consumers would be a major accomplishment that would prove a catalyst for further economic expansion. Such a market might reach five hundred million by the year 2000. Rusk added that it was the intention of the U.S. government to increase its economic aid to Latin America in order to accelerate both development and integration. He downplayed the setback Johnson suffered when his request to provide 1.5 billion dollars to Latin America was defeated 9–0 in the Senate Foreign Relations Committee. He claimed unconvincingly that the defeat was the result of a "procedural debate" between the president and Congress, but insisted that the Latin Americans were intent on utilizing their own resources to reach their goals.[111]

A more negative assessment came from Lincoln Gordon, the assistant secretary of state for inter–American affairs and former ambassador to Brazil. He explained that although a common market "might seem so obvious," there was in fact widespread opposition to such a scheme for various reasons, some of which were "legitimate ... and others reflecting vested interests in limited markets." It was the perennial problem of the poorer states arguing they could not open their markets because of the fear they would be inundated with cheap imports that would leave their population unemployed or underemployed. Gordon asserted that these attitudes were a tragedy for the region because many of the potential benefits that would accrue to all the states within a common market were being forfeited, such as more capital investment. Gordon challenged the assertion that U.S. capital was only interested in repatriating its capital. He argued that since the end of World War II, U.S. investors had "typically reinvested a larger share of their profits than they have withdrawn in capital or dividends." He urged American corporations to form new partnerships with Latin American business to ease the possibility of any tensions.[112]

By 1967, while pro-integrationist Latin Americans waited for further developments, the economy of the region continued to stagnate, causing alarm in American circles. Officials in the Central Intelligence Agency expressed concern over the region's general economic condition, explaining that Latin America's economic development had been "constrained" by economic policies that were unsuitable for the region. It cited inflation as a major problem, although it rejected the notion that defense expenditures were unduly high. Another problem of critical importance was the flight of foreign capital, cited as a factor that would hinder any substantial economic growth. The report explained that military expenditures were not a problem per se, as was commonly elaborated, arguing that defense spending was in fact "below average for the underdeveloped world and economic benefits from any foreseeable decrease in defense spending would be small."[113] The study claimed it was impossible to accurately measure capital flight, but suggested that the balance of payments problem should be used as a yardstick. This situation was exacerbated by the claim that "Latin American businesses and individuals had about two billion dollars deposited in U.S. banks at the end of 1966, an increase of $950 million over 1961," although it was noted that some of these funds were in fact working capital investments.[114]

With respect to economic integration, the CIA report explained that there were two major impediments to the integration process. First, it was suggested that the economies of the area were "more competitive than complimentary." Second, it reiterated the traditional arguments that distance, topography and poor transportation networks were barriers to further cooperation in the realm of integration (these notions were undoubtedly gleaned from the Latin Americans). It expressed optimism that Latin Americans appeared to be engaged in serious negotiations, although it was noted that any definite creation of an all–Latin American Common Market would have to wait several years. It was noted that most of the concessions made on tariff negotiations involved items that did not pose a threat to native industries.[115] As the integration process came to a quick halt after the Punta del Este summit, U.S. officials quietly disengaged themselves from any further public stance on economic integration. The slow pace of negotiations, and LAFTA's floundering after 1970, finally exhausted the available energy of both Latin Americans and Washington.

How influential was the United States in the move towards Latin American integration? In comparison to U.S. support for European integration, official American influence in promoting Latin American integration was ineffectual. The greatest support for the economic integration of Latin America came from non-profit public policy groups such as the Council on Foreign Relations and the Council for Economic Development. The most important person serving in the U.S. government who energetically pursued the theme of integration was New York senator Jacob Javits, but in spite of all his drive and enthusiasm, he was bridled in his efforts because he lacked the constitutional authority to direct U.S. foreign policy.

It is clear that any U.S. support for integration projects in the future will continue to require the Latin Americans to subscribe to policies which promote free-market economic interests associated with Washington's foreign policy objectives. In sum, it may be concluded that U.S. support for integration in the late 1950s and 1960s was as genuine, consistent, and ineffective as it was self-serving.

XI

MERCOSUR

Formation of MERCOSUR: Origins and Purposes

The intensity of international economic competition spurred four South American countries to resume the integrationist agenda. They met in Asunción, Paraguay, on March 26, 1991, to sign an accord known as the Treaty of Asunción. The treaty called for the implementation of a new regional organization dedicated to the expansion of trade via the economic integration of the signatory states. Once that was accomplished, new trade and political opportunities might arise. The new organization was to be called MERCOSUR, which is the Spanish acronym for the Mercado Común del Sur (Common Market of the South). The four countries that approved the treaty were Argentina, Brazil, Paraguay and Uruguay. The treaty also created the machinery for the administrative vertebrae that would govern MERCOSUR. This treaty functioned as the constitution of the organization until January 1, 1995, when it was bolstered by the Protocol of Ouro Preto, which was signed on December 17, 1994. The Ouro Preto protocol is a supplementary addition to the Treaty of Asunción.[1] It provided for an expanded organization and bureaucracy, although the most important and fundamental aspects of the Asunción treaty remain. Article 53 of the Ouro Preto agreement invalidated those clauses of the Asunción treaty that conflicted with the new document. The Treaty of Asunción and its additions continue to provide the basic foundation for the establishment and organization of MERCOSUR, primarily trade liberalization, which has been its principal objective.

The foundations for the Treaty of Asunción had been laid long before its formal signing. Between 1984 and 1989, Argentina and Brazil had signed twenty-four bilateral agreements covering a wide array of commercial issues. In 1985 the two countries signed an agreement known as the Declaration of Foz de Iguazú, which created the High Combined Commission (Comisión

Mixta de Alto Nivel). It was established to study the possibility of integration between Argentina and Brazil. These two states had been rivals since independence, but their growing economic interdependency required new commercial approaches towards each other. These two states, which were the most economically advanced in South America, signed the Programa de Integración Argentino-Brasileña in July 1986. The purpose of the accord was to promote cooperation in the fields of agriculture, nuclear energy, commerce, culture, payment systems and even military cooperation. In 1990 both countries signed an agreement known as the Treaty on Economic Complementarity, which was intended to strengthen prior trade agreements between the two states. This bilateral treaty soon found Uruguay and Paraguay, whose economies were strongly linked to and dependent on Argentina and Brazil, agitating for inclusion into an integration scheme.[2]

On June 26–27, 1992, the presidents of the four countries met at Las Lenas, Argentina, to make arrangements for the final implementation of MERCOSUR and to iron out remaining technicalities. The primary objective of the organization was the free movement of goods and services throughout its borders by December 31, 1994, which would be initiated via a 47 percent cut in tariff duties beginning on June 30, 1991.[3] The treaty asserted that its primary purpose was the expansion of domestic markets for its members via the integration process, and that it viewed economic growth as essential for promoting social justice in Latin America. These objectives called for implementing joint coordination of macroeconomic policies and improving the infrastructure. The framers wrote that their objectives could best be met by a policy of "gradualism, flexibility and balance." It was also noted that the treaty was in keeping with the objectives of the Montevideo Treaty of 1980. It asserted that its objectives were the "free movement of goods, services and factors of production between countries ... the elimination of customs duties and non-tariff restrictions on the movement of goods ... the establishment of a common external tariff." The treaty also called on its novice members to combat the imports influenced by "subsidies, dumping or any other unfair practice."[4]

The agreement stipulated that there would be a transition phase to initiate the functioning of MERCOSUR. The transition period would last from the signing of the Treaty of Asunción until December 31, 1994. Signatory members were called to engage in the creation of general rules and the construction of a "system for the settlement of disputes." It required member states to "ensure equitable trade terms in their relations with third countries." The agreement reminded the member states of the importance of recognizing the task before them by stipulating that the success of the treaty depended on the recognition and good faith of their respective legislatures to deal with any number of problems that might appear in the normal course of trade relations with third-party countries. The treaty also emphasized the importance of the various states to engage in the "reciprocity of rights and obligations between the state parties."[5]

The mechanism for achieving these goals during the transition period was to be a program of eliminating trade restrictions. This would be achieved via the institution of "progressive, linear and automatic tariff reductions" to be paralleled by the eventual "elimination of non-tariff restrictions." The ultimate objective was the complete elimination of all tariffs and non-tariff measures by December 31, 1994. Even more importantly, the Treaty of Asunción called for the initiation of a common external tariff, which the MERCOSUR signatories asserted was necessary for encouraging the competitiveness of the member states. The adoption of the common external tariff is particularly important because its introduction is a necessary prerequisite for the proper functioning of a common market. Even more important, it signifies the intent of the member states to solidify closer relations among themselves. In addition the treaty called on members to coordinate their macroeconomic policies in conjunction with the elimination of both tariff and non-tariff barriers.[6] Article 7 of the treaty called for the various states to provide other member states the same treatment as "domestically produced products" with respect to taxation, so that any normal tax applied in one state might apply to all products or economic enterprises of foreign origin, even if they were member states. No special levy, however, could be applied to the products or businesses of the other member states.[7]

Organizational Structure of MERCOSUR

Like any other supranational organization, MERCOSUR has a structure to deal with the multitude of issues it was designed to confront. The organization of MERCOSUR is centered on the establishment of two organs: (1) The Council of the Common Market, which is known simply as the Council, and (2) the Common Market Group.

The highest organ of MERCOSUR is the Council. The responsibility of the Council is to provide the political leadership necessary for the functioning of the organization. The Council consists of the individual foreign economics ministers of the member states. Other individual ministers may be invited to attend these Council functions. The Council is supposed to meet whenever member states agree it is necessary to convene. Article 11 asserts that the Council shall meet at least once a year with the presidents of the various countries in attendance. The Council operates with a president who must rotate the position with the other members' states every six months.

The Common Market Group is the executive organ of MERCOSUR and is coordinated by the foreign ministries of the member states. It is responsible for the administration and implementation of the treaty. Its duties are monitoring compliance with treaty provisions, adopting measures to enforce decisions made by the Council, proposing measures for the implementation of the trade liberalization program, coordinating macroeconomic policies, and negotiating new agreements with member states outside of MERCOSUR.[8] The Common Market Group would also create several working groups to study various issues.[9] The Common Market Group consists of four members and four alternates from each country, which represent member states. The state organs that are represented are the Ministry of Foreign Affairs, the Ministry of Economics or its equivalent organ such as in the areas of foreign trade, industry and/or economic coordination. The bureaucratic task of recording and archiving the documents of the organization was left to an administrative secretariat that was established with its headquarters in Montevideo, Uruguay.

The Treaty of Asunción required that the executive branches of the member governments represented in MERCOSUR keep their respective legislatures informed of progress. This particular clause was initially very vague, but was clarified in the accord that followed the Treaty of Asunción, known as the Protocolo de Ouro Preto. This arrangement is designed to convey information to the various member state legislatures, although this data is to be transmitted via the executive branches of the respective governments. Such an arrangement makes for a complex and awkward system of consultation.[10] In order to facilitate discussion, a joint parliamentary commission was established. The members of this commission were to be appointed by their respective legislatures. It was to have the power to submit recommendations to the Common Market Council and the Common Market Group. In addition, the parliamentary commission was given the autonomy to regulate its internal affairs. How effective this commission has been is unclear at the present moment.[11]

The Treaty of Asunción stated that it would be an agreement of "unlimited duration," which would be open to accession via negotiation by other member countries of the Latin American Integration Association (ALADI).[12] Article 20 asserted that states belonging to subregional groupings such as the Caribbean Common Market, the Central American Integration System, and the Andean Community (Comunidad Andina-CAN) could enter MERCOSUR five years after the effective date of the treaty. Nevertheless, a provision was made stipulating that states not belonging to other regional integration programs could apply for admission prior to the five-year deadline if they belonged to ALADI. Such approval would require unanimous consent from member states.

On November 6–8, 1991, the ministers of justice of the four member states met in Buenos Aires to discuss the possibility of forming a common judicial system. A recommendation was sent out by the respective ministers in December 1991 at a meeting in Brasília. It called for the implementation of measures to foment judicial cooperation necessary for the formation of a common market. The agreement emphasized the need for "compromise on behalf of the member parties to harmonize their legislation in pertinent areas in order to fortify the integration process." Member states made it explicitly clear, however, that this would be based on respecting the principles of national sovereignty. Because of suspicions about encroachments on the state judiciaries, Brazil announced in October 1996 that it would not participate in MERCO-SUR judicial hearings, claiming such an act endangered the stability and effectiveness of the Common Market.[13] For scholars studying MERCOSUR, special attention will have to be devoted to surveying the level of adherence to its judicial organ, which will serve as an effective barometer of integration progress.

Trade Liberalization Program

The Treaty of Asunción stipulated tariffs would be eliminated by December 31, 1994, when the Common Market was to officially begin its operation. It provided for a scheduled timetable stipulating that by certain dates each member state would have to reduce its tariffs by a certain percentage. The agreement defined "duties and charges" as customs duties along with any other monetary charges that might affect foreign trade. The term "restrictions" was defined as "any administrative, financial, foreign exchange or other measures by which a state party unilaterally prevents or impeded reciprocal trade." This clause was intended to eliminate the practice of instituting various mechanisms utilized for frustrating the efforts of foreign producers to penetrate local markets.[14]

The Treaty of Asunción stipulated that Paraguay and Uruguay would be given further time to reach these tariff reduction quotas. A further hindrance was the list of items submitted by the four signatories that would not be subject to tariff reductions. The number of items that did not apply, per country, is as follows[15]:

Argentina:	394 items
Brazil:	324 items

Paraguay: 439 items
Uruguay: 960 items

The nomenclature system used by the parties to classify these items was based on the system utilized by ALADI, which still exists and which conducts necessary and extensive technical research for other integration schemes. Because it is staffed by researchers from various countries, ALADI remains apolitical, thus providing a valuable tool for MERCOSUR.

MERCOSUR provides a genuine possibility that the objectives of pro-integrationists can be met. MERCOSUR encompasses in its organization an estimated 190–220 million people with a GNP estimated at $420 billion. Significantly, it has signaled it will attempt to follow the path of the EEC with the issuance of a MERCOSUR passport, which allows the citizens of the four respective countries to travel freely within its borders. The creation of this organization demonstrates the determination to proceed with the establishment of a genuine integration program free of the disruptive tendencies of other states. The establishment of MERCOSUR negates the specious argument that special and complex provisions need to be implemented for states that are at different levels of economic development. Argentina and Brazil are both relatively economically developed and have a high standard of living, although in Brazil there are huge pockets of poverty that are typical of Third World states. Uruguay has a relatively high standard of living, but it has only three million people, which limits the amount of industrial development it can engage in due to economies of scale. Paraguay and Venezuela are countries that might be considered Third or even Fourth World states. They suffer from high illiteracy, high unemployment, inadequate housing, malnutrition, insufficient resources for education, a shortage of medical personnel facilities and an inadequate infrastructure.

The two original signatories of MERCOSUR, Argentina and Brazil, are the more economically advanced states, both of which are on the verge of exploding onto the world stage as Second or even First World economic powers. Both states have often expressed the view that their countries were destined to provide leadership in Latin America as well as the world. The failure of MERCOSUR would be devastating to these states since they would lose the most in economic terms.

An analysis of the European experience (EEC) and the MERCOSUR experience clearly demonstrate that integration is fomented by the more advanced economic states.[16] It is the advanced industrial countries that have the most to lose in economic terms since they are the most dependent on trade in order to export their surplus production. These nations have an intense interest in securing new markets. The economically weaker states have less at stake because their potential of benefiting from the acquisition of secure markets that common markets provide is too small; indeed, in most instances, their economies do not depend on the requirement of expanding to new external markets.

Signature of the Neoliberals

Why did the MERCOSUR agreement come into being at that particular point in time? There were many reasons for this, some of which have been previously cited. First and foremost was the restoration of democratic government in the MERCOSUR countries by the neoliberals who brought their convergent ideology of political economy to all four MERCOSUR states. The neoliberals sought to strengthen both democratic political systems and market economies through the removal of all trade restrictions. The neoliberals were the old conservatives who had returned to power throughout Latin America in the mid–1980s. The principal difference between them and their conservative precursors from the 1930s was that the old conservatives had come from the landowning elite. The new conservatives represented the permanent presence of native and foreign capital that had come to dominate the political and economic landscape. Their interests coincided with the desire to forge stronger and more durable bonds via a supranational organization such as MERCOSUR.

One of the principal concerns facing the neoliberals in the 1980s and 1990s was the need to keep their countries economically competitive in the face of intense commercial rivalry emanating from all corners of the globe. These leaders feared that their countries would not be able to compete in this new environment. Neoliberal leaders took note of the new reconfiguration of the global economy that centered on regional economic blocs: the European Union, the North American Free Trade Agreement (NAFTA), and the various Latin American subregional groupings. Talk of an East Asian economic organization headed by Japan spurred recognition by southern-cone political figures of the need to create their own regional economic organization. President Saúl Menem of Argentina addressed the problem by stating that MERCOSUR membership would permit "the possibility of uniting [its members efforts] to compete in a new global market in which the strength of trade blocs has become more important than that of individual countries." It was also noted by supporters of MERCOSUR that it would give the Latin Americans greater leverage in securing trading concessions (agreements) from the United States, the European Union, Japan and other rising economic powers.[17]

Perhaps even more important, the neoliberals who created MERCOSUR had as one of their objectives the consolidation of democracy in Latin America. This objective was to be achieved by mandating a requirement that all member states of MERCOSUR be democratic governments.[18] The political scientist Alberto van Klaveren wrote that the "transitions to democracy coincide with and are, at least in part, responsible for the quest for integration. [MERCO-SUR] ... is based on the assumption that membership is restricted to demo-cratic governments and that, as in the European case, integration can be seen as a guarantee against coup d'état."[19] In addition MERCOSUR considers the maintenance of regional peace and security a primary objective. Political ana-lyst V. Whiting noted that the "lessened need for cross-regional security alliances increases the likelihood of regional integration."[20] Indeed, the merger of these states signals an end to the intense rivalry that had plagued both Argentina and Brazil, with their pretensions to regional power status, which resulted in the importation of very costly and technologically sophisticated weapons systems, including the purchase of aircraft carriers. At one time, both states had maintained nuclear weapons development programs, which were curtailed via a nuclear non-proliferation treaty in 1991.[21]

Problems of MERCOSUR

MERCOSUR is not without its own problems. Luigi Manzetti argued that the organization's weakness is in its institutional structure. He pointed out that the Treaty of Asunción was "conceived by its signatories as a point of departure for the setting up of a common policy agenda, rather than as the end product of lengthy negotiations over a period of years." He observed that the Asunción treaty was based upon the existing agreement already accepted by Argentina and Brazil and acquiesced to by Paraguay and Uruguay.[22] The rapid decision by the four member parties of MERCOSUR to sign the Asun-ción treaty was the result of their decision to avoid lengthy deliberations that would have postponed the integration process.[23] It was therefore agreed "to find a minimum common denominator among the four partners that could lead to the rapid establishment of a regional accord." To achieve this objective the signatory members deliberately left out various issues that continue to remain outstanding and that are to be dealt with by presidential summits and the individual governments in the future.[24]

One of the most glaring deficiencies of the Asunción treaty is the lack of an institutional framework that can grapple with problems independent of the individual governments, unlike the European Community, which has its own law making organs. From the very beginning the four signatory states have depended heavily on their state structures, especially their executive branches, to undertake the necessary initiatives for implementation of MER-COSUR, although both Argentina and Brazil have established congressional committees for evaluating MERCOSUR. The function of the organization is still heavily dependent on initiatives from the presidents and their foreign ministers.[25] This is not so unusual, since nation-states prefer to leave negotiations on sensitive foreign trade issues in the hands of the executive branch (the Trade Expansion Act of 1963 in the United States and NAFTA are good examples).

Accession Efforts in MERCOSUR

Whatever flaws MERCOSUR may possess in its institutional framework are more than compensated for by the innumerable opportunities afforded the Latin American countries to work together to attempt to solve some of the problems they face together, especially the problem of striving to maintain an advantage in a much more competitive global struggle for economic growth. Various countries sought to secure the benefits that are acquired with associate membership in MERCOSUR. Chile is now an associate membership in the organization.[26] Mexico and Ecuador initiated talks with MERCOSUR in order to achieve associate and full member status in January 1997.[27] That same month, Panama's ambassador informed Paraguay's president, Juan Carlos Wasmosy, that Panama was interested in associate membership in the common market.[28]

The prospects of closer cooperation within MERCOSUR and the promise of continued growth for the organization portends positive and further integration of the member states. Recognizing this possibility, the European Union and MERCOSUR sent each other powerful political signals on the need for closer cooperation. These signals include proposals for a bilateral agreement between the two regional blocs—the European Union (EU) and MERCOSUR, which were posited after the meeting of foreign ministers at the fourth EU–Rio Group meeting in São Paulo on April 22–23, 1994. This group was designed to meet annually. Its purpose is to foster dialogue between the highest ranking officials of both regional blocs.[29] At the June 24–25, 1994, meeting of the European Council held in Corfu, Greece, the importance of forging stronger links between the EU, MERCOSUR and Mexico was emphasized to the attending delegates. In September of 1994, Jacques Delors, the president of the European Union and an ardent Europeanist, made his second visit to Latin America within eighteen months, a clear indication of the increasing interest between the European Community and MERCOSUR. The vice president of the European Union, Manuel Marín of Spain, who also acted as commissioner for relations with Latin America, had headed several missions to that region in 1994.[30]

The importance of regional economic integration to Latin Americans led to several surveys conducted by Latinobarimetro in 1997. These surveys indicated that most Latin Americans were aware of the integration process and that they would support a trading bloc for their region, while at the same time supporting expanded trade with the world.[31] Later studies conducted by the United Nations Agency for Development and the Institute for the Integration of Latin America and the Caribbean studied elite attitudes on integration, globalization and the impact of identity with respect to MERCOSUR and FTAA to determine how these perspectives influenced their preferences. The UN report showed that although most elites supported MERCOSUR, they also favored an eventual hemispheric-wide free-trade zone. Given the fervor of middle- and working-class nationalism, it is unlikely that a hemispheric-wide trade pact can be implemented at this time.

The beginning of the twenty-first century saw nationalist and center-left political coalitions come to power in the southern cone countries. These groups took advantage of their ideological affinity to agitate for closer political and economic ties. By the year 2004 unionists saw their aspirations gain momentum, thereby signaling that unionism was no longer a marginal movement. On July 6–8, 2004, the MERCOSUR presidents met at Puerto Iguazú, Brazil, to consider the application of Mexico as an associate member and voted to accept Venezuela as an associated state, although Caracas also sought plenary status. This was the most important expansion in fourteen years because it accelerated MERCOSUR's growth, influence and potential for enlargement.

The application of Mexico for associate membership as a prelude to full membership in MERCOSUR was a major development for the organization.[32] The application was made because it was generally agreed upon by all quarters of Mexican society that their country was the "net loser" in NAFTA, which also included the United States and Canada. Experts varied in their opinions as to whether or not Mexico City would succeed in its endeavors. Most analysts agreed that Mexico would probably join the organization, but Gustavo Magariños objected, claiming Mexico would not be able to join MERCOSUR as a full member because it was a member of NAFTA, thus raising a question about MERCOSUR's nature. Was the organization solely about trade concessions and tariff rates? Was a large economic entity such as Mexico, with the largest GDP in Latin America, to be denied admission because of tariff matters, despite the fact that its accession would radically alter the status of political and economic relations in the hemisphere? President Vicente Fox of Mexico affirmed his commitment to join MERCOSUR, claiming that it was his intention to have Mexico enrolled in both trade blocs and that there was no contradiction in such a proposal, despite objections from other MERCOSUR members.[33]

Mexico's announcement that it would officially accelerate its application for full admission to MERCOSUR came at the IV Americas Summit on November 4–5, 2005, at Mar del Plata, Argentina. President Vicente Fox stated he would treat the application to MERCOSUR as a marriage proposal: "My love is ample for both agreements, for MERCOSUR and NAFTA. If there's no love, if there is no yes to my marriage proposal, well I'll keep insisting and I will continue offering more love to MERCOSUR and more love to NAFTA. That is my position which is not contradictory."[34] This was the strongest public pronouncement made in favor of economic integration in Mexican history. It is also one of the most important declarations in the history of unionism. The possibility of Mexico's admission was enthusiastically greeted by Uruguayan president Tabaré Vásquez, a member of the center-left who sought to utilize Mexico City as a balance of power against larger states such as Argentina and Brazil. He said, "We believe that to achieve better internal balance in MERCOSUR we need the participation of countries like Mexico, and hence we are strongly supporting its entry."[35] If Mexico were to be granted full accession to MERCOSUR there would be no reason for other Latin American states to stay out of the organization, save to protect the interests of monopoly capitalism. Those states choosing to remain outside of MERCOSUR would simply become the victims of history. Oddly enough, the Mexican foreign ministry was very quiet and vague on the matter. The press in the United States, Mexico and Latin America paid little if any attention to Mexico's application. The reason for the lack of interest is unclear. It is possible that the media questioned the sincerity of Mexico City's request. Perhaps there was doubt as to whether MERCOSUR would accept the application of Mexico, or fear that Mexico City was a Trojan horse sent by Washington to create a balance of power in the rising political and economic power bloc. Simultaneously, the United States and Mexico became embroiled in various issues that had previously been dealt with in a private manner. The controversies of immigration, narcotics smuggling and border violence, and the construction of a 700-mile wall along the U.S.-Mexican border, which was hundreds of times longer than the Berlin Wall, were now brought into public view by politicians and the corporate news media. Were Mexico's accession effort and the emerging controversies coincidences? In politics coincidences do not exist.

U.S. elites were infuriated that Mexico would not play according to the script it had been assigned. Mexico's accession efforts quietly faded away.[36] With the construction of a wall on the U.S.-Mexican border, the initiation of anti–Hispanic immigration policies and hostility to MERCOSUR, the United States had initiated a policy of economic warfare against Latin America.[37]

Venezuela's Accession Efforts

A very contentious and public accession debate occurred with the Puerto Iguazú announcement (July 2006) regarding Venezuela's request for full admission into the organization. The Venezuelan application for full membership was the most significant milestone in MERCOSUR's evolution since its inception.[38] It was the first state to apply for plenary membership and actually enter the accession process since the founding of the organization. The moment was the most dramatic in the history of unionism because it signaled the desire of the political class to seriously expand the unionist process beyond original membership of a viable trade bloc that could lead to further integration. This political achievement was led by the center-left, which utilized its ideological rationale to congeal a unionist alliance. This leftist coalition came to power on the heels of their predecessor neoliberal governments. Coincidentally, these pro-unionist governments came to power in all five states at almost the same time.

The formal application of Venezuela for full membership into the organization came on July 4, 2006. The event was attended by the presidents of the four plenary states, who met in the Teresa Carreño Theater in Caracas. The application gained widespread media attention in Latin America. The application was extremely controversial because its center-left president Hugo Chávez was an outspoken critic of Washington. He had promoted policies that many feared were intended to stifle public dissent and had cultivated a close relationship with Fidel Castro, suggesting he might mimic the Castroite revolution.

The fact that he was democratically elected did not deter criticism. Allegations were made that his populist rhetoric would turn Venezuela into a full-scale communist dictatorship. Indeed, Uruguay's former president Luis Alberto Lacalle stated that Venezuela's admission "would only bring us ills."[39] Fears circulated that Chávez would "short circuit" other countries in the region. Venezuela, however, could not be ignored, since it had the third largest GDP in South America. Its admission would ensure a steady supply of oil and natural gas to member states, a necessary requirement of Latin America's economy, which requires cheap energy to grow.[40] It was initially believed by MERCO-SUR's leadership that the twin applications of Mexico and Venezuela would provide a political and ideological balance of power within its ranks because Mexico maintained a center-right government. Since Mexico's application quietly faded, only the Venezuelan effort would have any relevance to unionists.

Argentina and Uruguay quickly reviewed and approved the application of Caracas, but intense and lengthy debates about the desirability of incorporating Venezuela were initiated in Brazil and Paraguay. Brazil eventually approved the entry of Venezuela, but at this point in time, history awaits the verdict of Paraguay. Presidents Lula (Brazil) and Lugo (Paraguay) sought to counter conservative opposition to Caracas by buying time for the entry of Venezuela and keeping the issue alive in their respective legislatures. The center-left Venezuelan opposition to Chávez played a crucial role in convincing moderates and their counterparts in Brazil to approve Venezuela's application. Antonio Ledezma, the mayor of Caracas (Social Democrat) and the most prominent critic of the president, argued before the Brazilian legislature that the only way to contain Chávez was to incorporate Venezuela into MERCO-SUR and other international organizations, where he could be effectively monitored and challenged. Venezuelan accession would "put limits to his actions that would be most positive for Venezuelan democracy." Without MERCO-SUR, Ledezma argued, "Chávez could be more dangerous if left isolated." Ledezma was later invited to address the Foreign Affairs and Defense Committee of the Brazilian senate on October 27, 2009. At the meeting he was able to convince enough senators about the need to admit Venezuela to the point that supporters of Venezuela began to claim victory.

In essence, Ledezma called on MERCOSUR to adopt a U.S.-style policy similar to Washington's treatment of Communist China—a strategy of promoting democracy via inclusion through integration into the global capitalist economy.[41] Recognizing the potential of economic integration for Venezuela, Ledezma told the Brazilian senators that they should differentiate between Chávez and Venezuela by clearly distinguishing the government from the "state, which is permanent." Failure to recognize the difference would allow Chávez to play the game of "isolationism."[42] Ledezma later addressed Brazilian journalists, arguing, "Leaders are only passengers, states are permanent." He added that for this "reason we ask that you support the entry of Venezuela into MERCOSUR; not for economic motives, but for political reasons."[43] The head of the pro–Lula coalition on the committee, Senator Romero Juca, stated, "If there's a lack of democracy in Venezuela, as the opposition argues, then it's one more reason to include the country—to add some transparency, dictatorships don't relate with democratic nations." The pro–Venezuela vote was assisted by the massive trade surplus between the two countries in favor of Brazil.[44]

The business community also entered the heated fray with its strong support for Venezuelan accession. José Francisco Marcondes, president of the Federation of Venezuelan-Brazilian Chambers of Commerce, stated that integration could "not be seen from a political point of view, since it creates an unnecessary polarization" inimical to economic development. He added that Brazil alone had business contracts in Venezuela totaling between 15 and 20 billion dollars.[45] Marcondes stated that the political situation in Venezuela did not concern him so much because "when MERCOSUR was created in 1991, the political conditions were hardly any better." He stressed the importance of Chávez's leading opponent supporting integration, but lamented ideological issues were at hand: "I only wish that he [Ledezma] were opposed [to Chávez] for economic rather than political reasons."[46]

The visit of Ledezma made a huge impression on the committee, leading to a final victory in the committee. Unionists and their pragmatic supporters finally scored a major success on October 29, 2009, when the senate committee voted a resounding 12 to 5 for sending a recommendation to the Brazilian senate for a full vote supporting the entry of Venezuela into MERCOSUR. The victory came with a compromise clause introduced by Senator Tasso Jereissati after almost four hours of debate. The clause called for the defense of democracy and human rights in Venezuela. It was introduced to alleviate the fears of the Brazilian center-right, although no mechanism for achieving this goal was mentioned.[47] The final victory came on December 15, 2009, when the Brazilian senate voted on the proposed bill, known as PDS 430/08.[48] The vote was a comfortable 35 to 27 votes in favor of Venezuelan admission to MERCOSUR.[49] Opposition senator Arturo Virgilio had argued futilely against the adhesion of Caracas, claiming its admission would only jeopardize an economic bloc that was already in a "state of agony." Unionists, however, proved able to carry the day when Senator Aloizio Mercadante argued during the deliberations that "political isolation between nations never resolved problems."[50] How long this pragmatism will be maintained is unclear, but the enlarging economic links promise to turn ideological conflicts into expanding economic possibilities that will strengthen unionism. The *sui generis* wisdom and practicality of Ledezma, Juca and Marcondes is unparalleled in the history of unionism, which has always been plagued by ideological conflicts and subterfuge. These men and the groups they represent recognize that the institution of MERCOSUR had to be separated from Chávez the individual as the main issue, lest the many opportunities be lost due to one man and ideological differences.

In Paraguay the situation regarding Venezuelan accession to MERCO-SUR took a turn for the worse when Paraguayan president Fernando Lugo withdrew his request to congress to accept Venezuela. His foreign minister, Hector Lacognata, claimed the withdrawal was made so as to avoid a defeat in congress and hence avoid complications with Venezuela. Lugo added that he hoped to resubmit the proposal at a later time when it would succeed.[51] Paraguayan opposition to Chávez grew as his statist attacks on opposition media networks and newspapers intensified. On July 21, 2009, the Paraguayan Chamber of Commerce sent a letter written by its president, Domingo Daher, to Miguel Carrizosa, president of the Paraguayan senate, stating, "President Hugo Chávez intends to access MERCOSUR in order to expand the founda-tions of his regime, which evolves in the opposite direction to the principles of the regional economic bloc." Daher claimed the Chávez government "pro-moted conflict rather than cooperation." He stated that Chávez was more interested in promoting class warfare than in "looking for common stances," hence the entrance of Venezuela had to be suspended until such time as a polit-ical reversal occurred.[52] In August 2010, the moderate, centrist Colorado Party in Paraguay let it be known that they would resume negotiations on Venezue-lan accession, but these quickly crumbled.

Despite frustrating rejections, Chávez would not relent. He was abso-lutely relentless in his pursuit of Venezuelan entrance into MERCOSUR. In 2011, Chávez, on the suggestion of Brazilian president Lula da Silva, arranged for a meeting in Brazil with the retired army general and prominent Paraguayan senator Lino Oviedo. The meeting lasted four hours and included a telephone call to senator and ex–Paraguayan president Nicanor Duarte (2003–2007), who remained obstinate in his refusal to admit Caracas. According to Chávez, he told Duarte that it was inevitable that Caracas would eventually be admitted into the union.[53]

The accession of Venezuela came in a most unexpected manner for most observers, as a result of events that unfolded in Paraguay. On June 15, 2012, a clash between police and protesters in that country ended with seventeen deaths. The Colorado Party of Paraguay, seeking to terminate the Lugo pres-idency, argued that the administration was ineffectual because it could not provide adequate security for its citizens and launched impeachment proceed-ings against the president. The vote taken on June 22, 2012, was 39–4 in the senate and 73–1 in the chamber of deputies and resulted in the ouster of Pres-ident Lugo that very day.

It just so happened that the 43rd Presidential Summit of MERCOSUR countries, which was also attended by the Union of South American States (UNASUR) member countries, began its meeting on June 25, 2012. The conference immediately reacted to the impeachment of Lugo by unanimously agreeing to temporarily suspend Paraguay's political rights in official MER-COSUR functions (*not* as a MERCOSUR member) until new elections could be held in 2013. The MERCOSUR states specifically argued that the removal of President Lugo was anti-democratic and illegal.[54] The pro–MERCOSUR faction complained that the successful removal of Lugo had resulted in a down-grade of its credit rating by Standard and Poor's to BB—and hence it was important to suspend Paraguay due to an implied threat to the regional economy.[55] The UNASUR states concurred.[56]

Despite the fact that the suspension was viewed as a leftist plot, the conservative government of Chile, headed by Sebastián Piñera, voted for the suspension within the UNASUR bloc. With Paraguay suspended, the other three MERCOSUR states agreed to incorporate Venezuela at the July 31, 2012, MERCOSUR meeting in Rio de Janeiro, Brazil. The initiative came at the behest of Brazilian president Dilma Rousseff at the Mendoza conference behind closed doors. According to Uruguayan foreign minister Luis Almagro, José Mujica (Uruguay's president) originally opposed the idea but then relented when the other two states agreed not to impose economic sanctions on Paraguay's new government.[57] The Paraguayan elites who had thought they were so shrewd to remove Lugo now found themselves completely outmaneuvered by the other three states and facing the incorporation of their feared enemy—Hugo Chávez. The only reply that came from conservative Paraguayan leaders was that they might leave MERCOSUR, which most observers felt was unlikely as 80 percent of its trade was with the bloc. Horacio Cartes, a candidate for the Paraguayan Colorado presidential nomination, concurred, telling young people at one of his political rallies, "Paraguay should in no way abandon Mercosur.... We have to hold on tight while they bash us a bit and keep low and do not play to being giants or annoyed." Cartes added, "Mercosur is a common market like Europe.... All countries are interconnected and it is out of the question to isolate Paraguay from other countries." He warned his countrymen to "avoid acting with arrogance," because there was too much at stake, reminding his audience that the Paraguayan people benefitted from the large internal markets of the MERCOSUR bloc and its tariffs.[58]

In an effort to calm the concerns of Paraguayan businessmen and conservatives, the MERCOSUR states made it clear they were admitting Venezuela and not Chávez. Pro-MERCOSUR observers tried to calm the fears of anti–MERCOSUR, anti–Chávez factions, stating openly in the press and polite society that Chávez was not a threat as he was battling a highly aggressive cancer and unlikely to survive another year. This did not stop Chávez from proclaiming a great victory. In a telephone interview with Telesur News,

Chávez stated, "This is a historic day for ... integration.... This is a win-win for everybody." Indeed, the MERCOSUR partners agreed. Brazilian president Dilma Rouseff stated that the admission of Caracas was necessary because "food and energy security are becoming more and more relevant" at every level. Alicia Barcena, director of the United Nations Economic Commission for Latin America and the Caribbean, articulated the significance of Venezuela's acceptance in economic terms: "MERCOSUR had a third of the world's water reserves, a third of arable lands, more than 45 percent of soy production ... and now with Venezuela's incorporation there's an expectation that energy integration could increase." Indeed, Venezuela holds the largest reserves of crude oil in the world, thus yielding the possibility of promoting a viable economic future for the regional bloc via a secure energy supply.[59]

Finally at the 43rd Extraordinary Summit of MERCOSUR, held in Brasília, Brazil, July 30–31, 2012, the plenary states minus Paraguay formally voted to incorporate Venezuela into the organization after a tumultuous six years of political wrangling, with the official signing on July 31, 2012.[60] The meeting was attended by all the leading dignitaries of the MERCOSUR bloc, including a rare appearance by Rosinés Chávez, daughter of the president.[61]

The incorporation of Venezuela was greeted with positive but cautious fanfare in Venezuela. Benjamin Tripier, president of the Chamber Advisory Council of Venezuela, claimed it was a great victory for the country that would expand its industrial base but warned that the future of the country was with free enterprise. He added, "I understand that Argentine and Brazilian businessmen have come to Venezuela, waiting for timing to settle down in the country." In response to Paraguayan claims that the accession was illegal, Juan Korody, an attorney, stated in a speech at the Venezuelan-Argentine Chamber of Commerce that the entry of Caracas was "fully legal and constitutional." He added that the new business opportunities afforded by the union meant that the new economic expansion required "standardized economic policies" and would provide a "tremendous momentum of the regional economy."[62] The coordinator of Venezuela's admission process, Isabel Delgado, called Venezuela's entry a milestone for the economic development of the country.[63]

A comuniqué from the Brazilian government stressed the fact that MERCOSUR was a spectacular success, citing that the organization would have 270 million people with the entry of Venezuela or 70 percent of the population of South America, and that trade between member states had increased from 4.1 billion to 104.9 billion dollars in 2011. It noted that the new GDP for the organization was 3.3 trillion U.S. dollars and that it now comprised 12.7 million km^2 (72 percent of South America's area).[64] Congratulations came in from everywhere, save the extreme right.

Brazilian experts were delighted with the victory. Carlos E. Abijaodi, director of industrial development for the Brazilian Confederation of Industry, pointed out that Venezuela was heavily dependent on manufactured goods from Brazil. He observed that they required "just about everything. We can very easily diversify in that market." Clemens Nunes, an economist at the Brazilian FGV School of Economics, added, "It is a good opportunity opening up, especially for the industrial sector," which had been sluggish. He added that the many bureaucratic problems faced by Brazilian businessmen would now be ameliorated as a result of Venezuela's membership.[65] Colombian economists were not blind to the impact Venezuela's entry would have on their country. Mauricio Reina of the Centro de Investigación Económica y Social de Desarrollo stated that the new member widened the market for Argentina and Brazil and that it would be difficult for Bogotá to compete. Economist Armando Barrios stated that it was only logical that Caracas would seek admission into MERCOSUR, as commerce between Venezuela and Brazil had quintupled between 2003 and 2011.[66] Support for Venezuela's admission also came from Uruguay when its former president, Jorge Batlle (2000–2005), leader of the centrist Colorado Party, asserted the necessity and positive impact Venezuela's entry would have on the trade bloc: "It is good for Uruguay that Venezuela becomes a market inside Mercosur." To assuage right-wing fears he pointed out that Chávez was not immortal.[67]

No sooner had Venezuela entered the union when charges of bribery began to be made by both sides. Chávez stated that a group of senators had solicited bribes (names were not given) for their approval of Venezuela into the organization, stating, "A little bunch of them pretended millions of dollars to vote in favor of Venezuela." Chávez, however, did not give names and probably used the term "pretended" to avoid potential charges of defamation.[68] The Paraguayan newspaper *Ultima Hora* soon ran an article in which Paraguayan senator Jorge Oviedo Matto claimed that several agents were sent to Paraguay at the behest of Chávez's brother, and that offers of up to $100,000 were made. Oviedo Matto claimed that the information was not new as it had been made public in the Paraguayan senate as early as October 2011.[69]

The accession of Venezuela was a great victory for MERCOSUR and a major blow to its detractors. With the entry of Caracas, MERCOSUR became self-sufficient in energy, food and hydroproduction, capable of meeting the immediate demands of a massive internal market extending from the Caribbean to Ushuaia (near Cape Horn). Nothing succeeds like success. No sooner had Venezuela joined MERCOSUR when an announcement was made on August 5, 2012, that Ecuador had initiated negotiations for full accession to the union. (This was not particularly new, as Ecuador's president Rafael Correa had requested admission in December 2011 at the Montevideo MERCOSUR summit, but the entry of Caracas was a major impetus to Quito's request.)[70] On the same day, August 5, 2012, Chávez stated at a news conference that he expected Bolivia, Ecuador and Colombia would eventually join the union as plenary members.[71] On September 7, 2012, the Bolivian deputy foreign minister Juan Carlos Alurralde stated his country would pursue full membership in MERCOSUR. The Uruguayan government, represented by Roberto Conde, promptly gave its support to the request. Conde, the deputy foreign minister of Uruguay, indicated that eventually a gas pipeline would be built from Bolivia to Montevideo and that Bolivian products would now have access to Uruguay's Atlantic port "with no need to pay any tariffs when they are moved." Both governments announced that negotiation for plenary accession would begin in January 2013.[72] Curiously, the MERCOSUR Secretariat does not have a mechanism for recruiting new members. This task must be initiated either by the state desiring incorporation or via a member state. It is believed that the Brazilian foreign ministry is orchestrating the accession of Bolivia and Ecuador.

U.S. Opposition to MERCOSUR

Since the creation of MERCOSUR the United States has opposed it. This is in stark contrast to Washington's support for the economic integration of Latin America in the 1960s. This opposition has utilized the ideology of free trade promoted by Washington since the demise of the Soviet Union. Since the United States could no longer utilize its irrational fear of communist ideology it began to place a stronger public emphasis on the virtues of free trade that became known as the Washington Consensus. The policies elaborated by Washington were accepted *en masse* throughout Latin American circles in the 1980s and 1990s. Utilizing the free trade concept, Washington has been able to oppose MERCOSUR with silk gloves rather than with overtly hostile rhetoric. The primary method used by Washington has been to encourage rivalries between Latin American states through two mechanisms.

The first tool is the bilateral trade agreement, which the United States has zealously pursued. The United States has had relative success in frustrating MERCOSUR with bilateral agreements. These treaties have had the most success with the poorer countries of Latin America, where the gentry and its agricultural interests prevail. Anxious that no other agricultural or commodity-exporting state should gain an advantage, these governments have succumbed to Washington's offers.

The second instrument is the promotion of rival regional trade blocs.

The first example of a competitor bloc was initiated by President George H.W. Bush in 1990 when he founded the Enterprise for the Americas initiative, which later became known as the Free Trade Area for the Americas (FTAA—the Spanish acronym is ALCA).

The FTAA approach, which eventually failed, is an old objective hailing back to the 1880s, when the United States decided it needed a method for eliminating industrial surpluses. In 1889 the U.S. secretary of state, James G. Blaine, decided to promote a hemispheric free trade organization. This approach became known as Pan-Americanism. When the countries of America gathered in 1889–90 to discuss such a treaty, they rejected it, claiming that under the arbitration process the independent Latin American states would have less rights under the treaty than any of the 43 states of the U.S. federation. Although this effort failed, it did not stop Washington from pursuing similar proposals. The FTAA was a duplicate of the 1889–90 conference. The 1990 proposal was an effort by Washington to stem the tide of what it felt was a movement it could not control.

FTAA is an example of globalization. The Latin Americans have made it clear that while they do not favor globalization, they do support *mondialization*. Globalization concerns itself solely with economic matters, whereas mondialization is concerned with the enhancement of free trade and quality of life issues, i.e., sustainability as defined by the United Nations and the quest for social justice. Former Argentine president Eduardo Duhalde asserted that as long as a hemispheric trade agreement is solely about economics rather than justice, such a treaty remains outside the scope of realization. As an example he stipulated that as prelude to a hemispheric treaty, the U.S.-Mexican wall must come down before talks resume.[73] The FTAA, which is a U.S. initiative, is the embodiment of both Pan-Americanism and globalization. MERCOSUR, on the hand, which is a genuine all–Latin-American institution, is the manifestation of mondialization, rooted in two centuries of struggle for closer bonds between Ibero-Americans and the quest for economic development and social objectives. The struggle between globalization and mondialization took form as the United States vigorously promoted the 1990 FTAA proposal until it was defeated by Brazilian leadership. This opposition was accelerated by the victory of the center-left in Brazil and Latin American nationalism. In lieu of the defeat, the United States has had to revert to the bilateral free-trade agreement and sponsoring new rival trade blocs.

An example of a rival free-trade organization is the newly formed Pacific Alliance. The new bloc was formed in June 2012, consisting of Mexico, Colombia, Peru and Chile. It was designed to foster free trade between member states with the alleged ultimate objective of eventually binding themselves in a free trade bloc with Asia. Its formation is a clear indication that the Andean Community is a total failure. It is unclear how Mexico joined the bloc when it is already a member of NAFTA. Certainly Mexico could have also acceded to the failed Andean Community, as the bloc functions through bilateral agreements, rendering that organization ineffectual.

In Latin America and the rest of the globe the Pacific Alliance is seen as a Washington-inspired organization. This view is not limited to Ibero-America but is held by outside observers as well. The former Indian ambassador to Argentina, Rengaraj R. Viswanathan, described the alliance as "a new force to counterbalance the Atlantic facing and Brazil-led Mercosur group" and identified Washington as "the hidden hand behind the formation of the Pacific Alliance to divide the region, hobble the growing Latin America autonomy and counter the rising leadership profile of Brazil."[74] A close examination of the new bloc shows that these are the countries with extremely weak state structures, as evinced by the grueling narcotics wars fought in both Colombia and Mexico. Likewise, the two countries are heavily linked economically to the United States, especially Colombia with its dependence on Washington's favorable concessions to its coffee imports. Viswanathan, an expert on the River Plate region, stated that the possibility of the new bloc ever becoming a dynamic economic entity was abysmally low and unnatural.[75] He observed that economically the alliance was mainly a political stunt (again designed to thwart MERCOSUR) rather than a serious organization based on any logical economic consideration, since the member states barely engage in any significant trade amongst themselves (trade between these states barely exceeds 3 percent), while the MERCOSUR states traded as much as 20 percent before their integration. Indeed, the new alliance will surely prove a step backward as these states have nothing exceptional to offer each other. A union with MERCOSUR would provide them with more commercial and diplomatic leverage with both the United States and China. By failing to reap the benefits of larger economic union, the new organization will only serve to facilitate a further waste of human potential.

A third mechanism for undermining MERCOSUR, according to many Latin Americans, is the press with its parade of negative articles highlighting every disagreement, however small or large. The consensus is that so many of these articles appear in pro–U.S. media outlets that it is part of a larger effort by U.S. intelligence agencies to undermine the organization. It is common knowledge that the CIA recruits heavily from the press corps, especially from international media organizations that have access to large populations, thereby providing the intelligence hierarchy and other enemies of MERCOSUR with a massive audience for the spread of misinformation.

United States opposition to MERCOSUR constitutes a return to the old hegemony and imperialism of the nineteenth and twentieth centuries. It is an abandonment of the enlightened policy of the 1960s, when the United States supported the economic integration of Latin America. Many of the Latin American countries that have signed bilateral trade accords with the United States have seen an increase in incoming revenues to their countries, but these policies are short sighted, as only a handful of people or corporations have been able to benefit from the increased trade. It is only a matter of time before the populations of these countries initiate another round of civil unrest reminiscent of the 1960s and 1970s. Likewise, U.S. efforts to undermine MERCOSUR are reckless, visceral and atavistic. The United States should return to its pro-integration 1960s policy for Latin America as a prelude to a hemispheric free-trade treaty, which is a genuine possibility if it is negotiated among parties that feel neither one shall have a grossly disproportionate advantage over the other. As Washington has done for Europe, so should it do for Latin America.

All-Class Opposition to FTAA

One of the consequences of MERCOSUR's growth was the eventual demise of its most important rival—the Free Trade Area for the Americas Initiative (FTAA—the Spanish acronym is ALCA). The first negotiations to discuss FTAA were not held until December 1994 in Miami, Florida. The FTAA proposal generated intense controversy throughout Latin America, especially within the MERCOSUR countries after the year 2000, when the nationalist inspired center-left seized the initiative when it came to power. Despite leadership from leftist quarters, this opposition became an all-class movement, with support from all sectors of society in multiple states. In Argentina, elections were held November 20–26, 2003, to determine whether Buenos Aires would support or oppose FTAA. The elections were sponsored by the "No to the FTAA" coalition, which was supported by various social groups, the church and political groups under an umbrella organization called Campaña Argentina contra el ALCA, which was part of a larger organization known as the Campaña Continental No al ALCA. The voters were asked: "Do you believe Argentina should enter the FTAA?" The total number of votes was 2,225,358, cast in 5699 ballot boxes. The final result was an overwhelming defeat for the FTAA, with 2,162,263 people, or 96 percent of the electorate, rejecting it. The yes faction provided only 67,570 voters or 3 percent for FTAA. A total of 22,525 votes or 1 percent of the ballots were voided.[76]

In Brazil the campaign against FTAA began even before the center-left candidate, Luiz Inácio Lula da Silva, became president. The Brazilian campaign against FTAA began in earnest in December of 2000 when over 700 trade union representatives from the MERCOSUR bloc met in Florianópolis, Brazil, to protest any adhesion to Washington's initiative. They demanded that all 34 countries in the Western Hemisphere submit the FTAA proposal to their people via national plebiscites.[77] On September 1–7, 2002, at the behest of 60 Brazilian civil organizations, the question of FTAA membership was included in an unofficial referendum in the municipal elections involving 3,894 municipalities, in which an estimated 10 million people voted overwhelmingly against the FTAA. The results were staggering. Of the 10,149,542 votes cast, 9,979,964, or 98 percent of the participating electorate, voted against FTAA adhesion.[78] This was followed by a November 6–9, 2003, conference in Belo Horizonte (the capital of Minas Gerais) attended by more than 20,000 attendees representing 1,500 organizations that voted overwhelmingly to reject FTAA. They also called for the issue to be put again before the people in a plebiscite during the October 2004 municipal elections.[79]

The attack on FTAA was adroitly led by President Lula da Silva after his inauguration in January of 2003. He conducted an intense and ruthless campaign against Washington's hemispheric proposal. As FTAA negotiations began in February 2004 at Puebla, Mexico, the Brazilians had quietly come to the conclusion that further negotiations were useless. Brazil's chief commercial negotiator for FTAA, the cagey and canny Adhemar Bahadian, let it be known before the Puebla talks began that Brasília felt the negotiations were futile. Bahadian publicly told reporters that the FTAA was like "a stripper in a cheap cabaret. At night under the dim lights, she is a goddess, but in the daytime she is something different. Maybe she is not even a woman." With these devastating comments Bahadian informally let it be known that the FTAA negotiations were effectively moribund.[80]

In the meantime pro–MERCOSUR activists railed against FTAA. In September of 2004, with the municipal elections, which were to decide the fate of MERCOSUR, the anti–FTAA campaign heated up. One activist cleverly stated he was opposed to FTAA because "municipal elections define the future of our cities and free trade agreements can limit local government's capacity to define policies and run their own territory." The FTAA would force municipalities, he argued, to purchase their goods and services via internal bids, leading to unemployment. He cited the North American Free Trade agreement (NAFTA) and its negative impact on Mexico as an example of what would happen to Brazil and the rest of Latin America. He concluded with the statement, "Sow these ideas! Life is not a business! Yes to sovereignty and solidarity! No to free trade!"[81] Extensive opposition to FTAA came from all segments of society. In Uruguay, business journalist Carlos Luppi echoed the sentiments of many people when he wrote in November of 2003, "FTAA is dead ... MERCOSUR more than ever."[82] The monsignor of Montevideo, Pablo Galimberti, criticized the lack of transparency in the complex FTAA negotiations. He also argued that there was no evidence that Washington's scheme would promote trade between the Latin Americans per se.[83] Galimberti cited a report by the Council of Canadian Bishops stating that FTAA would result in total vassalage for the American people.[84] The monsignor stated that the Latin American integration movement had the wholehearted support of the Roman Catholic Church, and that the church had always been an integrating force.[85] Hector Gros Espiell, a professor of constitutional law, cited the need for vigilance with the FTAA due to the secretive nature of the negotiations and their origin with the United States: "We are in the shadows. Only four or five negotiators who have carefully guarded their silence on this theme are familiar with its clauses.... We do not know the actual content of the negotiations. All we know is that they initiated with the United States for the purpose of creating a free-trade zone over all of America." Gros Espiell maintained that more favorable trading terms could be achieved via Uruguay's natural trading partners in MERCOSUR.[86] The notary public María Sara Corbelle, director of the Christian Association of Entrepreneurial Directors, protested FTAA, claiming it was only concerned with economic issues that would benefit a few, whereas MERCOSUR had adopted a more flexible approach of combining a political, economic and social agenda.[87] In the end President Silva's efforts to derail Washington's efforts and substitute them with MERCOSUR had the overwhelming support of Latin American nationalists, the center-left and agricultural interests (the gentry).

By December of 2006 President Lula, who had led the Latin-American offensive against FTAA, stated at the inauguration of MERCOSUR's parliament that FTAA was effectively dead as nobody ever spoke of it.[88] This animus from Brazil and the rest of Latin America arose from the traditional antagonism that the political left felt for the United States and because of the reluctance of the U.S. government to eliminate its $20 billion agricultural subsidies (a highly sensitive political issue in the USA). Indeed, the great rival to Washington's free trade bloc was Latin America's agricultural interests of the conservative Latin American gentry that delivered their countries into MERCOSUR. By agreeing to protect Latin American agri-business, the center-left had laid a successful ambush for FTAA, knowing full well that Washington would refuse to acquiesce on the subsidies issue.

Other Developments in the Integration Movement: IIRSA and the Córdoba Conference

One of the objectives of unionists is to promote economic integration by promoting the development of the region's infrastructure. It is believed that increasing physical linkage between states will facilitate additional trade between the Latin American states and thereby promote economic union. In 2000 the Initiative for the Integration of the Regional Infrastructure of South America (IIRSA) was initiated by twelve South American states. The objective is to build roads, modernize telecommunications, develop riverine transportation, and modernize air and sea ports. The group has organized South America into ten axes that revolve around geographical subregions of the continent. These vast and very expensive projects require financial assistance from the Inter-American Development Bank, whose primary objective is to finance regional integration projects. IIRSA will certainly promote expanded trade, but closer political links will be determined by political will, as evinced by the Spanish crown in colonial times; consequently unionists need not be dismayed if these massive projects are cancelled or fail to live up to their promise.[89]

In 2006, Bolivia announced it sought admission to MERCOSUR and was publicly supported by the assistant secretary for economic integration of the Argentine Foreign Ministry, Eduardo Sigal: "It is the desire of Argentina that Bolivia enter as a plenary member of MERCOSUR, since it was already an associated member." Sigal maintained that MERCOSUR had sought to facilitate Bolivia's entry into the organization for at least ten years.[90] While Bolivia and Venezuela sought to escape the moribund and ineffectual Andean Community (CAN), Chile announced it would seek readmission to CAN while maintaining its associate membership status with MERCOSUR, thereby continuing its puerile balance-of-power politics.[91] This policy was actively supported by Chilean president Michelle Bachelet and former president Eduardo Frei Ruiz-Tagle, the son of ex-president Eduardo Frei, who had formed CAN.[92] The readmission of Chile to CAN was viewed positively by some, though that organization was effectively null because its member states continued to sign bilateral treaties with other countries, diluting the purpose of the Andean Community as a customs zone. Opposition to Bachelet's decision came from Communist Party chairman Guillermo Teillier, who argued that as long as his country was not a plenary (full) member of MERCOSUR it would remain a "spectator," isolated from mainstream Latin America.[93] Likewise, Chilean intellectual Mireya Baltra criticized the press in her country for ignoring the earlier July 2006 Córdoba summit. She cited the newspaper *El Mercurio* as an example of this indifference and bias, claiming that the paper sought to diminish the prestige of the conference by not providing it any publicity.[94]

A few days later on July 20, 2006, the plenary and associate members of MERCOSUR met at Córdoba, Argentina, for the Córdoba Conference to discuss problems facing the organization as well as the future expansion of the bloc. The plenary states were Argentina, Brazil, Paraguay, and Uruguay. The associate states in attendance were Bolivia, Chile and Venezuela. Fidel Castro of Cuba attended as an observer. At the conference, President Néstor Kirchner of Argentina called for the establishment of "lifeguard and compensatory" clauses in case any of the economies, especially that of Argentina, should suffer from economic competition. This is the same policy that brought the ruin of LAFTA. Likewise, Kirchner added that the conference was "not about which country is smarter than the other. Solidarity is the banner of our actions." Evo Morales, the newly elected Marxist president of Bolivia, enthusiastically provided an ideologically oriented statement, arguing that the ambitions of the trade bloc needed to be the amelioration of the regions problems: "MERCO-SUR should be a solution for the victims of an economic model that has never resolved the economic problems of our families and our countries." His message clearly implied that his country's application was conditioned on whether or not MERCOSUR might become an ideologically oriented organization.[95]

The presence of Castro, Chávez and Morales highlighted the serious ideological disputes facing Latin America and MERCOSUR. Nonetheless, the end of the highly successful conference brought a call for the creation of a "Merco-America." The specifics of this plan were not outlined, but it was implied that further political and economic unification would be on the agenda. Brazilian president Lula added, "The rich are still rich, but today they are hardly going to hold a meeting without taking into account MERCOSUR." He stressed, "Opportunities do not depend on our rivals, on our enemies, but on the understanding and the need to stand together and build alternatives to improve the lives of our peoples." Lula denied the organization was suffering a crisis and claimed, "Our central aims are more effective than ever before." He warned MERCOSUR's supporters to remain alert about the organization's enemies, warning that the "long nourished anxieties of conservative sectors that have long been working to finish off MERCOSUR" were furiously at work.[96] Fidel Castro echoed support for Lula, claiming, "Our integration has centuries old enemies and they are certainly not happy when they hear about this meeting."[97]

The presidents at the Córdoba Conference took the opportunity to condemn skeptics and critics of expansion, claiming they were no different than the "Euroskeptics."[98] Nonetheless, criticisms would not abate. One Argentine journalist feared the new MERCOSUR might be used by the center-left to become a "trampoline for demagoguery," a clear reference to Chávez. Gustavo Magariños made it clear he opposed Chávez and accused him of trying to politicize MERCOSUR by creating a political structure and ideological hue for the organization.[99] The appearance of Chávez gave ample ammunition to the enemies of political and economic integration. One analyst criticized the advancement of the organization by claiming, "Before the incorporation of Venezuela, the regional bloc was an imperfect customs union and political bloc. With Venezuela, it is possible both imperfections will be accentuated."[100] Former Brazilian president Fernando Henrique Cardozo, once the leading proponent of "dependency theory," stated it would be a mistake for the organization to create a political structure.[101] The Brazilian Confederation of National Industries also voiced its opposition to what it perceived as state-building by MERCOSUR.[102] The new developments in the integration process were stimulated by the development of the Bolivarian Alliance for the Americas (ALBA) and the Union of South American Nations (UNASUR).[103] ALBA was begun at the behest of Hugo Chávez as an alternative to the free trade MERCOSUR. It consists of nine member states that happen to be among the poorest in the hemisphere or have the least control of their economic future. The organization is funded by Venezuela's petrodollars. It is not an all–Latin-American structure, as its members include several English-speaking Caribbean states. It is an ideological alliance rather than a body with any potential for future development. A change in the ideological hue of any government would immediately alter the composition of the group.

The Union of South American Nations (UNASUR) was initiated on December 8, 2004, at the third South American Summit, which formulated the Cuzco Declaration, signed by twelve South American states, with Mexico and Panama in attendance as observer states. UNASUR selected the phrase "Integration for a just development" as its motto, thereby signifying its commitment to mondialization rather than globalization. The purpose of the summit was to merge the Andean Community with MERCOSUR. The two-page Cuzco declaration stated that the objective was to form a common market similar to the European Union. The former secretary general of the Andean Community, Allan W. Tizón, stated that he felt a viable unification could occur by 2019. A special meeting known as the First South American Community of Nations Heads of State Summit was held on September 29–30, 2005, in Brasília, Brazil, to work out the structure of the proposal. UNASUR was formally established on May 23, 2008, when its Constitutive Treaty was signed by the 12 member states and two observer countries, Mexico and Panama.[104] The treaty was signed at the Third Summit of Heads of States, which was situated in Brasília, Brazil. The organization is not strictly an Ibero-American organization, since it includes Guyana and Suriname, which is a first in the unionist movement. This is somewhat unusual as unionism has always been a Pan-Hispanic or Pan-Latin-American movement; however, the introduction of the latter states does not negate the organization as a Pan-Hispanic organization as the populations of these countries are very small and large numbers of people speak Spanish and Portuguese. The official languages of the organization are Spanish, Portuguese, Dutch and English with efforts to include Guaraní.

The constitution of UNASUR stipulated that Quito, Ecuador, would be the site of the secretary-general. The treaty also called for a South American parliament to be established at Cochabamba, Bolivia. A Bank of the South, proposed by Hugo Chávez, is to be established at Caracas, Venezuela. The objective of the bank is to be adequately financed by the member states in order to minimize loans from the World Bank or the International Monetary Fund. The bank would primarily fund infrastructure projects needed to facilitate the physical and economic integration of member states.

As of this date the institutions of UNASUR are still developing. One of the goals of the organization is to create a single currency. At present all twelve monetary systems are still in use. Originally, UNASUR did not even maintain an independent website. The website attributed to the organization was maintained by the Andean Community. Nevertheless, the organization has made its presence felt in international American affairs. On May 5, 2010, it announced its support for Argentina's claim to the Malvinas (the Falklands Islands). It also condemned the draconian anti-immigrant law passed by the state of Arizona, SB1070, that singled out Hispanic Americans for discriminatory treatment. Likewise, the organization pledged to devote resources to combating narcotics smuggling as well.[105] In June 2010, UNASUR had its first meeting to determine the administrative vertebrae of the organization. In attendance were the Indigenous and Amazonian congresses, designed to give Native Americans a voice in the new organ. This inclusion is a testimony to the enlightened achievement of meaningful and participatory democracy in Latin America.[106]

A serious danger to UNASUR and MERCOSUR lies in the ideological divisions that threaten the region. In spite of the ideological schisms that have occurred in Latin America, no ideological group owns unionism. In February of 2007, Carlos Álvarez, the president of the Commission of Permanent Representatives of MERCOSUR, stated to an audience in Havana, Cuba, that ideological rigidity was inimical to the pursuit of union.[107] The conflict between left and right wing dogmatists threatens to diminish MERCOSUR into merely an ideological bloc that will abate the effectiveness of the organization and the possibility of deeper integration.

A second danger to the organizations are the bilateral free-trade proposals (FTAs) introduced by the United States in its efforts to corral the Latin American economies closer into its orbit, which are being pursued in the aftermath of the FTAA debacle. These FTAs ultimately serve as a mechanism for undermining MEROCSUR and UNASUR. These efforts are counterproductive to both Latin America and the United States. It will be recalled that during the 1960s Washington supported Latin American economic integration as a means of promoting the integration of that region into the global economy. This approach needs to be resumed as the most efficient mechanism for promoting capital integration and enhancing the economies of both the United States and Ibero-America.

A third danger is the sense of indifference among Latin Americans themselves. Polling surveys show that most Latin Americans support regional economic integration, but depend too much on the political class for promoting initiatives.

A fourth danger and by far the most serious is the decisions by some states such as Argentina to raise protectionist measures against MERCOSUR associates and the world by simply disregarding the wishes and needs of the member states. The above three problems can be overcome, but the continual raising of tariffs and non-tariff barriers against the MERCOSUR states will defeat the purpose of the organization. Only the future will reveal how this problem is to be resolved.

Not all aspects of the integration movement are fully understood, due to the fact that all integration movements today revolve around economic coordination. Little is known about specific integration negotiations as they are conducted because they are undertaken in secret by elites and are highly sensitive, thereby eluding efforts to promote transparency. It will take extensive work in archives to determine the impact of instructions given to negotiators by presidents or bureaucratic agencies, sectoral commissions or various trade or industrial organizations. An intriguing question that investigators must pursue is why the trade barriers tackled by NAFTA have been so successful while the MERCOSUR countries continue to seek advantage over each other and elude treaty obligations. Could it be that the various trade groups oftentimes dominated by U.S. corporate interests seek to derail MERCOSUR from within?

The people of Latin America need to understand that their only chance of competing with these larger and much more viable economic states and blocs is through the expansion of MERCOSUR and UNASUR. This recognition requires them to develop a militant awareness and to demand further integration. It demands that unionists handle the agendas of political parties and perhaps form their own continent-wide unionist party as a rival and power broker. Unionists need to develop visual symbols in support of MERCOSUR and UNASUR just as is done by any other political, economic, religious, social or cultural movement. They must also develop stronger and more proactive unionist organizations for all groups, especially among young people who now hold the unionist torch.

CONCLUSION

We still have a colonial mentality, and if we don't break those mental barriers, we'll never advance.—Celso Amorim, in an address to the International Labor Organization in Geneva, November 23, 2010

The primary reason for past failures to promote Latin American integration is the development of the state system and its consequent offspring, the political class, which has served as its shield. The political leadership of Latin America has habitually, and successfully, thwarted every effort to promote a viably integrated Latin America. They even stifled the efforts of the dynamic Simón Bolívar, a man who could hardly be considered a mere dreamer. Likewise, the political class was able to thwart the efforts of the region's most notable intellectuals and diplomats in both the nineteenth and twentieth centuries. The political class had good reason to oppose a pro-unionist agenda. Coadunation would have involved absorbing the problems and political factions of other governments. Throughout most of the nineteenth century, the region was a cauldron of chaos with conservatives battling liberals, moderates and Jacobins in polarizing political struggles, leading to all sorts of crises. In the post–1945 era, this situation was intensified by the rise of Fidel Castro, whose appearance suggested that the communist system might successfully challenge capitalism in Latin America. Both communists and liberals emphasized that a merger of their economic and political systems was incompatible with any program of economic integration, to say nothing of political unification.

The state system took on a life of its own in Latin America, and it has been as indestructible as it has proved self-defeating. Since the departure of the Spanish and Portuguese monarchies, the present state model has been accepted as a way of life for the last two centuries. These countries are not

256

genuine nation-states per se, so much as they are states where the mass of people share the same nationality based on culture. The fragmentation created by the state structure has led to numerous consequences, primarily economic problems, which have always led to political instability. Nevertheless, many Latin Americans have recognized the flaws inherent in the state system. Every generation of unionists has emphasized the negative ramifications and inadequacies of the state model. Their continual agitation demonstrates how unsatisfied they have been with "this system or lack of system" that exists in the region. The continuation of the status quo assures that the people of the region will not be able to solve the problems foisted on them by the state system "with or without psychiatric aid."[1]

Of course, it may be argued that the state system exists in Latin America because the people have given their explicit and implied consent to it. It must, however, be noted that at the beginning of the revolutionary period in the early 1800s, a mechanism did not exist whereby the public could explicitly express its approval of the emerging fragmentation. During this period there was never a Latin American equivalent to the Continental Congress formed in the United States. Nor were there individuals similar to a Bismarck, Cavour, Garibaldi or Lincoln in Latin America who advocated violence to create a unified state, or prevent political fragmentation by "blood and iron." Likewise, there was never an equivalent of the Italian Carbonari, utilizing terrorism and uprising to promote unification in the Ibero-American world. The use of such force is not the Latin American way for promoting political and economic integration. Unionism has always advocated peaceful consensus for political and economic integration. This is not surprising, since unionism is an ideology that has affiliated itself with classical liberalism, or liberal socialism. Even Simón Bolívar avoided using force to unify the region. What has been lacking is an authentic recognition by the mass of people of the economic limits of their respective countries. Recognition of the nature of these problems could have brought extensive pressure on the political leadership to spur the integration efforts. Celso Amorin, the Brazilian foreign minister, has argued that the animus confronted by MEROCSUR and its future problems were the result of a "colonial mentality." He added that the citizens of Latin America need to recognize America as their natural locus and said, "If we don't break those mental barriers, we'll never advance."[2] However, fault must not be placed with the majority of people seeking to live out their daily lives. The reason for the many past failures of the integration movement must be cast on the political class. In April of 2005 at a conference on the region hosted at the prestigious Yale Club in New York City, not a single Latin American leader spoke of integration, save the Spaniard Rodrigo de Rato, managing director of the

International Monetary Fund, who twice emphasized the necessity for Latin Americans to promote economic integration.[3] It is incumbent on the political elite to provide the moral and governmental leadership for political and economic integration. This, of course, has been lacking in Latin America during the so-called "national" existence. As a result of the inability to cast the state system aside, fierce suspicions and rivalry have arisen among the people of the region. Economic interests have also suffered from failed integration efforts. This was particularly apparent with LAFTA, where the sectoral commissions responsible for reducing tariff barriers served as obstacles to promoting stronger economic bonds in the region. The sectoral commissions were the representatives of the various industries situated in Latin America, which represented both domestic and foreign enterprises. Hence, it was the various economic sectors (typical of economic corporatism) that made public policy. The political class deserted its responsibilities by providing the sectoral commissions with a free hand in determining which concessions would be made, resulting in the abandonment of the integration process. A successful common market program could have been established regardless of these economic differences if the political will had existed. Such a program would have corrected any imbalances that occurred through any number of mechanisms, such as the movement of displaced workers to more prosperous zones. While it is easy to blame the Latin Americans for failing to make the necessary trading concessions during LAFTA's lifetime, it must be remembered how easy it is for politicians to offend interest groups. A glaring example comes from the United States, which was unwilling to make trading concessions to the Latin American states on the question of agricultural subsidies to U.S. farmers totaling $20 billion dollars during the FTAA negotiations, which ultimately failed.

A further explanation of why political and economic integration efforts have floundered is that the levels of economic development vary among the Latin American countries. This begs the question: If such differing levels of development between the various Latin American states are so profound as to pose a barrier to genuine political and economic integration, why has this not been the case with the European Union, or for that matter the United States, where the member states are at dissimilar levels of development? If differences in economic development are sufficient to preclude economic integration, then logically Spain, Greece, and Portugal should have been excluded from the European Union (EU). Taking these factors into account, there is no tenable reason why the Latin American states could not form the same type of organization. Another pedestrian argument lobbed against integration is that geography inhibits it. The argument has been made so many times that even some unionists have used it to explain the region's fragmentation, despite effective rule by the Spanish crown over all of America and the Philippines. Certainly geography has not impeded such large countries as India, China or Brazil from exercising effective political control. Hence, it is inane to argue or assume Latin America cannot be reunited in a hypostatic union between state and nation.

Another obstacle faced by pro-unionists is that many of the states have not effectively integrated their own societies. It would seem that this situation would have made political or economic integration easier if the politicians had chosen to exploit it. The lack of a strong identity within a particular country would have actually made it easier to create bonds with a politically or economically unified state. In many cases artificial patriotic (nationalist) ideologies arose, focusing on a neighbor state as a potential enemy instead of emphasizing what unified societies could accomplish. In many cases this so-called patriotism was limited to the small middle class, with the masses too busy in their quest for survival to entertain abstract notions developed by political elites. These competing ideas of patriotism are the product of politicians who believe their primary obligation is the protection of the state system. The result has been the descent of Latin America into delusion and self-destruction. Indeed, as Senator Jacob Javits (R–NY) noted, the true enemies of integration are those who have said it is impossible.

An additional impediment to consolidating the objectives of unionists has been the long history of political unrest in Latin America. In the case of LAFTA, for example, the region experienced tumultuous political upheavals in the 1960s, which grew worse as time passed. Post–1967 Latin America soon turned on itself in a series of polarizing political struggles between left-wing insurgents and right-wing governments. The result was a wave of dictatorships that replaced institutions of representative government in many Latin American countries. Consequently, Latin Americans refocused their energies on political, economic and social problems in their own countries, which they considered more pressing. The issue of political and economic integration thus became relegated to the realm of utopianism and unpleasant memories.

Considering the many frustrations of unionists, what is the future of the integration movement? The return of democratic institutions to Latin America in the 1980s paved the way for a bold new attempt to revive economic integration efforts, leading to the creation of MERCOSUR. In spite of being a subregional organization, MERCOSUR has the potential to incorporate more members and perhaps evolve into an all–Latin American organization. No other Latin American subregional organization holds this possibility, because only MERCOSUR has the necessary demographic, financial and industrial resources. President Inácio Lula da Silva of Brazil and President Néstor Kirchner of Argentina have created a parliament for MERCOSUR after many years of work, although this organ has practically no power.[4] Of course, such a structure implies a political union, which would be a monumental achievement, paralleling efforts to provide a constitution for the European Union. Of special significance is that initiative originated from the political left, the first time since the 1930s under Haya de la Torre that the left has viably seized the initiative to promote economic and political integration.

Originally, the United States supported the economic integration of Latin America during the 1960s, but it eventually set up the Free Trade Area for the Americas (FTAA) as a rival to MERCOSUR. The defeat of the FTAA was a significant moment in the history of the region. It marks the victory of Latin Americanism (mondialization) as represented by MERCOSUR over Washington's failed dream of Pan-Americanism (globalization) embodied by FTAA. Despite the demise of FTAA, the United States continues to oppose the economic integration of Latin America via bilateral free-trade treaties. This opposition is likely to grow as Washington's new foreign policy agenda, while quieter than the previous administration of George W. Bush, continues to be based on self-interest. On March 7, 2011, it was revealed in *Pagina 12*, an Argentine Web publication, that Wikileaks had divulged to them top-secret cables from the U.S. State Department that claimed MERCOSUR was anti–U.S, because of its center-left governments. The conclusion was articulated by a group of U.S. ambassadors posted to the southern cone region who met in Rio de Janeiro in May of 2007. There they articulated the view that they hoped Venezuela's Hugo Chávez would clash with President Lula da Silva of Brazil. The leaks confirm suspicions about U.S hostility towards regional economic integration in the area and Washington's duplicity.[5] The intense competition created by the European Union, Brazil, Russia, China and India (BRIC states), as well as contemporary efforts to replace the dollar with either the euro or Chinese yuan, along with the distinct possibility that some countries will cease to trade oil with the dollar, indicate that Washington may become more atavistic in seeking to contain the growth of Latin American economies via international trade organizations, by using the WTO with its stringent intellectual property requirements limiting technology transfers. The massive subsidies the United States provides to its military, scientific, industrial, and research university complex cannot be effectively challenged by Third World states, because they lack the political and economic strength to do so, thus limiting any challenges from these countries.[6]

Despite problems, MERCOSUR remains firmly grounded with the possibility of future growth. Guzmán Carriquiry and Lídice Gómez Mango have noted how the MERCOSUR countries are bracing for further consolidation and expansion by requiring the study of Portuguese and Spanish.[7] Venezuela, with the third largest GDP in South America, has been formally accepted into MERCOSUR trade bloc. Peru has signed several accords to strengthen its ties to the organization. The leading Peruvian electronic newspaper *El Peruano* stated the new agreements "insured that South American integration was not solely commercial and economic, but also social, political and cultural." Brazilian president da Silva stated that these gestures "could change the physiognomy of South America."[8] Argentine president Eduardo Duhalde's call on government officials, intellectuals and the common man to accept a new national consciousness demonstrates that unionism is no longer a marginal movement for romantics.[9] On March 3, 2011, Miguel López Perito, the cabinet chief of Paraguayan president Lugo, stated that the government would seek to persuade conservative elements in Paraguay opposed to the entry of Chávez into Mercosur with the inducement of increased food sales to Venezuela and cheaper energy costs for Paraguayans.[10] A promising development for unionists has been the issuance of a MERCOSUR passport (similar to the all–European passport) for inhabitants of member states. This could lay the foundation for a proto-federalism.

Another promising development for Latin American unionism is the *Declaration of Cancún*, issued in Cancún, Mexico, on February 34, 2010. It called for closer links between the heads of state that form UNASUR and for the development of administrative organs to deal with arbitration matters. It also stated the need for closer political and economic links for the purpose of promoting economic development and justice and a "priority push for regional integration."[11] A measure of the growing self-confidence of these states was their exclusion of the United States and Canada. Likewise, the document condemned the last remnants of colonialism in the New World by unanimously calling on Britain to return the Falkland/Malvinas Islands to Argentina. At the meeting Hugo Chávez called on Queen Elizabeth II to proceed with all deliberate speed to arrange the transfer of the isles.[12]

Other positive indicators of success come from the *Wall Street Journal*, which reported that trade between the four member states had risen from $4.5 billion in 1991 to $41 billion in 2010.[13] Another breakthrough came on August 2–3, 2010, when the 39th MERCOSUR summit, which met at San Juan, Argentina, instituted a long-awaited customs code that had taken several years to prepare.[14] The conference was greeted as a spectacular success by businessmen and foreign governments alike. Almost overnight, on August 4, 2010, the German foreign minister, Guido Westerwelle, initiated a new trade strategy for German investment in Latin America.[15]

Another positive development for MERCOSUR's expansion is the effort to increase trade with the European Union and the People's Republic of China. As a result of the MERCOSUR Presidential Summit held in Mendoza, Argentina, on June 24–30, 2012, it was announced that both MERCOSUR and the People's Republic of China sought to increase trade between the two to $200 billion by 2016.[16] Increased economic contacts among these trading partners will help to cement bonds among the four Latin American states and induce other countries to seek full membership. Observers from outside the hemisphere agree. India's ex-ambassador to Argentina, Paraguay and Uruguay has characterized MERCOSUR as an organ that "gives collective strength.... It is a win-win for all members."[17] Mexican experts view MERCOSUR as "well integrated and as a permanent fact" that will not go away, but will expand even further and deepen its economic integration. José de J. Sosa López, a Mexican university professor, added that Mexican academics and non-governmental organizations view MERCOSUR with great enthusiasm and optimism because "they see the capacity for innovation and the possibility of reducing differences, [trade] asymmetries and generating further talk of cooperation ... whereas NAFTA is dominated by the fact that asymmetries are unresolvable."[18] The constitutions of both Brazil and Uruguay require their governments to promote economic integration. Indeed the manuals for Brazilian diplomats state that MERCOSUR is of primary importance for Brazil and have instructed them to create closer links with all plenary and associate members.[19] The most positive development for the bloc is the decision at the July 31, 2012, meeting to incorporate Venezuela after six long years of wrangling negotiations within the member states.[20] This act represents a major defeat for the enemies of MERCOSUR.

Washington has recently sent mixed signals on the direction of U.S. policy on Latin American integration, as evinced by its recent statements that it supported the objectives listed in the Declaration of Cancún. Phillip Crowley, spokesperson for the U.S. Department of State, informed the press that he saw no problem with the development: "We think it's a good thing when countries in the region come together to talk about how they can cooperate more effectively. And this can take place in many regional forms. We consider the meeting in Mexico as consistent with our goals for the hemisphere."[21] Arturo Valenzuela, assistant secretary of state for Latin America, stated that Washington had no problem with the new development: "We do not see the fact that the countries of Latin America are trying to put together some of their mechanism for integration as, in any way, deleterious to the objectives that the United States are pursuing—quite the contrary. If in fact, through efforts at integration they can build better confidence measures between countries, if they can avoid protectionisms which they often have between their countries in order to expand trade, if they can build a better sense of integration, this reduces intrastate conflict. All these things are important. They're not deleterious to U.S. interests."[22] Are these mere words? A cautionary indicator for observers of the integration process will be the degree to which Washington pursues bilateral free-trade agreements with Latin American states. As of this point in time the United States has shown no sign of abandoning this activity. Indeed the evidence suggests that Washington continues to view the Latin American states of North America as its exclusive sphere of influence, as evinced by NAFTA and the free trade agreements with the Central American states and the Dominican Republic. This approach would be in keeping with a historical view of the American hemisphere that the United States should be the hegemon of North America while South America should have more latitude to conduct its internal affairs.

Perhaps a new statesman such as Eisenhower, Kennedy or Javits will appear who will reinvigorate support for Latin American integration. Only an educated and enlightened public in the United States can reverse the trend. An economically unified Latin America will create a robust economy capable of absorbing U.S. products, without the specter of hostility with Washington or other trade blocs since they will become more interdependent. There is no evidence to suggest unionists seek to create an autarkic society. They only seek better commercial concessions and the opportunity to work on common problems unshackled by a hoary state system. Just as the European monarchs and the United States struggled for political and economic control of America, so Latin America can be expected to fight for its commercial and political interests within itself.

Presently, there is no reason to believe that the views of unionists are utopian or impractical. Unionism should become the new ideology of Latin Americans. Unionists need to work on consolidating their gains and strengthening the links between their countries so that no political groups or ideologies may weaken their gains. Unionists need to become more militant and defiant. They must enlist the mass public to their cause. This must include students, academics, professionals, workers, peasants, and the middle class. Most importantly unionists urgently need to enlist new supporters, especially among young people.

It can be realistically anticipated that agitation for economic and political unity will intensify with the growing competitiveness posed by other economic blocs and the globalization of trade. Only when the masses of the region achieve "a federal future" (a unified state) will they have a viable opportunity to fully develop their human potential via more stable democracies and economies. We may very well see this in our time.

CHAPTER NOTES

Introduction

1. José Vasconcelos, *La Raza Cósmica: Misión de la Raza Iberoamericana* (Madrid: Agencia Mundial de Libreria, 1925). The term *American* is used here to refer to the inhabitants of Latin America.
2. John A. Crow, *The Epic of Latin America,* 4th ed. (Los Angeles: University of California Press, 1992), 86.
3. Vasconcelos, 11.

Chapter I

1. The exception to this pattern was Brazil, which became independent and maintained its territory intact under a new monarchy, independent of the Portuguese throne.
2. This situation presently continues in both Latin America and Europe.
3. Interview with Senator Elbio C. Pezzati, December 30, 2000, Montevideo, Uruguay.
4. Manuel A. Matta, "La Unión Americana y el Gobierno de la Confederación Argentina," in *Colección, de Ensayos I Documentos Relativos a la Unión I Confederación de los Pueblos Hispano-Americanos* (cited hereafter as *Colección*), ed. José Victorino Lastarria, Álvaro Covarrubias, Domingo Santa María, and Benjamín Vicuña Mackenna, 2 vols. (Santiago de Chile: Imprenta Nacional, 1867), 2:80.
5. Mark Van Aken, *Pan-Hispanism: Its Origin and Development to 1866* (Berkeley: University of California Press, 1959), 72.
6. Ibid., 141.
7. Francisco Muñoz del Monte, "España y las Repúblicas Hispano-Americanos," *Revista Española de Ambos Mundos* 1 (Madrid 1853): 268.
8. Ibid., 260.
9. Ibid., 265.
10. Van Aken, 77.
11. José María Samper, "La Confederación Colombiana," Lastarria, *Colección* 1: 349.

12. José María Samper, "La Cuestión de las Razas," *La América: Crónica Hispano-Americana* 2 (November 8, 1858): 2–3.
13. José María Samper, "España y Colombia," *La América: Crónica Hispano-Americana* 2 (May 8, 1858): 4.
14. Ibid., 2–4.
15. Edward S. Milenky, *The Politics of Regional Organizations* (New York: Praeger, 1973), 10.

Chapter II

1. C. Villanueva, *Historia Diplomática de la Primera República de Venezuela* (Caracas: n.p., 1969), 111–12.
2. Reginald Francis Arragon, "The Congress of Panama" (Ph.D. diss., Harvard University, 1923), 9.
3. Ibid., 8.
4. Jonte to Cabildo of Santiago de Chile, ca. 1810, in Alejandro Álvarez, *La Diplomacia de Chile Durante la Emancipación y la Sociedad Internacional Americana* (Madrid: Editorial-América, 1910), 70.
5. Arragon, *Congress of Panama*, 3–4.
6. The *cabildos* were the municipal councils that were elected either for life or for very lengthy periods. Voting privileges were reserved for the gentry or very wealthy merchants.
7. Miguel L. Amunátegui, *Camilo Henriquez* (Santiago de Chile: Imprenta Nacional, 1889), 1: 90–91, cited in Arragon, *Congress of Panama*, 5.
8. Alejandro Alvarez, *La Diplomacia de Chile Durante la Emancipación: Y la Sociedad Internacional Americana* (Madrid: Editorial-América, 1910), 257–61.
9. Ibid.
10. Bernardo O'Higgins, "Manifesto a los Pueblos de Chile del 6 de Mayo de 1818," Lastarria, *Colección* 1: 380.
11. Norberto Galasso, *América Latina: Unidos*

o Dominados (Buenos Aires: Editorial Convergencia, 1975), 42–43.

12. San Martín to General Guido, October 20, 1845, cited in Galasso, *América Latina*, 44–45.

13. Artigas to Junta of Paraguay, December 7, 1811, cited in Galasso, *América Latina*, 54–55.

14. Artigas to government of Buenos Aires, June 29, 1813, Galasso, *América Latina*, 56.

15. Artigas to Cabildo of Montevideo, May 9, 1815, cited in Galasso, *América Latina*, 56.

16. Artigas to Bolívar, July 29, 1819, cited in Galasso, *América Latina*, 57.

17. C.L. Fregeiro, *Don Bernardo Monteagudo: Ensayo Biográfico* (Buenos Aires: Igon, 1879), 14–15.

18. Ibid., 256–57.

19. Galasso, *América Latina*, 46.

20. Bernardo Monteagudo, *Sobre la Necesidad de una Federación General Entre los Estados Hispanoamericano*, vol. 40 (Mexico City: Universidad Nacional Autónoma, Centro de Estudios Latinoamericanos, 1979), 13. Reprint from original 1825 publication.

21. Ibid., 6.

22. Ibid., 9. The government of Pedro I was in fact a constitutional monarchy, though it could hardly be considered a democracy. It was representative government from above. According to the Brazilian Constitution of 1824, senators served for life. Their names were submitted by provincial officials whereupon the emperor determined which individuals would sit in the senate. It was the emperor's duty to select provincial governors. Voting rights were limited and the lower house was chosen indirectly.

23. Ibid.

24. The most illuminating analysis of federal and confederal governments may be found in Alexander Hamilton, James Madison, and John Jay, *The Federalist*, ed. Benjamin F. Wright (New York: Barnes and Noble Books, 1996), 1–88. The perspicacity of these individuals and the editorial analysis provided by B.F. Wright is unsurpassed.

25. The genuine accomplishment of the United States is the establishment of the world's first genuine federal republic. The federal system is not truly appreciated by most observers within the United States, or the rest of the world. In practice, it is an extremely complex form of government, made all the more difficult because of the many interpretations and multitudinous problems that can arise over matters of jurisdiction. Nevertheless, in the United States the federal system has proliferated in size, without serious impediments to the advancement of meaningful representative government and with increasing inclusion for more of its citizens, a clear testimony to the checks and balances provided by embracing many governments. The successful creation and continuity of a federal republic possessing vast tracts of territory is also a major achievement of the United States. Prior to the establishment of that country, it was believed that only city-states could successfully operate republics without slipping into tyranny. The United States has proved critics wrong on both issues.

Chapter III

1. Jorge Pacheco Quintero, *El Congreso Anfictiónico de Panamá y la Política Internacional de los Estados Unidos* (Bogotá: Editorial Kelly, 1971), 5.

2. Simón Bolívar, "Contestación de un Americano Meridional a un Caballero de Esta Isla," September 6, 1815, in Simón Bolívar, *Obras Completas* (Caracas: Ediciones Lisama, 1960), 1: 159.

3. Bolívar to Juan Martin Pueyrredón, June 12, 1818, in *Obras Completas*, 1: 294.

4. Arístides Silva Otero, *El Congreso de Panamá* (Caracas: Instituto de Invesetigaciones Económicas y Sociales, 1969), 9.

5. Bolívar to Francisco Paula de Santander, December 23, 1822, in *Obras Completas*, 1: 708.

6. Bolívar made these comments in *El Patriota de Guayaquil*, quoted in Joseph Lockey, *Pan-Americanism: Its Beginnings* (New York: Macmillan, 1920), 301–302, and in Arragon, *Congress of Panama*, 144.

7. Bolívar, "Views on the Congress of Panama," February 1826, in *Selected Writings of Bolívar*, ed. Vicente Lecuna and Harold A. Bierck (Caracas: Bolivarian Society of Venezuela, 1951), 2: 561.

8. Bolívar, "Contestación de un Americano Meridional a un Caballero de Esta Isla," September 6, 1815, in *Obras Completas*, 1: 170.

9. Ibid.

10. Otero, *El Congreso*, 7.

11. Antonio de la Peña y Reyes, ed., *El Congreso de Panamá y Algunos Otros Proyectos de Unión Hispano-Americana, Archivo Histórico Diplomático Mexicano*, vol. 19 (Mexico City: Publicaciones de la Secretria de relaciones exteriores, 1926), iv.

12. Quintero, *Congreso Anfictiónico*, 21–22.

13. Daniel Florencio O'Leary, *Memorias del General Daniel Florencio O'Leary: Narración* (Caracas: Imprenta Nacional, 1952), 2: 503.

14. Bolívar to Bernardo O'Higgins, January 8, 1822, in *Obras Completas*, 1: 618–619.

15. Simón Bolívar and José Sánchez Carrión to the governments of Gran Colombia, Mexico, Rio de la Plata, Chile and Guatemala (Central American Republic), December 7, 1824, in *Obras Completas*, 2: 52–54. At this time, Bolívar served as ruler of Peru. The note was co-signed by Sánchez Carrión, the Peruvian foreign minister.

Paraguay was not invited because its dictator, José Gaspar Rodríguez de Francia, was rabidly opposed to foreigners and outside governments. Brazil was later invited to attend the congress, but it is unclear what role it was expected to play by the other states. Opposition to Brazilian participation was due to its monarchical system, rather than cultural reasons. As a result, the congress became a forum for attending Spanish-speaking states. Originally five Hispanic-American countries emerged from the revolutionary wars; they eventually disintegrated into more states.

16. Bolívar to Manuel Lorenzo Vidaurre, August 30, 1825, in *Obras Completas*, 2: 206.

17. Bolívar and Sánchez Carrión to the republics of Gran Colombia, Mexico, Rio de la Plata, Chile and Guatemala (Central American Republic), December 7, 1824, in *Obras Completas*, 52–53.

18. M. Dominique de Pradt, *Congreso de Panamá* (Paris: Bechet Aine, Libraire-Editeur, 1825), 1–2. Spanish translation in *Congreso de Panamá* (Paris: Libreria de Bechet Mayor, 1825), 1–2. Translated by D.J.C. Pàges, royal interpreter. Citations are from the latter, which contains original French text. English translation is the author's. Interestingly, the U.S. Department of War received a copy of the work on September 7, 1885; this is rather odd, considering it was published in 1825 and that the work did not discuss military strategy, tactics or technology. Obviously, Washington considered the idea and the movement a threat to its hegemony. At this time Washington was promoting Pan-Americanism as a concept that would forge stronger economic links between the United States and Latin America through free trade.

19. De Pradt, *Congreso de Panamá*, 49.

20. Ibid., 28.

21. Peña y Reyes, *El Congreso de Panamá*, 19: xii.

22. See Arragon, *Congress of Panama*, 295–96, n247.

23. O'Leary, *Memorias*, 2: 543.

24. Canning to Hurtado, January 23, 1826, in Arragon, *Congress of Panama*, 299.

25. Canning to Dawkins, March 18, 1826, in Arragon, *Congress of Panama*, 299.

26. Canning to Hurtado, January 23, 1826, in Arragon, *Congress of Panama*, 299n259.

27. Canning to the Earl of Liverpool, June 6, 1825, in Edward J. Stapleton, *Some Official Correspondence of George Canning* (London: Longmans, Green, 1887), 1: 273–74, and in Arragon, *Congress of Panama*, 298n257.

28. Canning to Dawkins, March 18, 1826, in Arragon, *Congress of Panama,* 302-03n280-281.

29. Bolívar to Santander, October 21, 1825, in *Obras Completas*, 2: 251.

30. Arragon, *Congress of Panama*, 304n284.

31. Arragon, *Congress of Panama,* 303n282, from "The Representative," quoted in *El Peruano*, semestre 1, no. 26, August 26, 1826.

32. Bolívar, "Views on the Congress of Panama," in Lecuna, *Selected Writings*, 2: 561.

33. Bolívar to Sir Richard Wellesley, May 27, 1815, in *Obras Completas*, 1: 136–37.

34. Bolívar to Maxwell Hyslop, May 19, 1815, in Lecuna, *Selected Writings*, 1: 131–32.

35. Arragon, *Congress of Panama*, 277n181.

36. Ricketts to Canning, July 14, 1826, in Arragon, *Congress of Panama*, 288n218.

37. Ibid.

38. Manuel Lorenzo de Vidaurre and Manuel Pérez de Tudela to unnamed Peruvian official, n.d., in Manuel Lorenzo de Vidaurre, *Suplemento a las Cartas Americanas* (Lima: Imprenta Republicana de Concha, 1827), 131. Vidaurre noted the letter was only a rough draft and that it was unclear if the note was sent because his assistant lost the copies of many originals. He was also unsure if this note had a co-author and claimed it "appeared to be a letter directed by Mr. Tudela and me to the government."

39. Revenga to Bolívar, October 5, 1825, in Daniel F. O'Leary, *Memorias del General Daniel Florencio O'Leary: Publicadas por Su Hijo Simón B. O'Leary* (Caracas: Imprenta Nacional, 1879–1884), 6: 499–501.

40. Bolívar to Revenga, February 17, 1826, in *Obras Completas*, 2: 306–07. In employing the term "become men," Bolívar referred to the maturation of political institutions designed to foment and strengthen representative government. Like other educated people of his day, Bolívar believed that the successful foundations of representative political institutions were built over a lengthy period of time, as in Great Britain. Bolívar attributed the continuity and stability of British political institutions to the continued presence of the House of Lords.

41. Ibid., 2: 307.

42. Bolívar to Santander, May 30, 1825, in *Obras Completas*, 2: 145.

43. O'Leary, *Memorias*, 28: 556.

44. Peña y Reyes, *El Congreso de Panamá*, 19: xv–xvi.

45. Bolívar to Santander, October 21, 1825, in *Obras Completas*, 2: 251.

46. Peña y Reyes, *El Congreso de Panamá*, 19: xii.

47. Pedro Gual to Colombian Foreign Ministry, May 26, 1827, in Lockey, *Pan-Americanism*, 314–15; O'Leary, *Memorias*, 24: 383–84.

48. Peña y Reyes, *El Congreso de Panamá*, 19: ix. Michelena was later appointed by Mexico as one of its two representatives to the Panama Congress.

49. Ibid.

50. Gameiro (Gameyro) to Hurtado, written

in London, October 30, 1825, in O'Leary, *Memorias*, 24: 287–88. This letter is attributed to Gameiro but was signed "El Caballero de Janeiro." The Brazilian minister's name is spelled differently in various works.

51. O'Leary, *Memorias*, 2: 543 and 28: 575.

52. Peña y Reyes, *El Congreso de Panamá*, 9: ix–x.

53. Bolívar to Santander, January 6–7, 1825, in *Obras Completas*, 2: 68.

54. Bolívar to Santander, April 7, 1825, in *Obras Completas*, 2: 117.

55. Bolívar to Santander, January 6, 1825, in *Obras Completas*, 2: 69.

56. Ibid.

57. Ibid.

58. Bolívar to Santander, January 23, 1825, in *Obras Completas*, 2: 77.

59. Bolívar to Santander, February 9, 1825, in *Obras Completas*, 2: 80–81.

60. Bolívar to Santander, February 9, 1825, in *Obras Completas*, 2: 81.

61. Bolívar to Santander, March 11, 1825, in *Obras Completas*, 2: 104.

62. Bolívar, "Views on the Congress of Panama," February 1826, in Lecuna, *Selected Writings*, 2: 561.

63. Bolívar to José Rafael Revenga, February 17, 1826, in *Obras Completas*, 2: 307.

64. Bolívar to Santander, May 30, 1825, in *Obras Completas*, 2: 145–46.

65. Ibid., 144.

66. Ibid., 144–145.

67. Bolívar to Santander, October 10–11, 1825, in *Obras Completas*, 2: 229.

68. Bolívar to Santander, May 7, 1826, in *Obras Completas*, 2: 361.

69. Bolívar to Antonio José de Sucre, May 12, 1826, in *Obras Completas*, 2: 366.

70. Bolívar to Revenga, February 17, 1826, in *Obras Completas*, 2: 308.

71. Bolívar to Santander, July 10, 1825, in *Obras Completas*, 2: 169–70.

72. Bolívar to Revenga, February 17, 1825, in *Obras Completas*, 2: 308.

73. Bolívar to Santander, May 7, 1826, in *Obras Completas*, 2: 361–62.

74. Arragon, *Congress of Panama*, 29.

75. O'Leary, *Memorias*, 28: 558–59.

76. In 1825, Bolívar was president of three states (Gran Colombia, Peru and Bolivia) at the same time. Naturally this led to suspicions about his motives. Bolívar presided over Gran Colombia from December 1819 to May 1830. In Peru he ruled from February 1824 to January 1827 and in Bolivia he governed from August 1825 to December 1825.

77. Bolívar to Santander, February 21, 1826, in *Obras Completas*, 2: 311. The Roman general Sulla took power from the military dictator

Marius, claiming he would rule as a dictator for the purpose of restoring the senate.

78. O'Leary, *Memorias*, 28: 557–59.

79. Briceño Méndez to Simón Bolívar, April 12, 1826, in O'Leary, *Memorias*, 8: 188–89.

80. Méndez to Bolívar, April 26, 1826, in O'Leary, *Memorias*, 8: 200.

81. Ibid.

82. Vidaurre to Peruvian foreign minister, June 23, 1826, in *Archivo Diplomático Peruano: El Congreso de Panamá, 1826*, ed. Raúl Porras Barrenechea (Lima: La Opinión Nacional, 1930), 1: 388.

83. Bolívar to Revenga, February 17, 1826, in *Obras Completas*, 2: 308–09.

84. Arragon, *Congress of Panama*, 97n34.

85. Santander to Bolívar, February 2, 1825, in O'Leary, *Memorias*, 24: 256.

86. Briceño Méndez to Bolívar, December 23, 1825, in O'Leary, *Memorias*, 8: 183.

87. Ibid., 186.

88. Briceño Méndez to Bolívar, July 22, 1826, in O'Leary, *Memorias*, 8: 210.

89. Pedro Gual to Bolívar, July 17, 1826, in O'Leary, *Memorias*, 8: 449.

90. Briceño Méndez to Bolívar, December 23, 1825, in O'Leary, *Memorias*, 8: 183–84. Bolívar never arrived in Panama.

91. Bolívar to Santander, April 7, 1825, in *Obras Completas*, 2: 116.

92. Briceño Méndez to Bolívar, December 23, 1825, in O'Leary, *Memorias*, 8: 186.

93. Pedro Gual to Bolívar, February 26, 1826, in O'Leary, *Memorias*, 8: 435.

94. Bolívar to José Maria Pando, February 26, 1826, in O'Leary, *Memorias*, 30: 173–74 and 28: 503–04, and Arragon, *Congress of Panama*, 94.

95. Manuel Vidaurre, "Discurso Dirijido por el Señor D.D. Manuel Lorenzo Vidaurre Ministro Plenipotenciario de la República Peruana Cerca de la Gran Asamblea Americana, à los Señores Ministros Plenipotenciarios de los Demás Estados," *Suplemento a las Cartas Americanas*, 146–47, and in "Discurso del Plenipotenciario Don Manuel Lorenzo Vidaurre en el Congreso Americano de Panamá, al Instalarse la Gran Asamblea en 22 de Junio de 1826," in O'Leary, *Memorias*, 24: 329–34.

96. Raúl Porras Barrenechea, ed., Vidaurre to Bolívar, July 22, 1826, in *Obra Gubernativa y Epistolario de Bolívar: El Congreso de Panamá* (Lima: Comisión Nacional del Sesquicentenario de la Independencia del Peru, 1974) (hereafter referred to as *Obra Epistolaria*), 14: 437.

97. Ibid.

98. Arragon, *Congress of Panama*, 96.

99. Ibid., 95. Arragon claims this passage was omitted.

100. Ibid., 526. The Dutch agent Colonel

Jan Van Veer appeared with no credentials from his government and was left out of the Panama meetings, relying on information provided him by delegates at their discretion (Arragon, *Congress of Panama*, 585).

101. Ibid., 523.

102. Gual to Bolívar, April 11, 1826, in O'Leary, *Memorias*, 8: 439.

103. Vidaurre to Peruvian foreign minister, June 23, 1826, in Barrenechea, *Obra Epistolaria*, 1: 388.

104. Gual to Bolívar, April 11, 1826, in O'Leary, *Memorias*, 8: 436–40.

105. Arragon, *Congress of Panama*, 157–58, and in O'Leary, *Memorias*, 24: 262 and 28: 559.

106. Gual and Briceño Méndez to Revenga, April 10, 1826, in O'Leary, *Memorias*, 24: 313–15.

107. Gual to Bolívar, April 11, 1826, in O'Leary, *Memorias*, 8: 439.

108. Gual to Bolívar, April 27, 1826, in O'Leary, *Memorias*, 8: 445.

109. Gual to Bolívar, April 12, 1826, in O'Leary, *Memorias*, 8: 443.

110. Arragon, *Congress of Panama*, 569.

111. Ibid., 522–24.

112. Vidaurre, *Suplemento*, 146–47.

113. Ibid., 148.

114. Ibid., 144.

115. Ibid., 153.

116. Ibid., 147.

117. Ibid., 148.

118. Ibid., 152–53.

119. Ibid., 148–49.

120. Lastarria, *Colección*, 1: 37.

121. Ibid., 38–39.

122. Ibid., 41–42.

123. Ibid., 42–43.

124. This clause respecting private property may have originated from a concern regarding the rights of slaveholders, but most likely emanated from a concern to protect the commercial and agricultural interests of citizens from other states.

125. Lastarria, *Colección*, 1: 46–48. The original and entire text of the treaties and ancillary accords are in this work, 1: 37–48.

126. Arragon, *Congress of Panama*, 567–69.

127. Ibid., 588.

128. Ibid., 588n223.

129. Bolívar to Briceño Méndez, September 14, 1826, in *Obras Completas*, 2: 471–72, and in O'Leary, *Memorias*, 2: 528.

130. Dawkins to Canning, July 5, 1826, in Arragon, *Congress of Panama*, 588n222.

131. Lastarria, *Colección*, 1: 48–53.

132. Ibid., 1: 48–61.

133. International American Conference, *Reports of Committees and Discussions Thereon, IV, Historical Appendix, The Congress of 1826, at Panama and Subsequent Movements Toward*

a Conference of American Nations (Washington, DC: Government Printing Office, 1890) (hereafter cited as IAC), 199, and in O'Leary, *Memorias*, 24: 368.

134. Bolívar to Briceño Méndez, September 14, 1826, in *Obras Completas*, 2: 471–72, and in O'Leary, *Memorias*, 24: 368.

135. Lastarria, *Colección*, 39.

136. IAC, 195.

137. IAC, 199.

138. Bolívar to Briceño Méndez, September 14, 1826, in *Obras Completas*, 2: 471–72.

139. Ibid., 2: 471–72.

140. Briceño Méndez to General Mariano Montilla, July 17, 1826, in *Obras Completas* 8: 317.

141. Briceño Méndez to Simón Bolívar, July 22, 1826, in *Obras Completas*, 8: 208–09.

142. Ibid.

143. Van Aken, *Pan-Hispanism*, 79.

144. Arragon, *Congress of Panama*, 559.

145. Bolívar to Santander, July 8, 1826, in *Obras Completas*, 2: 430.

146. Bolívar to General José Antonio Páez, August 8, 1826, in *Obras Completas*, 2: 458–59.

147. Vidaurre to Peruvian Foreign Ministry, June 23, 1826, in Barrenechea, *Obra Epistolaria*, 1: 388.

148. Arragon, *Congress of Panama*, 534.

Chapter IV

1. Pedro A. Zubieta, *Congresos de Panamá y Tacubaya: Breves Datos para la Historia Diplomática de Colombia*, 2d. ed. (Bogotá: Imprenta Nacional, 1926), 109.

2. O'Leary, *Memorias*, 28: 555.

3. Gual to Colombian foreign minister, October 25, 1826, in O'Leary, *Memorias*, 24: 377–78.

4. Vidaurre to Peruvian Foreign Ministry, June 23, 1826, in Barrenechea, *Obra Epistolaria*, 1: 388.

5. Pérez de Tudela, to Peruvian Foreign Ministry, September 15, 1826, in Barrenechea, *Obra Epistolaria*, 1: 389–90.

6. Pérez de Tudela to Peruvian Foreign Ministry, October 31, 1826, in Barrenechea, *Obra Epistolaria*, 1: 389–91.

7. Gual to Colombian foreign minister, January 29, 1827, in O'Leary, *Memorias*, 24: 380.

8. Gual to Colombian foreign minister, April 20, 1827, in O'Leary, *Memorias*, 381–82.

9. Gual to Colombian foreign minister, May 26, 1827, in O'Leary, *Memorias*, 379.

10. Gual to Colombian foreign minister, November 29, 1826, in O'Leary, *Memorias*, 379.

11. Gual to Colombian foreign minister, May 26, 1827, in O'Leary, *Memorias*, 384.

12. Ibid.

13. Gual to Colombian foreign minister,

January 21, 1828, in O'Leary, *Memorias*, 391–94.

14. Gual to Colombian foreign minister, January 29, 1828, in O'Leary, *Memorias*, 396.

15. Gual to Colombian foreign minister, March 10, 1828, in O'Leary, *Memorias*, 398.

16. Gual to Colombian foreign minister, April 18, 1826, in O'Leary, *Memorias*, 399.

17. Gual to Colombian foreign minister, May 30, 1828, in O'Leary, *Memorias*, 403. The American minister claimed he was responsible for the creation of the Masonic York lodge, which became politically active in the turbulent politics of Mexico. The York faction favored a pro-republican and pro-federalist government for the Mexican state.

18. Zubieta, *Congresos de Panamá y Tacubaya*, 119–21.

19. Ibid., 122.

20. Ibid., 121.

21. Ibid., 122–24.

22. Ibid., 224.

23. Gual to Colombian foreign minister, September 6, 1827, in O'Leary, *Memorias*, 24: 387, and also in Zubieta, *Congresos de Panamá y Tacubaya*, 125–30.

24. Zubieta, *Congresos de Panamá y Tacubaya*, 126–30.

25. Gual to Colombian foreign minister, July 2, 1828, in O'Leary, *Memorias*, 24: 404. Gual did not provide a date as to when the article was written.

26. Gual to Colombian foreign minister, August 6, 1828, in O'Leary, *Memorias*, 405.

27. Gual to Colombian foreign minister, October 14, 1828, in O'Leary, *Memorias*, 406.

28. Gual to Colombian foreign minister, November 7, 1828, in O'Leary, *Memorias*, 407. The Venezuelan Ministry of Foreign Affairs has named its advanced school of international affairs after Pedro Gual. It is known as the *Instituto de Altos Estudios Diplomáticos Pedro Gual*.

29. "A Panoramic View of Spanish America," no specific date, 1829, in Lecuna, *Selected Writings*, 2: 740–41. Lecuna and Bierck state that this letter was written anonymously, but its inclusion in the volume indicates they viewed it as Bolívar's work.

30. Bolívar to Francisco de Paula Santander, May 29, 1825, in *Obras Completas*, 2: 136–37.

31. "A Panoramic View of Spanish America," in Lecuna, *Selected Writings*, 2: 743.

32. Gual to Bolívar, May 29, 1829, in O'Leary, *Memorias*, 8: 449.

Chapter V

1. Guadalupe Victoria to Bolívar, February 23, 1825, in O'Leary, *Memorias*, 24: 256.

2. Lúcas Alamán to Bolívar, February 23, 1826, in O'Leary, *Memorias*, 258.

3. Author unknown, "Bases para las Instrucciones de los Ministros para la Asamblea de Panamá," in Peña y Reyes, *El Congreso de Panamá*, 19: 9. Although the names of the authors are not cited in sources, the instructions logically had to come from their superiors—Mexico's president, Guadalupe Victoria, or the foreign affairs minister, Sebastián Camacho.

4. Author unknown, "Atribuciones Peculiares del Congreso," in Peña y Reyes, *Congreso*, 9–10.

5. Domínguez and Michelena to president, Council of Ministers, March 9, 1826, in Peña y Reyes, *Congreso*, 17–18.

6. President, Council of Ministers, to Domínguez and Michelena, March 9, 1826, in Peña y Reyes, *Congreso*, 18–19.

7. Domínguez and Michelena to president, Council of Ministers, March 9, 1826, in Peña y Reyes, *Congreso*, 17–18.

8. President, Council of Ministers, to Domínguez and Michelena, March 9, 1826, in Peña y Reyes, *Congreso*, 18–19.

9. Alamán to Bolívar, August 4, 1825, in O'Leary, *Memorias*, 24: 264.

10. Domínguez and Michelena to president, Council of Ministers, March 9, 1826, in Peña y Reyes, *El Congreso de Panamá*, 19: 18–19.

11. Manuel Díez de Bonilla to Mexican Foreign Ministry, November 18, 1831, in Peña y Reyes, *El Congreso de Panamá*, 154.

12. The United States was not the premier economic power in Latin America until the early 1900s due to British commercial predominance, but its growing military and political power was evident to all.

13. IAC, 202.

14. Manuel Díez de Bonilla to Mexican Foreign Ministry, November 18, 1831, in Peña y Reyes, *El Congreso de Panamá*, 19: 154.

15. Ibid., 157.

16. J.M. Torres Caicedo, *Unión Latino-Americana: Pensamiento de Bolívar para Formar una Liga Americana: Su Origen y Sus Desarrollos* (Paris: Librería de Rosa y Bouret, 1865), 42.

17. Ibid.

18. Peña y Reyes, *El Congreso de Panamá*, 19: xx–xxl.

19. Torres Caicedo, *Unión Latino-Americana*, 42. The term translates as "Every man for himself."

20. Juan Nepomuceno de Pereda to Mexican Foreign Ministry, March 27, 1857, in Peña y Reyes, *El Congreso de Panamá*, 19: 163. The term *raza* has many different translations depending on the context in which it is used. In this instance Nepomuceno employed the term as synonymous with civilization and culture.

21. Ibid., 173.

22. Ibid., 188.
23. Ramon Fernandez to Mexican Foreign Ministry, October 11, 1886, no. 18, in Peña y Reyes, *El Congreso de Panamá*, 215–16.
24. Ibid., 217.
25. Ibid.
26. Ibid., 218.
27. Ibid.
28. Alfonso Lancaster Jones, Emilio de León and Luis F. Borja, "Congreso Proyectado por el Gobierno del Ecuador: 1895–1896," in Peña y Reyes, *El Congreso de Panamá*, 261.
29. Central America had formerly been a part of the Viceroyalty of New Spain. Shortly after Mexican independence, the Central Americans separated from Mexico. Secession was peaceful, as the Central American governments did not conduct a war for independence.
30. Galasso, *América Latina*, 50.
31. Bolívar to Santander, April 7, 1825, in *Obras Completas*, 2: 117–18.
32. Juan Nepomuceno de Pereda to Mexican Foreign Ministry, March 27, 1857, in Peña y Reyes, *El Congreso de Panamá*, 19: 172.
33. Ibid., 173–74.
34. Ibid., 177–78.
35. D. José Cecilio del Valle, "Sonaba el Abad de San Pedro; Y Yo También Se Sonar," in *El Amigo de la Patria,* quoted in D. Ramón Rosa and Rómulo E. Durón, *Obras de D. José Cecilio del Valle,* vol. 1 (Tegucigalpa, Honduras: Tipografía Nacional, 1906), 1: xxxv.
36. Ibid.
37. Ibid., 158–59.
38. Bolívar, "A Panoramic View of Spanish America," 1829, in Lecuna, *Selected Writings*, 2: 744.
39. Rosa and Durón, *Obras de José Cecilio del Valle,* 1: 1–xxxvii.
40. Ibid., cii.
41. IAC, 202–203, and in Torres Caicedo, *Unión Latino-Americana*, 111–12.
42. Lastarria, *Colección*, 1: 67. The original phrase is *alhagüeñas esperanzas,* which translates as "sweetened hopes." The term *alhagüeño* can also mean alluring, attractive, or flattering.
43. Ibid., 82.
44. Ibid., 79.
45. Ibid., 69.
46. The text of the treaty may be read in its entirety in Lastarria, *Colección*, 67–81.
47. Author unknown, "Observaciones Hechos por Algunos de los Plenipotenciarios, I Extractadas de los Protocolos del 16 i 20 de Diciembre de 1848," Lastarria, *Colección*, 82.
48. J. Manuel Del Rio to Peruvian foreign minister, January 3, 1848, Lastarria, *Colección*, 93.
49. Ibid., 95.
50. Benjamín Vicuña Mackenna in *Voz de Chile,* May 1862, cited in Lastarria, *Colección*, 152.

51. D.J. Benavente to Ferreirós, September 10, 1848, Lastarria, *Colección*, 97.
52. Ibid., 98.
53. Ibid.
54. Ibid., 99.
55. Ibid., 100.
56. Ibid., 101.
57. Milenky, *Politics of Regional Organization*, 5.
58. Van Aken, *Pan-Hispanism*, 82.
59. Ibid., 83.
60. Juan Manuel Carrasco Albano, "Memoria Presentada Ante la Facultad de Leyes de la Universidad de Chile por Don Juan Manuel Carrasco Albano, en el Mes de Marzo de 1855, Sobre la Necesidad I Objetos de un Congreso Sud-Americano," in Lastarria, *Colección*, 1: 257.
61. Ibid., 262–63.
62. Ibid., 261.
63. Van Aken, *Pan-Hispanism*, 82.
64. Ibid., 83.
65. M. Ancízar to Francisco de Paula Vigil, June 1, 1855, in Lastarria, *Colección*, 1: 331–42.
66. The Bidlack Treaty created the first protectorate of the United States.
67. Octavio Méndez Pereira, *Justo Arosemena* (Panama: Imprenta Nacional, 1919), 252–53.
68. Van Aken, *Pan-Hispanism*, 83–84.
69. Ibid., 43n38.
70. Ibid., 84.
71. "Circular, República del Perú, Ministério de Relaciones Exteriores," Juan Antonio Ribeyro, Peruvian foreign minister, to other foreign ministries, in Torres Caicedo, *Unión Latino-Americana,* 281. Note: The date given in Torres Caicedo's work is January 11, 1861, on p. 277. This is a typographical error. Elsewhere the date is correctly given as January 11, 1864, on p. 81. The reply from the Bolivian government to the Peruvian Foreign Ministry dated February 26, 1864, also refers to Ribeyro's note dated January 11, 1864, which is also in the Torres Caicedo compendium, p. 289. The 1864 date is also found in IAC, 209.
72. Ibid., 282.
73. Ibid., 278–79.
74. Ibid., 281.
75. Ibid., 282–83.
76. There is no evidence that suggest Brazil was invited to the conference. Torres Caicedo states Ribeyro's note "invited all the republics" (p. 81), which precluded Brazil because that country still possessed a monarchy. On p. 85 he writes, "Shall we ignore if the government of Brazil was invited or not...," and then writes, "We cannot doubt that the policy of the Emperor and his ministers is not favorable to the principles that have been proclaimed." Torres Caicedo included in his compendium (pp. 301–303) a note from the Brazilian government signed by João Pedro Dias Vieira to the Chilean

foreign minister, Manuel A. Tocornal, from Rio de Janeiro dated June 7, 1864, in which the Brazilians promised whatever assistance they could provide the Spanish-Americans in their dealing with Spain. There was, however, no mention of supporting any type of political union. Whether or not Dias Vieira was responding to a formal invitation to participate in the Lima Congress is unclear. It is known that the Colombian foreign minister Antonio María Pradilla called for an exclusive Hispanic-American meeting (Torres Caicedo, p. 296). Torres Caicedo also mentioned that he did not possess official replies from Venezuela, Argentina, Guatemala, Honduras, El Salvador, Nicaragua, Costa Rica, or Paraguay (p. 82).

77. Manuel Tocornal to Peruvian Foreign Ministry, February 18, 1864, in "Aceptación del Congreso Americano por Parte de Chile," Torres Caicedo, *Unión Latino-Americana*, 285.

78. Ibid., 286.

79. Antonio María Pradilla to Peruvian Foreign Ministry, June 2, 1864, in "Respuesta del Gobierno Colombiano a la Invitación de del Perú," in Torres Caicedo, *Unión Latino-Americana*, 296–297.

80. Ibid., 300.

81. Rafael Bustillo to Peruvian Foreign Ministry, February 26, 1864, in "Aceptación del Congreso Americano por Parte de Bolivia," in Torres Caicedo, *Unión Latino-Americana*, 289–290.

82. Ibid., 290–291.

83. Justo Arosemena, *Estudio Sobre la Idea de una Liga Americana* (Lima: n.p., 1864), 153–55.

84. Ibid.

85. Arosemena, *Liga Americana*, 95.

86. Ibid., 93–95. Arosemena is referred to as a Panamanian. Arosemena was perhaps born in Panama, but at the Lima Congress in 1864, he was a Colombian citizen.

87. Ibid., 8.

88. Torres Caicedo, *Unión Latino-Americana*, 86, 303.

89. Ibid., 304–305. There is a typographical error in Torres Caicedo's citation. His source is *El Peruano Extraordinario*, dated April 14, 1864. This date is incorrect. The document identifies the speech of Paz Soldán as an address to the opening congress, given alongside the speech of the Peruvian foreign minister, Mr. Calderon, which was on November 14, 1864.

90. Arosemena, *Liga Americana*, 107–09.

91. The full text of the proposed treaty is in Arosemena, *Liga Americana*, 159–70.

92. Galatians 3: 3 in Lastarria, *Colección*, 1: 257.

Chapter VI

1. José María Samper, "La Confederación Colombiana," *Ferrocarril*, January 1859, in Lastarria, *Colección*, 1: 350.

2. Ibid., 358.

3. Ibid., 360.

4. Ibid., 357–60.

5. Ricaurte Soler described the membership of the Unión Americana as emanating from the "petite bourgeoisie," in Lastarria, *Colección*, 1: vi. More likely than not, the directorate emanated from the patrician families of Chile, while the rank-and-file members probably came from the middle class strata.

6. Author unknown, "Sesión del 28 de Abril de 1862," in Lastarria, *Colección*, 2: 13–19.

7. Juan Gregorio de Las Heras, Isidoro Errázuriz, Aniceto V. Albano and Guillermo Matta, "Junta Preparatoria de la Sociedad Unión Americana: Sesión del 11 de Mayo 1862," in Lastarria, *Colección*, 21.

8. Ramón Dehesa, José Torres and Juan R. Muñoz to Unión Americana de Valparaíso, in Lastarria, *Colección*, 36.

9. Author unknown, "Advertencia," September 1, 1862, in Lastarria, *Colección*, 8.

10. "Introducción," in Lastarria, *Colección*, 2: 8–9.

11. Ibid., 8.

12. Ramón Dehesa, José Torres and Juan R. Muñoz to Unión Americana de Valparaíso, in Lastarria, *Colección*, 2: 36.

13. Ibid.

14. M. Espínola to Secretaria de la Junta Patriótica del Distrito Mejicana, October 12, 1862, in Lastarria, *Colección*, 67.

15. La Comisión Directiva de la Unión Liberal, "Invitación para Todos," in Lastarría, *Colección*, 2: 18.

16. Ibid., 19.

17. Ramón Dehesa, José Torres and Juan R. Muñoz to Unión Americana de Valparaíso, in Lastarria, *Colección*, 35.

18. Ricardo Donoso Novoa, *Don Benjamín Vicuña Mackenna: Su vida, Sus escritos, y Su Tiempo, 1831–1886* (Santiago de Chile: Imprenta Universitaria, 1925), 354.

19. Benjamín Vicuña Mackenna, "Estudios Históricos," *Voz de Chile*, May 1862, in Lastarría, *Colección*, 1: 149.

20. Ibid., 157.

21. Ibid., 156–57.

22. Pedro Felix Vicuña, *Único Asilo de las Repúblicas Hispano-Americanas* (Santiago de Chile: n.p., n.d.), in Lastarria, *Colección*, 176. The source does not provide the publisher or the date of publication, but Vicuña calls for an end to the war with Peru in the essay (p. 225), which places its publication between 1836 and 1839.

23. Lastarria, *Colección*, 203–05.

24. Ibid., 210–11.

25. Ibid., 213.

26. Ibid., 209, 213.

27. Ibid., 223.

28. Ibid.
29. Ibid., 216–17.
30. Ibid., 217.
31. Ibid., 217–19.
32. Ibid., 220.
33. Juan Bautista Alberdi, "Memoria Sobre la Conveniencia I Objetos de un Congreso General Americano-Leída Ante la Facultad de Leyes de la Universidad de Chile Para Obtener el Grado de Licenciado," in Lastarria, *Colección*, 228. The exact date of publication of this essay is not given. It was probably written in 1834, the year that Alberdi received his law degree. The title indicates the essay was written to receive a "grado" in law. The term *grado* is somewhat nebulous. The term corresponds to either an exam or a degree. The essay was certainly written before the 1860s because he mentions (p. 252) the large tract of territory controlled by Russia in North America.
34. Ibid., 253.
35. Ibid., 230.
36. Ibid., 232.
37. Ibid., 237.
38. Ibid., 232–33.
39. Ibid., 240–41.
40. Ibid., 251.
41. Ibid., 252–53.
42. Pedro Pablo Figueroa, *Historia de Francisco Bilbao: Su Vida y Sus Obras* (Santiago de Chile: Imprenta de "El Correo," 1898), II and 241.
43. Francisco Barquín Bilbao, "Iniciativa de la América. Idea de un Congreso Federal de las Repúblicas," in Lastarria, *Colección*, 1: 276.
44. Ibid., 281.
45. Ibid.
46. Ibid., 280–83.
47. Ibid., 290.
48. Ibid., 293.
49. Ibid., 285.
50. Ibid., 284–85.
51. Ibid., 283.
52. Ibid., 295–96.
53. Ibid., 298.
54. Ibid., 289.
55. Francisco de Paula Vigil, "Paz Perpétua en América o Confederación Americana," in Lastarria, *Colección*, 319.
56. Ibid., 330.

Chapter VII

1. José Enrique Rodo to unknown recipient, 1916, in Servando Cuadro, *Los Trabajos y Los Días: Hacia la Federación Hispanoamericana* (Montevideo: Ediciones Nexo, 1960), 43.
2. Manuel Ugarte, *The Destiny of a Continent* (New York: Alfred A. Knopf, 1925), 26.
3. Ibid., 28.
4. Manuel Ugarte, *La Patria Grande*, 2d.

ed. (Santiago de Chile: Ediciones Ercilla, 1939), 15.
5. Ibid., 26.
6. Ugarte, *Destiny of a Continent*, 25.
7. Ibid., 233.
8. *O Paiz* of Rio de Janeiro, September 12, 1913, quoted in Ugarte, *Destiny of a Continent*, 237.
9. Ugarte, *La Patria Grande*, 13.
10. Ugarte, *Destiny of a Continent*, 23.
11. Ugarte, *La Patria Grande*, 19.
12. Ugarte, *Destiny of a Continent*, 5.
13. Ibid., 3–5.
14. Ibid., 8–9.
15. Ibid., 7.
16. Ibid.
17. Ibid.
18. Ibid., 7, 9.
19. Ibid., 8.
20. Ibid., 23–25.
21. Ibid., 67, 78.
22. Ibid., 78.
23. Ibid., 83.
24. Ibid., 69.
25. *El Imparcial*, February 4, 1912, quoted in Ugarte, *Destiny of a Continent*, 82.
26. Ibid., 215.
27. Ugarte, *La Patria Grande*, 56–57.
28. Ugarte, *Destiny of a Continent*, 152.
29. Ibid., 287.
30. Mendieta's political party was the first to embrace political union into its platform; however, Víctor Raúl Haya de la Torre's APRA party, which also included political integration as one of its principal objectives, was intended as an international party that was to be situated in all the Latin American states.
31. Mendieta's works are listed in the bibliography.
32. Salvador Mendieta, *La Enfermedad de Centro-América*, vol. 1 (Barcelona: Maucci, 1910), 270.
33. Arthur P. Whitaker and David C. Jordan, *Nationalism in Contemporary Latin America* (New York: Free Press, 1966), 163. The term *Indo-Spanish America* was influenced by Víctor Raúl Haya de la Torre and his APRA movement, which utilized the term *Indo-America*.
34. Hector Vargas Haya, *Amazonia, Realidad o Mito* (N.p, n.d.), 205–206., quoted in Mario Peláez Bazán, *Haya de la Torre y la Unidad de América Latina* (Lima: E. Delgado Valenzuela, 1977), 530.
35. Gabriel del Mazo, *Vida de un Político Argentino* (Buenos Aires: Plus Ultra, 1976), 141.
36. Ibid., 143.
37. Peláez Bazán, *Haya de la Torre*, 316.
38. Víctor Raúl Haya de la Torre, *La Defensa Continental*, 3d. ed. (Buenos Aires: Editorial Americalee, 1946), 11.
39. Víctor Raúl Haya de la Torre, *A Dónde*

va *Indoamérica?* (Santiago de Chile: Editorial Ercilla, 1935), 7.

40. Jean-Francis Billón, "Latin American Federalism," *The Federalist* (Pavia, Italy) 35, no. 1 (1993): 21–27.

41. Ibid., 23.

42. Peláez Bazán, *Haya de la Torre*, 39.

43. Haya de la Torre, *A Dónde va Indoamérica?*, 29.

44. Haya de la Torre, *La Defensa Continental*, 19.

45. Ibid., 23.

46. Ibid., 17, 20.

47. Ibid., 19.

48. Peláez Bazán, *Haya de la Torre*, 14.

49. Ibid., 130.

50. Ibid., 17.

51. Ibid., 278.

52. Ibid.

53. Carols Deambrosis Martins to Haya de la Torre, September 1928, cited in Haya de la Torre, *A Dónde va Indoamérica?*, 280.

54. Haya de la Torre, *A Dónde va Indoamérica?*, 240.

55. Ibid., 241.

56. Víctor Raúl Haya de la Torre, *El Antimperialismo y el APRA* (Santiago de Chile: Ediciones Ercilla, 1936), 36.

57. Ibid., 107.

58. Ibid., 37–38.

59. Ibid., 40.

60. Ibid., 30.

61. Parlamento Latinoamericano, "Andrés Townsend Ezcurra," http://parlatino.org/es/conozca-el-organismo/galeria-de-fundadores/94-andres-townsend-ezcurra.html, accessed June 28, 2010.

62. Andrés Townsend Ezcurra, *Las Provincias Unidas de Centroamérica: Fundación de la República* (Guatemala City: n.p., 1958).

63. The English translation of *crisol* is "boiling pot" or "crucible," symbolic of the youthful fury and energy of the writers.

64. "Nuestros Propósitos," *Crisol,* October 1946, no. 1, p. 1.

65. "Algunos Detalles," *Crisol,* December 1946, no. 2, p. 1.

66. "Nuestros Propósitos," *Crisol* October 1946, no. 1, p. 1.

67. Rubén A. Bonsignore, "Palabras del Presidente de la Asociación Juvenil Americana en la Apertura de la Asamblea General de Fundación," *Crisol,* October 1946, no. 1, p. 1.

68. "La Hora de Nuestra América Ha Llegado," *Crisol,* October 1946, no. 1, pp. 1, 3.

69. Interview with Luis D. Schinca, February 10, 2004.

70. "Nuestros Propósitos," Crisol, October 1946, no. 1, p. 1.

71. Interview with Luis D. Schinca, February 10, 2004.

72. Interview with Ariel B. Collazo, February 19, 2004.

73. Interview with Alberto Methol Ferré, February 16, 2004.

74. Roberto Ares Pons, "Introduction," in *Los Trabajos y Los Días: Hacia la Federación Hispanoamericana* (Montevideo: Ediciones Nexo, 1958), 9.

75. Cuadro, *Los Trabajos,* 7–13.

76. Ibid., 7–13. President Lula of Brazil made the same observation after the treaty forming UNASUR was created.

77. Interview with Ariel B. Collazo, February 19, 2004.

78. Ibid., 16–17.

79. Ibid., 17.

80. Ibid., 38.

81. Roberto Ares Pons, "Ha Muerto Servando Cuadro," *MARCHA,* March 13, 1953, file no. 7999/4, Biblioteca Nacional, Montevideo, Uruguay.

82. Alberto Methol Ferré and Alver Metalli, *La América Latina del Siglo XXI* (Buenos Aires: Edhasa, 2006).

83. Alberto Methol Ferré, "Juventud Universitaria y Mercosur," in *Grupo de Reflexão Prospectiva Sobre MERCOSUR,* ed. Clodoaldo Hugueney Filho and Carlos Henrique Cardin (Brasília: Ministério das Relações Exteriores/FUNAG, 2002).

84. Interview with Alberto Methol Ferré, December 30, 2007, and January 15, 2008, in Montevideo, Uruguay.

Chapter VIII

1. Victor Bulmer-Thomas, *The Economic History of Latin America Since Independence* (New York: Cambridge University Press, 1994), 196, 257–258.

2. Ibid.

3. United Nations, "Report by the Secretariat: Significance of the Common Market for the Economic Development of Latin America," *The Latin American Common Market* (New York: United Nations Dept. of Ecomomic Affairs, 1959), 8 (E/CN.12/C.1/9).

4. United Nations, *Economic Survey of Latin America 1949* (New York: United Nations Dept. of Ecomomic Affairs, 1951), 9–11 (E/CN.12/164/Rev.1).

5. Milenky, *The Politics of Regional Organization,* 10.

6. Raúl Prebisch, *Hacia una Dinámica del Desarrollo Latinoamericano* (Mexico City: Fondo de la Cultura Económica, 1963), xi–xii.

7. Willard L. Beaulac, *The Fractured Continent: Latin America in Close-Up* (Stanford: Hoover Institution Press, Stanford University, 1980), xi.

8. Interview with Mrs. Raúl Prebisch (Eliana

Díaz de Prebisch), in Buenos Aires, January 3, 1999.

9. Ibid.

10. Walter Krause and F.J. Mathis, *Latin America and Economic Integration* (Des Moines: Iowa University Press, 1970), 7.

11. Armando de Filippo, "La Visión Centroperiferia Hoy," Revista de CEPAL, Número Extraordinario, 1998, http://www.eclac.org/publicaciones/SecretarialEjecutiva/7/lcg2037/difil.htm, 1–4. The theory was named for Prebisch and Hans W. Singer.

12. Bulmer-Thomas, *Economic History of Latin America*, 276.

13. Ibid., 281.

14. Willard Beaulac, former U.S. ambassador to Argentina under Eisenhower, wrote that the ECLA was viewed as a front for communist ideologues by former Chilean president Jorge Alessandri. Beaulac claimed that Pedro Vuskovic and Carlos Matus, formerly of the ECLA, were Marxists who later served under President Salvador Allende (*Fractured Continent*, 108). For an excellent review of ECLA thought see Ricardo Bielschowsky, "Evolución de las Ideas de la CEPAL" (Revista de CEPAL, Número Extraordinario, 1998, http://www.eclac.org/publicaciones/SecretariaEjecutiva/7/lcg2037/bielchow.htm, 1). The objective of Prebisch was to promote import duties as a means of strengthening domestic private enterprise, which met opposition from some U.S. quarters. The Prebischean method was based on U.S. economic policy of the 19th and 20th centuries, which favored import tariffs in order to facilitate industrialization.

15. John Toye and Richard Toye, "Raúl Prebisch and the Limits of Industrialization," in *Raúl Prebisch: Power, Principle and the Ethics of Development*, Special Series, ed. Edgar J. Dosman (Buenos Aires: Inter-American Development Bank-Institute for the Integration of Latin America and the Caribbean [INTAL], 2006), 27, http://www.iadb.org.intal.

16. United Nations, *Economic Survey of Latin America* (New York: United Nations Dept. of Ecomomic Affairs, 1949), 5 (E/CN.12/164/Rev.1).

17. United Nations, "The Latin American Regional Market," *Economic Bulletin for Latin America* 3, no. 1 (March 1958): 1 (E/CN.12/531).

18. Ibid., 1–2.

19. Working Group on the Regional Market, "Bases for the Formation of the Latin American Regional Market," *Economic Bulletin for Latin America* 3, no. 1 (March 1958): 3.

20. Ibid.

21. Ibid., 4–7.

22. United Nations, "Recommendations Concerning the Structure and Basic Principles of the Latin American Common Market: Report of the Second Session of the Working Group," *The Latin American Common Market*, 39 (E/CN.12/531).

23. Ibid., 40–41.

24. Ibid., 50.

25. Ibid.

26. United Nations, "Summary Record of the Meetings Held at the Headquarters of the United Nations Economic Commission for Latin America, Santiago, Chile (April 6–17, 1959)," *The Latin American Common Market*, 100 (E/EN.12/C.1/11/Add.I).

27. United Nations, "Memorandum Transmitted by the Governments Members of the European Economic Community to the Latin American Governments," April 11, 1958, *The Latin American Common Market*, 108.

28. Letter from Arnaldo Tomás Musich to author, June 12, 2003.

29. "Report of the Second Session of the Trade Committee," in *The Latin American Common Market* (New York: Secretariat of the Economic Commission for Latin America, 1959), 113.

30. Raúl Prebisch, "Statement Made by Mr. Raúl Prebisch, Executive Secretary of the Economic Commission for Latin America, on 11 May 1959," *The Latin American Common Market*, 130.

31. Ibid.

32. Ibid., 131.

33. Ibid.

34. "Report of the Second Session of the Trade Committee," in *The Latin American Common Market*, 113.

35. Ibid., 119.

36. Ibid., 124. Regarding resolution 6 (II), the Arabic numeral represents the sequence of resolution from the previous session of the Trade Committee. The Roman numeral represents the second session of the Trade Committee.

37. Ibid., 126.

38. Jan Tinbergen, "Heavy Industry in the Latin American Common Market," *Economic Survey of Latin America* 5, no. 1 (March 1960): 3–5.

Chapter IX

1. Centre of National Statistics and International Trade of Uruguay, *Practical Manual of LAFTA* (Montevideo: [PUBLISHER], 1969), 3, 11.

2. Interview with Gustavo Magariños, December 19, 1998.

3. Centre of National Statistics, *Practical Manual of LAFTA*, 13.

4. Ibid., 27.

5. Sidney Dell, *A Latin American Common Market?* (London: Oxford University Press, 1966), 228.

6. Centre of National Statistics, *Practical Manual of LAFTA*, 13.

7. Banco de la República, *Tratado de Montevideo Que Crea la Asociación Latinoamericana de Libre Comercio* (Bogotá: Talleres Gráficos del Banco de la República, 1961), 3.

8. Nino Maritano, *A Latin American Economic Community: History, Policies, and Problems* (Notre Dame: University of Notre Dame Press, 1970), 60.

9. Central Intelligence Agency Office of Current Intelligence, *Special Report: The Latin American Free Trade Association,* Document ID #9153, October 19, 1961, 1.

10. Centre of National Statistics, *Practical Manual of LAFTA*, 11.

11. Jon M. Gasserud, "Economic Integration in Latin America," January 16, 1961, Council on Foreign Relations, Study Group Reports (SGR), 1–2. All SGR were written by Gasserud. The attached date identifies each report.

12. Ibid., 2–3.

13. Ibid., 4–5.

14. Ibid., 6.

15. Gasserud, *SGR*, April 6, 1961, 2–3. Alemann's parents, who were from Switzerland, published the Buenos-Aires-based German language paper *Argentinisches Tageblatt,* founded in 1874.

16. Walter Krause and F. John Mathis, *Latin America and Economic Integration: Regional Planning for Development* (Iowa City: University of Iowa Press, 1970), 17.

17. Ibid., 20.

18. George Jackson Eder, "Economic Integration in Latin America: The Next Fifty Years," in *The Movement Toward Latin American Unity,* ed. Ronald Hilton (New York: F.A. Praeger, 1969), 165.

19. Interview with Gustavo Magariños, December 29, 1999.

20. Ernst B. Hass and Phillipe C. Schmitter, *The Politics of Economics in Latin American Regionalism: The Latin America Free Trade Association After Four Years of Operation,* The Social Science Foundation and Graduate School of International Studies Monograph Series in World Affairs, vol. 3, monograph 2, 2965–66 (Denver: University of Denver, 1965), 7.

21. Since CACM was a small and relatively ineffectual organization, it shall not be discussed in depth. Several works on the organization have been published.

22. Centre of National Statistics, *Practical Manual of LAFTA*, 13.

23. Eduardo Frei to Carlos Lleras Restrepo, August 5, 1966, Archive of Fundacion Frei, File #1954.

24. Other regional trade areas exist today. It is not the intention here to discuss each one, but rather to focus exclusively on those that have been the most significant for the promotion of genuine economic or political integration in Latin America. Some other subregional groupings are the North American Free Trade Agreement (NAFTA), which came into effect in 1994; and the Caribbean Common Market, comprising the English-speaking Caribbean, which was established in 1973. Since these organizations do not deal exclusively with Latin America, they will not be discussed.

25. Under the military government, Chile began a massive campaign to induce foreign investment as the only means to maintain its survival, a policy that has outlived military control. No other Latin American government in recent times has made such strenuous efforts to open its doors to foreign investment, the free market and elimination of government-sponsored programs such as the pension system.

26. Peter Calvert, *The International Politics of Latin America* (Manchester: Manchester University Press, 1994), 183.

27. Maritano, *Latin American Economic Community*, 167; interview with Gustavo Magariños, December 29, 1999.

28. Maritano, *Latin American Economic Community*, 24.

29. Joseph Grunwald, Miguel S. Wionczek and Martin Carnoy, *Latin American Economic Integration and U.S. Policy* (Washington, DC: Brookings Institution, 1972), 113; see also Hass and Schmitter, *Politics of Economics*, 13–14, 25. For information on private capital enterprises in Latin America see Marcos Kaplan, ed., *Corporaciones Públicas Multinacionales para el Desarrollo y la Integracion de la América Latina* (Mexico City: Fondo de la Cultura Económica, 1972).

30. Hass and Schmitter, *Politics of Economics*, 25.

31. Jack Behrman, *The Role of International Companies in Latin American Integration: Autos and Petrochemicals* (Lexington, MA: Lexington Books, 1972), 60.

32. Hass and Schmitter, *Politics of Economics*, 25.

33. Centre of National Statistics, *Practical Manual of LAFTA*, 107–08.

34. Maritano, *Latin American Economic Community*, 132.

35. Centre of National Statistics, *Practical Manual of LAFTA*, 114–16.

36. President Frei to Mayobre, Herrera, Sanz de Santamaría, and Prebisch, January 6, 1965, in José Antonio Mayobre, Felipe Herrera, Carlos Sanz de Santamaría and Raúl Prebisch, *Hacia la Integracion Acelerada de América Latina: Proposiciones a los Presidentes Latinomericanos* (Mexico City: n.p., 1965), 1–6.

37. Ibid., 1–3.

38. Ibid., 1.

39. Ibid., 7–8.
40. Ibid., 19.
41. Ibid., 8–13.
42. Ibid., 14.
43. Ibid., 13–17.
44. Ibid., 26.
45. Ibid., 31.
46. Ibid., 58.
47. Ibid., 51.
48. Ibid., 181.
49. Ibid., 192.
50. Department of State Bulletin, May 8, 1967, 712, and in "Declaracion de los Presidentes de America Sobre Integración," *Boletín de la Integración* 17 (April 1967): 162–74.
51. Department of State Bulletin, May 8, 1967, 719.
52. Ibid.
53. Ibid., 714.
54. Marcos Gabay and Carlos María Gutierrez, *Integración Latinoamericana? De la Alianza Para el Progreso a la OLAS: Recopilación y Análisis Documental* (Montevideo: Ediciones Cruz del Sur, 1967), 121–13.
55. U.S. State Department, *The Inter-American Meeting of Presidents; Punta del Este, April 12–14, 1967* (Washington, DC: Government Printing Office, June 19, 1967), 18.
56. Author unknown, "Latin America: Now the Action? *Senior Scholastic*, April 22, 1967, 21.
57. Salvador Allende, *Punta del Este: La Nueva Estrategia del Imperialismo* (Montevideo: Editorial Dialogo, 1967), 58.
58. Ibid., 56.
59. Ibid., 57.
60. Ibid., 12.
61. Felipe Herrera, *América Latina Integrada* (Buenos Aires: Editorial Losada, 1967), 323. Hallstein insisted that economic unification ultimately led to political union (Walter Hallstein, "The European Economic Community," *Political Science Quarterly* 78, no. 2 [June 1963]: 165).
62. The most prominent members of EFTA were Britain, Austria, and Sweden.

Chapter X

1. Address of Sol Linowitz to the Conference of New York Chambers of Commerce in Washington, DC, *Department of State Bulletin*, May 29, 1967, 824.
2. George F. Kennan, *Memoirs: 1925–1950* (Boston: Atlantic-Little Brown, 1967), 476–81.
3. Ibid., 483.
4. Roger R. Trask, "George F. Kennan's Report on Latin America (1950)," *Diplomatic History* 2 (Summer 1978): 307–11.
5. Kennan, *Memoirs*, 94.
6. J. Warren Nystrom and Nathan A. Haverstock, *The Alliance for Progress* (Princeton: Van

Nostrand, 1966), 27; Emmet John Hughes, *The Ordeal of Power: A Political Memoir of the Eisenhower Years* (New York: Atheneum, 1963), 145–46.
7. Ibid.
8. Ibid.
9. Douglas MacArthur II to Senator John Sparkman, October 12, 1965, U.S. Congress, Joint Economic Committee, Subcommittee on Inter-American Economic Relationships, *Latin American Development and Western Hemisphere Trade*, Eighty-Ninth Congress., First Session., September 8, 9 and 10, 1965 (Washington, DC: Government Printing Office, 1965) (hereafter cited as Joint Economic Committee), 173; "Address Before a Joint Session of the National Congress of Chile, March 1, 1960," U.S. President, *Public Papers of the Presidents of the United States: Dwight D. Eisenhower*, no. 73 (Washington, DC: Office of the Federal Register, National Archives and Records Service, 1961), 260.
10. "Toast to President Alessandri at a Dinner Given in His Honor by the President, March 1, 1960," U.S. President, *Public Papers of the Presidents of the United States: Dwight D. Eisenhower*, no. 75 (Washington, DC: Office of the Federal Register, National Archives and Records Service, 1961), 262.
11. Joint Economic Committee, 173–74.
12. Ibid.
13. Lyndon B. Johnson, *The Vantage Point* (New York: Holt, Rinehart and Winston, 1971), 351.
14. Ibid., 347–48.
15. Interview with Senator Elbio C. Pezzati, December 23, 1998.
16. Harley Notter, "American Interests in the Economic Unification of Europe with Respect to Trade Barriers" (New York: Council on Foreign Relations Study, September 14, 1942), no. E-B56, 1–2. The issue of creating an autarkic economy was of great concern to American policy makers with respect to European integration. The study expressed concerns regarding the creation of a Europe that might develop "along autarkic or semi-autarkic lines." The study asserted, "A political danger would be created by making Europe into a single power bloc outside the range of American influence."
17. Raymond F. Mikesell, *Liberalization of Inter-Latin American Trade* (Washington, DC: Dept. of Economic and Social Affairs, Pan American Union, 1957), 1.
18. Ibid., 47.
19. Ibid., 75.
20. Ibid., 72.
21. Ibid., 2.
22. Ibid., 28.
23. Stacy May to committee members, October 4, 1960, *Study Group on Economic Integration in Latin America*. Council on Foreign

Relations New York: Council on Foreign Relations, December 7, 1960, 2.

24. Walter J. Sedwitz, "The Latin American Common Market: Emerging Patterns and Issues," December 7, 1960, Council on Foreign Relations, *Economic Integration in Latin America* Working Paper No. 1. New York: Council on Foreign Relations, December 7, 1960, 1–2.

25. Ibid., 5.

26. Ibid., 9–10.

27. Ibid., 16–20.

28. Sedwitz, "Latin American Common Market," 1.

29. Ibid., 3.

30. Walter J. Sedwitz, "Latin American Economic Integration and Development," January 16, 1961, Council on Foreign Relations, *Economic Integration in Latin America*, Working Paper No. 2. New York: Council on Foreign Relations, January 16, 1961, 5–6.

31. Gasserud, SGR, December 7, 1960.

32. Ibid., 6.

33. Ibid.

34. Ibid., 4–5.

35. Gasserud, SGR, February 23, 1961, Working Paper No. 2, 10. The possibility of creating one tax zone for U.S. business via economic integration in Latin America has not been found to be a major theme in American documents reviewed by the author. It is nevertheless an intriguing issue that was probably entertained by the Washington bureaucracy and policy makers. To what extent it was a concern considered by U.S. multinational corporations operating in Latin America is unclear, but it is known that corporations such as Gillette and Xerox of Mexico lobbied against further Mexican participation in LAFTA.

36. Gasserud, SGR, December 7, 1960, 5–6.

37. Ibid., 6–7.

38. Ibid., 8–9.

39. Gasserud, SGR, Working Paper No. 2, 22–23.

40. Walter J. Sedwitz, "Economic Development in the Framework of a Central American Customs Union and of LAFTA," February 23, 1961, Council on Foreign Relations, *Economic Integration in Latin America*, Working Paper No. 3. New York: Council on Foreign Relations, February 23, 1961, 3.

41. Gasserud, SGR, February 23, 1961, 6.

42. Gasserud, SGR, Working Paper No. 3, 12–13.

43. Gasserud, SGR, April 25, 1961, 1.

44. Walter J. Sedwitz, "Latin American Economic Integration: The Problem of Trade and Payments," April 6, 1961, Council on Foreign Relations Working Paper No. 4. New York: Council on Foreign Relations, April 6, 1961, 1–2.

45. Walter J. Sedwitz, "Latin American Economic Integration: Some Major Conclusions," December 12, 1961, Council on Foreign Relations, Study Group on Economic Integration in Latin America, Working paper No. 5. New York: Council on Foreign Relations, December 12, 1961, 2.

46. Ibid., 15–17.

47. Committee for Economic Development, *Cooperation for Progress in Latin America*, 5th ed. (New York: Committee for Economic Development, 1966), 15.

48. Committee for Economic Development, *Economic Development Abroad and the Role of American Foreign Investment* (New York: Committee for Economic Development, 1956), and cited in Committee for Economic Development, *Cooperation for Progress*, 10.

49. Committee for Economic Development, *Cooperation for Progress*, 11.

50. Ibid., 10.

51. Ibid., 35.

52. Central Intelligence Agency, Office of Current Intelligence, *Special Report: The Latin American Free Trade Association*, Document ID# 9153, October 18, 1963, 1.

53. Ibid., 2–3.

54. Ibid., 4.

55. Ibid.

56. U.S. President, *Public Papers of the Presidents of the United States: Lyndon B. Johnson* (Washington, DC: Office of the *Federal Register*, National Archives and Records Service, 1965), 2: 887.

57. Joint Economic Committee, 209.

58. Ibid., 218–19.

59. Salvador Rivera, "Jacob K. Javits and Latin American Economic Integration," *Cuaderno de Negocios Internacionales e Integración* (July–December 2007): 34–59.

60. Jacob Javits, "Last Chance for a Common Market," *Foreign Affairs* 45, no. 3 (April 1967): 457.

61. Interview with Mrs. Marion Javits, October 1, 2003.

62. Joint Economic Committee, 218–219.

63. Ibid., 6.

64. Ibid., 29.

65. Ibid., 20.

66. Ibid.

67. "Report by the Operations Coordinating Board to the National Security Council," *Foreign Relations of the United States*, 1958–1960, V, American Republics, 139. Report also known as "Report on Latin America (NSC 5902/1)."

68. Joint Economic Committee, 27.

69. Ibid., 32–36.

70. Ibid., 49.

71. Ibid., 50.

72. Ibid., 53.

73. Ibid., 64.

74. Ibid., 77.

75. Ibid., 72.
76. Ibid., 56.
77. Ibid., 53.
78. Ibid., 57.
79. Ibid., 87.
80. Ibid., 90–91.
81. Ibid., 143.
82. Ibid., 167.
83. Ibid., 145.
84. Ibid., 144.
85. Ibid., 145.
86. Ibid.
87. Ibid.
88. Ibid., 67.
89. Hugh Sidey, "LBJ's Diplomatic Foray into South America," *Life* 62, no. 15 (April 14, 1967): 38B.
90. Sol Linowitz, *The Making of a Public Man: A Memoir* (Boston: Little, Brown, 1985), 21.
91. "Optimism and Obstacles," *Newsweek*, April 26, 1967, 42–43.
92. U.S. State Department, *The Inter-American Meeting of Presidents: Punta del Este, April 12–14, 1967*, June 19, 1967. Washington, DC: U.S. Department of State, June 19, 1947. There is no serial or file number attached to this document. It is probably listed as an *After Action Report*. The author has a copy of this publication in his private possession. The State Department officials who placed their names at the end of the report are listed as SDEaton and HVFunk. These names appear exactly as in the document.
93. Ibid., 10.
94. "Optimism and Obstacles," 43.
95. Hugh Sidey, "The Benefactor Sealed Off from the Benefited," *Life* 62, no. 16 (April 21, 1967): 36B.
96. "American Chiefs of State Meet at Punta del Este," Department of State Bulletin, May 8, 1967. Washington, DC: Office of Media Services, Bureau of Public Affairs, 1967, 708.
97. Ibid., 709.
98. U.S. State Department, *Inter-American Meeting*, 35–38.
99. Ibid., 35.
100. "Optimism and Obstacles," *Newsweek*, April 24, 1967, 42–43.
101. Prologue, U.S. State Department, *Inter-American Meeting*.
102. Ibid., 2.
103. Ibid., 2–3.
104. Ibid., 45–46.
105. "The Road from Punta del Este," Department of State Bulletin, May 29, 1967. Washington, DC: Office of Media Services, Bureau of Public Affairs, 822–25.
106. Javits, "Last Chance," 449–50.
107. Ibid., 461.
108. Ibid., 453–56.
109. Ibid., 461.
110. Ibid., 449.
111. "Secretary Rusk Discusses the Punta del Este Conference and Viet-Nam on *Meet the Press*," Department of State Bulletin, May 8, 1967. Washington, DC: Office of Media Services, Bureau of Public Affairs, 722–25.
112. Lincoln Gordon, "Punta del Este Revisited," *Foreign Affairs* 45, no. 4 (July 1967): 626–27.
113. Central Intelligence Agency, *Economic Trends and Prospects in Latin America*, National Intelligence Estimate No. 80/90-67, July 20, 1967, 1–2.
114. Ibid., 18.
115. Ibid., 24.

Chapter XI

1. The Spanish text pertaining to the relationship between the Ouro Preto Protocol and the Treaty of Asunción reads as follows: "...Este Nuevo Protocol es parte integrante del Tratado de Asunción...," in "Protocol of Ouro Preto" (Montevideo, Uruguay: Comisión Sectorial para EL MERCOSUR), article 48.
2. *Informe Sobre EL MERCOSUR* (Montevideo: Comisión Sectorial para EL MERCOSUR, Centro de documentación y difusión) Periodo 26.3-31.12.94 Doc# cdd 012/95, 1.
3. Tratado de Asunción, Anexo 1—Programa de Liberación Comercial, 10.
4. Tratado de Asunción (Montevideo: Comisión Sectorial para EL MERCOSUR, Centro de documentación y difusión), 1–2.
5. Ibid., 3.
6. Ibid.
7. Ibid., 4.
8. Ibid., 6.
9. Ibid., 25.
10. Ibid., 9.
11. "Protocolo Adicional al Tratado de Asunción Sobre la Estructura Institucional del MERCOSUR-Protocolo de Ouro Preto,"(Montevideo, Uruguay: Comisión Sectorial para EL MERCOSUR), Articles 23–27.
12. ALADI serves to promote bilateral and multilateral trade agreements. It is financed by member states and also functions as a think tank. It is based in Montevideo, Uruguay.
13. Carlos Mata Prates and Eduardo Tellechea Bergman, "Creación por el Consejo del Mercado Común del Sur de la Reunión de los Ministros de Justicia, Brasília, December 1991," in *Normativa Sobre Derecho Internacional Procesal: Civil, Comercial, Laboral y Contencioso Administrativo de la República Oriental del Uruguay-Regulaciones Supranacionales y de Fuente Nacional* (Montevideo, Uruguay: Ministerio de Educación y Cultura, 1994), 233.
14. Tratado de Asunción, Anexo 1, 10.
15. Ibid., 1, 12.

16. The economy of Paraguay has been so inextricably linked to that of Argentina and Brazil that it was forced into MERCOSUR by sheer necessity. Uruguay is also dependent on economic trends within Brazil and Argentina.

17. Luigi Manzetti, "The Political Economy of MERCOSUR," *Journal of Interamerican Studies and World Affairs* 35, no. 4 (Winter 1993–94), 110.

18. Peter Smith, ed., "The Politics of Integration: Concepts and Themes," *The Challenge of Integration: Europe and the Americas* (Coral Gables, FL: University of Miami, North-South Center, 1993), quoted in Luigi Manzetti, "The Political Economy of MERCOSUR," *Journal of Inter American Studies and World Affairs* 35, no. 4 (Winter 1993–94): 109.

19. Alberto van Klaveren, "Why Integration Now? Options for Latin America," in *The Challenge of Integration: Europe and the Americas*, ed. Peter H. Smith (Coral Gables, FL: University of Miami North-South Center, 1993), 119.

20. Manzetti, "Political Economy of MERCOSUR," 109.

21. Ibid.

22. Ibid., 119.

23. Monica Hirst, *Avances y Desafíos en la Formación del MERCOSUR* (Buenos Aires, Argentina: Facultad Latinoamericana de Ciencias Sociales, 1992), 8.

24. Manzetti, "Political Economy of MERCOSUR," 119.

25. Ibid., 118.

26. "Senado de Chile Aprobara el Jueves Asociación con Países del MERCOSUR," *El País*, October 1, 1996.

27. "Mexico, MERCOSUR Talk," *Latin Trade*, January 1997, p. 16.

28. "MERCOSUR Alliance Sought," *Latin Trade*, January 1997, p. 19.

29. Institute for European-Latin American Relations, *Annual Report, 1994* (Madrid, Spain: Institute for European-Latin American Relations, 1995), 1.

30. Ibid.

31. "1997 Annual Survey," Latinobarimetro, http://www.latinobarometro.org.

32. "MERCOSUR Incorporo a Venezuela y Negocia con México," Oficina de la Prensa de ALADI, July 8, 2004.

33. "Mexico to Join MERCOSUR First Half of 2006," *Mercopress*, November 6, 2005.

34. Ibid.

35. "Uruguay After a 'More Balanced' MERCOSUR with Mexico," *Mercopress*, April 28, 2006.

36. President Fox of Mexico had stated for several years that he favored unification with the rest of Latin America. These statements were ignored by the press, but Fox's public announcement to pursue plenary MERCOSUR membership corresponded with tremendous animosity in the United States against everything Mexican. The prospect of Mexico leaving the American orbit infuriated the American elite. The 109th Congress, led by the Republican Party and the news media, both bastions of corporate America, unleashed a wave of anti–Mexican hysteria in the United States. They began calling for a program of ethnic cleansing through population transfer of undocumented Latin Americans living in the United States. They also demanded the criminalization of these individuals. The prospect of having the U.S. government holding President Fox's fellow nationals as hostages led him to abandon public talk of seeking full incorporation into MERCOSUR. A call for the boycott of the U.S. firm in charge of Mexico's public relations (Allyn and Co. of Dallas, Texas) was also announced. These reactionaries burned the Mexican flag in various quarters of the United States. This is particularly odd, because during the Korean, Vietnam and Iraq wars there was never any public burnings of the flags of these countries. Mexico's entry into MERCOSUR would have been a serious blow to the North American Free Trade Agreement (NAFTA). Such a defection could have destabilized the capitalist class in the United States, which views NAFTA as a critical pillar of its power (notwithstanding the claims of right-wing extremists led by Patrick Buchanan, who called for the elimination of NAFTA). In light of the economic wreckage caused by the financial crisis of 2008, U.S. elites cannot afford to be isolated from any trade bloc.

37. There is no wall on the Canadian border, despite the massive influx of undocumented immigrants and narcotics from and to that country. Inhabitants on the U.S. side have complained that low-flying planes have parachuted cargoes of drugs for decades. At the time the United States began construction of the wall, Ottawa inquired if Washington was intending to build a wall against Canada. Observers abroad and in the USA agree that the wall was part of a larger "keep America white" movement. The construction of the U.S.–Mexican wall coincided with a wave of human rights violations, pogroms and other repressive measures taken against Hispanic-Americans and undocumented immigrants from all over the world.

38. Oficina de la Prensa de ALADI, July 5, 2006.

39. Resumen de Noticias: Secretaria General de la Comunidad Andina, July 3, 2006.

40. "El Nuevo Socio del Sur," Editorial, *Diario La Nación*, July 25, 2006.

41. "Caracas Opposition Wants Brazil to Accept Venezuela in MERCOSUR to Rein in Chávez," *Brazzil Magazine*, October 13, 2009, http://www.brazzilmag.com/content/view/

11297/1/1, accessed October 13, 2009. Chávez had previously referred to Ledezma as "the most dangerous oligarch on the payroll of the empire."

42. Martin Araujo, "A Horas del Desenlace, Ledezma Pidió al Senado Brasileño el Voto para el Ingreso de Venezuela: Sarney y Jereissati en Duda," Somos Mercosur, November 2, 2009, http://www.somosmercosur.net/boletin/a-horas-de-la-votacion-ledezma-pidio-al-senado-brasileno-el-voto-para-el-ingreso-de-venezuela-al-mercosur.html, accessed November 2, 2009.

43. Ricardo Scagliola, "El Alcalde de Caracas, Oposito a Chávez, Comparece en el Senado Brasileño para Defender el Ingreso de Venezuela al Bloque," Somos Mercosur, November 2, 2009, http://www.somosmercosur.net/boletin/la-comision-de-relaciones-exteriores-del-senado-brasileno-recibe-al-alcalde-de-caracas-partidario-del-ingreso-de-venezuela-al-mercosur.html, accessed November 2, 2009.

44. María Luisa Rabello and André Soliani, "Brazil Opposition Senators Seek Chávez Defeat in MERCOSUR Vote," Bloombergwww, October 29, 2009, http://bloomberg.com/apps/news?pid=20601086&sid=aBtmQ4Mq6E7U, accessed October 29, 2009.

45. "Brazilian Businessmen Support Venezuela's Entry into MERCOSUR," *El Universal*, October 27, 2009, http://www.eluniversal.com/2009/10/27imp_en_eco_esp_brazilian_busi nessme_27A295 ... http://www.eluniversal.com/, accessed October 30, 2009.

46. Ricardo Scagliola, "El Alcalde de Caracas, Oposito a Chávez, Comparece en el Senado Brasileño para Defender el Ingreso de Venezuela al Bloque," Somos Mercosur, November 2, 2009, http://www.somosmercosur.net/boletin/la-co mision-de-relaciones-exteriores-del-senado-brasileno-recibe-al-alcalde-de-caracas-parti dario-del-ingreso-de-venezuela-al-mercosur. html, accessed November 2, 2009. Italics are the author's.

47. Jornal do Senado, "Venezuala Esta Agora mais Perto do MERCOSUR," Brasília, October 30, 2009, http://www.senado.gov.bnr/jornal/iNoticia.asp?codNoticias=90520,

48. For a copy of the bill, see Senado Federal, Secretária-Geral da Mesa, Atividade Legislativa-Tramitação de Matérias, Projetos e Matérias Legislativas at http://www.senado.gov.br/sf/atividade/materia/detalhes.asp?p_cod_mate=88888.

49. Jornal do Senado, "Adesão da Venezuela ao Mercosul é Aprovada Pelo Plenário do Senado," Ano 15, no. 3.158 (quarta-feira) December 16, 2009. See at www.senado.gov.br/jornal with reference to date.

50. Senado Federal do Brasil, "Senado Aprova Entrada de Venezuela no Mercosul," http://www.senado.gov.br/jornal/iNoticia.asp?cod Noticia=92555, accessed December 16, 2009.

51. "Gobierno Paraguayo Retira Petición de Adhesión de Venezuela al MERCOSUR," August 13, 2009, http://www.telesurtv.net/noti cias/secciones/nota/imprimir.php?ckl=55756, accessed August 14, 2009.

52. El Universal, "Paraguayan Businesspeople Reject Venezuela's Entry into MERCO-SUR," July 22, 2009, http://www.eluniversal.com/2009/07/22/en_eco_art_paraguayan-busi nessp_22A2529445.shtml, accessed August 14, 2009.

53. "Chávez Claims Paraguayan Senators Tried to Blackmail Him to Vote for Venezuela in Mercosur," MERCOPRESS, http://en.mercopress.com/2012/08/03/chavez-claims-paraguayan-senators-tried-to-blackmail-him-to-vote-for-venezuela-in-mercosur?utm_source=newsletter&utm_medium=email&utm_campaign=daily, accessed August 3, 2012.

54. "Declaración Sobre la Incorporación de la República Bolivariana de Venezuela al MER-COSUR," Montevideo, Secretaria de MERCO-SUR, June 29, 2012; "Comunicado Conjunto de los Presidentes de los Estados Partes del MERCOSUR," Montevideo, Secretaria de MERCOSUR, June 29, 2012.

55. "La Ruptura del Orden Constitucional en Paraguay," MERCOSURABC, July 2, 2012, http://www.mercosurabc.com.ar/nota.asp?Id Nota=3355&IdSeccion=3, p. 6, accessed July 2, 2012.

56. UNASUR 2012, *Reunión Extraordinaria del Consejo de Jefas y Jefes de Estado y de Gobierno de UNASUR.* (Quito, Ecuador. Secretaria General de UNASUR June 29, 2012). Decisión No. 26/2012.

57. "Uruguay Says It Was BRAZIL That Forced the Incorporation to Mercosur of Venezuela," MERCOPRESS, July 2, 2012, http://en.mercopress.com/2012/07/02/uruguay-says-it-was-brazil-that-forced-the-incorporation-to-mercosur-of-venezuela, accessed July 3, 2012.

58. "Paraguayan Presidential Hopeful Said the Country Should in No Way Abandon Mercosur," MERCOPRESS, July 13, 2012, http://en.mercopress.com/2012/07/13/paraguayan-presidential-hopeful-said-the-country-should-in-no-way-abandon-mercosur, accessed July 14, 2012.

59. Guido Nejamkis and Ana Flor, "Mercosur Welcomes Venezuela, Suspends Paraguay," Reuters, June 29, 2012, http://www.reuters.com/assets/print?aid=USBRE85S1JT201206 30, accessed June 30, 2012.

60. MERCOSUL/GMC EXT/ACTA No. 02/12, *XLI Reunião Extraordinária do Grupo do Mercado Comúm* (Montevideo, Secretaria General de MERCOSUR, 2012).

61. President Chávez has rarely been seen with his family. Indeed, they have seldom been mentioned or photographed by the press.

62. Mariela León, "Experts Recommend Depoliticized Mercosur," *El Universal*, July 17, 2012.

63. "Venezuela's Entry into Mercosur an Economic Milestone," http://www.bernama.com/bernama/v6/newsworld.php?id=686246, accessed August 8, 2012.

64. Nota a imprensa no. 190, "Cúpula Extraordinária dos Chefes de Estado do MERCOSUL-Brasília, 31 de julho de 2012" (Brasília: Ministério das Relações Exteriores de Brasil, July 30, 2012).

65. "Venezuela's Mercosur Entry Cheers Brazilians," http://www1.folha.uol.com.br/internacional/en/finance/1131871-venezuelas-mercosur-entry-cheers-brazilian-industry.shtml, accessed August 6, 2012.

66. "Colombia Verá Afectado Su Comercio con Venezuela por Ingreso a Mercosur," http://www.hoy.com.ec/noticias-ecuador/colombia-vera-afectado-su-comercio-con-venezuela-por-ingreso-a-mercosur-557648.html, accessed August 6, 2012.

67. "Venezuela en el Mercosur Sirve a Uruguay: Chávez es Mortal," http://www.elpais.com.uy/120805/pnacio-656002/politica/-venezuela-en-el-mercosur-sirve-a-uruguay-chavez-es-mortal-/, accessed August 6, 2012.

68. "Chávez Claims Paraguayan Senators Tried to Blackmail Him to Vote for Venezuela in Mercosur," http://en.mercopress.com/2012/08/03/chavez-claims-paraguayan-senators-tried-to-blackmail-him-to-vote-for-venezuela-in-mercosur?utm_source=newsletter&utm_medium=email&utm_campaign=daily, accessed August 3, 2012.

69. "Hermano de Chávez Habría Ofre Cido Dinero para Entrar a Mercosur," http://www.ultimahora.com/notas/549604-Hermano-de-Chavez-habria-ofrecido-dinero-para-entrar-a-Mercosur, accessed August 6, 2012.

70. "Mercosur Comenzara a Negociar Ingreso de Ecuador en Septiembre, Según Medio Brasileño," http://www.elcomercio.com/polit ica/Mercosur-comenzara-negociar-Ecuador-septiembre_0_749925046.html, accessed August 6, 2012.

71. "Chávez Espera que Bolivia, Ecuador y Colombia Se Unan en el Futuro a Mercosur," http://www.ultimahora.com/notas/549806-Chavez-espera-que-Bolivia,-Ecuador-y-Colombia-se-unan-en-el-futuro-a-Mercosur, accessed August 6, 2012.

72. "Bolivia Will Formally Request Mercosur Full Membership in 2013," *Mercopress*, September 8, 2012.

73. Eduardo Duhalde, *Comunidad Sudamericana: Logros y Desafíos de la Integración* (Buenos Aires: Editorial Planeta, 2006), 16.

74. Rengaraj R. Viswanathan, "The Pacific Alliance, yet Another Bloc in Latin America," *Mercopress*, June 13, 2012.

75. Ibid.

76. Javier I. Echaide, "Construcción de Herramientas de Resistencia Contra el ALCA. El caso de la Consulta Popular de 2003 en Argentina," in *Informe Final del Concursos: ALCA, Procesos de Dominación y Alternativas de Integración regional*. Programa Regional de Becas CLASCO, Buenos Aires, Argentina, 2005, http://bibliotecavirtual.clasco.org.ar/ar/libros/becas/2005/alcajov.echaide.pdf, accessed August 14, 2009.

77. Mario Osava, "Brazil: Unions Want FTAA Put to Popular Vote," Inter-Press Service, December 15, 2000, http://www.corpwatch.org/article.php/id=296&printsafe=1, accessed August 14, 2009.

78. Mario Osava, "10 Million Brazilian Votes Against Hemisphere's FTAA," Inter-Press News Service, September 18, 2002, http://commondreams.org/headlines02/0918-07.htm,

79. Mario Osava, "Trade Americas: MERCOSUR Defends Autonomy Despite Internal Dissent," Inter-Press Service, November 20, 2003, http://ipsnews.net/print.asp?idnews=21213, accessed August 14, 2009.

80. Jane Bussey, "Brazil, U.S. Deadlocked on Eve of FRAA Deadline," *Miami Herald*, February 6, 2004, http://www.miami.com/mld/miamiherald/2004/02/06/business/7886167.htm, accessed February 6, 2004.

81. Anonymous, "10 Reasons Why My Vote Is Against the FTAA, Free Trade and Foreign Debt," América Latina en Movimiento, September 9, 2004, http://alainet.org/active/6866, accessed August 14, 2009.

82. Centro de Estudio y difusión de la doctrina Social Cristiana, *El ALCA: Un Abordaje Actual y Diferente* (Montevideo: Centro de Estudio y Difusion de la Doctrina Social Cristiana, 2004), 48.

83. Ibid., 54.

84. Ibid., 57.

85. Ibid., 59.

86. Ibid., 37–38.

87. Ibid., 77.

88. Anonymous, "Brazil's Lula Inaugurates MERCOSUR Parliament and Declares FTAA Dead," December 14, 2006, http://www.brazilmag.com/component/content/article/43/7679-brazils-lula-inaugurates-mercosur-parliament-and-declares-ftaa-dead.html, accessed August 14, 2009. The Parliament of MERCOSUR was agreed upon in December of 2004 at a conference of MERCOSUR presidents. It was formally inaugurated in December 2006. It has virtually no power.

89. IRSA homepage, www.IIRSA.org.

90. Resumen de Noticias: Secretaria General de la Comunidad Andina, July 3, 2006.

91. Ibid. The CAN was formerly known as the Andean Pact.

92. "Mayor Compromiso con la CAN

Demanda Frei," Resumen de Noticias: Secretaria General de la Comunidad Andina, August 14, 2006. CAN is designed to promote the interests of monopoly capitalism. Its links to an agenda for middle and working classes are nil. CAN headquarters is situated in Lima, Peru, but 54 percent of 500 people surveyed in that city did not know its location and had never heard of the organization ("Mayoría de los Limeños Desconche Existencia de CAN," Resumen de Noticias: Secretaria General de la Comunidad Andina, August 14, 2006.

93. "Bachelet Under Flak at Home Because of MERCOSUR Summit," *Mercopress*, July 24, 2006.

94. Mireya Baltra, "El Nuevo Concepto de Integración Presente en el MERCOSUR," La Nación.cl, July 29, 2006.

95. Oficina de la Prensa de ALADI, July 21, 2006.

96. "MERCOSUR Is Changing the World's Commercial Geography," *Mercopress*, July 28, 2006.

97. "Castro Praises Latin American Unity," *Mercopress*, July 28, 2006.

98. "Surescépticos: Los Incrédulos de la Integración," Oficina de la Prensa de ALADI, July 25, 2006.

99. Interview with Gustavo Magariños, December 2005.

100. "Surescépticos: Los Incrédulos de la Integración," Oficina de la Prensa de ALADI, July 25, 2006.

101. "El MERCOSUR Está Perdiendo Su Esencia," Oficina de la Prensa de ALADI, August 9, 2006.

102. "Brasil: Industriales Preocupados por Venezuela en MERCOSUR," Oficina de la Prensa de ALADI, July 28, 2006.

103. The formal Spanish title of ALBA is *Alianza Bolivariana para los Pueblos de Nuestra América*. ALBA was formerly known as the *Bolivarian Alternative for the Americas*. The name was changed on June 24, 2009.

104. "Tratado Constitutivo de la Unión de Naciones Sudamericanas," http://comunidad andina.org/unasur/tratado_constitutivo.htm.

105. Oficina de la Prensa de ALADI, May 5, 2010.

106. "UNASUR Congressional Heads and Sec. Gen Kirchner Meet in Ecuador," *Mercopress*, June 16, 2010.

107. "Latinoamérica Deber Aprender y Evitar la Tentación Ideologista," Oficina de la Prensa de ALADI, February 12, 2007.

Chapter XII

1. These phrases were used by C. Wright Mills in *The Sociological Imagination* (New York: Oxford University Press, 1959), 10.

2. "The Challenge of Breaking Mental Barriers to Promote Mercosur and Unasur," *Mercopress*, November 23, 2010, http://en.mercopress.com/2010/11/23/the-challenge-of-breaking-mental-barriers-to-promote-mercosur-and-unasur.

3. "Workshop Addresses Challenges in the Americas," *Newsletter for the Atlas Network*, Spring 2005, 3.

4. Ana Pastorina, "Reflexiones (II) Sobre la Propuesta de un Parlamento MERCOSUR," *La Onda Digital* 143, http://www.uruguay.com/LaOnda/143/A2.htm, July 10, 2003.

5. Martin Granovsky, "El MERCOSUR es Antinorteamericano," http://www.pagina12.com.ar/imprimir/diario/elpais/1-163623-2011-03-07.html, 12, accessed March 8, 2011. Wikileaks, an international media organization begun in 2007, is dedicated to divulging information that is kept secret by various governments in the interest of a free press. Efforts were made to access the Wikileaks archive but they were unsuccessful. This may have been due to technical problems with the web site itself. It has been reported in the press that the U.S. government and groups sympathetic to Washington have sought to block public access to the site.

6. Ha-Joon Chiang, *Kicking Away the Ladder* (Cambridge: Cambridge University Press, 2008).

7. Lidice Gómez Mango, *Perspectivas de un Reencuentro de las Lenguas Español y Portuguesa* (Murcia, Spain: Quadema Editorial, 2007), 97–102.

8. "Peru Ingresa al MERCOSUR," El Peruano, http://www.editoraperu.com.pe/edc/2003/08/26/portada.asp, August 26, 2003.

9. Eduardo Duhalde, *Comunidad Sudamericana: Logros y Desafíos de la Integración* (Buenos Aires: Editorial Planeta, 2006), 159.

10. "Venezuela, MERCOSUR, Unasur Top of the Agenda for Paraguay's Congress," *Mercopress*, March 3, 2011, http://en.mercopress.com/2011/03/03/venezuela-mercosur-unasur-top-of-the-agenda-for-paraguay-s-congress, accessed March 4, 2011.

11. "Declaración de Cancún," Prensa de ALADI, February 23, 2010.

12. "Queen of England, I'm Talking to You: Hugo Chávez Demands Britain Return the Falklands to Argentina," MailOnline, http://www.dailymail.co.uk/news/article-1252870/Falkland-Islands-oil-row-British-rig-set-drill-despite-Argentinian-opposition.html, February 25, 2010.

13. "Despite Their Spats, Trade Among MERCOSUR Countries Soaring," *Wall Street Journal*, July 30, 2010, http://online.wsj.com/article/BT-CO-20100730-717870.html, accessed July 31, 2010.

14. Portal Oficial de MERCOSUR, MER-

COSUR/CMC/Acta No.01/10, Consejo del Mercado Común; "MERCOSUR Establishes Customs Code, at Long Last," *Bridges Weekly Trade News Digest* 14, no. 29 (August 4, 2010), http://ictsd.org/i/news/bridgesweekly/82081/#comment-33630, accessed August 5, 2010.

15. "Germany Recognizes Latin America's New Economic and Diplomatic Might," *Merco-Press*, August 5, 2010.

16. "China, MERCOSUR Eye 200 Billion-USD Trade in 2016," Xinhua/English.news.cn, http://news.xinhuanet.com/english/china/2012-06/30/c_131685876.htm, accessed July 2, 2012.

17. Letter of Indian ambassador Rengaraj R. Viswanathan to author, June 27, 2012.

18. Graciela Baquero, "En el Mercosur Se Puede Pensar en Territorio Común Compartido," *MERCOSUR ABC,* September 3, 2012, http://www.mercosurabc.com.ar/nota.asp?IdNota=3459&IdSeccion=1, accessed September 3, 2012.

19. See list of books and manuals for diplomats from the Fundação Alexandre de Gusmão, Ministério das Relações Exteriores, Brasília, Brazil.

20. The formal ceremony to incorporate Venezuela was held in Brasília, Brazil, on July 31, 2012.

21. "New Latam Block Consistent with U.S. Goals for the Hemisphere," http://en.mercopress.com/2010/02/24/new-latam-block-consistent-with-us-goals-for-the-hemisphere, accessed February 24, 2010.

22. Department of State News Conference for February 26, 2010, "Special Briefing on Secretary Clinton's Travel to Latin America," *U.S. Department of State-Diplomacy in Action*, Washington, DC, http://www.state.gov/p/wha/rls/rm/2010/137343.htm.

BIBLIOGRAPHY

Primary Sources

Documents

Archivo Histórico Diplomático Mexicano. *El Congreso de Panamá v Algunos Otros Proyectos de Unión Hispano-Americana*. Ed. Antonio de la Peña y Reyes. Vol. 19. México: Secretaria de Relaciones Exteriores, 1926.

Archivo Diplomático Peruano. *El Congreso de Panamá: 1826*. Ed. Raúl Porras Barrenechea. Vol. 1. Lima: Imprenta La Opinión Nacional, 1930.

Barrenechea, Raul Porras, ed. *Obra Gubernativa y Epistolario de Bolivar: El Congreso de Panamá*. Lima: Comisión Nacional del Sesquicentenario de la Independencia del Perú, 1974.

Bolívar, Simón. *Obras Completas*. 3 vols. Caracas: Ediciones Lisama, 1960.

Central Intelligence Agency Office of Current Intelligence. *The Latin America Free Trade Association*. October 18, 1963. OCI No. 0302163A. Washington, DC: Central Intelligence Agency, 1963. Released via Freedom of Information Act.

Central Intelligence Agency: *Economic Trends and Prospects in Latin America National Intelligence*. National Intelligence Estimate No. 80/90-67. July 20, 1967. Washington, DC: Central Intelligence Agency, 1967. Released via Freedom of Information Act.

Colección Documental de la Independencia del Perú. *Obra Gubernativa y Epistolario de Bolívar: El Congreso de Panamá*. Ed. Raúl Porras Barrenechea. Vol. 14. Lima: Comisión Nacional del Sesquicentenario de la Independencia del Perú, 1974.

Congress of the United States, Joint Economic Committee. *Hearings Before the Subcommittee on Inter-American Economic Relationships*. Eighty-Ninth Congress, First Session, September 8, 9, 10. 1965. Washington, DC: GPO, 1965.

Consejo de Estado. *Tratado de Montevideo, 1980*. Montevideo, October 14, 1980.

Council on Foreign Relations. *Study Group on Economic Integration in Latin America. The Latin American Common Market: Emerging Patterns and Issues*. New York: Council on Foreign Relations, 1960–1961.

Department of State Bulletin. "American Chiefs of State Meet at Punta del Este." *Department of State Bulletin*, May 8, 1967.

Diario de Sesiones de la Cámara de Representantes. Montevideo, December 1, 1969, and July 1, 1991.

Diario de Sesiones de la Cámara de Senadores. Montevideo, June 11, 1969; May 7, 1991; May 8, 1991; May 9, 1991; May 14, 1991; May 15, 1991; May 21, 1991; and May 22, 1991.

International American Conference. *Reports of Committees and Discussions Thereon*. Vol. 4. *Historical Appendix: The Congress of 1826 at Panama and Subsequent Movements Towards a Conference of American Nations*. Washington, DC: Government Printing Office, 1890.

Joint Economic Committee, Congress of the United States. *Hearings Before the Subcommittee on Inter-American Economic Relationships*. Eighty Ninth Congress; First Session, September 8, 9, 10, 1965. Washington, DC: Government Printing Office, 1965.

Lastarria, José Victorino. *Unión y Confederación de los Pueblos Hispano Americanos*. 2 vols. Ed. Álvaro Covarrubias, Domingo Santa María, and Benjamín Vicuña Mackenna. Santiago de Chile: Sociedad de La Unión Americana, 1862–67.

Latin American Free Trade Association. *Practical Manual of LAFFA.* Montevideo: Centre of National Statistics and International Trade of Uruguay, 1969.

Lecuna, Vicente. *Cartas de Santander.* 3 vols. Caracas: Edición del Gobierno de Venezuela, 1942.

_____ and Harold A. Bierck, Jr. *Selected Writings of Bolívar.* 2 vols. Caracas: Banco de Venezuela, 1951.

O'Leary, Daniel F. *Memorias del General Daniel Florencio O'Leary: Narración.* 3 vols. Referred to as *Narración.* Caracas: Imprenta Nacional, 1952.

_____. *Memorias del General O'Leary: Publicadas por Su Hijo Simón B. O'Leary.* Ed. Simón B. O'Leary. Referred to as *Memorias.* Caracas, 1879–1882; reprint, Venezuela: Ministry of Defense, 1981.

Public Papers of the Presidents of the United States. *Dwight D. Eisenhower. 1959.* Washington, DC: U.S. GPO, 1960.

_____. *Dwight D. Eisenhower. 1960–1961.* Washington, DC: U.S. GPO, 1961.

_____. *Lyndon B Johnson.1963–1964.* 2 vols. Washington, DC: U.S. GPO, 1965.

_____. *Lyndon B. Johnson 1965.* 2 vols. Washington, DC: U.S. GPO, 1966.

_____. *Lyndon B. Johnson. 1966.* 2 vols. Washington, DC: U.S. GPO, 1967.

_____. *Lyndon B Johnson. 1967.* 2 vols. Washington, DC: U.S. GPO, 1968.

_____. *Lyndon B. Johnson. 1968–1969.* 2 vols. Washington D. C.: U.S. GPO, 1970.

_____. *John F. Kennedy. 1961.* Washington, DC: U.S. GPO, 1962.

_____. *John F. Kennedy. 1962.* Washington, DC: U.S. GPO, 1963.

_____. *John F. Kennedy. 1963.* Washington, DC: U.S. GPO, 1964.

_____. *Richard M. Nixon. 1969.* Washington, DC: U.S. GPO, 1971.

_____. *Harry Truman. 1948.* Washington, DC: U.S. GPO, 1964.

Registro Nacional de Leyes, Decretos del República Uruguaya. *Se Apruebe el Tratado de Montevideo 1980.* Montevideo: Consejo de Estado, October 1980.

Secretaria del Senado. *MERCOSUR Estudio Sobre Su Problemática Actual y Perspectivas.* Montevideo: Comisión de Asuntos Internacionales, June 1998.

_____. *Transporte de Cargas y de Pasajeros en el Área del MERCOSUR: Evolución Productiva del País y la Importancia Estratégica de Nuestro Territorio.* Montevideo:

Comisión de Transporte y Obras Públicas, 1998.

United Nations Economic Commission for Latin America. *The Latin American Common Market.* Document E/CN.12/531. New York: United Nations, 1959.

_____. *Towards a Dynamic Policy for Latin America.* Document E/CN. 12/680/Rev.1. New York: United Nations, 1963.

United Nations Economic Commission for Latin America and the Caribbean. *The Economic Development of Latin America in the Post-War Period.* Document No. FICN.12/659/Rev.l. New York: United Nations, 1964.

U.S. Department of State. *Foreign Relations of the United States, 1958–1960.* Vol. 4. *Foreign Economic Policy.* Washington, DC: U.S. Government Printing Office, 1992.

_____. *Foreign Relations of the United States, 1958–1960.* Vol. 5. *American Republics.* Washington, DC: U.S. Government Printing Office, 1991.

_____. *Foreign Relations of the United States, 1961–1963.* Vol. 12. *American Republics.* Washington, DC: U.S. Government Printing Office, 1985.

_____. *The Inter-American Meeting of Presidents: Punta del Este, April 12–14, 1967.* Internal Report. Washington, DC: U.S. Department of State, June 1967.

Vidaurre, Manuel Lorenzo de. *Suplemento a las Cartas Americanas.* Lima: Imprenta Republicana de Concha.

Organizations and Contemporary Sources

Asociación Latinoamericana de la Integración. *La Asociación Latinoamericana de Integración: Un Análisis Comparativo.* Depósito Legal No. 285.344/92. Montevideo: Secretaria General, 1980.

Banco de la República. *Tratado de Montevideo y Resoluciones Aprobadas por la Conferencia de la Asociación Latinoamericana de Libre Comercio.* Bogotá, Colombia: Banco de la República, 1964.

Banco Interamericano de Desarrollo. *América Latina a Principios del Siglo XXI: Integración. Identidad y Globalización-Actitudes y Expectivas de la Elites Latinoamericanas.* Eds. Diego Achard, Juan I Garcia Peluffo and Luis Eduardo Gonzalez. http://www.iadb.orglintal. 2 (XJI). Buenos Aires: Instituto para la Integración de América Latina y el Caribe (INTAL), 2001.

Banco Interamericano de Desarrollo. *La Inte-*

gración Económica de América Latina Real-izaciones, Problemas y Perspectivas. Buenos Aires: Instituto para la Integración de América Latina (INTAL), 1968.

Banco Nacional de Comercio Exterior. *Misión a ALALC*. México: Banco Nacional de Comercio Exterior, 1964.

Blanco-Fombona, Rufino. *El Pensamiento Vivo de Bolívar*. Buenos Aires: Editorial Losada, 1942.

_____, ed. *Simón Bolívar: Discursos y Procla-mas*. Paris: Casa Editorial Garnier Her-manos, 1913.

Boletín de la Integración. *Declaración de los Presidentes de América Sobre Integración*. Buenos Aires: Instituto para la Integración de América Latina (INTAL), April 1967.

_____. *II Reunión de Cancilleres de la Cuenca del Plata*. Buenos Aires: Instituto para la Integración de América Latina, June 1968.

Castelar, Emilio. "La unión de España y Amér-ica." *La América: Crónica Hispano-Ameri-cana* 1 (February 24, 1858): 1–2.

Committee on Foreign Law. *Economic Integra-tion in Latin America*. New York: Association of the Bar of the City of New York, 1962.

Gabay, Marcos, and Carlos María Gutierrez. *Integración Latinoamericana? De la Alianza Para el Progreso a la OLAS: Recopilación y Análisis Documental*. Montevideo: Edi-ciones Cruz del Sur, 1967.

Herrera, Felipe. *América Latina Integrada*. Buenos Aires: Editorial Losada, 1967.

Institute for European-Latin American Rela-tions (Instituto de Relaciones Europeo-Lati-noamericanas). *Annual Report 1994*. Madrid: IRELA, 1994.

Instituto Interamericano de Cooperçäo para a Agricultura. *Agricultura no Mercosul: Chile Mais Bolivia*. Montevideo: MERCOSUL, 1998.

Inter-American Development Bank. *The Latin American Integration Process in 1976*. Buenos Aires: Institute for Latin American Integra-tion (INTAL), 1976.

_____. *Multinational Investment in the Eco-nomic Development and Integration of Latin America*. Bogotá: Round Table Conference of the Inter-American Development Bank (INTAL), 1968.

_____. *Special Series: Raúl Prebisch: Power, Principle and the Ethics of Development*. Ed. Edgar J. Dosman. Buenos Aires: Institute for the Integration of Latin America and the Caribbean (INTAL), 2006. http://www.iadb.org/intal.

Instituto Interamericano de Estudios Jurídicos Internacionales. *Derecho de la Integración Latinoamericana: Ensayo de Sistematiza-ción*. Washington, DC: Ediciones Depalma, 1969.

Mayobre, José Antonio, Felipe Herrera, Carlos Sanz de Santamaría and Raúl Prebisch. *Hacia la Integración Acelerada de América Latina: Proposiciones a los Presidentes Lati-noamericanos*. Mexico City: Fondo de la Cultura Económica, 1965.

Mikesell, Raymond F. *Liberalization of Inter-Latin American Trade*. Inter-American Eco-nomic and Social Council: Organization of American States. Economic Research Series. Washington, DC: Department of Eco-nomic and Social Affairs-Pan American Union, 1957.

Notter, Harley A. "American Interests in the Economic Unification of Europe with Re-spect to Trade Barriers." New York: Council on Foreign Relations Study, No. E-B56, 1–2, 14 September 1942.

Research and Policy Committee of the Com-mittee for Economic Development. *Coop-eration for Progress in Latin America*. New York: Committee for Economic Develop-ment, 1966.

Snow, Freeman. *Treaties and Topics in Ameri-can Diplomacy*. Boston: Boston Book, 1894.

Torres Caicedo, J.M. *Unión Latino-Americana: Pensamiento de Bolívar para Formar una Liga Americana: Su Origen y Sus Desarrollos*. Paris: Librería de Rosa y Bouret, 1865.

United Nations Economic Commission for Latin America and the Caribbean. *Raúl Pre-bisch: Un Aporte al Estudio de Su Pensa-miento*. Santiago de Chile: Comisión Econo-mica para *América* Latina y El Caribe, 1987.

World Trade Organization. *The General Agree-ment on Tariffs and Trade: Text of General Agreement*. Geneva, 1986. http://www.wto.org.english/docs_ellegal_e/gatt47.pdf.

Memoirs and Participant Literature

Abreu, Bonilla Sergio. *Mercosur e Integración*. Montevideo: Fundación de Cultura Univer-sitaria, 1991.

_____. *Mercosur: Una Década de Integración*. Montevideo: Fundación de Cultura Univer-sitaria, 2000.

Allende, Salvador. *Punta del Este: La Nueva Estrategia del Imperialismo*. Montevideo: Editorial Dialogo, 1967.

Collazo, Ariel B. "La Federación de Estados: Única Solución para el Problema de América Latina." Unpublished paper, private papers of Ariel B. Collazo. Montevideo: n.p., 1967.

Cuadro, Servando. *Los Trabajos y Los Días: Hacia la Federación Hispanoamericana.* Montevideo: Ediciones Nexo, 1960.

De Pradt, M. Dominique. *Congrès de Panamá.* Paris: Bechet Aine, Libraire-Editeur, 1825.

_____. *Congreso de Panamá.* Paris: Libreria de Bechet Mayor, 1825. Spanish version translated by D.J.C. Pagès, Royal Interpreter.

Duhalde, Eduardo. *Comunidad Sudamericana: Logros y Desafíos de la Integración.* Buenos Aires: Editorial Planeta, 2006.

Furtado, Celso. *La Fantasia Organizada.* Buenos Aires: Editorial Universitario, 1988.

Haya de la Torre, Victor Raúl. *El Antimperialismo y el APRA.* Chile: Editorial Ercilla, 1936.

_____. *A Dónde va Indoamérica?* Santiago de Chile: Editorial Ercilla, 1935.

_____. *La Defensa Continental.* 3rd ed. Buenos Aires: Editorial Americalee, 1947.

Johnson, Lyndon B. *The Vantage Point.* New York: Bantam, 1971.

Linowitz, Sol. *The Making of a Public Man: A Memoir.* Boston: Little, Brown, 1985.

Kennan, George F. *Memoirs: 1925–1950.* New York: Bantam, 1969.

Magariños, Gustavo. *Comercio e Integración Mundo-Continente-Región.* 3 vols. Montevideo: Fundación de Cultura Universitaria, 1994.

_____. *Evaluación del Proceso de Integración de la ALALC.* Montevideo: Asociación Latinoamericana de Libre Comercio, 1969.

_____. *Integración Económica Latinoamericana Proceso ALALC/ALADI, 1950–2000.* 3 vols. Montevideo: Asociación Latinoamericana de Integración, 2006.

_____. *Integración Multinacional: Teoría y Sistemas.* Montevideo: Universidad ORT and Asociación Latinoamericana de Integración, 2000.

_____. *Uruguay en el Mercosur.* Montevideo: Fundación de Cultura Universitaria, 1991.

Mendieta, Salvador. *Alrededor del Problema Unionista de Centro-América.* 2 vols. Barcelona, Spain: Ediciones Maucci, 1934.

_____. *Cómo Estamos y Qué Debemos Hacer.* Managua, Nicaragua: Tipografía Moderna, 1911.

_____. *La Enfermedad de Centro-América.* 3 vols. Barcelona, Spain: Ediciones Maucci, 1934.

_____. *Paginas de Unión.* 1902. This work is from Mendieta's PhD dissertation. Honduras: Tipografía de J. C. Gurdian & Ciá, 1902.

Monteagudo, Bernardo. *Sobre la Necesidad de una Federación General Entre los Estados Hispanoamericanos.* Series: Latinoamérica: Cuadernos de Cultura Latinoamericanca, vol. 40. 1825. Reprint, Mexico City: Universidad Nacional Autónoma de México, Coordinación de Humanidades, Centro de Estudios Latinoamericanos, Unión de América Latina, 1979.

Prebisch, Raúl. *Cinco Etapas de Mi Pensamiento Sobre el Desarrollo.* Mexico City: El Trimestre Económico, 1983.

Rodo, José Enrique. *Ariel.* Madrid: Colección Austral, 1975.

Ugarte, Manuel. *La Patria Grande.* Santiago de Chile: Editorial Ercilla, 1939.

_____. *The Destiny of a Continent.* New York: Alfred A. Knopf, 1925.

Secondary Sources

Specialized Historical and Contemporary Studies

Allen, Robert Loring. "Integration in Less Developed Countries." *Kyklos* 3 (1961): 315–336.

Arosemena, Justo. *Estudio Sobre la Idea de una Liga Americana.* Ed. Ricaurte Soler. Lima: Imprenta de Huerta y Co, 1864. Reprint, Panamá: Edición del Comité del Sesquicentenario del Congreso Anfictiónico, 1976.

Arragon, Reginald Francis. *The Congress of Panama.* Ph.D. dissertation, Harvard University, 1923.

Beaulac, Willard L. "*The Fractured Continent: Latin America in Close-Up.*" Stanford: Hoover Institution Press, 1980.

Behrman, Jack N. *The Role of International Companies in Latin American Integration: Autos and Petrochemicals.* New York: Committee for Economic Development, 1971.

Billón, Jean-Francis. "Latin American Federalism." *The Federalist* 35, no. 1 (1993): 21–27.

_____. "Movimiento Pro-Federación." *The Federalist* 35, no. 2 (1993): 123–30.

_____. "The Process of Latin American Integration." *The Federalist* 38, no. 1 (1996): 26–43.

Bradford, Colin I. *The New Paradigm of Systemic Competitiveness: Toward More Integrated Policies in Latin America.* Paris:

Organization for Economic Co-Operation and Development, 1994.

Brown, A.J. "Economic Separatism Versus a Common Market in Developing Countries." *Yorkshire Bulletin of Economic and Social Research,* May 1961, and November 1961.

Bonetti, Ernesto, Silvana Bruera, Francisco Gatto, et al. *Frontera, Integración y Después: El Desarrollo Regional Integrado: Un Aspecto Específico de la Integración Nacional.* Montevideo: Centro de Informaciones y Estudios del Uruguay, 1990.

Business International Corporation. *Operating in Latin America's Integrating Markets: ANCOM/CACM/CARICOM/LAFFA.* New York: Business International Corporation, 1977.

Carriquiry, Guzmán. *El Bicentenario de la Independencia de los Países Latinoamericanos.* Madrid: Ediciones Encuentro, 2011.

_____. *Una Apuesta por América Latina: Memoria y Destino de un Continente.* Buenos Aires: Editorial Sudamericana, 2005.

Carriquiry, Guzmán, and Gómez Mango, Lidice. *Perspectivas de un Reencuentro de las Lenguas Española y Portuguesa.* Murcia, Spain: Quadema Editorial, 2007.

Castañeda, Jorge. "Pan Americanism and Regionalism: A Mexican View." *International Organization* vol. 10 (August 1956): 373–89.

Chamberlain, Robert S. *Francisco Morazán, Champion of Central American Federation.* Coral Gables, FL: University of Miami Press, 1950.

Cochrane, James D. "The Movement Toward Economic Integration in Latin America: A Selected English Language Bibliography." *Southeastern Latin Americanist,* June 1974, 5–7.

Comisión Económica Para América Latina y el Caribe. *Raúl Prebisch: Un Aporte al Estudio de Su Pensamiento.* Santiago de Chile: Naciones Unidas, 1987.

Cossío del Pomar, Felipe. *Haya de la Torre: El Indoamericano.* Lima: Editorial Nuevo Día, 1946.

Delgado, Isabel Lirola. "Perspectivas Actuales del Proceso de Integración Europea: El Tratado de Amsterdam y la Agenda 2000." *Cuaderno de Negocios Internacionales e Integración* 4, no. 18/19 (July–October 1998): 2–14.

Dell, Sidney. *A Latin American Common Market?* London: Oxford University Press, 1966.

Del Valle, José Cecilio. *Obras del José Cecilio del Valle.* Vol 1. Ed. D. Ramón Rosa and Rómulo E. Durón. Tegucigalpa, Honduras: Comisionado por el Gobierno de la República para Ordenarlas y Editarlas, 1906.

Di Biase, Hector N. "Acuerdo MERCOSUR-UNION EUROPEA: Fotografía Revelada; Habrá Acuerdo de Libre Comercio?" *Cuaderno de Negocios Internacionales e Integración* 4, no. 18/19 (July–October 1998): 23–46.

Diffie, Bailey W. "The Ideology of Hispanidad." *The Hispanic American Historical Review* 23 (August 1943): 457–83.

Edwards, John David. "Economic Ideology and Economic Integration in Latin America: The Impact of ECLA on LAFTA." Ph.D. dissertation, University of Virginia, 1974.

Espiell, Hector Gros, Carlos F. Delpiazzo, and Felipe Rotondo. *El Derecho de la Integración del Mercosur.* Montevideo: Universidad de Montevideo, Facultad de Derecho, 1999.

Ferrero, Rómulo A. "Purposes and Realities of the Latin American Common Market: A Peruvian Viewpoint." *Statist,* March 1960, 161–163.

Finch, Elizabeth A. *The Politics of Regional Integration: A Study of Uruguay's Decision to Join LAFFA.* Monograph Series No. 4. Liverpool: University of Liverpool, Centre for Latin American Studies, 1973.

Fregeiro, C.L. *Don Bernardo Monteagudo: Ensayo Biográfico.* Buenos Aires: n.p., 1879.

Frei Montalva, Eduardo. "The Alliance That Lost Its Way." *Foreign Affairs* 45, no. 3 (April 1967): 437–448.

Gauhar, Altaf, ed. *Regional Integration: The Latin American Experience.* London: Third World Foundation for Social and Economic Studies, 1985.

Gómez Mango de Carriquiry, Lidice. *El Encuentro de Lenguas en el Nuevo Mundo.* Córdoba, Spain: CajaSur, 2000.

Gordon, Lincoln. "Punta del Este Revisited." *Foreign Affairs 45, no.* 4 (July 1967): 624–38.

Griffith, William J. "The Personal Archive of Francisco Morazán." *Philological and Documentary Studies* 2, no. 6 (1977): 197–286.

Grez Pérez, Carlos E. *Los Intentos de Unión Hispano Americana y la Guerra de España en el Pacífico.* Santiago de Chile: Imprenta Nascimento, 1928.

Grunwald, Joseph, Miguel S. Wionczek, and Martin Carnoy. *Latin American Economic*

Integration and U.S. Policy. Washington, DC: Brookings Institute, 1972.

Haas, Ernst B., and Philippe C. Schmitter. *Mexico and Latin American Economic Integration.* Research Series No. 5. Berkeley: University of California, Institute for International Studies, 1964.

_____ and _____. *The Politics of Economics in Latin American Regionalism: The Latin American Free Trade Association After Four Years of Operation.* Monograph Series in World Affairs, vol. 3. Denver: University of Denver Graduate School of International Studies, 1965.

Hackett, Charles Wilson. "The Development of John Quincy Adam's Policy with Respect to an American Confederation and the Panama Congress, 1822–1825." *The Hispanic American Historical Review* 8 (November 1928): 496–526.

Herrera, Felipe. "The Inter-American Development Bank and the Latin American Integration Movement." *Journal of Common Market Studies* 5.2 (December 1966): 172–80.

Hilton, Ronald, ed. *The Movement Toward Latin American Unity.* New York: Praeger, 1969.

Hirst, Mónica. *Avances y Desafíos en la Formación del MERCOSUR.* Buenos Aires: Facultad Latinoamericana de Ciencias Sociales (FLASCO), 1992.

Javits, Jacob K. "Last Chance for a Common Market." *Foreign Affairs* 45, no. 3 (April 1967): 449–62.

Kadar, Bela. *Regional Cooperation in Latin America.* Budapest: Institute for World Economics of the Hungarian Academy of Sciences, 1975.

Kaplan, Marcos. *Problemas del Desarrollo y de la Integración en América Latina.* Caracas: Monte Ávila Editores, 1968.

_____, ed. *Corporaciones Públicas, Multinacionales Para el Desarrollo y la Integración de la América Latina.* Mexico City: Fondo de la Cultura Económica, 1972.

Karnes, Thomas, *The Failure of Union: Central America 1824–1975.* Chapel Hill: University of North Carolina Press, 1960.

Krause, Walter, and F. John Mathis. *Latin America and Economic Integration: Regional Planning for Development.* Iowa City: University of Iowa, 1970.

_____ and _____. *The Latin American Common Market: Economic Disparity and Benefit Diffusion.* Bulletin No. 15. Atlanta: Georgia State College, School of Business Administration, Bureau of Business and Economic Research, June 1968.

Linowitz, Sol. "The Road from Punta del Este." *Department of State Bulletin,* May 29, 1967.

Mace, Gordon. "Regional Integration in Latin America: A Long and Winding Road." *International Journal* 43, no. 3 (Summer 1998): 405–27.

Manzetti, Luigi. "The Political Economy of MERCOSUR." *Journal of Interamerican Studies and World Affairs* 35, no. 4: 101–141.

Maritano, Nino. *A Latin American Economic Community: History, Policies, and Problems.* Notre Dame: University of Notre Dame Press, 1970.

Mathis, F. John. *Economic Integration in Latin America: The Progress and Problems of LAFTA.* Studies in Latin American Business Series, No. 8. Austin: University of Texas, Bureau of Business Research, 1969.

Mayobre, José Antonio, Felipe Herrera, Carlos Sanz de Santamaría, and Raúl Prebisch. "Proposals for the Creation of the Latin American Common Market Submitted to the Governments of Latin America in 1965." *Journal of Common Market Studies* 5 (September 1966): 83–110.

Mendoza, Juan Manuel. *Salvador Mendieta.* Guatemala City: Tipográfica Sánchez & De Guise, 1930.

Methol Ferré, Alberto. "La Integración de América en el Pensamiento de Perón." Unpublished paper, private papers of Alberto Methol Ferré.

_____. "Juventud Universitaria y Mercosur." In *Grupos de Reflexão Prospectiva Sobre MERCOSUL,* ed. Clodoaldo Hugueney Filho and Carlos Henrique Cardin. Brasília: Ministério das Relações Exteriores/FUNAG, 2002.

_____ and Alver Metalli. *La América Latina del Siglo XXI.* Buenos Aires: Edhasa, 2006.

Milenky, Edward S. *The Politics of Regional Organization in Latin America: The Latin America Free Trade Association.* New York: Praeger, 1973.

Mory, Warren H. "Salvador Mendieta: Escritor y Apóstol de la Unión Centroamericana." Thesis, University of Alabama, 1971.

Navarette, Jorge E. "Latin American Economic Integration: A Survey of Recent Literature." *Journal of Common Market Studies* 4 (December 1965): 168–77.

Peláez Bazán, Mario. *Haya de la Torre y la Unidad de América Latina.* Lima: Editorial Universal, 1977.

Peña, Félix. *Momentos y Perpectivas: La Argentina en el Mundo y en América Latina.* Buenos Aires: Universidad Nacional de Tres de Febrero, 2003.

Plaza, Galo. "For a Regional Market in Latin America." *Foreign Affairs,* July 1959, 607–616.

Prebisch, Raúl. *A Crise do Desenvolvimento Argentino: Da Frustração ao Crescimento Vigoroso.* 2nd ed. São Paulo, Brasil: Edições Vértice, 1987.

_____. *Hacia una Dinámica del Desarrollo Latinoamericano.* Mexico City: Fondo de la Cultura Económica, 1963.

_____. "El Mercado Común Constituye Una de las Grandes Reformas Estructurales de América Latina." *Revista de Ciencias Económicas* (São Paulo), June 1962, [PAGES].

Rivarola, Andrés Puntigliano. "Un Ideólogo de Integración." *Revista Contemporánea* (Montevideo) 1, no. 1 (2010): 247–250.

Rivera, Salvador. "Diplomats, Idealists, and Technocrats: The Long Quest for Latin American Integration." Ph.D. dissertation. Ann Arbor: University of Michigan Microfilms, 2004.

_____. "Jacob K. Javits and Latin American Economic Integration." *Cuaderno de Negocios Internacionales e Integración* (Montevideo) 13 (July–December 2007): 34–59.

_____. "Which Way for Unionism?" *Cuaderno de Negocios Internacionales e Integración* (Montevideo) 46/47/48 (November–December 2004): 2–6.

Sáez, Manuel Alcántara. *South American Legislatures: Thinking About Economic Integration and Defense Policy.* Washington, DC: Center for Strategic and International Studies, 2000.

San Martín de Dromi, María Laura. *Integración Iberoamericana: Declaraciones de Guadalajara Madrid, Salvador, Cartagena, Bariloche y Santiago.* Buenos Aires: Ediciones Ciudad Argentina, 1996.

Silva Otero, Arístides. *El Congreso de Panamá.* Caracas: Universidad Central de Venezuela, Instituto de Investigaciones Económicas y Sociales, 1969.

Smith, Peter H., ed. *The Challenge of Integration: Europe and the Americas.* Coral Gables: University of Miami, North-South Center, 1993.

Taiana, Jorge. *El Nacimiento del MERCOSUR.* Guatemala City: FLASCO, 1995.

Tellechea Bergman, Eduardo, and Carlos Mata Prates. *Normativa Sobre Derecho Internacional Procesal: Civil, Comercial, Laboral y Contencioso Administrativo de la República Oriental del Uruguay-Relaciones Supranacionales y de Fuente Nacional.* Montevideo: Ministerio de Educación y Cultura, Dirección General de Secretaria Asesoría: Autoridad Central de Cooperación Jurídica Internacional y Representación Ministerial a la Reunion de los Ministros de Justicia del MERCOSUR, 1994.

Undurraga, Aldunate José M. *Verdadero Origen de la Política de Integración Total Latinoamericana en lo Cultural, Económico y Político.* Santiago de Chile: Editorial Ricardo Neupert, n.d.

Van Aken, Mark J. *Pan-Hispanism: Its Origin and Development to 1866.* University of California Publications in History, vol. 63. Berkeley: University of California Press, 1959.

Zubieta, Pedro A. *Congresos de Panamá y Tacubaya: Breves Datos para la Historia Diplomática de Colombia.* 2nd ed. Bogotá: Imprenta Nacional, 1926.

General Works

Álvarez, Alejandro. *La Diplomacia de Chile Durante la Emancipación: Y la Sociedad Internacional Americana.* Madrid: Editorial-América, 1910.

Arcinegas, German. *The State of Latin America.* New York: Alfred A. Knopf, 1952.

Bulmer-Thomas, Victor. *The Economic History of Latin America Since Independence.* London: Cambridge University Press, 1994.

Chang Rodríguez, Eugenio. *La Literatura Política de Gonzalez Prada, Mariátegui y Haya de la Torre.* Mexico: Ediciones de Andrea, 1957.

Child, Jack. *Geopolitics and Conflict in South America: Quarrels Among Neighbors.* New York: Praeger Special Studies and Hoover Institution Press, 1985.

Deves Valdes, Eduardo. "El Pensamiento Latinoamericano en el Siglo XX. Entre la Modernización y la Identidad." Vol. 1, *Del Ariel de Rodó a la CEPAL: (1900–1950).* Santiago de Chile: Editorial Biblos, 2000.

Díaz, Loza Florentino. *Geopolitica para la Patria Grande.* Buenos Aires: Ediciones Temáticas SRL, 1987.

Dominguez, Jorge I. "Consensus and Divergence: The State of the Literature on Inter-American Relations in the 1970s." *Latin*

American Research Review 13, no. 1 (1977): 87–126.

Duarte-Pereira, Osny. *La Seudo-Rivalidad Argentino-Brasileña Pro y Contra de ITAIPU.* Trans. Neiva Moreira. Buenos Aires: Ediciones Corregidor, 1975.

Englekirk, John E. "El Hispanoamericanismo y la Generación de 98." *Revista Iberoamericana* 2 (November 1940): 321–51.

Lockey, Joseph B. "Diplomatic Futility." *The Hispanic American Historical Review* 10, no. 3 (August 1930): 265–94.

Mayer, Robert. "The Origins of the American Banking Empire in Lath America: Frank A. Vanderlip and the National City Bank." *Journal of Inter-American Studies and World Affairs* 15 (February 1973): 60–72.

Morse, Richard. "Toward a Theory of Spanish American Government." *Journal of the History of Ideas* 15 (1954): 71–93.

Rosenberg, Emily. "Emergency Executive Controls Over Foreign Commerce and United States Economic Pressure on Latin America During World War I." *Inter-American Economic Affairs,* Spring 1978, 81–96.

Rótulo, Daniel. *Política Exterior y Estrategia de Brasil en el Atlántico Sur (1964–1990): La Cancillería v el Mito de Golbery.* Montevideo: Universidad de la República, Departamento de Ciencias Sociales, 1999.

Trask, Roger R. "George F. Kennan's Report on Latin America: 1950." *Diplomatic History* 2 (Summer 1978): 307–11.

Popular Literature

Fuentes, Carlos. "Latin America's Alternatives: An Ibero-American Federation." *New Perspectives Quarterly,* Winter 1991, 15–17.

Galasso, Norberto. *América Latina: Unidos o Dominados.* Buenos Aires: Editorial Convergencia, 1975.

Lazcano Jiménez, Mauro. *Integración Económica e Imperialismo.* Mexico City: Editorial Nuestro Tiempo, 1968.

"Optimism and Obstacles." *Newsweek,* April 24, 1967, 42–43.

Pacheco Quintero, Jorge. *El Congreso Anfictiónico de Panamá y la Política Internacional de los Estados Unidos.* Bogotá: Editorial Kelly, 1971.

Sidey, Hugh. "The Benefactor Sealed Off from the Benefited." *Life* 62, no. 16 (April 21, 1967): 36-B.

_____. "LBJ's Diplomatic Foray into South America." *Life* 62, no. 15 (April 14, 1967): 38-B.

"What Punta del Este Lacked." *Business Week,* April 22, 1967, 209.

Periodicals and Magazines

Boletín de la Integración. Buenos Aires: Instituto Para la Integración de América Latina.

Cuaderno de Negocios Internacionales e Integración. Montevideo: International Business Department.

Foreign Affairs. New York: Council on Foreign Relations.

La América: Crónica Hispano-Americana. Madrid, Spain.

The Federalist: A Political Review. Pavia, Italy.

North American Review. Boston, Massachusetts.

Mercopress. http://en.mercopress.com/.

Newspapers

Crisol. Universidad de la República de Uruguay.

El País. Montevideo, Uruguay.

Financial Times. London, England.

Gaceta Mercantil. Montevideo, Uruguay.

Latin Trade. Miami, FL.

Archives and Libraries

ALADI. Montevideo, Uruguay.

Archivos del Senado Mexicano. Mexico, D.F., Mexico.

Archivos Legislativos de Uruguay. Montevideo, Uruguay.

Archivo Nacional de Chile. Santiago de Chile.

Archivos Nacional de Uruguay. Montevideo, Uruguay.

Biblioteca Nacional de Uruguay. Montevideo, Uruguay.

Central Intelligence Agency. Washington, DC.

Council on Foreign Relations. New York, New York.

Fundação Alexandre de Gusmão. Ministério das Relações Exteriores, Brasília, Brazil.

Fundación Frei. Santiago de Chile.

Instituto Artigas. Ministério de Relaciones Exteriores, Montevideo, Uruguay.

Instituto Pedro Gual. Ministerio de Poder Popular para Relaciones Exteriores de la República Bolivariana de Venezuela, Caracas.

Jacob Javits Papers. State University of New York at Stony Brook.

Library of Congress. Washington, DC.

Ministério das Relações Exteriores. Brasília, Brazil.

Ministério de Relaciones Exteriores. Montevideo, Uruguay.

Ministério de Poder Popular para Relaciones Exteriores de la República Bolivariana de Caracas. Venezuela.

National Archives. College Park, Maryland.

New York State Library. Albany, New York.

Secretaria General del MERCOSUR. Montevideo, Uruguay.

U.S. Department of Commerce. Washington, DC.

U.S. Department of State. Washington, DC.

Letters and Interviews

Abreu Bonilla, Sergio. Former Uruguayan minister of foreign relations. Telephone interview, December 2002.

Álvarez, Carlos. Former vice president of Argentina and secretary general of ALADI. Interviewed Jaunary 16, 2012, Montevideo, Uruguay.

Bustamante del Mazo, Silvia and Margarita. Interviewed January 4, 1999, Buenos Aires.

Carlevaro, Hector. Accountant and special adviser to LAFTA, ALADI and MERCOSUR. Interviewed January 2, 2002, Montevideo, Uruguay.

Carriquiry, Guzmán. Lay Catholic representative from Uruguay to the Vatican. Interviewed January 10, 2009, Montevideo, Uruguay, and via correspondence.

Chesterton, Maria. Manager of International Business Development for Blue Cross/Blue Shield of Delaware in Argentina and Uruguay. Interviewed September 25, 1998.

Collazo, Ariel B. Uruguayan senator and associate of Servando Cuadro. Interviewed February 19, 2004, and December 30, 2008.

Di Biase, Dr. Hector N. Director of International Business and Integration Programs, Universidad Catolica, Montevideo, Uruguay. Interviewed January 3, 2000.

Ford, Gerald. Former president of the United States. Correspondence.

Grunwald, Joseph. Professor of economics, University of California at San Diego. Interviewed November 1987.

Javits, Mrs. Marion. Widow of former New York senator Jacob K. Javits. Telephone interview, March 2004.

Johnson, Peter. Special assistant to David Rockefeller.

Leal, Jorge E. Brigadier general (ret.), Argentine army. Interviewed December 29, 1999, Buenos Aires.

Macario, Carla. United Nations Economic Commission for Latin America and the Caribbean. Interviewed October 1999.

Magariños, Gustavo. Secretary general of LAFTA. Interviewed December 19, 1998, and December 26, 2000, Montevideo.

Methol Ferré, Alberto. Vice director of the Port of Montevideo, Uruguayan writer, historian, lay Catholic representative to Vatican from Uruguay. Interviewed February 16, 2004, December 30, 2007, and January 15, 2008.

Pezzati, Elbio Carlo. Journalist, Minister of Physical Culture, and Uruguayan senator. Interviewed January 3, 1999, Montevideo.

Prebisch, Elena. Widow of Raúl Prebisch. Interviewed January 8, 1999, Buenos Aires.

Rostow, Walt Whitman. Special assistant to presidents Kennedy and Johnson. Correspondence.

Rotundo, Felipe. Professor of law, Universidad de la República de Uruguay. Interviews 2000–2002.

Schinca, Luis D. Editor of *Crisol.* Interviewed December 2002.

Szabo, Daniel. Special assistant to Senator Jacob K. Javits. Correspondence.

Tomás Musich, Arnaldo. Adviser to Argentine president Frondizi and board of directors of Buenos Aires Stock Exchange. Interviewed December 2001.

Urquidi, Víctor. Mexican representative to United Nations Economic Commission for Latin America. Interviewed October 2001.

Vaughn, Jack Hood. Assistant secretary of state for Inter-American Affairs under Lyndon B. Johnson. Interviewed 2001.

Viswanathan, Rengaraj R. Former ambassador to Argentina, Paraguay and Uruguay. Letter to author, June 27, 2012.

INDEX

www.ingramcontent.com/pod-product-compliance
Lightning Source LLC
Chambersburg PA
CBHW031409270326
41929CB00010BA/1386